PICTORIAL
ATLAS
OF THE
WORLD

Jarvis

This edition published 1992 by
Tormont Publications Inc.
338 Saint Antoine St. East
Montreal, Canada   H2Y 1A3
Tel. (514) 954-1441   Fax (514) 954-1443
© 1992 Colour Library Books Ltd.,
Godalming, Surrey, England

ISBN 2-89429-143-4
Printed in Canada

PICTORIAL ATLAS
OF THE
WORLD

TORMONT

FOREWORD

In 1636 a bound collection of maps was published by Gerard Mercator and John Hondt with a frontispiece illustrating the titan Atlas bearing the world on his shoulders. As a result, the word 'atlas' entered the vocabulary as a synonym for a book of maps. In the seventeenth century only the very rich could afford the luxury of an atlas. Cartographic masterpieces by Dutch map engravers offered their patrons the first view of a world the horizons of which were being swiftly broadened by maritime discovery.

Today, most households can afford an atlas even if they do not own one. Certainly, the need for and the attraction of the atlas have never been greater. Never have so many people been on the move around the world. Never have so many been concerned with the impact of world events. 'Atlas-eaters', Dylan Thomas called those who were hungry for world news. The atlas, through its co-ordinates of latitude and longitude, can answer the question 'Where?'. Or, perhaps, more precisely, the index to the atlas provides the answer – hence the importance of the extended index to the *Pictorial Atlas of the World*.

In an atlas, the science of map-making is married to the art of map presentation. Techniques of production are increasingly refined; sources of information are increasingly precise. Satellite imagery, photogrammetry and computerisation have transformed map production. Most of the *Pictorial Atlas of the World* consists of topographical maps, with our own respective home areas receiving generous treatment. Additionally, the pictorial section provides useful and fascinating information on the world's nations and peoples.

An atlas is no substitute for a globe. The two are complementary, for not even the larger globes can include a fraction of the information that is packed into an atlas. The task of projecting the globe onto a flat surface has taxed the ingenuity of mathematicians since the Greeks first attempted to measure the circumference of the Earth. The variety of formidably-named projections employed in the *Pictorial Atlas of the World* illustrates the extended range of options available to present-day cartographers.

Atlases have a romantic appeal as well as a utilitarian value. The novelist Alan Sillitoe, in a memorable essay on maps, recalls the flights of fancy set in motion by his 'first cheap layer-tinted atlas'. To turn the pages of the *Pictorial Atlas of the World* – to contemplate the controlling features of land and sea, to reflect upon the boundaries that define the outlines and shape the destinies of countries and to respond to the magic of the infinity of place-names – is to experience a stimulus to the imagination as well as to the intellect.

William R. Mead
PROFESSOR EMERITUS OF GEOGRAPHY, UNIVERSITY COLLEGE LONDON.

MAP LEGEND

SETTLEMENT

For scales larger than 1:2,000,000   Population

BIRMINGHAM   >1,000,000

GLASGOW   500,000–1,000,000

CARDIFF   250,000–500,000

LIMERICK   50,000–250,000

• **Dover**   10,000–50,000

• Lossiemouth   5,000–10,000

○ Church Stretton   <5,000

CROYDON   London Borough

For scales between 1:2,000,000 and 1:12,000,000

NEW YORK   >5,000,000

RANGOON   2,500,000–5,000,000

■ **KUYBYSHEV**   1,000,000–2,500,000

• **Hyderabad**   500,000–1,000,000

• Adelaide   100,000–500,000

○ Baden-Baden   <100,000

For scales smaller than 1:12,000,000

■ **DAR ES SALAAM**   >1,000,000

• **Maracaibo**   500,000–1,000,000

• Tiranë   <500,000

<u>Lisboa</u>   National capital   <u>Winnipeg</u>   State, provincial capital

COMMUNICATIONS

Motorway

Motorway under construction

Principal road

Principal road under construction

Other main road

Track, seasonal road

Road tunnel

Principal railway

Principal railway under construction

Railway tunnel

✈   International, main airport

BOUNDARIES

International

Undefined, disputed

Internal, state, provincial

Armistice, cease-fire line

The representation of a boundary in this atlas does not denote its international recognition and therefore the *defacto* situation has been depicted.

HYDROGRAPHIC FEATURES

River, stream

Intermittent watercourse

Waterfall, rapids

Dam, barrage

Irrigation, drainage channel

Canal

Lake, reservoir

Intermittent, seasonal lake

Salt pan, mud flat

• Oasis

Marsh, swamp

Reef

Depth of sea in metres

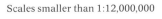

Scales larger than 1:12,000,000

```
0
200
3000
```

Scales smaller than 1:12,000,000

```
0
1000
5000
```

OTHER FEATURES

▲ 3798   Elevation above sea level (metres)

▼ –133   Depression, below sea level (metres)

≶   Pass

•—•   Oil, gas pipeline with field

ENVIRONMENTAL TYPES

Permanent ice and snow

Mountain and moorland

Tundra

Coniferous forest

Deciduous forest

Tropical forest

Prairie

Temperate agriculture

Mediterranean scrub

Savannah

Desert

This representation of the environment and its associated vegetation gives an overview of the landscape. It is not intended to be definitive.

CONVERSION SCALES

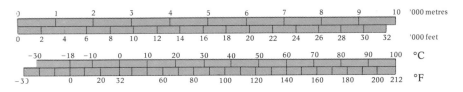

5

CONTENTS

First page: Victoria Falls span the Middle Zambezi River at one of its widest points. Title Page: the well-known resort of Bled, in the Slovenian Highlands.

◄ *Chicago, Illinois, one of the largest cities in the U.S.A.*

EUROPE

*A*s the cradle of Western civilisation and the industrial revolution which now dominates the world economies, Europe may justly claim to be the historical heart of the modern world. It was in Europe that technological advances made mass-production industry possible for the first time. This led to an economic dominance over the rest of the world, which continued until the same processes were taken up by the booming population of North America and the industrial lead crossed the Atlantic.

Geographically Europe is a highly diverse and fragmented continent without any of the vast plains, mountain ranges or deserts which characterise other land masses. In Europe everything is on a much smaller scale than elsewhere. The greatest mountain chain is the Alps, which stretch across northern Italy and on into eastern Europe, but these peaks are dwarfed by the Asian Himalayas or the American Andes. The largest plain is that of the Ukraine, now devoted to the production of grain crops, but again this is far smaller than the North American prairies or the Mongolian grasslands.

Europe is, however, immensely diverse, with a wide variety of landscape forms being found in relatively small areas. Fertile plains jostle with mountain ranges and dense forests with productive meadows. It is the sheer diversity of the geological make up that gives the continent its characteristic appearance. Nowhere is it possible to travel far without coming across a change in scenery.

Hidden beneath this fragmented landscape is a wide variety of mineral wealth. Pockets of every conceivable metal ore are to be found scattered across Europe. Though none occurs in the kind of mass deposit encountered on other continents, these ores have provided the raw materials for European industry for some centuries, and only now are being surpassed by bulk ores from elsewhere.

Until the immigration of racial groups from other continents in large numbers during the later 20th century, the population of Europe was remarkably homogeneous. Almost the entire population was descended from Indo-Europeans, who spread across the continent in antiquity. Earlier peoples were swamped by these new cultures, only surviving in isolated pockets, such as that of the Basques of northern Spain.

However, the populations of Europe have strong historic cultures and concepts of nationhood which transcend the rather academic classification of Indo-European. These nationalist identities are a powerful cultural impetus within Europe and sources of much pride. They may also lead to factional violence, and attempts at supra-national states have rarely survived. Among the most recent to fall before nationalist feelings is Yugoslavia, where civil war culminated in the declaration of independence by Croatia and Slovenia. The colossal USSR, too, crumbled following severe economic difficulties and the abortive coup of 1991. The Baltic States took the opportunity of leaving the union first, followed by the other republics, which remained bound together, however, within the hastily created Commonwealth of Independent States.

The keynote of Europe is diversity. There is diversity in landscape, in geology and in human culture. Packed into the smallest of the continents are over thirty countries based around identifiable national groupings. Even within countries nationalist divisions are to be found. The nation state of Italy was united only a century ago and strong regional differences of culture, language and lifestyle are still apparent. Europe is nothing if not a continent of contrasts.

◄ Iceland – 'Land of fire and Ice'.　　▲ Traditional costume, Bulgaria.　　▲ Dubrovnik, Croatia.　　▼ Pünderich, overlooking the Mosel, Germany.

ALBANIA

Population: 3.2 million
Area: 29,000 square kilometres
Capital: Tirana
Language: Albanian and Greek
Currency: Lek

The rugged mountain nation of Albania has been virtually cut off from the rest of Europe for decades. A province of first the Byzantine and later the Ottoman Empires, Albania gained independence as a kingdom in 1912 and as a Communist republic in 1946. The old-style Stalinist regime has retained a tight grip on running the country, and in 1991 President Ramiz Alia took full power to himself. Under Communism the nation has tried to revolutionise its economy by abandoning the traditional farming techniques which formerly employed the population. Today, less than half the workforce is in farming, the rest having moved to the towns to join the growing number of industrial workers. Copper, steel and electronics are among the growth industries.

ANDORRA

Population: 52,000
Area: 468 square kilometres
Capital: Andorra La Vella
Language: Catalan and French
Currency: French Franc and Spanish Peseta

The independent mountain state of Andorra has retained its freedom unchanged since 1278, when the rival powers of the region agreed on a compromise. Under the 700-year-old arrangement the state is ruled jointly by the Bishop of Urgel and the Count of Foix. As the estates of Foix have since passed to the French state, the present joint rulers are the Bishop of Urgel and the President of France. In practice the native Andorrans, who number around 10,000, govern themselves through a democratic system, though the agreement of the joint rulers is needed for all actions. Sheep are the mainstay of the agricultural economy, but tourism and duty-free shopping bolster the modern prosperity.

AUSTRIA

Population: 7.6 million
Area: 84,000 square kilometres
Capital: Vienna
Language: German
Currency: Schilling

Until 1918 the heart of the vast Hapsburg Empire, which encompassed the Danube Basin and much of the Balkans, Austria is now a democratic republic based upon the German-speaking parts of that Empire. The capital, Vienna, has a long tradition of sophisticated culture and excellence in the arts, music being particularly strongly represented. The economy of Austria is broadly based, though agriculture is limited by the terrain. The mountains, however, do attract large numbers of tourists who come to enjoy winter skiing and summer walking. The industrial sector was heavily nationalised after the Second World War, but has recently been returned to the private sector.

BELGIUM

Population: 10 million
Area: 31,000 square kilometres
Capital: Brussels
Language: Flemish, French and German
Currency: Belgian Franc

The present constitutional monarchy dates back to 1830, when the Belgian people rebelled against Dutch rule and invited a German prince to become their king. The constitution has been amended several times since, but consists of a two-chamber Parliament acting under the monarch. The Flemish- and French-speaking areas each enjoy a degree of regional self-government. The nation is predominantly urban, with industry and services leading the economy. The coal, steel and other metal industries dominate the scene, and these are in turn in the hands of a small number of conglomerates. Agriculture contributes only a small proportion to the economy, but Belgium is now almost self-sufficient in temperate-climate foods, only tropical fruits being imported in bulk.

▲ *An open-air restaurant, Brussels, Belgium.*

BULGARIA

Population: 9 million
Area: 111,000 square kilometres
Capital: Sofia
Language: Bulgarian
Currency: Lev

Bulgaria became independent of the Moslem Ottoman Empire in 1908 as a kingdom, and became a Communist republic following the Russian occupation in 1946. In 1989

▲ *Tranquil countryside, Finland.*

Above right: *The Schonbrunn Palace, Vienna, Austria.*

▼ *Old-world charm, Czechoslovakia.*

▼ *Nyhavn, in Copenhagen, Denmark.*

▲ *Corn harvest, Albania.*

▼ *An Orthodox priest, Cyprus.*

▲ *The Orthodox Cathedral, Tallinn, Estonia.*

▲ *Vineyards, Santenay, France.*

▲ *The mountain state of Andorra.*

street protests and demands for reform led the National Assembly to approve a multi-party democracy and free elections. In 1990 the Communist government stepped down to make way for a democratic election. The river valleys have fertile soils and a climate conducive to heavy grain crops and live-stock rearing. In recent years the traditional dominance of agriculture has been overtaken by a growing industrial sector producing large quantities of iron, steel, textiles and agricultural equipment.

CYPRUS

Population: 700,000
Area: 9,000 square kilometres
Capital: Nicosia
Language: Greek and Turkish
Currency: Cypriot Pound

For centuries part of the Ottoman Empire, Cyprus passed to Britain as security for a loan which was never repaid. Britain, however, granted independence in 1960 under a constitution designed to calm ethnic rivalries between the Greek and Turkish populations. In 1974 a coup by the Greeks threatened to join Cyprus to Greece, and Turkey invaded to block the move. Today, the island is divided between the Turkish northern third and the southern section inhabited by Greeks. The traditional agricultural products of olives, grapes and fruits remain important. Tourists, attracted by the beautiful scenery and beaches, provide much foreign currency, though this business has been disrupted by the partition. There is no communication across the demarcation line and northern Cyprus has declared itself an independent state.

CZECHOSLOVAKIA

Population: 16 million
Area: 127,000 square kilometres
Capital: Prague
Language: Czech and Slovak
Currency: Koruna

As its name suggests, this is a nation formed from two distinct ethnic groups. The Czechs inhabit the western regions and have a predominantly urban culture with strong German influences. The Slovaks of the eastern regions are more agricultural in outlook and their culture shows strong Hungarian influence. Formerly part of the Hapsburg Empire, Czechoslovakia became independent in 1918. Communists took power with Soviet aid in 1948, and an attempt at liberalisation in 1968, known as the Prague Spring, was crushed by Russian tanks. In November 1989 mass public demonstrations led to the resignation of the Communist

government and the legalisation of opposition parties. In December the dissident playwright Vaclav Havel became President. Czechoslovakia is a heavily industrialised nation with iron and steel, chemicals and food processing being prominent.

DENMARK

Population: 5 million
Area: 43,000 square kilometres
Capital: Copenhagen
Language: Danish
Currency: Krone

The rich soil and temperate climate of Denmark have aided the traditionally-strong agricultural sector. Grains, potatoes and vegetables are grown in quantities, but it is livestock which dominates. There are estimated to be over nine million pigs and sixteen million chickens in Denmark, and bacon is a major export earner. Recently the industrial sector has grown significantly, using imported raw materials which are then processed for export as finished goods. Manufacturing now outstrips agriculture in terms of economic value by about four times. The constitution is based on the monarch, who cannot act without the consent of the democratically-elected parliament. Parliament includes members from Greenland and the Faroes, which are dependencies of the Danish Crown.

ESTONIA

Population: 1.5 million
Area: 45,000 square kilometres
Capital: Tallinn
Language: Estonian and Russian
Currency: Rouble

In September 1991 Estonia was accepted as an independent nation for the first time since it annexation by the Soviet Union in 1939. The republic has been dominated by economic central planning from Moscow for over five decades and relies heavily on agriculture for employment and prosperity. Gas-rich shale and phosphates represent the only mineral wealth and industrial base for this small nation. Co-operation with the other Baltic states is already established and other foreign economic links are being vigorously pursued.

FINLAND

Population: 5 million
Area: 338,000 square kilometres
Capital: Helsinki
Language: Finnish
Currency: Markka

Ruled in turn by Denmark, Sweden and Russia, Finland gained independence in 1917, when the people took advantage of the chaos

following the Russian Revolution to seize power for themselves. In 1940 war with Russia resulted in Finland losing much territory around Lake Ladoga to the Soviets. Modern foreign policy emphasises the need for friendly relations with Russia and with Scandinavian nations. The economy of the nation is mixed and broadly based. The vast forests provide raw material for a lumber trade. The small area of land suitable for agriculture is heavily used for the raising of livestock, particularly cattle in the south and reindeer in the north. Industry is concentrated on the extraction and processing of iron deposits, though many other businesses flourish.

FRANCE

Population: 56 million
Area: 543,000 square kilometres
Capital: Paris
Language: French
Currency: French Franc

The modern state of France is generally traced back to the accession of the Capetian dynasty to the throne of the Western Franks in 987, though Frankish power was established in the region as early as 500 a.d. The monarchy was overthrown in the Revolution of 1789, after which France was ruled by republics, emperors and kings. The Fifth Republic was established in 1958. The present constitution allows for a democratically-elected parliament, which operates under the guidance of an elected President. The economy of the nation is highly developed, with industry and services being dominant employers. Agriculture remains largely in the hands of small-scale farmers and produces quantities of grain and fruits, most notably grapes, from which the famous French wines are produced.

GERMANY

Population: 80 million
Area: 357,000 square kilometres
Capital: Berlin
Language: German
Currency: Mark

Unity and division have been the hallmarks of German history. The disparate German tribes were united under the Frankish Empire in the 9th century, but this fell apart, to be replaced by the Holy Roman Empire of the Middle Ages. Initially strong, the Empire broke up into dozens of petty feudal states and city republics. The Napoleonic Wars swept this pattern away and in 1871 the German states were united under Prussian rule as the German Empire. This nation remained together until 1945, when Germany lost much territory and was divided as Communist East and Democratic West Germany. In 1990 the overthrow of the Communist regime in East Germany led to reunification. The strong West German economy is concentrating on raising the prosperity of East Germany. Agriculture is well developed throughout the country.

GREECE

Population: 10 million
Area: 132,000 square kilometres
Capital: Athens
Language: Greek
Currency: Drachma

Home of the ancient civilisation which has had such a profound influence on all Western culture, Greece is today working to join the front runners in European economies. The magnificent history, fine climate and attractive beaches have made Greece a favourite tourist resort for generations, and recent developments have boosted this business to the point where it welcomes over seven million visitors each year. Tourism is now the largest single industry in terms of foreign earnings. The mountainous terrain limits agriculture, but there are extensive olive groves and citrus orchards producing over a million tonnes of each product annually. Industry is less dominant than in other European nations and is concentrated on food processing, textiles and leatherwork. After a period of military rule in the 1970s, Greece has reverted to a democratic system.

HUNGARY

Population: 11 million
Area: 93,000 square kilometres
Capital: Budapest
Language: Magyar
Currency: Forint

Formerly a dominant state within the Hapsburg Empire, which ruled the Danube Basin from the Alps to the Black Sea, Hungary became independent in 1918. In 1949 a Communist government was imposed and the 1956 nationalist rising was put down by Russian tanks and troops. After popular protests and demands for reform, the Communist Party was disbanded in 1989 and opened the way for democratic elections, which took place in 1990. The great flat plain of Hungary has dominated the economy for generations. Its fertile soils and temperate climate make abundant crops possible. Wheat, maize and potatoes are the main crops, and large numbers of cattle and pigs are raised. In recent years industry has rapidly gained over agriculture and now dominates the economy, with metallurgy,

chemicals and electronics predominating.

ICELAND

Population: 253,000
Area: 103,000 square kilometres
Capital: Reykjavik
Language: Icelandic
Currency: Icelandic Krona

Viking settlers began arriving in Iceland in the 9th century, ousting the few Irish monks who had already established themselves. An independent society existed based on Viking social rules until 1264, when factional violence led to Norwegian control. In 1381 Iceland passed to the Danish crown, recovering full self-government in 1918 and severance from Denmark in 1946. The present republic operates with two chambers working under an elected President. Only two percent of land is farmed, producing potatoes, turnips and hay. Livestock is kept in small numbers. Fishing provides the basis of the economy, with Icelandic trawlers harvesting the rich reserves of white fish in the chill northern waters. Industry is very limited.

IRELAND

Population: 3.5 million
Area: 70,000 square kilometres
Capital: Dublin
Language: Gaelic and English
Currency: Irish Pound

After centuries of growing British influence, Ireland joined with Britain in 1801. In 1921 the Catholic southern counties of Ireland gained independence after an armed uprising and became the Republic of Eire in 1948, the Protestant counties of Ulster remaining part of Britain. Ongoing civil violence and terrorist activities have disrupted life in border counties and dominate Irish relations with Britain. The economy is traditionally agricultural. Large numbers of cattle produce dairy products, and sheep and pigs provide meat. The former reliance on potato crops has been reduced and larger areas are now under grains than under potatoes. Industrial activity has grown rapidly in recent years, and this is now more important to the economy than agriculture. Food processing, textiles and electrical engineering are the dominant industries.

ITALY

Population: 57 million
Area: 301,000 square kilometres
Capital: Rome
Language: Italian
Currency: Italian Lira

The various city states, kingdoms

and duchies of Italy were not united until 1861, and the republic was established in 1946. The present constitution allows for two chambers, the lower elected directly and the upper elected by the historic regions. The President is elected by the two houses of parliament. There are numerous political parties representing many shades of opinion, though fascism is banned. Southern parts of the country are generally less well developed than the north. Agriculture based on olives, wheat and sheep dominates in Sicily and the land south of Naples. More northerly farms tend to be large commercial concerns producing cash crops of sugar beet, tomatoes and fruits. Grapes are widely grown for wine production. Industry is concentrated in northern cities where textiles, food processing and the manufacture of machinery lead the sector.

LATVIA

Population: 2.6 million
Area: 64,000 square kilometres
Capital: Riga
Language: Latvian and Russian
Currency: Rouble

The troubled history of Latvia as an independent nation began with a democratic government being installed with British military support in 1919 after a brief Soviet regime and came to an end in 1940 when Soviet power was reimposed. Together with Lithuania and Estonia, Latvia became independent once again after the failed coup in Moscow of August 1991. Five decades of economic central planning has given Latvia a heritage of heavy industry, with steel, railway equipment and textiles dominating. The previous agricultural economic base has been reduced to a substantial minority of wealth-creating activity.

LIECHTENSTEIN

Population: 28,000
Area: 160 square kilometres
Capital: Vaduz
Language: German
Currency: Swiss Franc

The tiny principality of Liechtenstein dates back to 1434, when the Count of Vaduz gained control of Schellenberg. In 1712 the principality passed to the Liechtenstein family, which held it directly from the Holy Roman Emperor. When that empire collapsed in 1806 the family retained their domains, and in 1923 joined Switzerland in a customs and currency union. The present constitution places power in the hands of the Prince, though legislation needs approval of the democratically-elected parliament.

▲ *Dusk in Mykonos, Greece.*

▲ *A Round Tower, Co. Wicklow, Ireland.*

▼ *Luxembourg, one of Europe's smallest nations.*

▲ *The Principality of Monaco.*

▼ *The Principality of Liechtenstein.*

▲ *The River Danube, Budapest, Hungary.*

◄ *Heavy industry, Lithuania*

▲ *A characteristic view of Malta.*

▼ *The Old City, Riga, Latvia.*

◄ *The Colosseum, Rome, Italy.*

▲ *Kinderdijk, east of Rotterdam, Netherlands.*

The economy is based on a mixture of agriculture, light industry and commerce. Many companies have their nominal headquarters in Liechtenstein and their taxation contributes to the state income.

LITHUANIA

Population: 3.7 million
Area: 65,000 square kilometres
Capital: Vilnius
Language: Lithuanian and Russian
Currency: Rouble

With a population over 80 percent ethnic Lithuanians, the republic has long desired independence. In March 1991 an overwhelming majority voted for separation from the Soviet Union, but not until the failed coup of August 1991 did this freedom become a reality. Traditionally an agricultural nation, Lithuania is now dominated by industry. Heavy engineering and textiles dominate the economic scene, although forestry and agriculture are significant employers.

LUXEMBOURG

Population: 379,000
Area: 2,500 square kilometres
Capital: Luxembourg
Language: German and French
Currency: Luxembourg Franc

The tiny state of Luxembourg enjoyed varying degrees of self government until being conquered by France in 1795. In 1815 the current Grand Duchy came into being under the Dutch monarchy, and in 1890 full independence came when a junior branch of the Dutch royal family inherited Luxembourg. The Grand Duke is closely involved in administration with the democratically-elected parliament. The nation is part of a customs union with Belgium and Belgian currency can be used within Luxembourg. Industry is based on a thriving iron and steel business, though attempts are being made to diversify the economy. Agriculture plays a minor role in national life with the production of grain, market crops and meat as well as a small quantity of wine.

MALTA

Population: 354,000
Area: 316 square kilometres
Capital: Valletta
Language: Maltese and English
Currency: Maltese Pound

During World War II Malta was a vital British naval base and came under massive attack by German and Italian forces. In 1942 King George VI awarded the George Cross to the people of Malta. This medal is featured on the Maltese flag, together with the colours of the religious Knights of Malta, who ruled between 1530 and 1798. Malta gained independence from Britain in 1964, though economic ties remain close. Malta's strategic position in the Mediterranean makes commerce, trade and ship-building lucrative industries. Tourism has long been important and about 800,000 visitors arrive each year. Tourism is the biggest single earner of foreign currency for Malta. The constitution is a multi-party democracy in which two major parties dominate.

MONACO

Population: 30,000
Area: 1.5 square kilometres
Capital: Monaco
Language: Monegasque and French
Currency: French Franc

The small Principality of Monaco has been the domain of the Grimaldi family since 1297, placing itself under French protection in 1861. The traditional Grimaldi colours make up the flag, which is almost identical to that of Indonesia except that it is slightly shorter. The constitution allows for democratic government though the Prince retains much influence. The main economic base of Monaco is tourism, with nearly ten times as many visitors as residents in the course of a year. The scenic coastline and fine beach delight many tourists, but it is the famous casino which is the major attraction. The nightlife is hectic and provides entertainment for those tourists who have tired of gambling. Agriculture is virtually non-existent but the industrial sector is growing in importance.

NETHERLANDS

Population: 15 million
Area: 34,0000 square kilometres
Capital: Amsterdam and The Hague
Language: Dutch
Currency: Dutch Guilder

The present nation came into being in the late 16th century, when the prosperous Protestant cities rebelled against oppressive Catholic rule from Spain. Much of the Netherlands has been reclaimed from the sea by massive projects, culminating in over 1,000-square-kilometres being reclaimed from the Zuider Zee this century. Much of this land is devoted to agriculture, with potatoes, sugar beet and grain and dairy farming being important. The nation's position at the mouth of the Rhine has long ensured lucrative trade and commerce connections. The Netherlands still enjoy much transshipment trade and processes many raw materials for re-export.

13

NORWAY

Population: 4.2 million
Area: 324,000 square kilometres
Capital: Oslo
Language: Norwegian
Currency: Norwegian Krone

In 1905 Norway gained independence from Sweden and took Prince Carl of Denmark as its first monarch. The constitution places power in the hands of a democratically-elected parliament, though the monarch retains control of the armed forces and has the power to veto any legislation. The mountainous terrain makes agriculture difficult and much food needs to be imported. Hydro-electric power is produced in quantity and supplies ninety-nine percent of domestic needs. Offshore oil and gas has added to the energy self-reliance of Norway. Industry is prosperous and is based on the processing of domestic metals, agricultural products and timber from the vast upland forests.

▲ *The Lofoten Islands, Norway.*

POLAND

Population: 38 million
Area: 312,000 square kilometres
Capital: Warsaw
Language: Polish
Currency: Zloty

The powerful kingdom of Poland collapsed in the late 18th century and was divided between the growing Prussian, Hapsburg and Russian empires. Reconstitution and independence did not occur until 1918. The German invasion of Poland in 1939 sparked the Second World War, and following liberation in 1945 Poland was ruled by a Communist regime imposed by Russia. Communist rule ended in 1989 after several years of opposition from the Solidarity trade union. Free elections were called for 1991, with opposition parties campaigning for the first time in decades. The Polish economy is industrially based, with iron and steel, machine manufacture and textiles being the most important.

The agricultural sector is still important, producing wheat, rye and potatoes, together with large quantities of dairy produce.

PORTUGAL

Population: 10 million
Area: 92,000 square kilometres
Capital: Lisbon
Language: Portuguese
Currency: Escudo

The coup of 1974 overthrew the dictatorship which had governed Portugal since 1933, and in 1976 introduced a democratic constitution for only the second time in Portugal's 800-year history. The present constitution, adopted in 1982, allows for an elected President who chooses the Prime Minister from the Assembly, which is elected by universal suffrage. The economy is presently dominated by the dismantling of government control and privatisation of industry. Manufacturing is based on textiles and leather goods together with ceramics. Agriculture is based on grains and potatoes, and wine, cork and olives are important cash crops for export.

ROMANIA

Population: 23 million
Area: 238,000 square kilometres
Capital: Bucharest
Language: Romanian and Hungarian
Currency: Leu

The overthrow of the Communist regime of President Ceausescu was attended by street fighting and great confusion. A temporary government was elected in 1990 to draw up a new constitution based on democratic principles. Until the Communist takeover in 1947 Romania was a traditionally agricultural kingdom with little industry. The past decades have seen massive government encouragement of industry, which today has overtaken agriculture as an employer and is concentrated on iron and steel, chemicals and textiles. The farms continue to produce large quantities of wheat and maize, while shepherding is as important as it was before the advent of the Communist regime.

SAN MARINO

Population: 23,000
Area: 61 square kilometres
Capital: San Marino
Language: Italian
Currency: Italian Lira

Legend has it that the 4th-century Saint Marinus founded the republic as a self-governing Christian community to escape Imperial persecution. The republic won full independence from the Pope in 1631, and in 1862 concluded a treaty of friendship with the newly-created Italian nation, which secured continued independence. Agriculture is an important source of employment and wine is exported. Small-scale industrial activity includes chemicals, ceramics and paints. Much economic wealth comes from tourism and the sale of the unique coins and stamps of the republic.

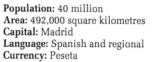

SPAIN

Population: 40 million
Area: 492,000 square kilometres
Capital: Madrid
Language: Spanish and regional
Currency: Peseta

Spain regained its monarchy in 1975 after an interruption of forty-four years. King Juan Carlos is carefully leading his nation to democracy and stability. The constitution vests power in a parliament named the *Cortes*, with a main body elected by proportional representation and a senate elected by province. The traditional agricultural economic base has now been overtaken by industry, but remains important. Wheat and barley are the major crops. Industry is dominated by motor vehicles, textiles, paper, and iron and steel, which together account for the majority of exports.

SWEDEN

Population: 8.5 million
Area: 450,000 square kilometres
Capital: Stockholm
Language: Swedish
Currency: Swedish Krona

Sweden acquired approximately its present boundaries a thousand years ago, but has since been united with other Scandinavian nations, and in the 17th century enjoyed Baltic hegemony. The present dynasty dates from 1809, when the highly-successful French general Jean Bernadotte was chosen to become king on the extinction of the native line. The constitution introduced in 1975 reduced the role of monarch to ceremonial and gave power to the democratic parliament. The highly-prosperous economy is based on iron ore deposits, the forests and immense hydro-electric power. Over half of all manufacturing is made up of metal smelting, metal machinery and other metal products. A further quarter of the sector is composed of timber, plywood and other wood products. Agriculture is well developed, but on a small scale.

SWITZERLAND

Population: 6.7 million
Area: 41,000 square kilometres
Capital: Bern
Language: German, French, Italian and Romansch
Currency: Swiss Franc

The confederation of twenty-three cantons which makes up Switzerland is famous for its neutrality. But the state had its origins in a defensive alliance between Uri Schwyz and Unterwalden in 1291, and saw many wars in its early centuries of existence. The constitution vests supreme power in the electorate which can demand laws and changes to the constitution without regard to the wishes of the two-chamber parliament. Each canton is self-governing, with its own parliament; the federal government being responsible for war, peace and treaties. Isolated Alpine valleys continue to practise agriculture on traditional lines, but most crops are grown on the fertile central plain. Manufacturing is a major activity and is based on textiles, chemicals and the processing of agricultural produce. Banking and finance is a well-established sector of the economy.

THE FORMER USSR THE COMMONWEALTH OF INDEPENDENT STATES

Successor to the Soviet Union, the Commonwealth of Independent States came into being following the August 1991 coup and the collapse of the old regime. Embracing most of the republics formerly within the USSR, it is intended that this loose and hastily designed structure handle only major central issues such as nuclear weapon deployment, with other powers being assumed by the individual nations.

ARMENIA

Area: 30,000 square kilometres
Population: 3.3 million
Capital: Yerevan
Language: Armenian, Russian, Kurdish
Currency: Rouble

Armenia's rugged terrain allows only limited agriculture based on olive groves, cotton and sub-tropical fruits. Wide ranging mineral deposits are more promising for the economy and efficient exploitation of these in the wake of freedom from central Soviet planning may lead to prosperity.

AZERBAIJAN

Area: 87,000 square kilometres
Population: 7 million
Capital: Baku
Language: Azerbaijani, Armenian, Russian
Currency: Rouble

Recently the scene of ethnic violence between the Azerbaijani majority and the Armenian minority, this republic is rich in natural resources. Industry is based on reserves of oil, iron ore, bauxite and various precious metals. Agriculturally, the republic produces rubber, grapes and tobacco along with other warm weather crops.

BELORUSSIA

Area: 208,000 square kilometres
Population: 10 million
Capital: Minsk
Language: Russian, Polish and other languages
Currency: Rouble

Belorussia has taken a lead in the development of the CIS and its institutions. The economy of the republic is based on the rich pasture land and pockets of agricultural land. The processing of the farm output accounts for much of the industry, but there are also large chemical and steel concerns.

GEORGIA

Area: 70,000 square kilometres
Population: 5.5 million
Capital: Tblisi
Language: Georgian, Armenian, Russian
Currency: Rouble

Vast manganese deposits form the basis for the prosperous mining industry of Georgia, though coal is also found in quantity and other minerals are expoited on a smaller scale. The warm climate enables production of silk, tea and wine in large quantities.

INFORMATION AWAITED SOVIET-STYLE FLAG STILL IN USE

KAZAKHSTAN

Area: 2,717,000 square kilometres
Population: 16.5 million
Capital: Alma-Ata
Language: Russian, Kazakh
Currency: Rouble

Since the collapse of the USSR, Kazakhstan has emerged as one of the Central Asian Republics of the CIS, a region with interests that are distinct from the other states of the new Commonwealth. Formerly a pastoral economy, agriculture and the mineral wealth are now exploited on a large scale.

INFORMATION AWAITED SOVIET-STYLE FLAG STILL IN USE

KIRGHIZIA

Population: 4.2 million
Area: 198,000 square kilometres
Capital: Bishbek
Language: Kirghiz-Turkish, Russian, Jagatai
Currency: Rouble

Traditionally a pastoral region, the economy of Kirghizia remains firmly based on livestock. Agriculture has become established in recent years, with grain crops and tobacco particularly important. Much of the industry is based on processing

agricultural products, though mining contributes to the economy.

MOLDOVA

Area: 34,000 square kilometres
Population: 4 million
Capital: Kishinev
Language: Romanian, Russian, Gagauzi
Currency: Rouble

Populated mainly with ethnic Romanians, the republic is economically dominated by agriculture and the processing of farm products. Only the production of concrete and other building materials breaks the pattern.

RUSSIA

Area: 17,075,000 square kilometres
Population: 148 million
Capital: Moscow
Language: Russian, numerous other languages
Currency: Rouble

The largest of the republics within the CIS. Industry is highly developed and is a major employer. Russia's economy has led the way in throwing off central state control and embracing free market principles.

▲ *The golden domes of the Kremlin, Moscow, Russia*

INFORMATION AWAITED SOVIET-STYLE FLAG STILL IN USE

TAJIKISTAN

Population: 5 million
Area: 143,000 square kilometres
Capital: Dushandbe
Language: Tajik-Persian, Jagatai, Russian
Currency: Rouble

The republic is largely dependent on agriculture, with irrigation enabling the production of warm-climate fruits including lemons, oranges, figs and olives on a large scale, while pasturelands support large herds of cattle and sheep. Coal, lead and zinc mining account for most industrial activity in Tajikistan.

INFORMATION AWAITED SOVIET-STYLE FLAG STILL IN USE

TURKMENISTAN

Area: 488,000 square kilometres
Population: 3.5 million

Capital: Ashkhabad
Language: Turkish, Russian, Jagatai
Currency: Rouble

Rich oil, coal and sulphur deposits form the basis for an industrial economy, although agriculture, notably cotton, maize, fruit and vegetables, provides the majority of the employment. Turkmenistan was the first of the Central Asian Republics to declare itself free of Moscow, in August 1990.

UKRAINE

Area: 604,00 square kilometres
Population: 52 million
Capital: Kiev
Language: Ukrainian and Russian
Currency: Rouble

The traditional grain basket of eastern Europe, the Ukraine is still a highly productive agricultural region, with nearly half of the crops of the CIS coming from this country. Large deposits of coal and oil have boosted the industrial sector in recent years.

UZBEKISTAN

Area: 447,000 square kilometres
Population: 20 million
Capital: Tashkent
Language: Jagatai, Russian, Tatar
Currency: Rouble

The Uzbek economy is based on intensive agriculture producing silk, rice, sub-tropical fruits and grapes with mineral exploitation on a modest scale. Industry is limited and is largely based on the rich deposits of oil, coal and copper.

UNITED KINGDOM

Population: 57 million
Area: 243,000 square kilometres
Capital: London
Language: English, Welsh and Gaelic
Currency: Pound Sterling

The United Kingdom is a constitutional monarchy governing Britain, the northern counties of Ireland and neighbouring islands. The kingdoms of England and Scotland were united in 1603 when King James VI of Scotland inherited the English throne. The Parliaments merged a century later, but administration and justice remain distinct to some extent. The constitution allows for a single elected chamber together with a part-appointed, part-inherited House of Lords. The monarch has far-reaching powers, but in practice follows the wishes of Parliament. Agriculture is well developed, and produces about half the nation's requirements. Industry and commerce are the basis of the economic wealth of this prosperous nation.

VATICAN

Population: 700
Area: 0.3 square kilometres
Capital: Vatican City
Language: Italian and Latin
Currency: Italian Lira

The Vatican is the smallest independent state in the world and exists solely as the residence of the Pope. Until 1860 the Pope ruled extensive areas of central Italy, but these were incorporated in the newly-created Kingdom of Italy, which in 1870 invaded Rome itself and confined the Pope to the complex of religious and administrative buildings known as the Vatican. In 1929 the Vatican was recognised as an independent state in return for the Pope relinquishing claims over Rome and surrounding territory. The Vatican has no industry, no agriculture and no commerce, though some income is gained from tourism. It is the administrative headquarters of the Catholic Church, which pays for its upkeep.

(Former)
YUGOSLAVIA

Population: 24 million
Area: 255,000 square kilometres
Capital: Belgrade
Language: Serbian, Croat, Slovene, Macedonian and others
Currency: Yugoslavian Dinar

Yugoslavia came into being in 1918 as a confederation of southern Slavonic peoples newly independent of the Hapsburg Empire. A new constitution of 1946 made the nation a grouping of six republics, in which Communism was the only legal political party. Agriculture still employs about a quarter of the workforce. Industry has increased rapidly, particularly in the north. Iron and steel, chemicals and textiles are the primary industries. Attempts in 1989-90 by the central government to curb the internal government of the republics led to widespread protest. The prosperous northern industrial republics of Slovenia and Croatia declared themselves independent in June 1991. In September 1991, the southern republic of Macedonia proclaimed its independence; no major foreign power has as yet accorded it recognition. The disintegration of the confederation continued with the declaration of independence by Bosnia-Herzegovina in March 1992, leading to fierce fighting and a fragile ceasefire.

CROATIA   SLOVENIA

BOSNIA-HERZEGOVINA

ASIA

*A*sia is the largest and most populated continent on Earth. Just two nations, China and India, between them account for nearly two billion inhabitants. An Asian country, Bangladesh is the most densely populated on Earth, with around 730 people to each square kilometre. This compares to a mere twenty-five per square kilometre in the United States.

The incredible population statistics are made possible by the remarkably fertile soils and productive climates of Asia. Bangladesh, for example, is almost ideal for rice cultivation. The monsoon climate provides the alternate wet and dry season needed by the cereal, while the flat landscape makes the flooding and draining of fields easy to accomplish. Massive crops are produced each year. Similar conditions prevail in eastern China, where rural populations have reached saturation point in some areas.

But if Asia has been endowed with vast, life-giving resources, it also has its share of natural disasters. Earthquakes, floods and typhoons are common. Given the concentrated populations, these calamities claim horrendous death tolls among the local peoples. Many regions of Asia have a history scattered with the records of bumper crops leading to population booms, the children of which are then wiped out by disaster and famine.

Not only does Asia contain some of the densest populations in the world, it also boasts some of the emptiest regions anywhere. The vast expanses of Siberia consist of open tundra bordering the Arctic Ocean and, further south, extensive boreal forests. These great coniferous forests cover a staggering 1,100,000,000 hectares and are though to contain about one-quarter of all the world's trees.

In central eastern Asia there are extensive grasslands on which pastoralist peoples lead traditional lives which have scarcely changed in centuries. Mongolia and neighbouring sections of both China and and the former Soviet Union are the home of ethnic Mongols, who herd cattle and horses on the open plains as their ancestors have done for millenia.

Ethnically, the population of Asia is incredibly diverse. In addition to recent immigrations of Europeans and Africans there is a wide range of indigenous peoples. In the far east Mongoloid races form the vast majority. In the sub-continent of India Indo-Europeans and Dravidians constitute the bulk of the population. Here, as elsewhere in Asia, there are remnant populations of far older peoples. The inland uplands of Sri Lanka are home to the Veddah, who are apparently unrelated to the majority population but have affinities with the Aboriginals of Australia. Similarly enigmatic are the Ainu of Japan.

Culturally, too, the Asians present a bewildering picture to the world. Asia has been the cradle of major world religions: Buddhism, Hinduism, Confucianism and Taoism all originated in Asia, and continue to find the bulk of their adherents on that continent. Islam, originating on the Arabian peninsula, has spread across much of southern Asia as far as the Pacific Ocean.

The vast continent of Asia is rich in both agricultural and human resources. However, much of the population continues to live at subsistence level. Great increases in the number of humans has kept pace with improved farming technology and crop increases, so that the per capita wealth remains low. National prosperity in most nations is devoted to finding food for their growing populations rather than in improving the standard of living. So long as this cycle of improved food production and increased population continues, the traditional lifestyles and general impoverishment of Asia looks set to continue.

▲ *The Himalayas, Nepal.*

▼ *Temple dancers, Bali, Indonesia.*

◄ *Lake Kawaguchi and Mount Fujiyama, Japan.*

▼ *A natural rock formation in Dukhan, Qatar.*

◄ *The back-breaking task of planting rice, Laos.*

▼ *The bustling city of Taipei, Taiwan.*

17

AFGHANISTAN

Population: 16 million
Area: 652,000 square miles
Capital: Kabul
Language: Pustu and Dari
Currency: Afghani

Afghanistan is a country in turmoil, and has been for generations. The Soviet invasion of 1979 led to the various factions uniting against the aggressor. The withdrawal of Soviet troops has allowed the chieftains and religious leaders to resume their internal disputes. The mountainous republic has a long tradition of tribal independence and weak government control. The social structure remains fragmented, with most of the population belonging to distinctly different ethnic groups united by the Islamic religion. The bulk of the population are subsistence farmers or nomadic herdsmen, the latter mainly in the south. Fruit, bread and mutton are the basis of the nation's self-produced food supply. The only mineral wealth is natural gas in the far north, which is piped directly to the USSR.

BAHRAIN

Population: 486,000
Area: 687 square kilometres
Capital: Manama
Language: Arabic
Currency: Bahraini Dinar

In 1882 the Emirate of Bahrain handed control of its foreign affairs to Britain, whose navy was in the process of suppressing the endemic piracy of the Arabian Gulf. In 1971 the arrangement was ended and the Emir proclaimed his nation's independence and soon after dismissed Parliament to rule the nation himself. Until 1931 Bahrain was an impoverished state subsisting on pearl fishing, small scale agriculture and the profits of trade. The discovery of oil changed everything and vast wealth poured into the nation. The thirty-three islands now support a flourishing manufacturing economy, including the production of aluminium alloys, ships and medical equipment. So many people now live in Bahrain that ninety percent of food needs to be imported and water supply is a chronic problem.

BANGLADESH

Population: 115 million
Area: 144,000 square kilometres
Capital: Dhaka
Language: Bangla and English
Currency: Taka

In a good year Bangladesh is almost ideally suited to intensive cultivation of rice. As many as three heavy crops can be grown on the rich soils within just twelve months. As a consequence the nation is extremely densely populated by peasant farmers growing vast crops for their own consumption and for sale. Unfortunately, recurrent natural disasters, such as floods and cyclones, take a heavy toll in human life and destroy crops. The extremely high birth rate causes an ever-growing population which ensures that the agricultural wealth is fully used feeding the people rather than in improving their living conditions. Other than glass sand, mineral deposits scarcely exist and industry is negligible. The government is notoriously unstable, having suffered numerous coups and military takeovers since independence from Pakistan in 1971.

BHUTAN

Population: 1.4 million
Area: 47,000 square kilometres
Capital: Thimphu
Language: Dzongkha, Nepalese, English
Currency: Ngultrum

The mountain kingdom of Bhutan is an anomaly in India, having managed to retain its quasi-independence when Britain withdrew from the subcontinent, while other kingdoms became merged into the new state of India. Bhutan receives an annual subsidy from India in return for abiding by that country's foreign policy. Internal government is conducted by the king, with the advice of an elected assembly. The electoral system is unusual in that each family has one vote regardless of its number, and monks are separately represented. Bhutan is made up of a number of valleys isolated from each other by precipitous mountains and sheer cliffs. The different ethnic groups have scarcely mixed and they retain their identities. The basis of the economy is agriculture, with many hill tribes surviving at subsistence level. Large mineral deposits have been found but the difficult terrain has hampered exploitation.

BRUNEI

Population: 267,000
Area: 5,700 square kilometres
Capital: Bandar Seri Begawan
Language: Malay and English
Currency: Brunei Dollar

The Sultan of Brunei is reputed to the be the richest man on earth, with a personal fortune in the region of twenty-six billion US Dollars. This massive wealth is based on the oilfields of Brunei and on the fact that all national finance is conducted through the Sultan. The first oil well was sunk in 1929, and since that time fresh reserves have been continually identified. Oil production remains high and is the basis of the nation's wealth. The Sultan is currently encouraging the growth of other businesses in order to limit his people's reliance on international oil prices. The traditional industries of boat-building, silver-smithing and weaving remain in operation, and the agriculture of the tropical country continues to produce rubber, fruits and rice.

BURMA

Population: 40 million
Area: 676,000 square kilometres
Capital: Rangoon
Language: Burmese, Thai, English
Currency: Kyat

Burmese history has been one of upheaval, fragmentation and unification. The process continues today, with vociferous separatist movements among the various minority populations which live in the country. Since Burma was granted its freedom by Britain in 1947 there have been numerous coups and attempted coups. The military junta which seized power in 1988 recently held democratic elections but power remains with the army, which numbers over 200,000. Burma is dominated by traditional agriculture, based on rice, cattle and pigs, which flourishes in the wet tropical climate of the region. Industrial activity is mainly concerned with processing cash crops of sugar and cotton or with manufacturing fertiliser and agricultural tools.

▲ *Temples in Rangoon, Burma.*

CHINA (PEOPLE'S REPUBLIC)

Population: 1,115 million
Area: 9,572,000 square kilometres
Capital: Peking
Language: Mandarin and numerous dialects
Currency: Renminbi Yuan

With a civilisation dating back at least 3,500 years, China has one of the oldest cultures on earth. Despite periods of civil war and instability, there has been a constant pressure for unity among the Chinese, principally to resist the incursions of foreign barbarians. The Empire collapsed in 1912, to be replaced by the rule of several warlords. The Communist Party restored unity in 1949 under Chairman Mao, and has held power since. China's economy is based on intensive cultivation of rice, wheat and beans together with the raising of cattle, pigs and sheep. Small scale, traditional industries are carried on within villages, but large, state-run factories in the cities produce silk, cotton and heavy industrial goods, both for internal consumption and export.

▲ *Tianzi Mountains, China.*

▼ *The ancient town of Dali, China.*

INDIA

Population: 843 million
Area: 3,166,000 square kilometres
Capital: New Delhi
Language: Hindi, English and various regional languages
Currency: Rupee

The most populous democracy in the world has experienced unrest in recent years with the assassination of two prime ministers and demands for independence by ethnic minorities. Despite this, however, the polyglot nation remains intact and the processes of democracy have not been overthrown. The present Indian state originated in 1947, when the provinces of British India gained independence and joined with several semi-independent monarchies to form a federal union. The economic base of the nation is agriculture, which has benefited from modern technology in recent years, ensuring that famines are a thing of the past. Rice and wheat are the main crops, though beans and sugar are also produced. Tea is grown in large quantities for export, and coffee production is increasing. Industry has grown in recent years, but remains at a low technical level and chiefly supplies local demand.

▲ *Dusty hill-country, Afghanistan.*

▶ *Tropical rain forest, Brunei.*

▲ *Zhang Jia Khou Pass, Great Wall, China.*

▲ *Ceremonial costumes, Bhutan.*

▼ *The 'Wailing Wall', Jerusalem, Israel.*

▲ *New development in oil-rich Bahrain.*

▼ *In the Golden Temple of Amritsar, India.*

▲ *Low-lying Bangladesh, veined by rivers.*

▼ *14th Ramadhan Mosque, Baghdad, Iraq.*

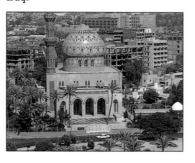

◀ *Tehran, capital of Iran.*

INDONESIA

Population: 180 million
Area: 1,920,000 square kilometres
Capital: Jakarta
Language: Malay, Indonesian, English and Dutch
Currency: Rupiah

The East Indies, of which area Indonesia occupies a large percentage, were previously famous as the Spice Islands, from which came mace, nutmeg, cinnamon and pepper to grace the cuisines of the world. So valuable was this trade that fierce battles were fought along the trade routes and for control of the islands themselves. In the early 17th century the Dutch gained dominance of the islands and remained the ruling power until the Japanese invasion of 1941. Independence came in 1949, since when the islands have experienced periods of both democracy and dictatorship, the former presently pertaining. Spices are now negligible in the Indonesian economy. Oilfields are dominant, producing most of southern Asia's oil, backed by copper and manufactured goods. Agriculture employs many people in the production of rice, cassava and sweet potatoes for local consumption and coffee, rubber and coconuts for export.

IRAN

Population: 54 million
Area: 1,648,000 square kilometres
Capital: Tehran
Language: Persian, Kurdish and Arabic
Currency: Rial

In 1979 a popular revolution overthrew the monarchy and established Islamic Republic under the religious control of the Ayatollah Khomeni. This event marked a fundamentalist revival of Islam, which has been felt elsewhere throughout the Islamic world. The basis of the modern Iranian economy is oil, which was discovered in 1908. The industry has suffered several setbacks with the destruction of refineries and ports during the Iran-Iraq War of 1980-88, but oil remains the chief export and currency earner. Other minerals exist in some quantity but are exploited on only a modest scale. Most of the country is unsuited to agriculture due to the lack of rain, but crops include wheat and barley. Millions of sheep, cattle and goats are grazed on the sparse grasslands.

IRAQ

Population: 17 million
Area: 435,000 square kilometres
Capital: Baghdad
Language: Arabic and Kurdish
Currency: Iraqi Dinar

The economy of Iraq was severely

disrupted by the Desert Storm War of 1990-91 and is not yet recovered. The war began in August 1990 when Iraq invaded Kuwait without warning and announced the annexation of that state. International forces gathered in Saudi Arabia while attempts were made to persuade Iraq to withdraw. On 16th January allied air strikes on Iraqi positions began and in February a lightning campaign codenamed Desert Storm crushed the Iraqi army and liberated Kuwait. International sanctions on Iraq crippled its economy, which before the war was based on oil exports. Internally agriculture is a major employer and large crops can be raised in the fertile Tigris-Euphrates Valley. Industry was poorly developed before hostilities. The nation is ruled by the Ba'th Party led by Saddam Hussein, the country's President.

ISRAEL

Population: 5 million
Area: 21,000 square kilometres
Capital: Jerusalem
Language: Hebrew, Arabic and English
Currency: Shekel

The six pointed Star of David dominates the flag of Israel, symbolising the overwhelming Jewish heritage of the nation. The state of Israel came into being in 1948 as a homeland for Jews from across the world. The demand for a Jewish state became especially strong after the persecution at the hands of the Nazis. As soon as Israel came into being it was invaded by Arab states, and the nation's history has been dominated by intermittent warfare and constant terrorist activities to the present day. Israel currently occupies large areas of territory which officially belong to neighbouring states. The nation has few mineral resources and agriculture is only possible in irrigated areas. Israel produces much of its own food and its manufacturing industries are healthy.

JAPAN

Population: 124 million
Area: 378,000 square kilometres
Capital: Tokyo
Language: Japanese
Currency: Yen

The Emperor of Japan belongs to a family which has occupied the throne for many centuries, reputedly since the sun goddess began the dynasty in around 600 BC. For many years the nation was actually ruled by powerful noblemen known as Shogun, but the Emperor regained power in 1867, and in 1947 the present democratic constitution was introduced. Since the devastation of the Second World War,

Japan has fully revitalised its industry and is now a major economic world power. The most important industries are iron and steel, electronics and chemicals, in which Japan leads the world in technical expertise as well as profitable productivity. The small area of land suitable for agriculture is intensively worked to produce rice, fruit and livestock, but the nation needs to import most of its foods.

JORDAN

Population: 3.2 million
Area: 91,000 square kilometres
Capital: Amman
Language: Arabic
Currency: Jordanian Dinar

The kingdom of Jordan is ruled by King Hussein, last surviving monarch of the four Arab kingdoms established following the collapse of the Ottoman Empire in 1918. Political parties have recently been legalised in the kingdom, though elections to Parliament have not been called. During the 1967 war with Israel, Jordan lost control of the West Bank of the River Jordan which remains under Israeli control. This entailed the loss of nearly half of the kingdom's fertile land, a serious blow to an economy dependent on agriculture. The farmland of Jordan produces large quantities of tomatoes, olives and citrus fruits. Livestock is grazed on the arid grasslands and near desert of the east. Industry is dependent on the mining and processing of phosphates and potash.

KAMPUCHEA

Population: 8 million
Area: 70,000 square kilometres
Capital: Phnom Penh
Language: Khmer and Chinese
Currency: Riel

In the last two decades the formerly wealthy kingdom of Kampuchea, has been plunged into a vicious maelstrom of violence, hardship and poverty. In 1970 Prince Sihanouk was ousted from power by a republican movement. When the Vietnam war spilled into Cambodia in 1975 the Communist Khmer Rouge movement took power. This new regime abolished money, expelled foreigners, closed the borders and forced city dwellers to move to the countryside. Mass executions followed any attempt at protest, and it is thought that fifteen percent of the population died in these years. Vietnamese troops imposed a new government in 1979. Nationalist resistance under both Prince Sihanouk and the Khmer Rouge began a civil war interrupted by fragile peace agreements which continues to this day. The former cash crops and industries have been

destroyed and the population relies on subsistence agriculture.

KOREA (NORTH)

Population: 22 million
Area: 121,000 square kilometres
Capital: Pyongyang
Language: Korean
Currency: Won

In 1945 the defeat of Japan in the Second World War led to a joint occupation of Korea by Russian and American forces. In 1948 the Russian zone declared itself the People's Democratic Republic of Korea and established a Communist state. At elections only one Communist candidate is allowed and, it is claimed, these attract the votes of over ninety-five percent of the electorate. President Kim Il Sung has been in office for two decades. Industry, developed during the Japanese occupation, has been enhanced by government plans and Korea now produces iron and steel in quantity and is a major shipbuilding power. Agriculture is also state-run, and rice, maize and potatoes are produced in large quantities.

KOREA (SOUTH)

Population: 42 million
Area: 100,000 square kilometres
Capital: Seoul
Language: Korean
Currency: Won

Following liberation from Japan, Korea was divided into Russian and American areas. In 1948 the American zone became the Republic of Korea, with a democratic constitution. In 1950 North Korea invaded in an attempt to reunite the nation under Communism. International forces backed the South, while China supported the Communist forces. In 1953 a ceasefire was agreed but no peace treaty has ever been signed. Political life in South Korea has been unstable, with military rule and political murders. The current democratic government began in 1980. Agriculture remains important in the South Korean economy, with large quantities of rice, radishes and fruits being produced. Industry has increased dramatically in recent years and now accounts for about half of the economy.

KUWAIT

Population: 2 million
Area: 17,000 square kilometres
Capital: Kuwait City
Language: Arabic
Currency: Kuwait Dinar

Kuwait is an hereditary Sheikdom on the Arabian Gulf which has been

▲ *Wadi Kum, Jordan.*

Above right: *The volcanic island of Mauritius.*

▲ *Stormy skies over the Maldives.*

▲ *A children's orchestra, North Korea.*

▼ *Waiting for petrol, Kuwait.*

▲ *Angkor Wat, Kampuchea.*

▼ *Rice field, Malaysia.*

▼ *Misfat Oasis, Oman.*

▶ *Beirut, capital of Lebanon.*

▲ *On the grass plains of Mongolia.*

▶ *Agriculture in South Korea.*

ruled by the same family since 1756. In 1899 the Sheikdom placed itself under British protection and regained full independence in 1961, though Britain promised aid if needed. In 1990 Kuwait was invaded and overrun by Iraqi forces which annexed the nation. British forces, together with allied troops under United Nations approval, liberated Kuwait in 1991 after fierce fighting. Kuwait's oil wells were left flaming by the war and many months later most were still on fire. The economy of Kuwait is almost entirely dependent on its vast oil reserves, which bring in large quantities of foreign money. The Sheik was attempting to use this money to diversify the economy before the war.

LAOS

Population: 4 million
Area: 237,000 square kilometres
Capital: Vientiane
Language: Lao and French
Currency: Kip

The modern state of Laos is unusual in having been founded by a Communist movement led by a royal prince. When the French relinquished colonial control of the Lao people in 1947, a constitutional monarchy was established. The discontented Prince Souphanouvong, however, allied himself with Communists from North Vietnam and began a rebellion. This culminated in 1975 with the collapse of the Royal government and the installation of a Communist state under the Pathet Lao party. The nation is predominantly agricultural, with many of the Lao raising rice in the valleys of the various rivers of Laos. The mountainous interior and poor communications have made exploitation of mineral deposits difficult and industry is at only a rudimentary level.

LEBANON

Population: 3 million
Area: 10,000 square kilometres
Capital: Beirut
Language: Arabic and French
Currency: Lebanese pound

Lebanon is best known for the factional violence which has torn this previously-prosperous nation apart. During the 1960s the Moslem Palestinian Liberation Organisation began using bases in southern Lebanon to attack Israel. This led to great tension between the Christians and Moslems within Lebanon and civil war broke out in 1975. Israel invaded in 1982, occupying much of southern Lebanon. Syrian troops are present in many areas of the country in an attempt to enforce a ceasefire among the factions.

Lebanon has a constitution with an elected assembly and a President, but real power remains with the factional guerillas. Lebanon is now a basically agricultural nation, having lost its banking, manufacturing and tourist industries during the civil war.

MALAYSIA

Population: 18 million
Area: 330,000 square kilometres
Capital: Kuala Lumpur
Language: Malay, Chinese and English
Currency: Ringgit

The government of Malaysia is unique in that the nine rajahs and sultans meet every five years to elect one of their number to be the supreme ruler, or Yang de-Pertuan Agong. Operating under the head of state is a Parliament elected from the states, in which political power is vested. The nation is among the most prosperous of Southeast Asia, having a highly diversified economy. Exports are dominated in value by manufactured goods, though agriculture provides employment for most people. The lush farmland not only produces food for internal consumption but also exports cash crops such as rubber, cocoa, tobacco, sugar cane and tea. There are substantial deposits of tin in the country, together with oilfields, which add to the national wealth.

MALDIVES

Population: 215,000
Area: 300 square kilometres
Capital: Male
Language: Divehi
Currency: Rufiyaa

Scattered across the Indian Ocean, southwest of India, the Maldives number around 1,200 islands, but only 202 are inhabited. The islands were dominated by the Arabs from around 1100 and Islam is the dominant religion among the mixed population of Arabs, and the Sinhalese from India. Britain established a protectorate over the local Sultanate in 1887 and returned full independence in 1965. The Sultan was overthrown and a republic established in 1968. The coral islands lack mineral wealth and only small patches of land are suitable for farming. The economy is based on fishing, tourism and the processing of coconuts and reeds into craftwork for sale abroad.

MAURITIUS

Population: 1 million
Area: 2,000 square kilometres
Capital: Port Louis
Language: English
Currency: Mauritius Rupee

Mauritius is composed of a number of islands in the Indian Ocean. The two largest islands, Mauritius itself and Rodrigues, are separated by over 500 kilometres of open ocean. The rocky volcanic islands have an economy based on the production of sugar. Sugar cane covers most of the arable land and industry is dominated by sugar refineries. Tobacco and tea are also grown for export, while maize, beef and goat meat are produced for internal consumption. Fishing also provides employment. The government is a democracy based on universal suffrage, producing an assembly which elects a prime minister who appoints a cabinet. The Queen of Great Britain is the head of state and is represented by a Governor General who fulfils her duties.

MONGOLIA

Population: 2 million
Area: 1,567,000 square kilometres
Capital: Ulan Bator
Language: Mongol
Currency: Tugrik

During the early 13th century the Mongols conquered a massive empire encompassing China, Central Asia and parts of eastern Europe. By the late 17th century, however, the Mongols had fallen under Chinese control. In 1924 the Mongols, with Soviet support, drove the Chinese out and declared an independent Mongolian nation. The new Communist government suppressed traditional Buddhist and Shamanist religions and pursued a policy of farm collectivisation and industrialisation, which has been partially successful. However, the majority of the population still leads a traditional nomadic lifestyle, caring for herds of livestock. Millions of cattle, horses, sheep and goats are driven across the vast grasslands by expert horsemen. In 1990 the Communist Party allowed free elections for the first time and retained power with a large majority.

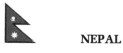

NEPAL

Population: 18 million
Area: 147,000 square kilometres
Capital: Kathmandu
Language: Nepali
Currency: Nepalese Rupee

The mountain kingdom of Nepal is unique in having the only flag which is not rectangular in shape. The traditional triangular banner carries a sun to represent the ruling Maharaja and a moon to symbolise the prime minister, until 1951 an hereditary post. Nepal pursued a policy of isolation until the mid 1950s, since when the economy has been slowly modernised. Many Nepalese live in inaccessible mountain valleys where they continue to practise traditional farming techniques. Others produce cash crops of herbs and potatoes or keep cattle to produce ghee, a form of clarified butter. A valuable source of foreign currency comes from the Gurkha troops recruited in Nepal to serve in the British army. Under a constitution introduced in 1990 the Maharaja permits political parties and free elections.

OMAN

Population: 2 million
Area: 300,000 square kilometres
Capital: Muscat
Language: Arabic
Currency: Rial

Until 1937 the Sultanate of Oman was a somewhat impoverished Moslem state relying upon fishing and date production for its livelihood. In that year, however, oil was discovered, and although reserves are not vast it is the petrochemical industry which dominates. The Sultan is attempting to diversify the economy by improving agriculture and the fishing industry. Copper mining in the interior is being encouraged, but further mineral exploitation is hampered by the fact that Oman's borders with both Saudi Arabia and the Yemen are in dispute. Oman has no constitution and is ruled by decrees issued by the Sultan. There is, however, a State Council composed of prominent citizens which the Sultan may call for consultation on important issues.

▲ *Honeymoon Lake, Pakistan.*

PAKISTAN

Population: 105 million
Area: 796,000 square kilometres
Capital: Islamabad
Language: Urdu, Punjabi, Sindi and English
Currency: Pakistan Rupee

The nation of Pakistan was created in 1947 by the British as an Islamic homeland after fears were expressed by the Moslems about joining a Hindu-dominated India. The population is united by its religion, but otherwise very diverse, with occasional calls for independence by various ethnic groups. Periods of democracy have alternated with military rule, and there have been frequent charges of corruption in both types of government. The economy is based upon agriculture, which employs over half the workforce. The irrigated plains around the Indus and its tributaries produce large quantities of rice, wheat and sugar for internal consumption and some cotton for export. Tax and economy laws favour the peasant smallholder with less than twenty-five acres to farm.

PHILIPPINES

Population: 60 million
Area: 300,000 square kilometres
Capital: Manila
Language: Filipino, Spanish, English and tribal languages
Currency: Philippine Peso

The Philippines contain over 7,000 islands, but very few of these are inhabited and most do not even have names. From about 1550 Spain gradually acquired control over the profitable Spice Islands of the Philippines and ruled until 1898, when the United States of America took over. Independence was achieved in 1946, since when a fragile democracy has been interrupted by military coups, fraudulent elections and massive corruption. The Philippines is an agricultural nation with rice, maize and coconuts as the main crops. Many coastal villages depend on fishing for income. The mining of nickel, zinc and copperlead the mining industry, while manufacturing is rapidly gaining in importance. The nation remains dependent on imported food and materials for survival.

▲ *Banaue rice terraces, Philippines.*

QATAR

Population: 375,000
Area: 11,000 square kilometres
Capital: Doha
Language: Arabic
Currency: Qatar Riyal

The long, streaming banner of the Emirate of Qatar is based upon the red and white banner imposed by Britain in the 19th century on all Gulf states which were party to an anti-pirate agreement. Britain controlled foreign policy until 1971, when the Emir was granted full independence. The Emir is an absolute monarch who rules by decree, but an Advisory Council of prominent citizens is consulted on major issues. Oil was first exploited during the 1950s, and since then has come to dominate the economy. Oil revenue is being used to improve agriculture and fishing, with the long term aim of the country becoming self-sufficient. Industry is also being encouraged. Most of Qatar is desert, thinly populated by nomadic Bedouin tribes. Lack of water is a perennial problem.

SAUDI ARABIA

Population: 12 million
Area: 2,200,000 square kilometres
Capital: Riyadh
Language: Arabic
Currency: Saudi Riyal

The religious kingdom of Saudi Arabia was carved out of the deserts by the aristocratic Saud family of the Wahhabi Islamic sect earlier this century, and was internationally recognised as recently as 1927. The king is also custodian of the holy mosques and the power structure is based upon Koranic law, though an assembly may be consulted by the king if he wishes. The desert kingdom began producing oil in 1937, and the economy rapidly shifted away from traditional reliance on dates and nomadic herds to concentrate on petrochemicals. Oil revenues are being used to improve agriculture with vast irrigation projects, and to re-equip the fishing fleet. There has also been some diversification into light industry and the production of plastics as a by product of oil refining.

SEYCHELLES

Population: 67,000
Area: 455 square kilometres
Capital: Victoria
Language: English and French
Currency: Seychelles Rupee

When Portuguese sailors discovered the Seychelles in the 16th century they were uninhabited, and not until the 1770s was permanent colonisation begun by France. Britain acquired the islands in 1810 and independence was granted in 1976. A coup took place within a year of independence and the Seychelles are now a one-party state. Tourism is the major industry on the islands, with about 100,000 people visiting each year. The idyllic coral islands, rugged granite peaks and tropical climate make the Seychelles a popular holiday

▲ *Istanbul, Turkey, at dusk.*

▶ *Abu Dhabi, United Arab Emirates.*

▲ *La Digue, Seychelles.*

▲ *The Singapore River, Singapore.*

▼ *Mecca, Saudi Arabia.*

▲ *Sailing junks, Vietnam.*

◀ *Stilt fishermen, Sri Lanka.*

▲ *A Yemeni landscape.*

▼ *Damascus, Syria.*

resort for those able to reach them. The large fishing fleet catches tuna for canning and export, while coconuts and cinnamon are the main cash crops.

SINGAPORE

Population: 2.7 million
Area: 625 square kilometres
Capital: Singapore
Language: English, Chinese and Malay
Currency: Singapore Dollar

The city state of Singapore was founded by Sir Stamford Raffles in 1819 as a trading port of the British East India Company. Since that date the city has flourished as a trading and manufacturing centre. Singapore passed from the Company to the British Government in the 19th century before acquiring independence in 1965. Though it has no mineral resources and virtually no farmland, Singapore is a leading economic power in Asia. Commercial and merchant banks number almost 200, and together provide the economic mainspring for much of Southeast Asia. The manufacturing base is diverse, including the processing of chemicals, foods, rubber and textiles. The state is a democracy with free elections though power is almost monopolised by a single party.

SRI LANKA

Population: 17 million
Area: 65,000 square kilometres
Capital: Colombo
Language: Sinhala, Tamil and English
Currency: Sri Lankan Rupee

Sri Lankan politics are dominated by ethnic violence between the majority Sinhalese and the Tamils, the largest minority. Many Tamils wish to form their own nation in the north of the island, and extremists undertake periodic terrorist action. Other minority groups include Europeans, Malays and the Veddah tribesmen who inhabit the forested mountains and are probably descendants of the original inhabitants. Agriculture dominates the economy, with rubber, coconuts and especially tea being grown as cash crops for export. Efforts are being made to improve rice production to reduce reliance on imported food. Industry centres on the processing of agricultural products, while precious stones are the only mineral resources of note.

SYRIA

Population: 12 million
Area: 185,000 square kilometres
Capital: Damascus
Language: Arabic
Currency: Syrian Pound

Arabs form the overwhelming bulk of the Syrian population and the Islamic religion is a strong unifying force. Government is by a democratically-elected Parliament, and the Arab Socialist Party has formed a majority since 1963, with President Assad holding executive power. Syria has been a major power in the Middle East, taking part in wars against Israel and maintaining a peace-keeping force in Lebanon. The economy is based on oil and textiles, which together make up about three-quarters of exports. Irrigated farmland in the Euphrates Valley and in the west produces quantities of wheat, barley and olives for domestic consumption. The southern deserts are sparsely populated by nomadic pastoralists raising livestock at subsistence level.

TAIWAN

Population: 20 million
Area: 36,000 square kilometres
Capital: Taipei
Language: Chinese dialects and Japanese
Currency: New Taiwan Dollar

When the Communist Party gained control of mainland China in 1949 the surviving nationalists fled to the island of Taiwan and set up a rival Republic of China, which is now usually referred to as Taiwan. Neither regime recognises the other as legitimate, and a continual propaganda war has been carried on. Until the Nationalist takeover, Taiwan was an agricultural island with intensively-farmed pockets of fertile land. Rice, pineapples and bananas are still produced in quantity on the few areas suitable for agriculture amid the mountainous terrain. Industrial development has been the keynote of Taiwan's economy since 1949. Light industry was encouraged first, but iron and steel works and shipbuilding yards are now well established, together with electronics.

THAILAND

Population: 56 million
Area: 513 square kilometres
Capital: Bangkok
Language: Thai
Currency: Baht

The kingdom of Thailand dates back many centuries, but the present dynasty came to power in 1782, when the founder threw off Burmese control. The kingdom never succumbed to European colonialism but was overrun by Japan in World War II. The royal dynasty remains on the throne, but political power has changed hands rapidly between Parliament and army factions as coups have been common in recent years. The majority of the population lives in rural areas, where the fertile soil and ideal climate allow Thailand to produce far more food than it needs. Rice is a substantial export. The beautiful old temples and notorious nightlife of Bangkok makes Thailand a popular tourist resort, attracting over five million visitors annually.

▲ *Buddhist priests, Bangkok, Thailand.*

TURKEY

Population: 51 million
Area: 779,000 square kilometre
Capital: Ankara
Language: Turkish
Currency: Turkish Lira

The Turks formerly ruled the vast Ottoman Empire, embracing the Balkans, the Near East and much of North Africa, and modern Turkey has a flag derived from that of the Empire. The modern republic was founded in 1923, when the last emperor was deposed. Democratic government has been interrupted by periods of military control, most recently in 1980-83. The interior plateau has a fertile soil and produces large quantities of grain, while the warmer coast produces heavy crops of olives, figs and citrus fruits. Flax and cotton form the basis of a flourishing textile industry. Agriculture employs over half the workforce, some at little above subsistence level. Industry is dominated by the production of iron and steel, motor vehicles and cement, and is growing under state encouragement.

UNITED ARAB EMIRATES

Population: 1.6 million
Area: 84,000 square kilometres
Capital: Abu Dhabi
Language: Arabic
Currency: Dirham

As the name suggests, the United Arab Emirates is a confederation of seven independent nations: Abu Dhabi, Dubai, Ash Shariqah, Ajman, Umm al Qaywayn, Al Fujayrah and Ras al Khaymah. The federation is ruled jointly by the seven Emirs, who appoint ministers to legislate and agree a joint budget. The federation came into being when Britain gave the Emirs full independence after a period when Britain controlled foreign policy in return for giving military protection. The bulk of the territory is desert, with little opportunity for agriculture, though fishing has potential and there is already a large export trade in prawns. The economy is basically dependent on oil, which is produced in large quantities. Oil revenues are used to promote a more diversified economy and to improve living conditions.

YEMEN

Population: 12 million
Area: 531,000 square kilometres
Capital: Sana'a
Language: Arabic
Currency: Riyal and Dinar

In May 1990 the former states of Yemen and the People's Democratic Republic of Yemen merged to form a single nation. The new constitution of the united Republic of Yemen allowed for free, multi-party elections after an interim period of two years, during which complicated arrangements for fusing the armies, administrations and economies would be put into effect. The two currencies, the riyal of the Yemen and the Dinar of the Peoples Republic remain in circulation side by side. The new nation has very little industry and most of the population is engaged in agriculture, usually at subsistence level. The arid nature of much of Yemen restricts agriculture to river valleys. Coastal villages supplement farming with fishing, with much of the catch being dried and exported.

VIETNAM

Population: 65 million
Area: 330,000 square kilometres
Capital: Hanoi
Language: Vietnamese
Currency: Dong

Vietnam formally came into being on 2nd July 1976 with the union of the former nations of North and South Vietnam after a long and costly war. Just two years later Vietnam invaded Cambodia, withdrawing only in 1988. The constitution claims that Vietnam is a proletarian dictatorship under Marxist-Leninism. In effect all power is in the hands of the Communist Party, which has followed a consistently pro-Russian stance, thus angering its neighbour China. This has led to border skirmishes in recent years. Well over half the population is directly dependent on agriculture. Over fifteen million tonnes of rice and two million tonnes of sweet potatoes are produced each year, but Vietnam still needs to import food. There is little heavy industry and light industry is localised and small scale.

AFRICA

*A*frica is, in general, an underdeveloped continent, where political violence and dictatorships are common. It is also, however, a continent of great potential, with a magnificent environmental heritage and the possibility of significant improvements.

It is usual to divide Africa, for cultural and geographical reasons, into two distinct sections. The first, North Africa, includes the Islamic states which fringe the Mediterranean and northern Atlantic coasts. These nations are united by a common language and religion which is the result of their Islamic past. Most have fertile coastal regions backed by vast desert interiors inhabited only by nomadic tribesmen. Oilfields are present in most of these nations, ensuring a national wealth which pays for schemes to improve the quality of life.

The second major region is sub-Saharan Africa, which stretches from the Sahara Desert to the Cape of Good Hope. This is a more diverse region, ranging from dense rainforest through open savannah to desert conditions, but united by having a mainly Negro population and having only recently gained independence from European colonial rule. There are, however, distinct differences between the regions.

West Africa is characterised by settled farming communities of great tribal diversity, where mineral exploitation and industry is well developed compared to elsewhere in Africa. East Africa is dominated by plains originally populated by semi-nomadic pastoral tribes, where minerals are less common and farming plays a more dominant role in the economy. Southern Africa is as diverse as the entire continent, with areas of fertile farmland, dense forests and open plains to be found within a short distance of each other.

Nations bordering the Sahara are subject to periodic droughts, which bring great misery in their wake. Population booms over the past decades have led to a reliance on good crops and when these fail famine follows. The worst of these famines was that which killed hundreds of thousands of people in Ethiopia and neighbouring countries. Elsewhere in Africa famine is not such a constant threat, but chronic poverty and poor medical services cause a low life expectancy.

Though the age of European colonisation is now over, the signs of those times are still clear. The official language of most nations is still that of the colonising power. The diverse tribal tongues of most nations (some have over 200 languages) make a lingua franca essential and it has been found most convenient to maintain that of the former ruling European power.

Most former French colonies in sub-Saharan Africa share a common currency: the Franc CFA. This currency is issued by the Banque Centrale des Etats de l'Afrique de l'Ouest, and is locked into the French Franc at a rate of 50 Francs CFA to one French Franc. This arrangement has advantages for those countries within it, but also has the effect of robbing them of total discretion over their own economies which, to some extent, remain vulnerable to outside control.

Perhaps due to an unfamiliarity with governmental machinery and the process of multi-party constitutions, many sub-Saharan states have abandoned democracy. In some cases this is due to the total dominance of a single party, which then outlaws opposition, but is more normally produced by a military coup. Nearly all sub-Saharan African states have experienced dictatorship at some stage and many are still ruled without democracy. There have been numerous accusations of human rights violations in these states. In some cases government forces have been responsible for horrific attacks and massacres.

Most attention has been focused on South Africa, where a White minority holds total control over the nation, without the right to vote being given to the Black majority. International pressure has been brought to bear on the nation and the government is now abandoning the policies of apartheid which enforced this control.

The mineral wealth of Africa is vast and underexploited. Effective capital investment and improved transport conditions would bring this wealth into the economy, but international companies are unwilling to invest heavily in nations subject to civil war or frequent coups.

Africa is undoubtedly a beautiful and potentially wealthy continent, but its endemic problems and recurring violence have locked it into a cycle of poverty which will prove difficult to break.

◀ *Sierra Leone beaches.*　　　▲ *People of Ethiopia.*

▲ *A village in Mozambique.*

▶ *A waterfall in Cameroon.*

▼ *Salisbury, Zimbabwe.*

25

ALGERIA

Population: 23 million
Area: 2,400,000 square kilometres
Capital: Algiers
Language: Arabic
Currency: Dinar

Algeria gained its independence from France in 1962 after nearly a decade of guerilla warfare. The bulk of the population lives along the Mediterranean coast and in the Atlas Mountains, where the climate is milder and the land more fertile than in the arid Sahara which makes up most of the country. The discovery of large natural gas fields has made Algeria relatively wealthy, and some of these resources are spent on free health treatment and high quality education. Many people continue to lead a traditional Islamic lifestyle, though European influences are strong in coastal towns. The single-party dictatorship which has held power since 1965 has recently announced its intention to allow rival political parties and to hold elections.

ANGOLA

Population: 10 million
Area: 1,200,000 square kilometres
Capital: Luanda
Language: Portuguese and various tribal languages
Currency: Kwanza

For most of its independent existence Angola has been racked by civil war between the communist MPLA party, which forms the central government, and the rebel UNITA organisation, which controls much of southern Angola. The long years of warfare have caused much hardship and have seriously disrupted the economy, making this one of the poorer African nations. However, oil production in the north and diamond mining provide a source of foreign capital which may lead to economic revival. The coastal region is the centre for industrialisation and urban lifestyles. The high plateau of the interior is heavily forested and inhabited by tribes which live in a traditional way with their own languages and religions.

BENIN

Population: 4 million
Area: 112,000 square kilometres
Capital: Porto Novo
Language: French and tribal languages
Currency: Franc CFA

The ideal of a revolutionary socialist state was recently abandoned in Benin, with the holding of free elections and the founding of several political parties. For the vast majority of the population the change probably meant little. Traditional agricultural lifestyles dominate in the interior, where tribal culture and animist cults are common. It is thought that about ninety percent of the population practice subsistence farming. In the mountainous far north Islamic culture has filtered down from the desert regions. Only on the coast is industry to be found, and even this is heavily based on the agricultural produce of the interior, particularly sugar and palm oil. A recently-exploited oilfield off the coast is expected to help boost the economy.

BOTSWANA

Population: 1.2 million
Area: 582,000 square kilometres
Capital: Gaborone
Language: English, Setswana
Currency: Pula

Botswana is rare among African nations in having maintained its democratic constitution throughout its period of independence. The constitution granted in 1966 allowed for an Elected Assembly of thirty-eight members and a House of Chiefs comprising the twelve tribal chiefs, and this arrangement is still in place. The vast majority of the population live in traditional villages, where cattle farming is the main activity, though some crops are also sown. Industry is limited to diamond and copper mining and many young men work in South Africa for some years in order to earn money for their families at home. The vast Kalahari Desert in the southwest of the nation is inhabited by nomadic bushmen tribes and they have little to do with national life.

BURKINA FASO

Population: 7.9 million
Area: 274,000 square kilometres
Capital: Ouagadougou
Language: French and tribal languages
Currency: Franc CFA

As one of the poorest and most unstable countries in Africa, Burkina Faso has experienced much hardship. Numerous coups and government changes have occurred, most recently in 1989. The nation is a largely artificial creation, being a former French administrative district covering the territory of several indigenous tribes. The vast majority of the population are engaged in subsistence farming in traditional tribal society. The country is periodically struck by drought and famine, being on the southern fringe of the Sahara. The recent discovery of gold and manganese deposits are unlikely to be exploited due to a poor transport system and lack of capital. The nation depends largely on foreign aid and remains chronically depressed.

BURUNDI

Population: 4.7 million
Area: 27,000 square kilometres
Capital: Bujumbura
Language: French, Kirundi and Swahili
Currency: Burundi Franc

Sometime in the 16th century Tutsi tribes invaded the area and conquered the Hutu peoples. Even today the nation is divided into the two ethnic groups, with the Tutsi wielding power. After a period of German and Belgian rule Burundi became independent in 1962 under a Tutsi monarch. In 1966 the king was overthrown by the Tutsi-dominated army, which has since suppressed Hutu unrest and dismissed Presidents at will. Tea and coffee plantations are the mainstays of both industry and the export economy. The majority of the population, however, remains dependent on subsistence agriculture based on bananas, maize and cattle. Less than one percent of the population is composed of pygmies, who inhabit dense forest and take little active part in national life.

CAMEROON

Population: 11.5 million
Area: 475,000 square kilometres
Capital: Yaounde
Language: English, French and tribal languages
Currency: Franc CFA

Much of the interior of Cameroon is virtually inaccessible during the rainy season, when torrential downpours wash away roads and flood large areas. This isolation is emphasised by ethnic diversity, with twenty-four languages and as many as 200 tribes. The fragmentation has slowed economic development, though the nation is relatively wealthy by African standards. The economy is based largely on agriculture, with coffee, cocoa and palm oil forming the bulk of export crops. The majority of farmland is, however, devoted to producing foods such as cassava, maize and groundnuts for local consumption. Industry is concentrated on aluminium smelting and the processing of agricultural products. Oil revenue has helped the government to invest in new projects.

CAPE VERDE

Population: 369,000
Area: 4,000 square kilometres
Capital: Praia
Language: French and Sangho
Currency: Cape Verde Escudo

The Cape Verde Islands have been independent only since 1975, when Portugal relinquished control. The

▲ *Farm workers in Angola.*

▲ *A scene on the Chobe River, Botswana.*

▲ *Celebrations on the anniversary of the Algerian Revolution.*

▲ A village in Chad.

▼ A domestic scene in Burkina Faso.

▲ Barren, drought-ridden scenery, Cape Verde.

▲ Riverboat seller, Benin.

▼ The Central African Republic.

▲ Bathers in the Comoros.

islands have strong historical links with Guinea Bisseau, also formerly Portuguese controlled, and have similar flags. The government is a single-party state, though the ruling elite joined several other African nations in 1990 by announcing an intention to allow democracy. The islands are small, rugged and arid, with little opportunity for farming. Coconuts, coffee and sugar are produced in small quantities on irrigated land. Fishing is far more productive for the local population with large numbers of tuna being landed each year. The climate and scenic coastline hold out the promise of an increase in tourism for the islands, though as yet this is underdeveloped.

CENTRAL AFRICAN REPUBLIC

Population: 2.9 million
Area: 622,000 square kilometres
Capital: Bangui
Language: French and tribal languages
Currency: Franc CFA

For thirteen years until 1979 this nation was ruled by Jean-Bedel Bokassa, who proclaimed himself Emperor and staged a lavish coronation ceremony. Bokassa was overthrown by the army and today the nation is a one-party state ostensibly committed to introducing democratic government. Though potentially rich in minerals and agriculture, the economy has been held back by political instability, poor communications, and particularly by the lack of a coastline. Diamond, gold and uranium mining lead the small industrial sector, while the majority of the population remain employed in subsistence agriculture. The southern rainforests are beginning to be exploited, though ecological damage may result unless sustainable replanting is undertaken.

CHAD

Population: 5.5 million
Area: 1,284,000 square kilometres
Capital: N'djamena
Language: French, Arabic and tribal languages
Currency: Franc CFA

Endemic civil war has marked the history of Chad since independence from France in 1960. The fighting between various ethnic factions is based upon a struggle between the nomadic, Moslem north and the agricultural and animist south. The situation has been confused by shifting alliances and foreign intervention. Chad remains a dangerous and unstable country and the British ambassador to Chad is resident in London. The warfare has prevented exploitation of recently-discovered oilfields and deposits of gold and uranium.

The population remains desperately poor and is dependent on subsistence agriculture varied by fishing on the shores of Lake Chad. A new government was installed in March 1991, and it is to be hoped that this leads to some stability.

COMOROS

Population: 500,000
Area: 1,800 square kilometres
Capital: Moroni
Language: Arabic, French and Swahili
Currency: Franc CFA

When the three Comoros islands of Mwali, Njazidja and Nzwani declared themselves to be independent of France in 1975, the fourth island, Mayotte, refused to join them. The newly-independent nation has suffered three successful coups and has chronic problems of disease and poverty. The islands have, over the centuries, received influxes of Africans, Indonesian, Arabic and European peoples and today have a mixed population. The majority of the population engage in subsistence farming, producing such crops as cassava, bananas, coconuts and maize. In recent years commercial production of vanilla, cloves and coffee has been undertaken and these now account for much of the nation's exports. Though independent, the Comoros remain economically dependent on France.

▲ The Congo's Sangha River.

CONGO

Population: 2.2 million
Area: 341,000 square kilometres
Capital: Brazzaville
Language: French and tribal languages
Currency: Franc CFA

Formerly a French colony, the Congo is now a single-party, Marxist-Leninist state in which the army has a dominant influence. The army has engineered a total of four coups since independence. The nation is relatively wealthy by African standards, with oil reserves offshore and productive gold mines. Industry is well established around the capital and produces cement and textiles among other products. However, more than three-quarters of the population remains engaged in farming, much of it at subsistence level. The vast bulk of the population is found in the southern parts of the country, for the northern regions are covered by dense forests and unfertile land.

DJIBOUTI

Population: 480,000
Area: 23,000 square kilometres
Capital: Djibouti City
Language: Somali, Afar, French
Currency: Djibouti Franc

Sandwiched between Ethiopia and Somalia, the tiny state of Djibouti is dominated by disputes between its ethnic Somalis and Afars. The hinterland is composed of arid grazing lands, although the bulk of the population lives in or around Djibouti City. The city has a long history as a trading centre and the economy is largely dependent on the port. Djibouti is a one-party state under President Hassan Aptidon.

EGYPT

Population: 50 million
Area: 1,000,000 square kilometres
Capital: Cairo
Language: Arabic
Currency: Egyptian Pound

Famous for its ancient history of pyramids and pharaohs, Egypt was conquered by the Arabs in 7th century, and today the nation is firmly Moslem in culture and outlook. People and prosperity are concentrated in the Nile Valley, as they have been since recorded history began here in around 3,000 BC. The waters of the Nile allow irrigation of the farmland which produces the bulk of the nation's food as well as export crops of cotton and citrus fruits. Industry is well advanced in the major towns and cities. Tourism plays a major role in the economy, with well over a million visitors to the country each year. The main attractions are the ancient temples and tombs, which are maintained by the government. Despite the assassination of President Sadat in 1981, Egypt has a relatively stable political system.

EQUATORIAL GUINEA

Population: 417,000
Area: 28,000 square kilometres
Capital: Malabo
Language: Spanish and tribal languages
Currency: Franc CFA

The single-party state of Equatorial Guinea is divided between the mainland territory on the Mbini River and the island of Bioko. Commercial farming has declined since independence in 1968, but cocoa and coffee remain important export crops. The majority of farmland is used for subsistence

agriculture, with cassava and sweet potatoes being the chief products. The wet, hot tropical climate produces vast forests in the interior and these are beginning to be exploited for their timber, which accounts for one quarter of all exports. Although over half the population lives in towns, there is virtually no industry in the nation and foreign capital is difficult to attract due to the unstable nature of politics in the country.

ETHIOPIA

Population: 50 million
Area: 1,221,000 square kilometres
Capital: Addis Ababa
Language: Arabic and tribal languages
Currency: Birr

Drought, famine and civil war have placed Ethiopia in the world's headlines for several years. Much of the country is in the hands of rebel factions, one of which recently overthrew the central government. The violence is largely due to the many ethnic groups included within the nation, many of whom desire independence from strong central rule. The great famine of 1981-83 claimed hundreds of thousands of lives, and the country lives under the perpetual threat of another drought. Despite this, farming is generally in good condition and in productive years can account for valuable exports of coffee and sugar. Much potentially fertile ground remains untilled due to political instability. Peace would undoubtedly help ease the desperate plight of the Ethiopian peoples.

GABON

Population: 1.2 million
Area: 267,000 square kilometres
Capital: Libreville
Language: French and tribal languages
Currency: Franc CFA

Made up largely of the drainage basin of the Ogooue River, Gabon has numerous natural resources but lacks the finance and population to take best advantage of them. Offshore oil is being exploited, as are deposits of uranium and manganese, but the economy remains based chiefly on agriculture. The Equator runs through the centre of Gabon, and this dictates the climate and range of crops which can be produced. Most of the population supports itself on subsistence agriculture, though sugar cane is grown in large quantities near the coast for export. Government under a single-party state has been stable since 1967, but this was recently dismantled and free elections held, though allegations of ballot-rigging were made.

▲ *Thatched huts in Equatorial Guinea.*

Above right: *Children in Guinea -Bissau.*

▼ *Filling water pots, Ghana.*

▲ *Women cleaning groundnuts, Gambia.*

▲ *The mountain village of Ha Thuhlo, Lesotho.*

▶ *Landscape of Gabon.*

▼ *Kenyatta Centre, Nairobi, Kenya.*

▶ *Abidjan, Ivory Coast.*

GAMBIA

Population: 875,000
Area: 11,000 square kilometres
Capital: Banjul
Language: English and tribal languages
Currency: Dalasi

The Gambia exists because of the river from which it takes its name. The nation is made up of a narrow strip of land rarely more than twenty kilometres wide which follows the twists and turns of the river from Koina to the ocean. Several tribes have their territories along the river and their chiefs have an established position within the constitution. The nation is basically agricultural and has only one export of any importance. This is the groundnut, thousands of tons of which are shipped out each year. More recently the government has tried to break this hazardous dependence on a single crop and production of cotton is on the increase. In 1982 Gambia joined with Senegal, which virtually surrounds it, to form the Confederation of Senegambia.

GHANA

Population: 15 million
Area: 239,000 square kilometres
Capital: Accra
Language: English and tribal languages
Currency: Cedi

As the first Black African state to become independent of a European colonial power, in 1957, Ghana has set several trends in African history. The colours of the Ghanaian flag – red, green and yellow – have been adopted by several other colonies on achieving independence, while the black star of African freedom has also become a popular motif. Ghana has experienced several coups and is currently ruled by a Provisional Council led by Flight Lieutenant Jerry Rawlings. The economy is relatively healthy and is based on cash crop agriculture, with cocoa being by far the most important, though tobacco, coffee and tropical fruits are catching up. The small-scale industrial activities are based around the mining of gold, diamonds and, more recently, oil.

GUINEA

Population: 6.7 million
Area: 245,000 square kilometres
Capital: Conakry
Language: French and tribal languages
Currency: Syli

Guinea followed Ghana to independence one year later and adopted the same colours for its flag, though they are arranged in vertical rather than horizontal stripes. Several tribal groupings are included within Guinea, with the Fulani being the largest at around forty percent of the population. The nation is under the control of a military junta which seized power in 1984 following the death of the former president. The nation has a tropical climate, with a summer monsoon which brings heavy rain and high temperatures. Combined with fertile soils this climate creates ideal conditions for a variety of crops including rice, sugar cane and tropical fruits. Vast reserves of bauxite are now being mined as are iron ore deposits and high-grade diamonds.

GUINEA-BISSAU

Population: 0.9 million
Area: 36,000 square kilometres
Capital: Bissau
Language: Portuguese and tribal languages
Currency: Peso

The single party which has ruled Guinea-Bissau since the coup of 1980 has recently announced that it will be working towards multi-party democracy, though little progress has so far been made. The fertile soil and tropical climate allow the production of large quantities of rice, rubber and groundnuts, much of which is exported. Most of the population remains dependent on subsistence agriculture and industry is virtually non-existent. Guinea-Bissau has a crushing foreign debt more than one hundred times the size of the government's annual budget. Ethnically the population is divided between the coastal Balanta and the Muslim Fulani of the inland regions, though there are several smaller tribes.

IVORY COAST

Population: 12.1 million
Area: 322,000 square kilometres
Capital: Abidjan
Language: French and tribal languages
Currency: Franc FA

This nation takes its name from the early trade in ivory which dominated the region when it was first discovered by Europeans in the 15th century. Since then slavery, and more recently coffee, have been the mainstays of the economy. Today the rich soil of the coastal regions has been turned to support a wide variety of crops including yams, cassava and a number of tropical fruits for export. Despite this fertility the economy of the Ivory Coast is held back by massive foreign debts and limited mineral resources. The single party state which has existed for many years recently announced that it would begin a process of democratisation and free elections have been held. The former sole party still retains power, having won over ninety percent of seats in Parliament.

KENYA

Population: 24 million
Area: 582,000 square kilometres
Capital: Nairobi
Language: English, Swahili and tribal languages
Currency: Kenya Shilling

Committed to the concept of "democracy with one party", the state of Kenya has enjoyed rather more stability than many other African nations since it achieved independence in 1963. This has combined with rich natural resources and a long history of international trade to make it economically viable, though not particularly wealthy. Most of the population inhabits the interior highlands, where coffee, tea and sugar are grown in large quantities for export, or the lower hills, where maize, cassava and sweet potatoes are produced for local consumption. The vast semi-arid plains are the home of gazelles, zebra and lions, which attract over half-a-million tourists each year, boosting the economy. The coastal towns have been trading with foreigners since the Arabs first arrived about the time of Christ and are thriving commercial centres.

LESOTHO

Population: 1.7 million
Area: 30,000 square kilometres
Capital: Maseru
Language: English, Sesotho
Currency: Loti

Lesotho is one of the few African tribal kingdoms to survive into modern times. Since a coup in 1986 the king acts on the advice of the army. In the early 19th century refugees from vicious warfare in the north fled to the mountains of Lesotho and became welded into a kingdom under Moshoeshoe I, who placed himself under British protection. This wise move ensured the Sotho clans retained some form of self-government throughout the colonial era, and in 1966 became independent outside the Union of South Africa. The country has few natural resources and little agricultural land. The young men work in South Africa for long periods of time, earning enough money to support their families and keep the fragile economy of the kingdom in balance.

LIBERIA

Population: 2.4 million
Area: 111,000 square kilometres
Capital: Monrovia
Language: English and tribal languages
Currency: Liberian Dollar

The flag of Liberia is similar to that of the United States of America, indicating the origins of the nation. In 1822 an American society landed a party of freed slaves on the coast in Monrovia in an attempt to establish a haven for such people. In 1847 the nation declared itself independent and adopted a constitution similar to that of the United States. Recent years have witnessed violent upheavals, with coups and civil war raging fiercely. The situation is not yet stable. Liberia has rich mineral resources, in particular massive iron ore deposits, which make up seventy percent of exports, together with gold and diamonds. The vast bulk of the population is engaged in farming, with numerous commercial farms growing coffee, rice and sugar cane.

▲ *A lake in the Fezzan desert, Libya.*

LIBYA

Population: 4 million
Area: 1,760,000 square kilometres
Capital: Tripoli
Language: Arabic
Currency: Libyan Dinar

Until recently one of the poorest Mediterranean nations, Libya is now one of the richest, following the discovery of massive oil fields in 1959. In 1969 King Idris was overthrown by an army faction led by Colonel Muammar Gadaffi, who established Libya as an Arab republic. The country has since vociferously supported Arab unity and nationalism, lending aid to various organisations such as the PLO and so earning Western enmity. The economy is based on natural oil and gas, which account for nearly all exports. Internally, however, agriculture dominates, with the most fertile lands of North Africa producing rich harvests of dates, citrus fruits and cereals. Ambitious irrigation projects are under way which aim at adding hundreds of square kilometres to the farmland.

MADAGASCAR

Population: 11.4 million
Area: 590,000 square kilometres
Capital: Antananarivo
Language: Malagasy and French
Currency: Malagasy Franc

The original kingdom, comprising a mixed population of Malaysians and Africans, was overrun by the French in 1897. In 1960 the island became independent as a republic, and since then has undergone several coups. It is now ruled by the Supreme Revolutionary Council and the President, who leads the sole political party. The economy of the nation is based on tropical agriculture and the exploitation of forests, both natural and planted. The fertile soils produce heavy crops of coffee, tobacco and tropical fruits, the processing of which forms the basis of the island's small-scale industries. Cattle breeding is a major activity in the highlands and there are nearly as many cattle on the island as people.

MALAWI

Population: 7 million
Area: 118,000 square kilometres
Capital: Lilongwe
Language: Chichewa and English
Currency: Kwacha

Ruled as a one-party state by Dr Kamuzu Banda, Malawi is a landlocked nation with few resources. Agriculture is the basic activity, with most of the population relying on subsistence farming for a livelihood. Tobacco and tea are grown for export, but occupy only a small part of the total agricultural land. Marble is the only major quarrying material and industry is restricted to local consumer goods. As a mountainous nation, however, Malawi has massive potential for hydro-electricity and this is now being exploited on a large scale. The economy remains reliant on its migrant workers, who leave Malawi for South Africa or Zambia to work in mines and factories to earn much needed income.

MALI

Population: 9 million
Area: 1,240,000 square kilometres
Capital: Bamako
Language: French, Bambara and tribal languages
Currency: Franc CFA

Mali is one of the world's poorest nations, being dependent on an agriculture at the mercy of drought and semi-desert conditions. The majority of the diverse population is concentrated in the southwest, where the Senegal and Niger rivers give a semblance of reliability to the water supply for irrigation.

Millet, cassava and sweet potatoes are the chief crops for local consumption, while cotton is produced on a modest scale for export. The northern and eastern regions are covered by desert and are virtually uninhabited. Mineral wealth remains untapped due to poor transport and a lack of capital. The military coup of 1968 produced a stable government which is still headed by the coup leader, General Traore, who heads the only legal political party.

MAURITANIA

Population: 2 million
Area: 1,031,000 square kilometres
Capital: Nouakchott
Language: Arabic and French
Currency: Ouguiya

The crescent and star on Mauritania's green flag indicates the Islamic heritage of this desert nation. The vast desert region of the north and east is the home of nomadic herdsmen, but the majority of the population inhabits the Senegal Valley in the southwest. In this region millet, rice and dates are produced in large quantities for local consumption. Coastal villages land large catches of Atlantic fish, which are dried or salted locally to form the bulk of exports by value. Industry is virtually non-existent, what there is being restricted to iron-ore mining or food processing. A long-running war with Morocco over the Western Sahara territory, which ended in 1979, drained the Mauritanian economy, which is still attempting to recover. The country is ruled by a Military Committee which seized power in the coup of 1978.

MOROCCO

Population: 24.5 million
Area: 446,000 square kilometres
Capital: Rabat
Language: Arabic, Berber, French
Currency: Dirham

The Islamic kingdom of Morocco became independent of France in 1956, though the Sultan had always enjoyed some degree of control. The Sultanate became a Kingdom in 1957. The king holds supreme authority over both secular and religious life, though the government is actually carried out by a democratically-elected Parliament. The bulk of the nation's wealth is based on its rich mineral deposits, particularly phosphates and lead ore, which are extensively mined and provide much employment. Most of the population remains dependent on agriculture, however, and traditional crops of cereals, fruits and tomatoes dominate. Morocco has been involved in a lengthy war in the

Western Sahara, where it claims large areas of territory.

MOZAMBIQUE

Population: 15 million
Area: 783,000 square kilometres
Capital: Maputo
Language: Portuguese and tribal languages
Currency: Metical

The national flag of Mozambique features a book, a hoe and a gun; symbols which are apt for this poverty-ridden nation in southern Africa. Since 1977 the Marxist Frelimo Party has been the only legal political party in Mozambique, though it recently announced its intention of allowing opposition. Opposition of a more violent kind has been maintained by the Renamo movement, which has been carrying on an armed struggle for many years. To counter this threat Mozambique maintains one of the largest armies in Africa, numbering 60,000 men. The hoe symbolises the agricultural base of the national economy, which relies on cereals, bananas and various types of nut. The long coastline on the Indian Ocean offers fine fishing opportunities and the prawn catch is substantial.

NAMIBIA

Population: 1.3 million
Area: 825,000 square kilometres
Capital: Windhoek
Language: English, Afrikaans and tribal languages
Currency: South African Rand

The vast desert nation of Namibia gained independence from South Africa in 1990, after many years of confused political instability. Cuban mercenaries from Communist Angola backed the SWAPO guerilla movement, while South Africa attempted to maintain its influence by enforcing a constitution. The independence elections resulted in victory for SWAPO, but not by the margin needed for them to fulfil their goal of one-party dictatorship. The political struggle was made more bitter by the vast mineral wealth of Namibia, which provides one the highest average incomes on the continent. Diamonds and uranium form the basis of the mineral industry. Most of the people are engaged in stock ranching of either cattle or sheep, which together outnumber humans in Namibia by six to one.

NIGER

Population: 7.5 million
Area: 1,268,000 square kilometres
Capital: Niamey
Language: French, Hausa and tribal languages
Currency: Franc CFA

▲ *A typical Senegalese, Senegal.*

▲ *Fertile river banks, Morocco.*

▼ *Terraced hillsides, Rwanda.*

▲ *Tanandava, Madagascar.*

▲ *Djenné, Mali.*

▲ *A young girl, Mauritania.*

◄ *Lumber workers, Lagos, Nigeria.*

▼ *The colourful natives of Malawi.*

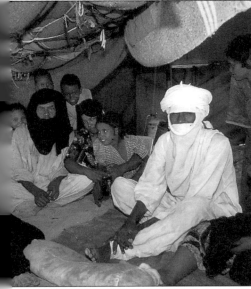
▲ *Refugees in Niger.*

▲ *Oranjemund, Namibia.*

Only around the southwestern borders is Niger a productive agricultural country. Here the Niger River provides water for irrigation and drinking. The bulk of the population is concentrated in this region, where they farm at a subsistence level. The capital, Niamey, stands on the banks of the Niger River and has some small-scale industry. Elsewhere through southern Niger a number of oases permit farming, but away from the Niger the land is generally devoted to grazing cattle, sheep and goats. In the northern regions the Sahara makes even grazing virtually impossible. In 1974 the government was overthrown by a military coup, and today the nation is ruled by a twelve-man military council.

NIGERIA

Population: 100 million
Area: 923,000 square kilometres
Capital: Lagos
Language: English, Hausa and tribal languages
Currency: Naira

Great confusion exist about Nigeria, its population and resources, due to decades of political instability and civil war. The population was reckoned in 1963 to be 55,670,000. Recent massive growths in population are known to have taken place, but estimates of the present number range from 89- to 119-million. Equally uncertain are the country's economic figures. The rich agricultural soil supports thriving farming communities, which produce heavy crops of millet, cassava and yams for local consumption. Export crops include cocoa and groundnuts. Industrial activity has been boosted by rich oil reserves, but no accurate picture of this sector is possible. The political troubles began in 1983 with a military coup, followed by another in 1985, and a civil war when the Biafra province attempted to become independent.

RWANDA

Population: 6.7 million
Area: 26,000 square kilometres
Capital: Kigali
Language: Kinyarwanda and French
Currency: Rwanda Franc

The independence celebrations of Rwanda in 1962 were nearly marred when it was realised that the intended national flag was almost identical to that already chosen by Mali. A large 'R' was hurriedly added and the events went ahead as planned. Independence from Belgium came in the wake of a savage internal struggle between the agricultural Hutu and the pastoral Watutsi. The latter had held power for centuries but were overthrown in the fighting, many fleeing to

neighbouring countries. Rwanda is a densely-populated agricultural country producing sweet potatoes and cassava for local use and coffee for sale abroad. The coup of 1973 brought the military to power, and today there is only one political party allowed in the country.

SAO TOME AND PRINCIPE

Population: 115,000
Area: 845 square kilometres
Capital: Sao Tome
Language: Portuguese and Fang
Currency: Dobra

As with many African nations, Sao Tome has now announced that it will be abandoning the one-party form of government for democracy. The move was agreed in 1990, but in the Presidential elections of 1991 there was, as usual, only one candidate. The economy of the islands is heavily dependent on two agricultural crops, cocoa and copra, and fluctuations in the international markets have great effects in Sao Tome and Principe. The government has recently tried to diversify crop production, but has had more success in building up a fishing industry to exploit the vast tuna shoals of the Gulf of Guinea. The flag of the republic features two black stars to symbolise the two islands and carries the green and yellow colours common to many African nations.

▲ *Sao Tome, capital of Sao Tome and Principe.*

SENEGAL

Population: 7.2 million
Area: 196,000 square kilometres
Capital: Dakar
Language: French, Wolof and tribal languages
Currency: Franc CFA

In 1960 Senegal became independent of France as part of the Mali Confederacy. After only a few months Senegal withdrew, adding a green star to the Mali flag to proclaim its independence. The nation was a one-party state for some years, but is now a democracy despite several coup attempts. The groundnut, or peanut, was introduced in the 1600s as a cheap food for slaves being transported to the Caribbean, and it remains the country's most important crop. Cotton is also grown for export and attempts at diversifying into other areas have been made. The nation has a good transportation system and this has encouraged modest industrialisation, though this is still largely confined to Dakar, which is an extremely busy port, handling both trade and fishing vessels.

SIERRA LEONE

Population: 4.1 million
Area: 73,000 square kilometres
Capital: Freetown
Language: English, Krio and tribal languages
Currency: Leone

Freetown was founded as a settlement for freed slaves by the British in 1787, but the area was not formally taken over as a colony until 1808. When independence came in 1961 Sierra Leone adopted a flag showing blue for the ocean, white for unity and green for agriculture. The nation is now a one-party state under the leadership of the army. The vast majority of the population engage in subsistence farming, with rice, cassava and livestock being the primary products. A small amount of both coffee and cocoa is exported, but the nation's economy is based on the mining of bauxite, diamonds and molybdenite. Local government in Sierra Leone is based on tribal units. Each chief is supported by a Council of Elders which is responsible for law and order in the area and which has limited powers to raise and spend taxes.

SOMALIA

Population: 6.3 million
Area: 638,000 square kilometres
Capital: Mogadishu
Language: Somali, Arabic, English and Italian
Currency: Somali Shilling

The Somali people are a widely-scattered nation of herdsmen whose members range widely across the arid grazing lands of the Horn of Africa. The desire of the Somalis in Ethiopia's Ogaden District to join Somalia has led to intermittent fighting. Somalia came into being when British Somaliland merged with Italian Somalia and became independent. In 1969 General Barre seized power in a coup. A long-running civil war caused Barre to flee the nation in 1991. The internal troubles have prevented exploitation of the iron ore and gypsum and the development of industry. Over three-quarters of the Somalis lead a traditional lifestyle based on cattle, goats, sheep and camels. A few engage in agriculture along the river banks, but this activity is continually under threat from drought.

SOUTH AFRICA

Population: 30.2 million
Area: 1,123,000 square kilometres
Capital: Pretoria
Language: Afrikaans, English and tribal languages
Currency: Rand

Conflict between the white minority and various factions among the Black majority, most noticeably the ANC and Inkatha, have overshadowed South African history in recent years. In 1991 the government announced the end of *Apartheid*, a policy of separate racial development. South Africa is without doubt the wealthiest nation in Africa. Its prosperity is founded on the efficient exploitation of a vast mineral wealth and large agricultural potential. Gold is mined in staggering quantity; 600 tonnes in 1990, and is only the most valuable of several mining exports. Industry is well developed, with food processing, metal smelting and machinery manufacture being the most productive. The massive economic base of South Africa makes several neighbouring nations dependent upon it and attracts large numbers of migrant workers. An unreliable climate ensures that agriculture remains unpredictable, though highly productive.

▲ *A Sudanese group, near Jonglei Canal, Sudan.*

SUDAN

Population: 26 million
Area: 2,505,000 square kilometres
Capital: Khartoum
Language: Arabic, English, tribal languages
Currency: Sudanese Pound

In 1989 the army overthrew the government and pledged itself to ending the bitter civil war between the Arabic and Islamic north, and the south, where Black Africans practising tribal religions form the majority. Despite this pledge the war continues to bring misery to millions of Sudanese. The war, combined with government control of the economy, led to a drastic food shortage in 1991. The nation is mainly desert or arid grassland, where cattle, goats and sheep are

grazed. Agriculture is concentrated along the Nile and in the south, where irrigation is possible. Cotton and sugar are grown for export as is gum arabic in the forested southwest. Land devoted to producing food is vulnerable to the periodic droughts of the region. The large mineral reserves are undeveloped due to political instability.

▲ *The coronation of Mswati III, Swaziland.*

SWAZILAND

Population: 681,000
Area: 17,000 square kilometres
Capital: Mbabane
Language: siSwati and English
Currency: Lilangeni

Sandwiched between Mozambique and South Africa, the Kingdom of Swaziland gained independence from Britain in 1968. Since 1973 the king has ruled without Parliament, though the new king, Mswati III, has allowed an advisory college to be elected. The flag depicts the traditional shield and spears with which the Swazi successfully defended themselves against Zulu aggression in the early 19th century. Today, Swaziland is a predominantly agricultural country with the bulk of the population being engaged in subsistence agriculture. European settlers operate large-scale farms producing sugar cane, citrus fruits and cotton for export. Industry is limited to the mining of asbestos, coal and iron ore, chiefly for export.

TANZANIA

Population: 25 million
Area: 945,000 square kilometres
Capital: Dodoma
Language: English, Swahili and tribal languages
Currency: Tanzanian Shilling

The republic of Tanzania is made up of over 100 tribes, each with its own language and customs. Since 1977 this diverse population has been kept together by a government based on a single political party, the leader of which, Ali Mwinyi, won the 1990 Presidential Election. He was the only candidate. The

nation came into being in 1964, when the African majority on Zanzibar overthrew the Islamic Sultan and joined mainland Tanganyika to form a new republic. Most of the population is engaged in agriculture, though the tsetse fly and drought make this difficult across much of the mainland. Crops such as coconuts, cardamoms and cocoa have been introduced in an attempt to gain much-needed export sales. Deposits of several metal ores have recently been found but remain unexploited.

TOGO

Population: 3.5 million
Area: 57,000 square kilometres
Capital: Lome
Language: French and tribal languages
Currency: Franc CFA

A white star for hope dominates the flag of Togo. This former German colony passed through French control after World War I before achieving independence in 1960. The first decade of freedom was marred by internal violence, but since 1969 power has been centralised in the hands of a single party under military control. Vast reserves of phosphates, bauxite and iron ore have provided a mineral backbone to the Togo economy since exploitation began in 1953. Most of the population is engaged in agriculture on the pockets of fertile land among the inland hills. Maize and cassava are the bulk crops for local consumption, though coffee, cocoa and cotton are produced for export. The short coastline is dotted with fishing villages which reap rich harvests in the tropical waters.

TUNISIA

Population: 7.7 million
Area: 163,000 square kilometres
Capital: Tunis
Language: Arabic and French
Currency: Tunisian Dinar

The Tunisian flag has been in use since 1835 when this was a province of the Turkish Empire, and it retains the crescent, star and red field of the Turkish flag. After a period as a French protectorate, Tunisia became an independent kingdom in 1956 and a republic the following year. Oil fields exist in Tunisia, but are not rich enough to dominate the economy in the same way as in other Arab countries. Mining of lead, iron and zinc ores is also an important source of mineral wealth. Tunisia remains, however, an agricultural nation, with nearly half the working population occupied on farms, mostly in the northern half of the country. Tomatoes, olives and citrus fruits are among the most important crops. Fishing is an important employment along the coast.

▲ *A crowded market, Togo.*

▲ *Mogadishu, Somalia.*

▼ *Ngorongoro Conservation Area, Tanzania.*

▲ *Typical Tunisian architecture.*

▲ *Kampala, Uganda's capital.*

▼ *Vineyards, South Africa.*

UGANDA

Population: 16 million
Area: 236,000 square kilometres
Capital: Kampala
Language: English, Swahili and tribal languages
Currency: Uganda Shilling

Uganda has experienced several coups and foreign invasions since independence, giving rise to numerous regimes, the most notorious being that of Idi Amin in the 1970s. The nation is made up of numerous tribes, none constituting more than one fifth of the total population, and each with its own language and culture. The political troubles have prevented the development of an industrial economy, though there is some copper mining. By contrast, agriculture is well developed and Uganda can feed itself while still producing cotton, sugar cane and coffee for export. Fishing on Lake Victoria is also a major occupation. Uganda was a British colony from 1894 to 1961. English is still widely spoken and the bulk of the population is Christian.

ZAIRE

Population: 32 million
Area: 2,345,000 square kilometres
Capital: Kinshasa
Language: French, Lingala, Swahili and tribal languages
Currency: Zaire

The highly-distinctive flag of Zaire is based on the emblem of the Popular Movement of the Revolution, the only legal political party in the country, which has held power since 1978. The vast interior of Zaire is largely covered by the Congo Basin, in which flourishes dense rain forest. Much of this area has never been properly explored and remains home to tribes leading traditional lifestyles. Best known are the pygmies, but several hundred other peoples maintain their languages and cultures. Government control is limited to regions along the Congo River and the more open regions. Here mineral mining is the mainstay of the economy, with exploitation of rich deposits of copper, oil and cobalt being predominant.

ZAMBIA

Population: 8 million
Area: 752,000 square kilometres
Capital: Lusaka
Language: English and tribal languages
Currency: Kwacha

The Zambian economy is almost entirely dependent on copper, over half-a-million tonnes of which are produced each year. The nation is therefore vulnerable to changes on the international commodities market. The bulk of the population is employed in agriculture, much of it subsistence. Maize and livestock are the main agricultural products, though some sugar cane is produced for export. The development of more sophisticated agriculture is hampered by the tsetse fly and occasional droughts. Forests cover nearly half the total land area, but there is no forestry industry. Independence from Britain came to Zambia in 1964, and since then it has been ruled by the United National Independence Party of Kenneth Kaunda.

▲ *Kapenta drying racks, Zambia.*

▲ *Plantation worker harvesting tea, Zaire*

ZIMBABWE

Population: 9 million
Area: 390,000 square kilometres
Capital: Harare
Language: English, Shona and Ndebele
Currency: Zimbabwe Dollar

Zimbabwe came into being in 1980, when the former white-ruled Rhodesia became a democracy under Black rule. President Mugabe moved the nation towards Marxism. The new nation was named after enigmatic stone ruins discovered in the region, which indicated an advanced civilisation that had vanished some centuries earlier. The country has a balanced economy, with mining, industry and agriculture all playing their part. Mining is based on the exploitation of gold, nickel and coal deposits. Agriculture is largely conducted by subsistence farmers producing maize and sorghum. Larger scale farms produce tobacco for export and fruits. The extensive industrial scene is dominated by the processing of mining and agricultural products.

The AMERICAS

*T*he Americas are continents of contrast, where wealth and poverty, wilderness and man-made landscapes can be found in the greatest diversity and extremes.

Stretching from the Arctic Ocean to the chill, stormy waters off Cape Horn, the Americas embrace the full range of climatic zones, from frozen tundra to tropical heat and so to bare, frozen plains again. Nor is the physical geology any less diverse. The vast prairies of North America are as flat and featureless as it is possible for open grasslands to be, and the Amazon Basin is a vast, alluvial depression where no land is more than a few metres above sea level. But in the Andes and Rockies the Americas can also boast one of the longest and most rugged mountain chains in the world. Heights nudge 7,000 metres in the southern Andes and top 6,000 metres in Alaska.

Associated with climatic and geographical variation are those of ecology and habitat. The tropical regions of South and Central America are the site of the largest and most diverse rainforests in the world. These forests cover vast areas of land and contain more species of plant and animal than the rest of the world put together. The sheer beauty and diversity of the rainforests are staggering. Yet it is in the Americas that destruction of the rainforests is at its most widespread. The vast boreal forests of the far north are less under threat, though they are heavily exploited for timber and pulp. Elsewhere, a combination of semi-aridity and suitable temperature produce vast grasslands on which graze huge herds of animals.

The human impact on the Americas has been immense. North America is generally more prosperous and has felt the influence of man more widely than either Central or South America. The open prairies have been emptied of the millions of bison and are now ploughed to produce massive crops of grain to feed the world. Those areas unsuited to grain agriculture are grazed by cattle and sheep, banishing the native fauna to special reserves.

The mineral wealth of the north has been exploited, and is still being extracted on a massive scale. Gold, silver, copper and other metals are gouged from the ground in huge quantities by large conglomerate companies.

These changes have resulted in a highly developed and prosperous economy for the peoples of North America. Large cities have sprung up across the nation, with populations numbering into the millions. Roads, railways and flightpaths provide good communications across the northern continent, allowing free trade and transport links further to aid prosperity.

By contrast, much of Central and South America is relatively untouched by human progress and living conditions are generally poorer. Though large areas of rainforest are being destroyed, the majority still stands untouched by anything except the activities of hunter-gatherer societies which have co-existed with the forests for millenia. Industry and mining are poorly developed and the bulk of the population rely on farming for a livelihood. Often the farmers operate at subsistence level, barely producing enough for their own needs. Many of the peoples of the interior have little contact with European-style civilisation. Both in the high Andes and in the dense forests there exist settlements which continue to live as their ancestors have done for generations. Technology and beliefs are much as they have always been, preserving cultures in tune with their surroundings, but giving poor life expectancy and low standards of living.

Many of the nations are poverty stricken and have fragile economies. Though the dominant and more prosperous nations give aid and help, the tiny island republics of the Caribbean remain devoid of natural resources, and have economies based on the growing of bananas or coconuts.

Taken together the Americas provide a startling contrast of landscapes, natural ecologies and human activities. If they are continents of wealth, plenty and beauty, they are also lands where poverty, deprivation and squalor are equally common.

◄ A hillside dwelling, Colombia.

▲ Lake and mountain scenery, Colorado, USA.

▶ Prickly Bay beach, Grenada, WI.

▲ Caracas, capital of Venezuela.

ANTIGUA AND BARBUDA

Population: 85,000
Area: 440 square kilometres
Capital: St John's
Language: English
Currency: East Caribbean Dollar

This nation of three islands take its name from the two populated islands, the third being Redonda. The islands were discovered by Christopher Columbus in 1493 but Spanish attempts at colonisation failed, as did those of France. Only when British settlers arrived to grow sugar cane in the late 17th century did a permanent settlement result. The sugar crop was abandoned in the 1970s in favour of more diversified agriculture, with cotton and fruit ranking high. The wealth of the nation, however, lies in tourism. The glittering white beaches and warm seas make this a paradise for those seeking a relaxing holiday. The government is a democracy based on universal suffrage, with the Queen of Great Britain as Head of State.

ARGENTINA

Population: 32.7 million
Area: 2,766,000 square kilometres
Capital: Buenos Aires
Language: Spanish
Currency: Austral

As one of the largest and richest countries in South America, Argentina has the potential to become a dominant influence in that region. Internal political troubles, however, have held back the massive growth which is still possible. The most recent military rule began in a coup of 1976, and collapsed after defeat in the Falklands War against Britain in 1982. The new government is attempting to bring together in harmony the mixed population. The largest ethnic groups are the native Indian peoples, the descendants of Spanish settlers, and more recent European arrivals. Agricultural fertility is noticeable. Sunflower oil and wheat are both produced in quantity, but the largest exports are beef and lamb from the pampas grasslands. Mining is a major contributor to national wealth, with coal, gold, silver and copper all being worked in quantity.

BAHAMAS

Population: 250,000
Area: 14,000 square kilometres
Capital: Nassau
Language: English
Currency: Bahamian Dollar

There may be as many as 1,700 islands and cays in the Bahamas, but only 700 are of any size, and a mere thirty are permanently inhabited. The low-lying coral islands support only a thin soil, a fact which has long hampered a more dynamic economy. The agricultural base of the islands remains sugar cane, though livestock and egg production for local consumption are important. Fishing the shallow tropical waters is a thriving industry and modern techniques of fish farming are boosting the catch. The business community is much larger than might be expected, due to the less-demanding tax laws which have turned the islands into a tax haven for foreign businessmen. The balmy climate and open beaches have made the islands a centre for tourism, which brings large quantities of foreign currency into the islands.

BARBADOS

Population: 260,000
Area: 430 square kilometres
Capital: Bridgetown
Language: English
Currency: Barbados Dollar

The trident dominates the flag of Barbados, symbolising the wealth of the sea. This is apt for, the island has long depended on the sea for its livelihood. The delectable flying fish of the island's waters are a noted delicacy, and during the season hundreds of boats put out in search of these creatures and the high prices they fetch. Recent tourist promotions have boosted the economy, with outsiders flocking to Barbados in search of the warm sea and wide beaches. The island is densely populated, ranking high in the world's population density league, though most of the people live in the countryside. The traditional sugar cane crop, part of which is turned to rum, remains important to the local economy. The country has a democratic constitution with the Queen of Great Britain as Head of State.

BELIZE

Population: 193,000
Area: 23,000 square kilometres
Capital: Belmopan
Language: English and Spanish
Currency: Belize Dollar

The small nation of Belize gained its independence from Great Britain in 1981. A British military garrison remains, however, to provide protection against Guatemala, which claims Belize for its own, as the latter's army consists of a single battalion and two small naval craft. Belize has a democratic government operating under a Governor General representing the Queen. Only the coastal region is heavily populated, with the interior being blanketed in dense forests which are, as yet, unexploited. The mainstay of the economy is agriculture, which accounts for over half of export values. Sugar cane is the chief crop, followed by citrus fruits which are processed into juice concentrates for export. Maize, rice and livestock are raised for local consumption, making Belize self-sufficient in food.

BERMUDA

Population: 60,000
Area: 53 square kilometres
Capital: Hamilton
Language: English
Currency: Bermuda Dollar

The islands of Bermuda lie in the Western Atlantic some 800 kilometres from the North American coast. Only about twenty of the 150 islands are inhabited, the rest being isolated islets and rocky outcrops. The economy is almost entirely reliant on tourism and insurance for survival. Over half a million tourists come to Bermuda each year to enjoy the balmy climate and excellent swimming waters. Several major insurance companies are based here to take advantage of favourable local laws. The islands are officially a colony of the United Kingdom, with a Governor General being appointed by the Crown. However, the democratically-elected Parliament is free to take what action it wishes in all matters other than foreign affairs, defence and the police. The Governor General himself is responsible for these matters.

▲ *A musician performing at a festival, Bolivia.*

BOLIVIA

Population: 6.5 million
Area: 1,098,000 square kilometres
Capital: Sucre
Language: Spanish and tribal languages
Currency: Boliviano

Bolivia has been landlocked since it lost its coastline to Chile in 1884, and all exports must leave via other nations, predominantly along the

▲ *Kings Landing Historical Settlement, Canada.*

▼ *English Harbour, Antigua.*

▲ *Normans Cays and Exuma Cays, Bahamas.*

▼ *Village children in Belize.*

▲ *A landscape in southern Chile.*

Below left: *Hawkins Island, Bermuda.*
▼ *The Careenage, Bridgetown, Barbados.*

◄ *Cartago, former capital of Costa Rica.*

▼ *Buenos Aires, Argentina.*

rail link to the Chilean town of Arica. The vast bulk of these exports are minerals, with tin leading the field by a large margin. It is planned to expand the smelting capacity of Bolivia so that more tin ore can be processed before export. Silver and gold are exploited in smaller quantities, as is zinc. The agricultural output includes coffee and potatoes grown in the mountains, together with increasing quantities of sugar cane and cotton in the eastern lowlands. Coca is a traditional crop which has recently boomed as a source of cocaine. The United States is sponsoring a government programme to destroy the coca crop. Bolivia is notoriously unstable politically, having experienced fourteen presidents and a military junta since 1966.

▲ *Rio de Janeiro, Brazil.*

BRAZIL

Population: 155 million
Area: 8,511,000 square kilometres
Capital: Brasilia
Language: Portuguese and tribal languages
Currency: Cruzeiro

The present democratic constitution of Brazil came into being in 1988 after two decades of military rule. The nation is the only South American state with Portuguese as the official language, a fact which dates back to a treaty between Spain and Portugal in 1494. The southern and eastern regions are the best developed and it is here that agriculture and industry are most heavily concentrated. Coffee is by far the most important crop, producing over three-million

tonnes annually. Various other tropical crops such as sugar cane, cotton, cassava and citrus fruits are also important. Industry is based on the exploitation of crops and minerals such as quartz, thorium, zirconium and chromium. The vast Amazon Basin contains the largest rainforest in the world, with an incredible diversity of wildlife. Conservationists throughout the world are concerned as large areas of this forest are felled each year to make way for agriculture and to extract the valuable timber.

CANADA

Population: 26 million
Area: 9,922,000 square kilometres
Capital: Ottawa
Language: English and French
Currency: Canadian Dollar

As the second largest country in the world, Canada has a surprisingly small population. The reason for this is that the vast majority of Canada's land lies in the harsh northern latitudes, where tundra or boreal forest cover the ground. The population is concentrated in the southern region, where the climate is kinder and agriculture is possible. Wheat production is the basis of the agricultural economy, with nearly 900 million bushels being produced each year. Beef output is almost as important, while market gardening and fur farming are important in certain localities. Vast mineral reserves include nickel, zinc, copper and gold. The industrial scene is highly diversified, with a wide range of products being produced both for internal consumption and for export. Canada is a federal democracy with each of the provinces retaining considerable powers. There are occasional demands for provincial independence.

CHILE

Population: 13 million
Area: 736,000 square kilometres
Capital: Santiago
Language: Spanish
Currency: Chilean Peso

The long, narrow strip of territory which makes up Chile is defined by the Pacific Ocean on the west and the watershed of the Andes on the east. The mountainous terrain has inhibited both communications and economic development and Chile remains one of the poorer South American states. Nonetheless the nation has some potential. The north has rich mineral deposits and these are being exploited on a large scale, especially copper, which accounts for forty percent of exports by value. Agriculture is restricted to valleys and terraced highlands. The most

important crops are fruits such as apples, plums and citrus. Chile has had a chequered political history, with military coups and a Marxist government featuring strongly. In 1989 the military regime handed rule over to a democratically-elected civilian government, but retained some powers to itself.

COLOMBIA

Population: 33 million
Area: 1,142,000 square kilometres
Capital: Bogota
Language: Spanish
Currency: Colombian Peso

When Colombia won its independence from Spain in 1819 it included modern Panama, Venezuela and Ecuador within its frontiers. These states broke away in 1830 and 1903, while an internal revolution stripped the remaining areas of power and centralised it in Bogota. Earlier political violence appears to have ended and the government now concentrates on improving the economy. The nation is perhaps best known for its coffee, which remains an important crop. Rubber is also cultivated, but the dominant food crops are potatoes and rice. The coca crop forms the basis of a flourishing cocaine trade and the government is engaged in a bitter struggle with drug barons to stamp out the industry. Minerals are found in abundance in Colombia, with gold and silver being the most important. The mountains produce half the world's emeralds, which are exported in quantity.

COSTA RICA

Population: 3 million
Area: 51,000 square kilometres
Capital: San Jose
Language: Spanish
Currency: Costa Rican Colon

Named 'The Rich Coast' when first discovered by Spain in the 16th century, Costa Rica has continued to support a thriving economy despite periodic disturbances. The nation is unusual in that its constitution forbids the raising of an army for any reason. However, the para-military Civil Guard undertakes many duties usually carried out by the army in other nations. Agriculture forms the basis of the economy, with the traditional crops of coffee and bananas still dominating. The two-million cattle which roam the interior grasslands make an increasing contribution to the economy, as does a burgeoning industrial sector which concentrates on processing local products. Since a civil war in 1948 government has been relatively stable and the constitution of 1949 is still in force.

CUBA

Population: 10.5 million
Area: 115,000 square kilometres
Capital: Havana
Language: Spanish
Currency: Cuban Peso

It is ironic that the Cuban flag is based on that of the United States, with a triangle added to symbolise Freemasonry, for the present regime is openly hostile to the United States and has a Communist system. The present flag dates to 1849 and remained unchanged when Fidel Castro seized power in 1959. Since then Castro has pursued a Marxist-Leninist programme and has lent support to similar movements in Third World nations. Agriculture remains the basis of the Cuban economy, with the traditional sugar cane being the chief crop. Tobacco growing is also important, as is cotton. Fishing is a major export earner, with numerous small craft putting out to fish the surrounding waters. Mining and associated processes make up the bulk of the industrial sector, with iron and nickel leading the production tables.

DOMINICA

Population: 82,000
Area: 750 square kilometres
Capital: Roseau
Language: English and French
Currency: East Caribbean Dollar

The tiny nation state of Dominica is a democratic republic within the Commonwealth and is one of the poorer Caribbean states. The economy is heavily reliant on agriculture. Bananas and coconuts are the principal crops, both of which are vulnerable to international price fluctuations. The crops are periodically devastated by hurricanes, most recently in 1980, bringing disaster to the country. Fishing promises to increase significantly and remove the dangerous reliance on agriculture. Tourism is also growing as visitors come to enjoy the sun on the broad sandy beaches of the island. The inland mountains have a diverse wildlife population, including a unique species of parrot, the sisserou, which features on the national flag.

DOMINICAN REPUBLIC

Population: 7.2 million
Area: 48,000 square kilometres
Capital: Santo Domingo
Language: Spanish
Currency: Dominica Peso

The capital city of the Dominican Republic is the oldest European city in the Americas, having been founded by Bartholomew

Columbus in 1496. During the bitter colonial struggles of the 18th century the western area of Hispaniola was captured by France, but the eastern section remained under Spanish control and this now forms the Dominican Republic. The nation became independent in 1844, since when the nation has experienced political instability and periods of occupation by United States troops. The economy remains dependent on sugar cane, with sugar refining the main industry. Sugar accounts for about a quarter of all exports, though coffee and cocoa also earn foreign cash. Minerals being exploited include bauxite, gold and silver.

ECUADOR

Population: 11 million
Area: approx 300,000 square kilometres
Capital: Quito
Language: Spanish and Quechua
Currency: Sucre

Perched high in the Andes, the capital of Ecuador, Quito, has witnessed much political instability since independence from Colombia in 1830. The past forty years have seen fifteen changes of government and confused party loyalties continue to complicate the power structure. There have been continual disputes with Peru over the border territories in the rainforest, and this quarrel most recently erupted into war in 1981, when the present border was grudgingly accepted. The discovery of oil in the rainforest region has helped boost the underdeveloped economy but has added fuel to the dispute with Peru. The mountains and coastal regions are the centre of agriculture, much of which is carried out at subsistence level by the Quechua Indians. Foreign cash is earned by the export of coffee, bananas and cocoa.

EL SALVADOR

Population: 5.2 million
Area: 21,000 square kilometres
Capital: San Salvador
Language: Spanish
Currency: Salvadoran Colon

Civil war and terrorism have dominated the political scene of El Salvador for over a decade. Despite this the nation is densely populated, and nearly every piece of fertile land is now under cultivation. Coffee and sugar are the main cash crops for export but large quantities of maize, beans and sorghum are produced for local consumption. There are few mineral resources and industry is based on food processing and the supply of internal requirements for clothing and other similar items. The interior forests are being exploited for

▲ A rural scene in Ecuador.

◄ Punta Cana, Dominican Republic.

► A diver at Acapulco, Mexico.

▼ Scotts Head Peninsula, Dominica, WI.

▼ Women washing clothes, Guatemala.

▲ Cigar making in Havana, Cuba.

▲ An agricultural scene, Haiti.

► Cutting cane, El Salvador.

▲ *A coconut palm plantation, Guyana.*

▲ *Tegucigalpa, capital of Honduras.*

commercial gain, principally for timber and tropical gums. The majority of the population is descended from Spanish settlers and indigenous tribesmen, the mixed-blood mestizos forming the large majority of the people.

GRENADA

Population: 110,000
Area: 344 square kilometres
Capital: St George's
Language: English and French
Currency: Eastern Caribbean Dollar

Since independence from Britain in 1974 Grenada has remained within the Commonwealth but has experienced violent changes of government. In 1979 the democratic government was overthrown by a Marxist coup, which was followed by an army takeover in 1983 and an almost immediate invasion by United States troops at the request of neighbouring nations worried by the turn of events. Democracy has now been restored. The economy is based on agriculture and tourism, which together account for almost all foreign earnings. The local agriculture has traditionally specialised in tropical spices, with nutmeg and mace remaining valuable crops. More usual Caribbean crops of cocoa, coconuts and bananas are also grown in quantity.

GUATEMALA

Population: 9 million
Area: 109,000 square kilometres
Capital: Guatemala City
Language: Spanish and Mayan
Currency: Quetzal

As with most Central American states, Guatemala has experienced periods of revolution, civil war and dictatorship. A constitution introduced in 1986 has restored democracy and free elections were held in 1990. The ancient Mayan civilisation dominated the region before the arrival of Spanish colonists, and Mayan is still spoken by the minority Indian population. Most of the people are Spanish or have adopted Spanish culture. The nation relies on agricultural produce for export earnings. Coffee alone accounts for nearly half of exports by value, with cotton, bananas and sugar making up much of the remainder. The bulk of the population is concentrated in the farming regions of the south, while the northern forests are sparsely inhabited.

GUYANA

Population: 1 million
Area: 214,000 square kilometres
Capital: Georgetown
Language: English
Currency: Guyana Dollar

The original inhabitants of Guyana, the local Indian tribes now make up barely ten percent of the population and live mainly in the southern highlands. The fertile coastal region is densely populated by the descendants of settlers and slaves of African, Indonesian, European and Chinese racial origins. These racial divides are reflected in the nation's politics, with parties often basing their support on the interests of sections of the population. The wealth of the nation lies in the agriculture of the coastal plain, where sugar cane and rice are grown in large quantities. Tropical fruits are also important crops and much is exported. The exploitation of minerals, particularly bauxite and diamonds, adds to the export drive.

HAITI

Population: 5.8 million
Area: 28,000 square kilometres
Capital: Port-au-Prince
Language: French and Creole
Currency: Gourde

With an economy based on subsistence farming mixed with some cash crops, Haiti is one of the poorest American nations. Haitian coffee is considered to be of good quality and commands a high price; however, inefficient farming methods ensure that the business is of only limited profitability. Sugar and rum are also exported, but again without producing dramatic profits. The nation may have extensive mineral deposits, but these have never been confirmed. Haiti became the first Black republic when the slaves revolted in 1791 and won independence from France in 1804. After periods as a republic, kingdom and empire, Haiti fell under United States occupation before regaining independence in 1934. Between 1957 and 1986 the nation was ruled by the notorious Duvalier regime, but a fragile democracy is now in place.

HONDURAS

Population: 4.5 million
Area: 112,000 square kilometres
Capital: Tegucigalpa
Language: Spanish
Currency: Lempira

In 1821 Honduras joined with El Salvador, Guatemala, Costa Rica and Nicaragua to declare independence from Spain. Once colonial rule had been ended, however, the union fell apart and Honduras became fully independent in 1838. Since then the nation has been subject to coups and military rule alternating with periods of democracy, one of which began in 1982. The mountainous interior and continual troubles have combined to ensure that Honduras remains economically backward. The wealth of the nation is derived from two crops, bananas and coffee, which together account for nearly all exports by value. Increasingly heavy catches of lobster and shrimps are beginning to feature in the economy. There is some small-scale mining and industrial activity.

JAMAICA

Population: 2.5 million
Area: 11,000 square kilometres
Capital: Kingston
Language: English
Currency: Jamaican Dollar

Though comparatively wealthy by Caribbean standards, Jamaica has continued to be troubled by a degree of poverty and periodic unemployment. The democracy established on independence in 1962 remains in force. The island nation has a mixed economy better able to withstand international price fluctuations than others in the region. Agriculture is dominated by the traditional Caribbean crops of sugar cane, bananas and citrus fruits, though less usual products such as spices are also to be found. The bulk of exports, however, are created through the mining of bauxite and gypsum. A substantial influence in the local business community, and the island's culture, is tourism. Over a million visitors come to the island each year and pump large quantities of cash into the economy.

▲ *St Elizabeth, Jamaica.*

MEXICO

Population: 81 million
Area: 1,972,000 square kilometres
Capital: Mexico City
Language: Spanish
Currency: Mexican Peso

Carved out of central America by invading Spaniards, Mexico was formerly the territory of the Aztecs and other tribes, who practised human sacrifice and sun worship. The bulk of the population, known as Mestizos, is today of mixed blood though substantial minorities of both Indians and Spaniards remain. Once notorious for revolutions and bandits, Mexico has preserved its democratic constitution since 1917, and is now a relatively wealthy Central American nation. This wealth is largely based on oil reserves and a booming tourist business. Silver, iron and uranium are also important minerals. Many people live on the land, producing quantities of maize, potatoes, fruits and wheat for internal markets.

NICARAGUA

Population: 3.8 million
Area: 128,000 square kilometres
Capital: Managua
Language: Spanish and English
Currency: Cordoba

Nicaragua has a democratic constitution, but the President has imposed a state of emergency which repealed many civil liberties and much democracy. The cause of the move was the long-running civil war between the government and supporters of the previous Somoza regime. The continuing troubles have ensured that Nicaragua has remained underdeveloped, with agriculture continuing to employ most of the population. Coffee, cotton and sugar make up the bulk of exports, though gold, silver and copper are being mined on a small scale. Crops of maize, rice and beans are raised for internal consumption, often by farmers operating at a subsistence level.

PANAMA

Population: 2.3 million
Area: 77,000 square kilometres
Capital: Panama City
Language: Spanish
Currency: Balboa

The Panama Canal has dominated Panamanian history and its economy ever since the nation came into being. Indeed, the province of Panama declared itself independent of Colombia in 1903 because the Colombian government had refused to sanction the construction of the Canal. The Canal eventually opened in 1914, providing both jobs and an incentive to local business. The land flanking it was held by the United States, but was returned to Panama in 1979. The late 1980s saw a succession of Presidents as power was manipulated by General Noriega. In 1989 the United States invaded the country and removed Noriega from control. Despite the economic dominance of the Canal, local food processing and manufacturing industries are important. Agriculture is restricted due to the lack of fertile ground and provides less than half of the nation's food.

PARAGUAY

Population: 4.1 million
Area: 407,000 square kilometres
Capital: Asuncion
Language: Spanish and Guarani
Currency: Guarani

West of the River Paraguay is a vast region of open grasslands known as the Chaco, where the indigenous Guarani Indians ranch millions of cattle. The bulk of the population is of mixed Guarani and Spanish ancestry and inhabits the more fertile southeastern parts of the country. Here cassava, maize and beans are produced in large quantities for local consumption, though coffee and tobacco are raised as cash crops. Industry is chiefly concerned with processing agricultural products as the mineral wealth of Paraguay is negligible. There is great potential for hydro-electricity and the largest such scheme in the world stands at Itaipu. A 1989 coup overthrew General Stroessner, who had held power since 1956, replacing him with General Rodriguez.

PERU

Population: 23 million
Area: 1,285,000 square kilometres
Capital: Lima
Language: Spanish, Aymara, Quechua
Currency: Sol

The mountain republic of Peru is unusual in that the bulk of its population is composed of indigenous Indians, with the Europeans and mixed-ancestry Mestizo in the minority. The Indians belong to the Aymara and Quechua tribal groups and generally lead traditional lifestyles in the Andes. The isolated villages and subsistence economy of the Indians have kept them outside the mainstream of Peruvian politics and national life. Along the coastal fringe coffee, cotton and sugar are produced as cash crops. Industrial activity is concentrated around the capital and is composed largely of iron and zinc works. The government of Peru has been notoriously volatile, but a democratic constitution has been in place since 1980.

ST CHRISTOPHER NEVIS

Population: 45,000
Area: 267 square kilometres
Capital: Basseterre
Language: English
Currency: East Caribbean Dollar

The tiny state of St Kitts Nevis, as it is often called, is populated almost entirely by the descendants of African slaves brought to the Caribbean during the 18th century, when sugar cane was the economic mainstay of the area. Sugar remains the major crop on the islands and industry concentrates on sugar refining. Cotton is the secondary crop and livestock is raised for local uses. Tourists, especially those from cruise ships stopping at the islands, are a welcome source of income for many of the citizens. The islands have a democratic constitution which guarantees Nevis the right to secede under certain conditions. After gaining internal self-government in 1967 the islands became fully independent in 1983.

SAINT LUCIA

Population: 150,000
Area: 617 square kilometres
Capital: Castries
Language: English and French
Currency: East Caribbean Dollar

When Saint Lucia was granted self government in 1967 a competition was launched to design a flag, and the winning entry remains the national flag now that full independence has been achieved. The blue ground symbolises the ocean while the black triangle represents the volcanic peak of Mount Gimie and the yellow signifies the sun. Since independence in 1979 Saint Lucia has struggled to diversify its economy and prevent urban deprivation. Despite a move into the production of spices and citrus fruits, bananas, cocoa and coconuts remain the three dominant factors in the economy. Industry is limited to the processing of these foods. Tourism is significant with more people visiting the island than actually live there.

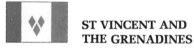

ST VINCENT AND THE GRENADINES

Population: 115,000
Area: 388 square kilometres
Capital: Kingstown
Language: English and French
Currency: East Caribbean Dollar

During the 18th century the sugar plantations of the Caribbean were a rich source of wealth, and they prompted rivalries between European powers. St Vincent was agreed to be neutral territory, but fighting between the British and French soon reached the island, which became a British colony in 1783. The islands achieved independence in 1979, since when the agricultural and tourist industries have continued to flourish. Agriculture is based upon bananas, cocoa, avocado pears and other tropical crops. Tourism attracts over 120,000 visitors each year, who come in search of the balmy climate and broad beaches lapped by warm waters. The constitution allows for a single elected chamber under the Governor

General, who acts on behalf of the Queen.

SURINAM

Population: 410,000
Area: 163,000 square kilometres
Capital: Parmaribo
Language: Dutch, English and others
Currency: Surinam Guilder

In 1667 Britain exchanged Surinam for Manhattan in a deal with the Netherlands. Dutch rule continued until 1975, when the nation gained independence. Since that time Surinam has been troubled by volatile politics and ethnic diversity. The major population groups are Indonesians and Creoles, with mixed European and Black ancestry, but significant numbers of Chinese, Javanese and Blacks form minority communities. The dense inland forests are inhabited by indigenous Indian tribes. Since independence there were several coups before democracy was established in 1988, to be ousted by a military coup in 1990. The country has a flourishing economy based on mining for bauxite, together with the growing of rice and bananas, as well as fishing.

TRINIDAD AND TOBAGO

Population: 1.3 million
Area: 5,000 square kilometres
Capital: Port-of-Spain
Language: English
Currency: Trinidad and Tobago Dollar

The two islands which make up this nation were joined administratively by Britain in 1889, but differences remain marked. Tobago has gained the right of limited self-government after agitation against control from Trinidad. The population of Tobago is almost entirely composed of the descendants of African slaves, while Trinidad has a more mixed people. As with other Caribbean islands Trinidad and Tobago produce quantities of cocoa, sugar and other tropical products and enjoys a thriving tourist business. However, the basis of the economy is oil, with major fields existing both on Trinidad and offshore. Unemployment remains high and substantial parts of the population suffer poverty despite government attempts to alleviate the situation.

UNITED STATES OF AMERICA

Population: 250 million
Area: 9,529,000 square kilometres
Capital: Washington, D.C.
Language: English
Currency: US Dollar

The United States is the dominant economic power in the world. All sectors of the economy are

▲ *Nevis Peak, St Christopher Nevis WI.*

▼ *Loading a schooner, St Vincent, WI.*

▲ *Machu Picchu, Peru.*

▲ *Washing clothes, Nicaragua.*

▼ *Punta del Este, Uruguay.*

▼ *Parmaribo, Surinam.*

▲ *Englishman's Bay, Trinidad and Tobago.*

▼ *The Panama Canal, Panama.*

▲ *Petit Piton and Soufrière, St Lucia, WI.*

▶ *Asuncion, Paraguay.*

highly developed and extremely productive. Throughout the large area occupied by the nation are to be found deposits of a wide range of minerals, including oil, various metals and gemstones. The fertile soils are extensively farmed to produce huge crops; over two billion bushels of wheat alone. Industry is highly developed with high-tech industries leading the world in developing new processes. In other fields, too, the USA leads the industries of the world with a highly diversified range of businesses producing almost every type of goods imaginable. The nation is a democratic federal union of fifty states in which individual states have some rights of self-government, but the most important powers are held by the central administration.

URUGUAY

Population: 3.1 million
Area: 176,000 square kilometres
Capital: Montevideo
Language: Spanish
Currency: Uruguayan Nuevo Peso

A province of Brazil until it won its independence in 1828 after a brief war, in which Uruguay enjoyed Argentinian support. Uruguay then adopted a flag sharing the same colours and the Sun of May symbol as that of Argentina. In 1989 democratic elections were held after more than a decade of military intervention in government. The chief wealth of Uruguay is its land, which supports a flourishing pastoral economy. There are about

eleven million cattle and twenty-five million sheep grazing on the rich grasslands of Uruguay, together with large numbers of farm animals. The processing of meat and leather are major industries in Uruguay, as is the spinning and weaving of wool. The nation has virtually no mineral resources and only a limited industrial base.

VENEZUELA

Population: 9.3 million
Area: 912,000 square kilometres
Capital: Caracas
Language: Spanish
Currency: Bolivar

The Republic of Venezuela came into being in 1830, when the area broke away from Colombia just nine years after jointly winning independence from Spain. Venezuela is more heavily dependent on industry than most other South American nations and has large and densely populated cities. Nearly ninety per cent of the population live in towns, far more than in neighbouring states. Vast oil reserves have recently been discovered and are slowly being exploited. More established is the mining of bauxite, which supports an aluminium smelting business. Iron ore similarly forms the basis of a metal working industry. Agriculture has steadily declined in importance, with more than half of those now employed in agriculture living at subsistence level.

AUSTRALASIA

*T*he nations of Australasia do not occupy a single continental entity, as do those of Asia, Africa or Europe. Instead they are united by cultural and ethnic traits more closely linked to the human populations than to the geographical limits of that region commonly called Australasia.

Strictly speaking, Australasia consists of the island continent of Australia, New Guinea, the Solomon Islands and possibly New Caledonia and New Zealand, though these latter are separate geological entities. The remaining islands strung across the vast spaces of the Pacific are isolated outcrops of volcanic rock or coral reefs with no geological or geographical connection at all.

These far flung islands and islets are, however, united by their human inhabitants. Several centuries ago, the ancestors of Polynesian and Melanesian islanders sailed across the vast, open stretches of the Pacific Ocean from Southeast Asia to colonise the remote islands of the tropical and sub-tropical regions. With them they brought taro, yams and other tropical crops with which to support themselves. Common ties of culture and religion bound these peoples together. Long voyages in open canoes were often undertaken between the various islands, preserving ties of technology and belief.

When European seamen arrived, from the 16th century onwards, they found the islands densely inhabited by peoples so similar that the entire region of Oceania came to be viewed as a cultural entity. European settlers and missionaries radically altered the society and cultures of the islands, though many features of Polynesian society remain even today.

The modern nations of Australasia are clearly divided into cultural and physical regions. The divides between the regions has as much to do with the economies and lifestyles of the peoples as with the physical location of the islands.

Dominating all is the great landmass of Australia. The Australian nation has a mixed culture based on the various immigrant groups, chiefly from Europe. To a much lesser extent Australian culture rests on the indigenous Aboriginal peoples who are now largely restricted to the Outback. The bulk of Australia is covered by arid deserts, where settlements are few and far between. The only populous centres are mining towns thriving on the exploitation of the rich mineral content of the nation's rocks.

Kinder climatic regions around the coasts are more densely populated, with farming communities producing crops according to the prevailing climate. All the major cities are on the coast, centred on the sites of historic ports. Here the population is engaged in industrial and service occupations more akin to developed western economies than to the prevailing culture of Australasia.

Sharing much of the flavour of Australia is New Zealand, with its largely European population and small indigenous element. The economy and lifestyle here is more rural than in Australia, while the temperate climate dictates the crops and livestock which can be produced.

Away from these economic giants of the region, the nations are far smaller and less developed, though the original cultures are more apparent. Nations may be as small as a single island with a population of just 7,000. The largest consist of archipelagoes spread across thousands of square kilometres of ocean, but even these never top one million in population. The cultures of the smaller nations are closely allied to the indigenous peoples. Christianity has generally replaced the violent ceremonies and beliefs of the former religions, and settlers from Europe and elsewhere often form sizeable minorities among the population.

The disparate nations of Australasia form a complex pattern of human adaptation to harsh environments. From the Australian deserts to the open ocean, Australasia is a place of extremes and superlatives. The differing cultures of European settlers and native populations are sometimes blended together and elsewhere stand in stark contrast to each other. But everywhere there is the great Pacific Ocean, dividing the nations and yet uniting them.

▲ Mount Tasman, New Zealand.

▶ A native girl on the beach, Kiribati.

◀ The world-famed Opera House, Sydney, Australia.

▲ *An isolated beach, Nauru.*

▶ *A highly-decorated native, Papua New Guinea.*

AUSTRALIA

Population: 17 million
Area: 7,682,000 square kilometres
Capital: Canberra
Language: English
Currency: Australian Dollar

The vast nation continent of Australia was the last major landmass to be discovered by Europeans, remaining largely unknown until the 18th century. Immigration, initially from the UK but later from the rest of Europe, and most recently from Asia, produced the dominant social profile of modern Australia. The extensive grazing lands support large numbers of sheep and cattle, while the smaller areas of arable land produce wheat, rice and market crops. The large desert regions are rich in mineral deposits. Industry is well developed, with a wide range of consumer goods and engineering equipment being produced. The nation is a federation of six states, with the central government being responsible for the Northern Territory. It came into being on the first day of the 20th century, when former British colonies joined to form the Commonwealth of Australia.

FIJI

Population: 730,000
Area: 18,000 square kilometres
Capital: Suva
Language: English, Fijian and Hindustani
Currency: Fijian Dollar

Britain annexed the 330 islands of Fiji in 1874 and stamped out the endemic tribal warfare. Independence was granted in 1970 and a troubled history has resulted. The population is almost equally divided between native Fijians of Melanesian and Polynesian ancestry and immigrants from India, who arrived during British rule. In 1987 an Indian coalition won power in Parliament. Within months a coup organised by the native Fijians placed the army in power. A new constitution has been imposed, which places political power in the hands of the native Fijians. The economy is based on agriculture, with sugar cane, coconuts and ginger being the primary crops. Industry is concentrated on processing the crops, while mineral wealth is restricted to two small gold mines.

KIRIBATI

Population: 66,000
Area: 717 square kilometres
Capital: Tarawa
Language: English, Gilbertese
Currency: Australian Dollar

Although Kiribati is independent it has no currency of its own, and its citizens use the Australian dollar. The islands are generally small but are spread over an immense area of the Pacific Ocean, being grouped into three coral archipelagos and one volcanic island. The islands voluntarily became British protectorates in 1892 and regained independence in 1979. The democratically-elected government consists of one chamber and a President. The agricultural economy of the islands relies almost exclusively on coconuts and copra, which make up over ninety percent of exports by value. The coconut tree grows well in the thin soil and tropical climate of Kiribati. Pigs, chickens and breadfruit trees are produced for local consumption, as is a local vegetable named *babai*.

NAURU

Population: 8,100
Area: 21 square kilometres
Capital: Yaren
Language: Nauruan and English
Currency: Australian Dollar

With a population among the lowest in the world, Nauru does not support its own currency, using instead the Australian dollar. The population is a mix of Polynesian and Melanesians who arrived generations ago and have merged to produce a single racial group. The island fell under German control in 1881, passed to Australia in 1914, and became independent in 1968. The constitution allows an assembly elected every three years under a President. Nauru remains within the Commonwealth. The traditional crop of coconuts is widely grown and exported, while vegetables and livestock are kept for local consumption. Tourism is a growing business. The island nation's wealth, however, depends on phosphates mined on the island. This gives Nauru the highest per capita income in the Pacific islands and the wealth is being invested against the time when deposits run out.

NEW ZEALAND

Population: 3.4 million
Area: 268,000 square kilometres
Capital: Wellington
Language: English and Maori
Currency: New Zealand Dollar

Descendants of European immigrants form the bulk of New Zealand's population, though the native Maori form the largest minority. The exports of New Zealand have traditionally been agricultural and the pattern continues, with chilled meat, live animals, dairy products and wool far outstripping manufactured goods in value. However, industry

▼ *Niutao Island church, Tuvalu.*

▲ *Lefaga Beach, Upolu, Western Samoa.*

◀ *Yasur volcano, Vanuatu.*

▼ *Mananuca Islands, Fiji.*

is of growing importance internally, with iron and steel works and aluminium smelting being the largest heavy industrial works. The attractive scenery and relaxed lifestyle of the islands makes New Zealand an increasingly popular holiday attraction, with nearly a million tourists visiting each year. The government is based on universal suffrage, though some seats in the Assembly are reserved for Maoris and have an exclusively Maori electorate.

PAPUA NEW GUINEA

Population: 3.8 million
Area: 463,000 square kilometres
Capital: Port Moresby
Language: English, Motu and tribal languages
Currency: Kina

The rugged highlands of New Guinea are divided into isolated valleys covered by dense forests in which travel is difficult and communications are poor. The numerous tribes speak as many as 700 different languages, though the Motu form of pidgin English is a common *lingua franca*. Many of these tribes were untouched by the outside world, having no knowledge of Whites until the 1940s, and they still lead traditional lifestyles and pursue traditional tribal wars. Agriculture for export is concentrated around the coasts and produces coffee, copra and cocoa. Gold is mined on a commercial scale and there are large copper reserves on the island of Bougainville, though an active secessionist movement has disrupted mining. The constitution is based on that of the UK.

▲ *Native dance, Honiara, Solomon Islands.*

SOLOMON ISLANDS

Population: 309,000
Area: 28,000 square kilometres
Capital: Honiara
Language: English and tribal languages
Currency: Solomon Island Dollar

The Melanesian tribes of the Solomons retained their freedom until Britain declared a protectorate in 1893. The Japanese invaded during World War II, and Britain granted full independence in 1978. The country is governed by a Parliament elected by universal

suffrage. The Governor General, who represents the Queen, is appointed on the advice of the Parliament. The islands are predominantly agricultural, with property ownership held collectively by tribes and clans. Cocoa and coconuts are grown for export while yams, taro and sweet potatoes are consumed locally. The large fishing fleet exploits the tuna shoals of the region and the catch is canned before export. Industry is limited to processing crops for export.

▲ *The Tongatapu Island coastline, Tonga.*

TONGA

Population: 100,000
Area: 700 square kilometres
Capital: Nuku'alofa
Language: Tongan and English
Currency: Pa'anga

The kingdom of Tonga dates back to the early 19th century, when the warlike King Tupou of the Ha'apai conquered all the island tribes. Tupou overthrew the rule of petty chiefs and established a rudimentary democracy before Britain declared a protectorate in 1899. Internal government continued under the royal family and full independence came in 1970. The present constitution is based on that of King Topou. The Assembly consists of nine chiefs elected by the chiefs, nine people elected by the people and eleven privy councillors appointed by the king. The main exports are coconuts, fish and vanilla, while tourism brings in substantial quantities of foreign capital. Industry is virtually non-existent.

TUVALU

Population: 8,000
Area: 24 square kilometres
Capital: Fongafale
Language: Tuvaluan and English
Currency: Australian Dollar

As with other tiny Pacific states, Tuvalu uses the Australian dollar. However, it mints its own coins with unique and attractive designs. A British protectorate from 1892 to 1968, Tuvalu has a Parliament elected by universal suffrage and consisting of just twelve members,

four of whom are ministers. There are no political parties and candidates stand as individuals. The nine islands of the group are coral atolls with thin soils capable of supporting little other than coconut trees. Coconuts and copra comprise the main exports, with vegetables being grown for local consumption. The flag is highly symbolic, with the blue field representing the Pacific Ocean, the nine stars the nine islands, and the Union Jack standing for membership of the Commonwealth.

VANUATU

Population: 142,000
Area: 12,000 square kilometres
Capital: Vila
Language: Bislama and English
Currency: Vatu

On independence in 1980 the islands changed their name from New Hebrides to Vanuatu. The former name was given by Captain Cook because the rugged mountainous interiors reminded him of the Scottish islands, though the tropical climate is very different from that of the Scottish Hebrides. Power resides in an elected Parliament together with the tribal chiefs who sit in a separate Council. The Council advises primarily on matters of custom and tradition. The basis of the economy is the coconut tree, cocoa and coffee, which flourish in the hot, moist climate. A livestock industry based on cattle is becoming established. Tropical crops such as yams and taro are grown for local markets. Industry is limited to processing export crops and freezing the plentiful fish catch brought in by the numerous fishing boats.

WESTERN SAMOA

Population: 163,000
Area: 2,800 square kilometres
Capital: Apia
Language: English and Samoan
Currency: Tala

Formerly a German colony governed since 1920 by New Zealand, Western Samoa became independent in 1962. His Highness Malietoa Manumalfili became head of state for life, but after his death future heads of state are due to be elected. Though now independent, Western Samoa maintains direct diplomatic links only within the Pacific. Elsewhere New Zealand acts on its behalf. The economy of the islands is basically agricultural, with coconuts, bananas and cocoa being among the most important crops. Despite the tropical climate and a marked dry season, tourism is only poorly developed. Industry is limited to the processing of agricultural products.

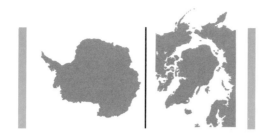

POLAR REGIONS

*T*he polar regions have an image of being blizzard-swept wastes inhabited only by penguins and polar bears. In fact the polar regions are far more than that. It is true that both the North and South Poles are ice-bound throughout the year, but the wildlife of the regions is incredibly varied. In the north polar bears, seals and whales make up the mammal population and the oceans are teeming with fish. The south, which has the advantage of a solid rock continent, is home to a variety of fauna, including penguins.

Both poles have been divided between various nations which maintain scientific bases and conduct research. As the Arctic is open ocean beneath the ice, it is technically not subject to any state. However, those nations which have Arctic coasts maintain various bases, often military, in the area and patrol it regularly.

The political situation of Antarctica is more fraught. Officially, the vast continent is divided between Australia, New Zealand, France, Norway and Britain. Other nations, however, including Chile and Argentina, claim sections of the continent. All these nations, and others, maintain scientific research stations on Antarctica. The population of these outposts varies greatly with the season and from year to year, but there are rarely more than a thousand people on the continent. English is now the recognised scientific language, but each nationality speaks its own language on the continent.

In 1959 the Antarctic Treaty was signed by nations involved on the continent, and has since expanded to include thirty-eight nations. The Treaty bans military activity and tightly regulates commercial and scientific activity in Antarctica. It is unlikely that either polar region will ever maintain a sizeable human population but both remain rich in wildlife and environmental interest. It is to be hoped that international co-operation will ensure the continued existence of these great wilderness areas.

▲ An Eskimo in a hunting kayak, north-west Greenland.

▶ As temperatures drop, the sea near Signy Island starts to freeze.

▼ *Macaroni penguins on Bird Island, South Georgia.*

▲ *Heavy-bodied walruses resting on the beaches at Round Island, Alaska.*

▼ *Probing newly-formed ice in Antarctica.*

Mercator Projection

1:85,000,000 (Scale at the Equator)

49

50

1:12,500,000

West of Greenwich   East of Greenwich

| 0 | 100 | 200 | 300 | 400 | 500 | 600 | 700 | 800 KILOMETRES |

| 0 | 100 | 200 | 300 | 400 | 500 STATUTE MILES |

© COLOUR LIBRARY BOOKS

Miller Oblated Stereographic Projection

Designed and produced by E.S.R.

Transverse Mercator Projection

1:1,175,000

© COLOUR LIBRARY BOOKS

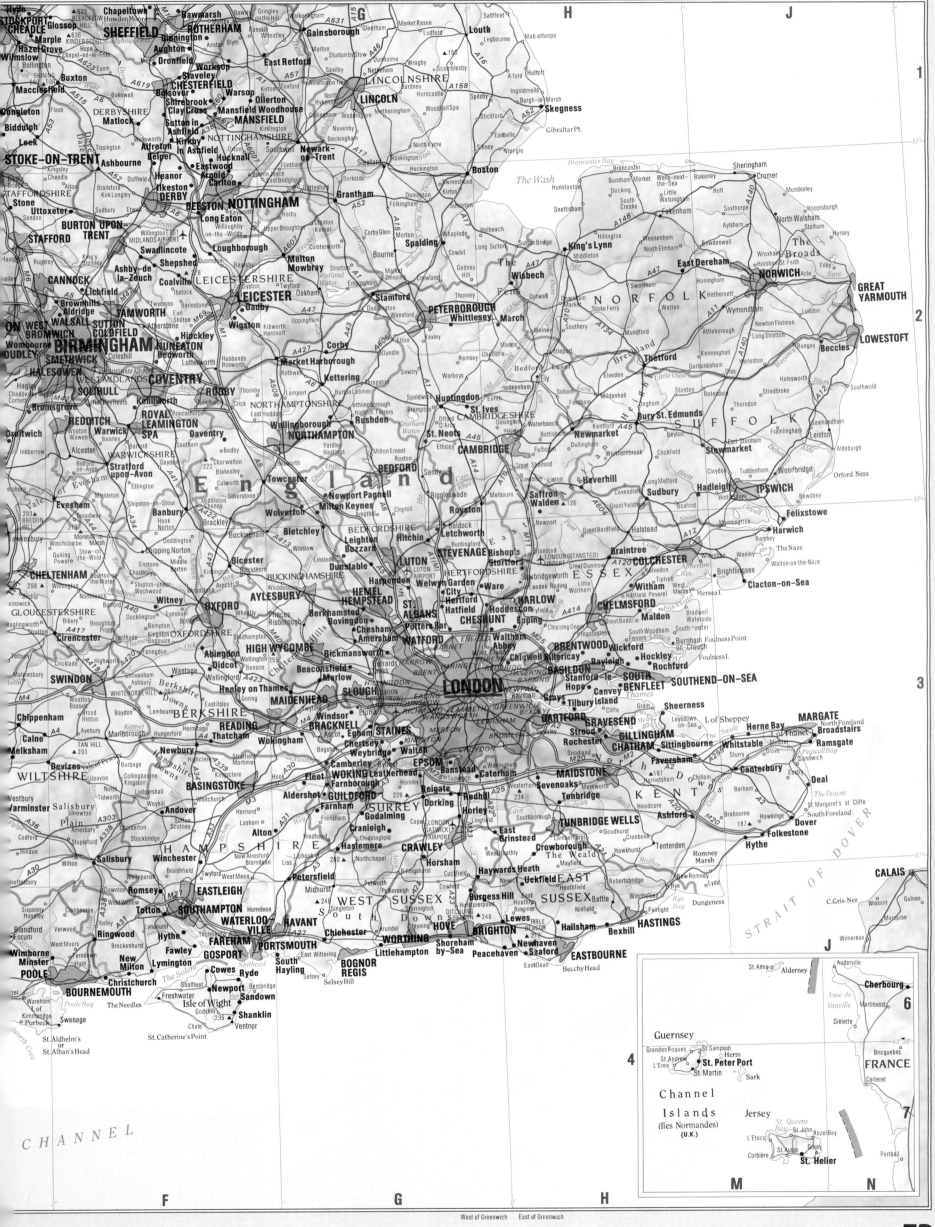

Designed and produced by E.S.R.

Transverse Mercator Projection

1:1,175,000

| 0 | 10 | 20 | 30 | 40 | 50 | 60 | 70 | 80 KILOMETRES |

| 0 | 10 | 20 | 30 | 40 | 50 STATUTE MILES |

© COLOUR LIBRARY BOOKS

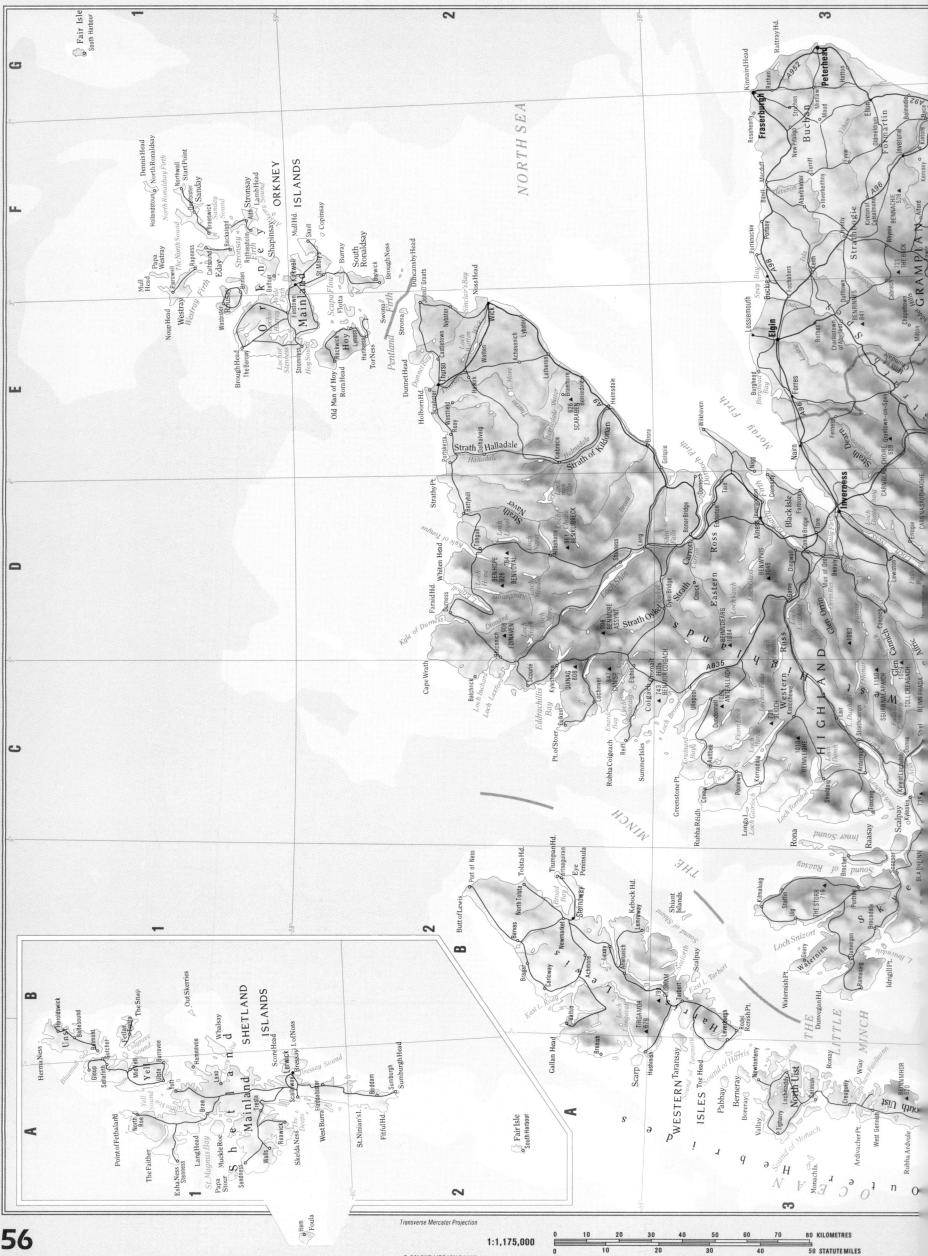

Transverse Mercator Projection

1:1,175,000

| 0 | 10 | 20 | 30 | 40 | 50 | 60 | 70 | 80 KILOMETRES |

| 0 | 10 | 20 | 30 | 40 | 50 STATUTE MILES |

© COLOUR LIBRARY BOOKS

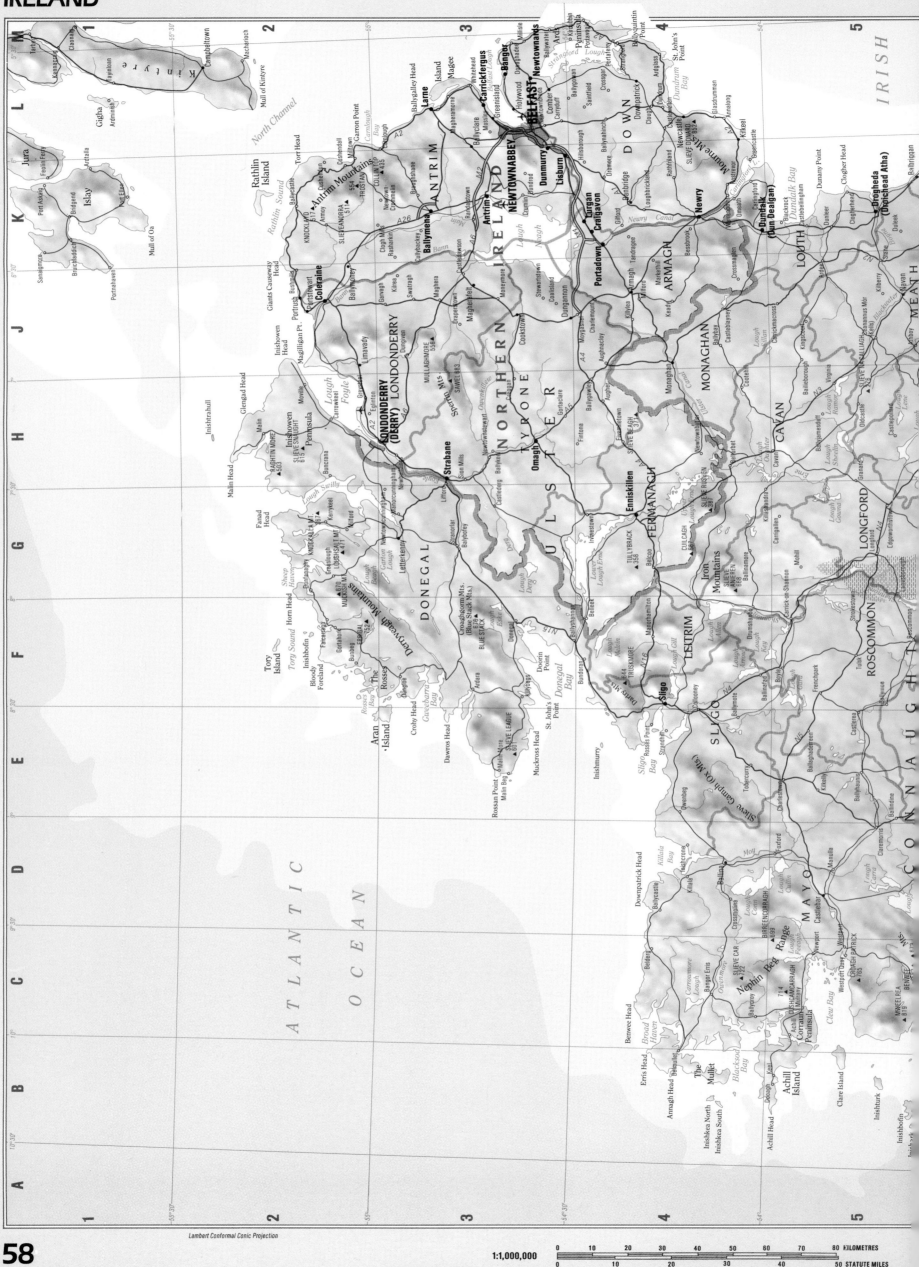

Lambert Conformal Conic Projection

© COLOUR LIBRARY BOOKS

1:1,000,000

| 0 | 10 | 20 | 30 | 40 | 50 | 60 | 70 | 80 KILOMETRES |

| 0 | 10 | 20 | 30 | 40 | 50 STATUTE MILES |

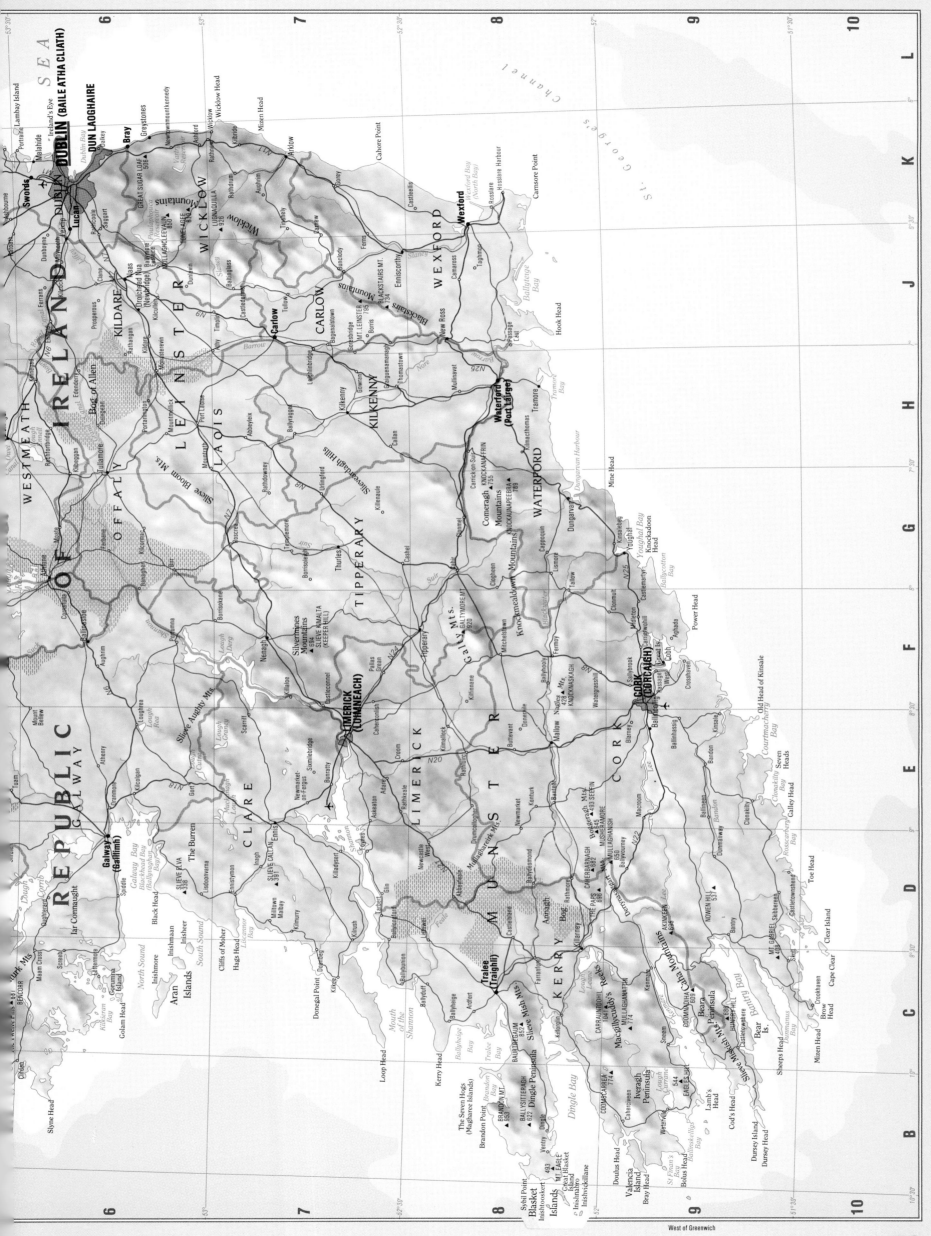

59

1:5,000,000

© COLOUR LIBRARY BOOKS

West of Greenwich | East of Greenwich

0   50   100   150   200   250   300   350   400 KILOMETRES

0   50   100   150   200   250 STATUTE MILES

Designed and produced by E.S.R.

Miller Oblated Stereographic Projection

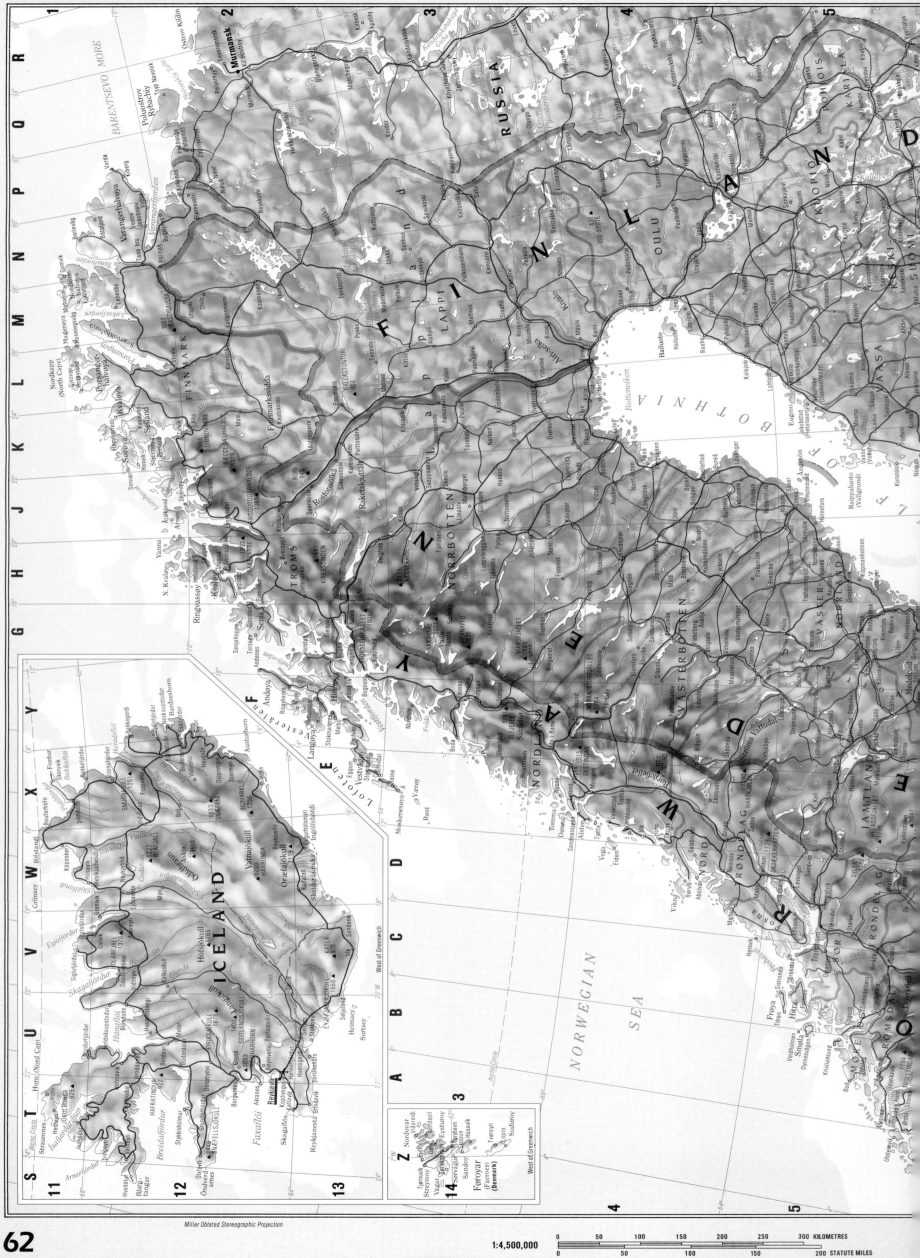

Miller Oblated Stereographic Projection

1:4,500,000

© COLOUR LIBRARY BOOKS

| 0 | 50 | 100 | 150 | 200 | 250 | 300 KILOMETRES |

| 0 | 50 | 100 | 150 | 200 STATUTE MILES |

NORTH SEA
SKAGERRAK
KATTEGAT
BALTIC SEA
Gulf of Danzig
GULF OF FINLAND
(SUOMENLAHTI FINSKIJ ZALIV)
Bottenhavet
Rizhskiy Zaliv
(Gulf of Riga)
DENMARK
GERMANY
POLAND
RUSSIA
LITHUANIA
LATVIA
ESTONIA
BELORUSSIA
KØBENHAVN
(COPENHAGEN)
STOCKHOLM
BERLIN
Oslo
Helsinki
(Helsingfors)
Tallinn
Riga
Vilnius
(Vilna)
MINSK
LENINGRAD
(SANKT PETERBURG)
Göteborg
(Gothenburg)
Malmö
HAMBURG
Bremen
Hannover
Szczecin
Gdańsk
(Danzig)
Bydgoszcz
(Bromberg)
Kaliningrad
(Königsberg)
Kaunas
Grodno
Bornholm
(Denmark)
Gotland
Öland
Saaremaa
Hiiumaa
Åland
(Ahvenanmaa)
Rügen
Nord-
Friesische
Inseln
Ostfriesische
Inseln
Designed and produced by E.S.R.
East of Greenwich

BENELUX AND FRANCE

© COLOUR LIBRARY BOOKS

1:3,000,000

Conic Projection

0   25   50   75   100   125 STATUTE MILES
0   25   50   75   100   125   150   175   200 KILOMETRES

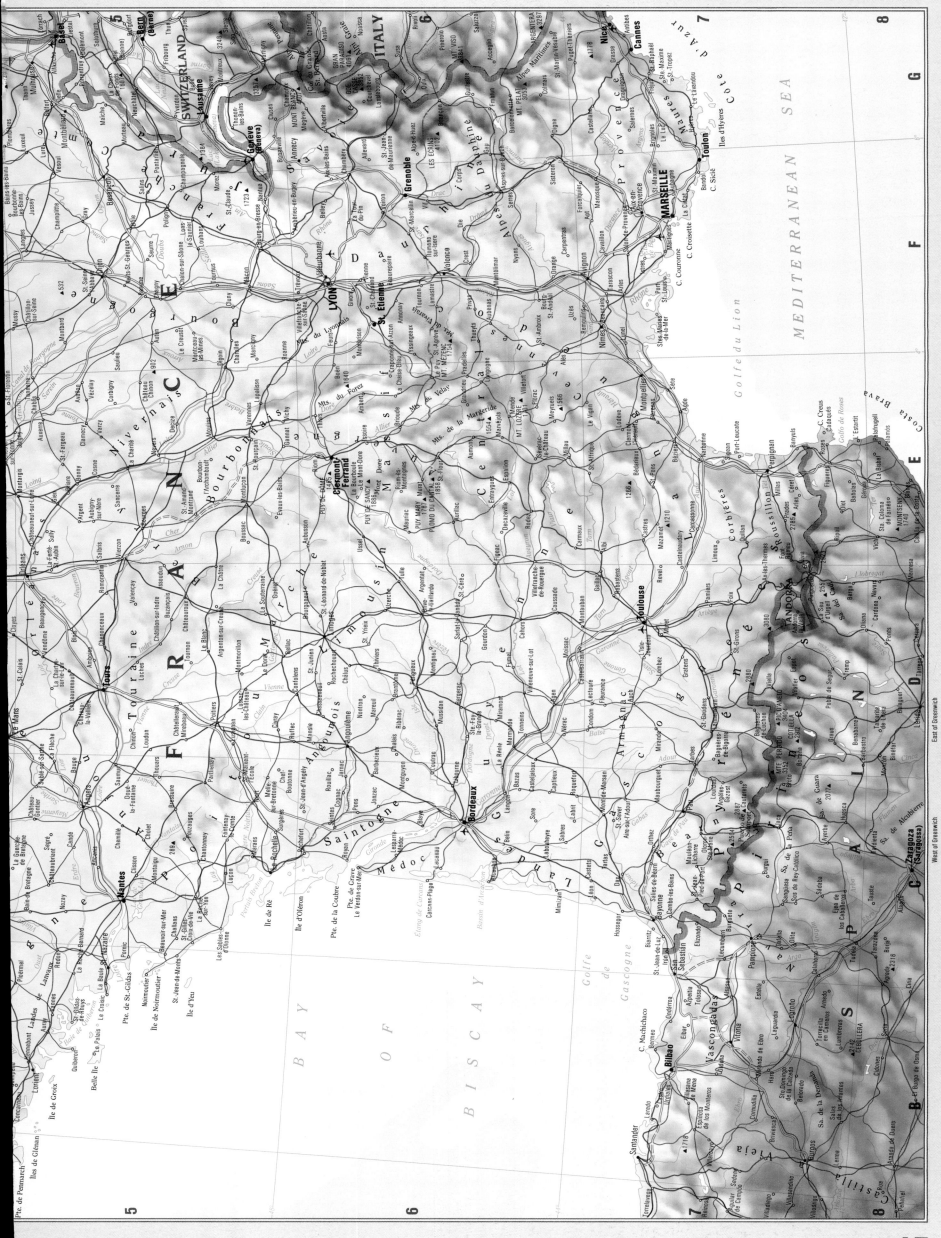

Conic Projection

1:3,000,000

© COLOUR LIBRARY BOOKS

| 0 | 25 | 50 | 75 | 100 | 125 | 150 | 175 | 200 KILOMETRES |
| 0 | | 25 | 50 | | 75 | 100 | | 125 STATUTE MILES |

Golfo de Gascuña

Armagnac

F R A N C E

L a n g u e d o c

Provence

Toulouse

Pyrénées

P i r i n e o s

ANDORRA

Roussillon

Perpignan

Golfe du Lion

MARSEILLE

Toulon

Iles d'Hyères

1

Zaragoza (Saragossa)

C a t a l u ñ a

BARCELONA

Hospitalet

Costa Brava

2

Costa Dorada

Golfo de San Jorge

C. de Tortosa

C. Caballeria

Menorca (Minorca)

Ciudadela

Mahón

3

N

Islas Columbretes

Golfo de Valencia

Puerto de Pollensa

Palma

Mallorca (Majorca)

VALENCIA

Ibiza (Iviza)

Cabrera

I s l a s   B a l e a r e s
(Balearic Islands)
(Spain)

Formentera

Pta. Rota

M u r c i a

Alicante

Costa Blanca

Murcia

C. de Palos

Cartagena

La Unión

4

M E D I T E R R A N E A N   S E A

C. Gata

EL DJAZAÏR (ALGIERS)

Golfe de Béjaïa

Kabylie

Petite

Djurdjura

LALLA KHEDIDJA

A L G E R I A

Mts. du Hodna

Oran

C. Ferrat

D a h r a

M a s s i f   d e   l ' O u a r s e n i s

5

West of Greenwich   East of Greenwich

Designed and produced by E.S.R.

67

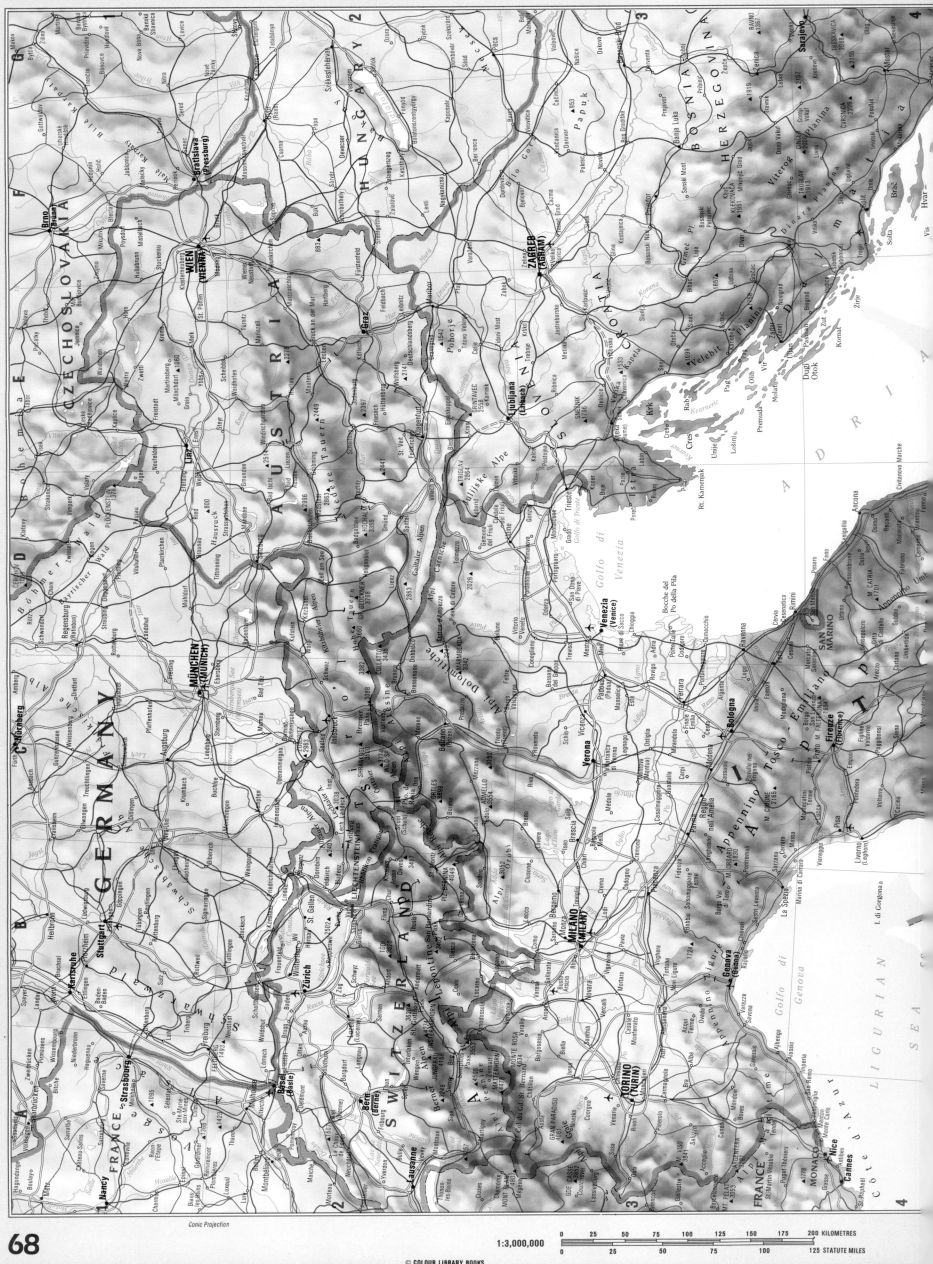

Conic Projection

1:3,000,000

| 0 | 25 | 50 | 75 | 100 | 125 | 150 | 175 | 200 KILOMETRES |

| 0 | 25 | 50 | 75 | 100 | 125 STATUTE MILES |

© COLOUR LIBRARY BOOKS

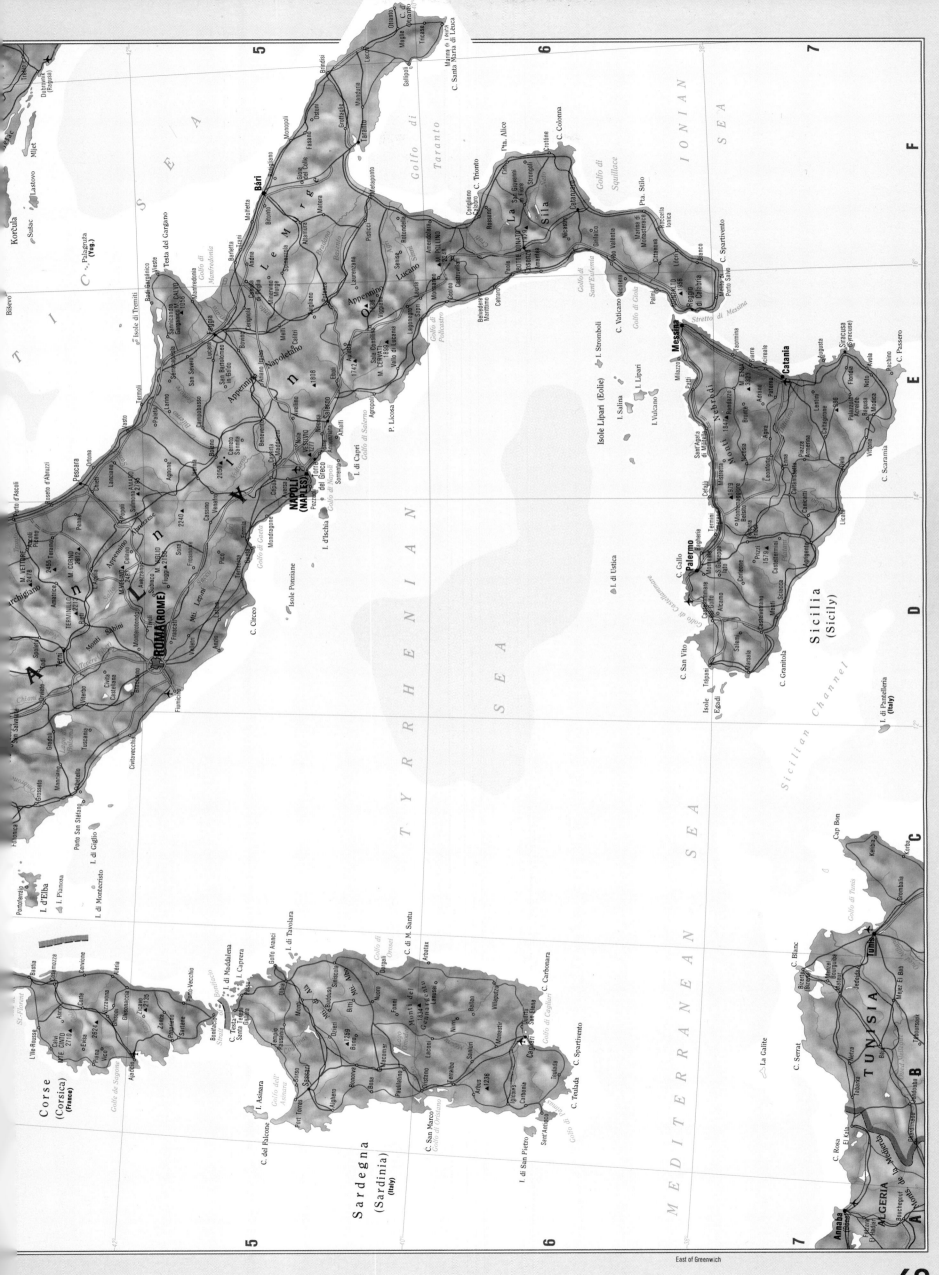

Designed and produced by E.S.R.

East of Greenwich

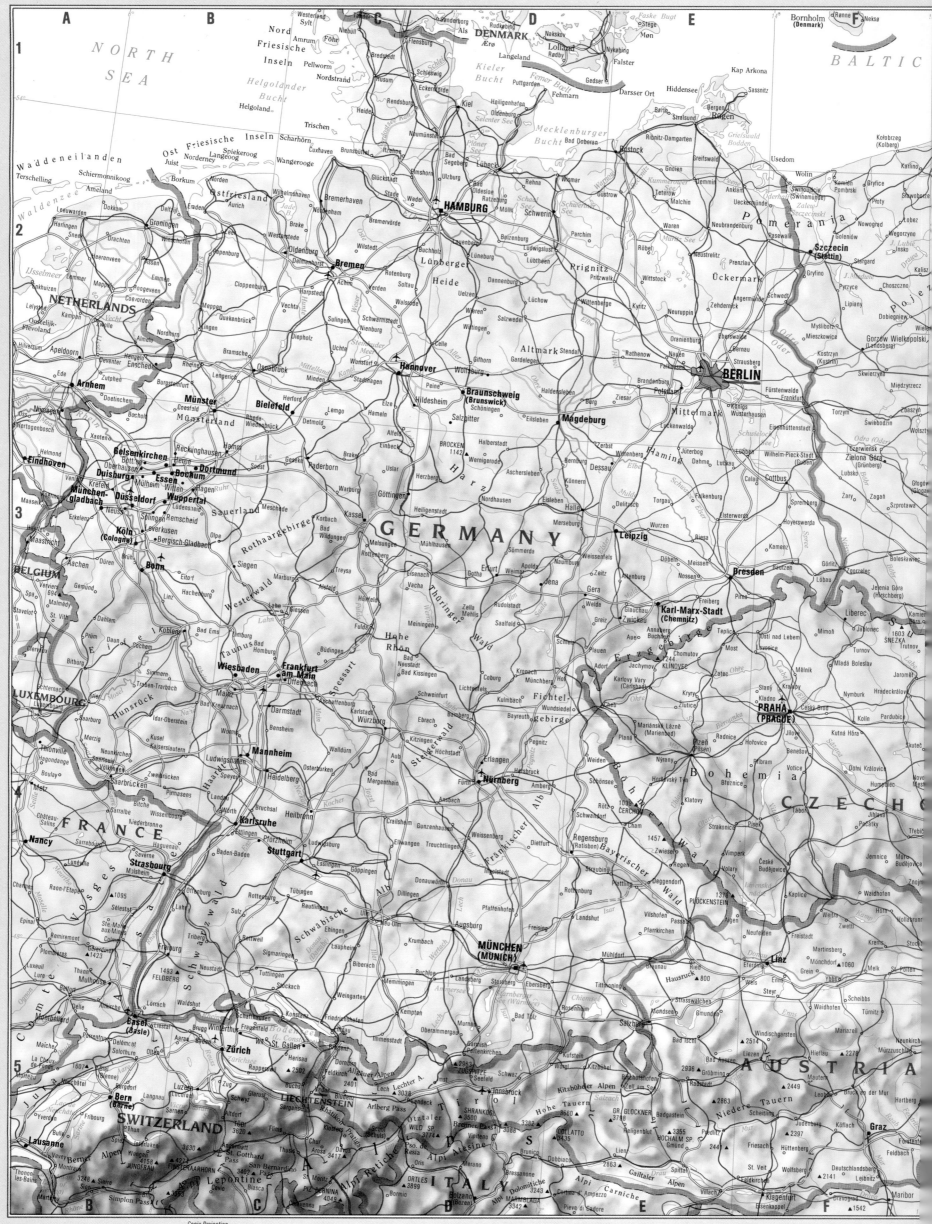

Conic Projection

1:3,000,000

| 0 | 25 | 50 | 75 | 100 | 125 | 150 | 175 | 200 KILOMETRES |

| 0 | 25 | 50 | 75 | 100 | 125 STATUTE MILES |

© COLOUR LIBRARY BOOKS

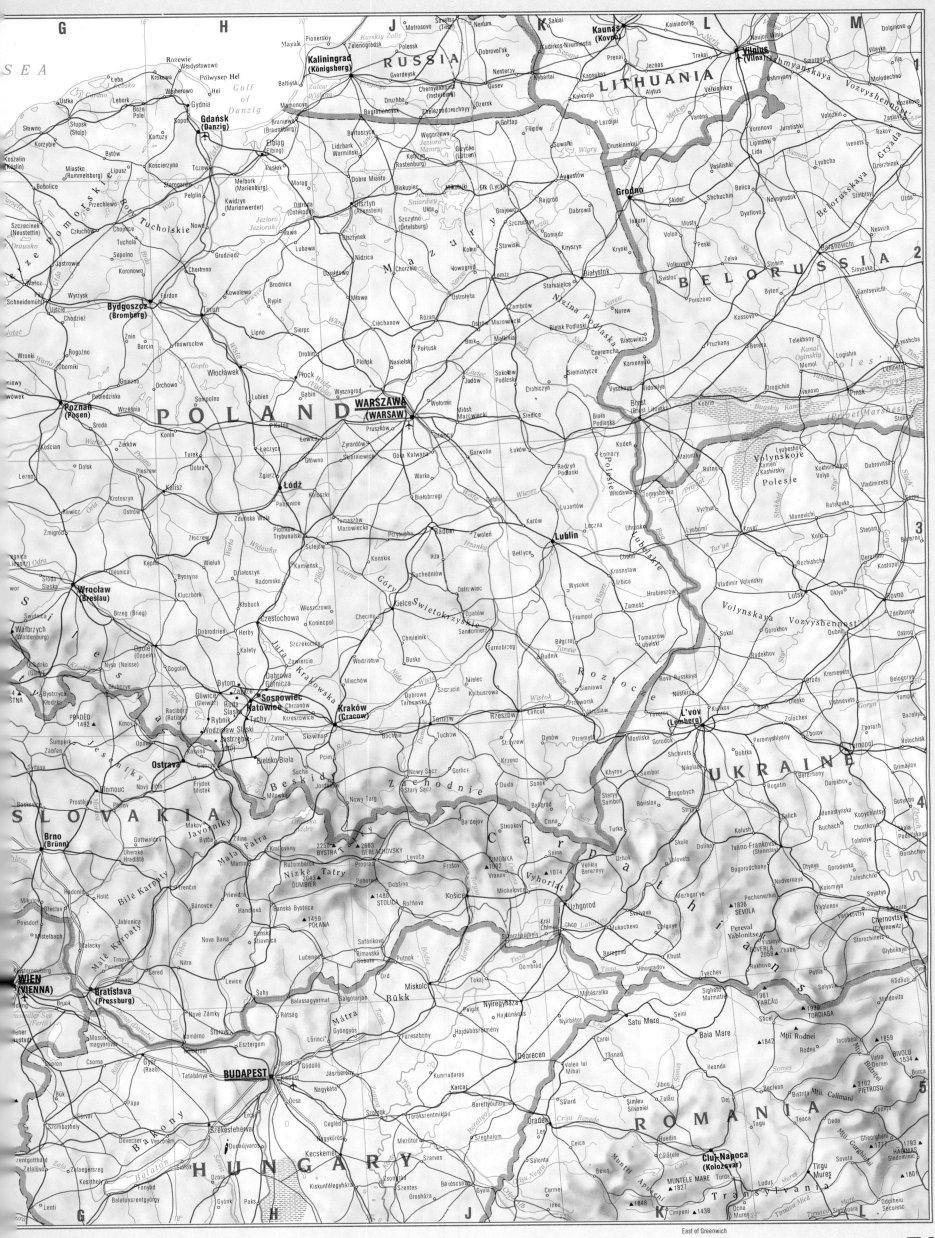

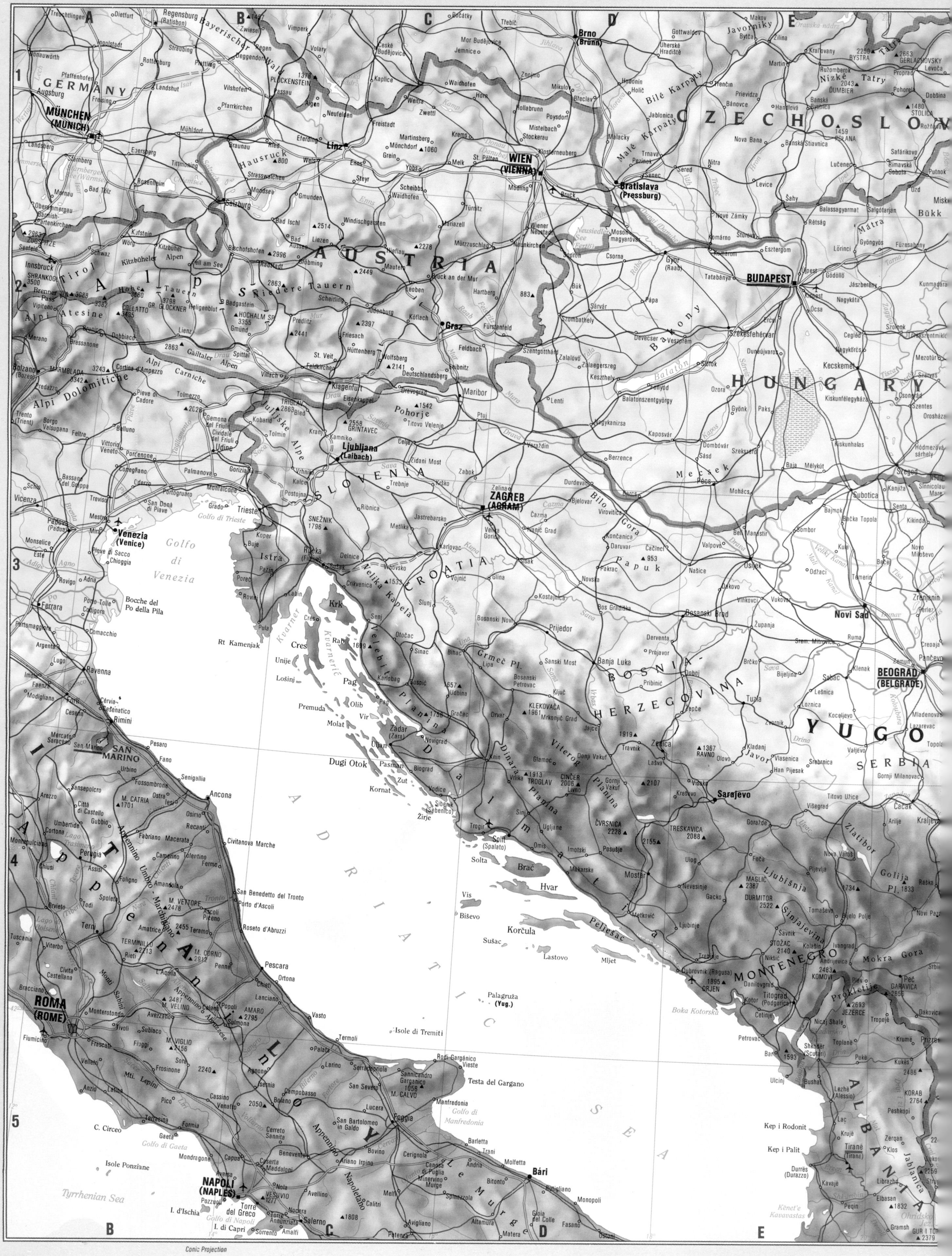

(Former) YUGOSLAVIA, HUNGARY, ROMANIA AND BULGARIA

GERMANY

MÜNCHEN (MUNICH)

AUSTRIA

WIEN (VIENNA)

Bratislava (Pressburg)

Brno (Brünn)

CZECHOSLOV

Linz

Salzburg

Graz

Innsbruck

BUDAPEST

HUNGARY

Balaton

SLOVENIA

Ljubljana (Laibach)

ZAGREB (AGRAM)

CROATIA

Trieste

Venezia (Venice)

Golfo di Venezia

Istra

Rijeka (Fiume)

Pula

Krk

Cres

Lošinj

Pag

Zadar (Zara)

Dugi Otok

BOSNIA-HERZEGOVINA

Banja Luka

Novi Sad

BEOGRAD (BELGRADE)

YUGO

SERBIA

Sarajevo

Split (Spalato)

Brač

Hvar

Korčula

Lastovo

Mljet

MONTENEGRO

Titograd (Podgorica)

Dubrovnik (Ragusa)

ITALY

ROMA (ROME)

San Marino

Ancona

Pescara

Appennino

Foggia

Bári

NAPOLI (NAPLES)

Tyrrhenian Sea

ADRIATIC SEA

ALBANIA

Tiranë (Tirana)

Durrës (Durazzo)

1:3,000,000

0 25 50 75 100 125 150 175 200 KILOMETRES

0 25 50 75 100 125 STATUTE MILES

Conic Projection

© COLOUR LIBRARY BOOKS

Conic Projection

1:3,000,000

| 0 | 25 | 50 | 75 | 100 | 125 | 150 | 175 | 200 KILOMETRES |

| 0 | 25 | 50 | 75 | 100 | 125 STATUTE MILES |

© COLOUR LIBRARY BOOKS

Designed and produced by ESR

BLACK SEA

BULGARIA

GREECE

İSTANBUL
(CONSTANTINOPLE)

İzmit

Marmara Denizi
(Sea of Marmara)

Bursa (Brusa)

ANKARA

Balıkesir

Eskişehir

T U R

İZMİR
(SMYRNA)

Kayser

Konya

Tuz Gölü

Antalya
(Adalia)

Antalya Körfezi

Toros

Mersin
(İçel)

Ada

Dhodhekanisos
(Dodecanese)

Ródhos
(Rhodes)

Kríti
(Crete)

CYPRUS

Levkosía
(Nicosia)

Famagusta
(Ammókhostos)

Larnaca
(Lárnax)

MT. TROODOS
(OLYMPUS)

Limassol
(Lemesós)

M E D I T E R R A N E A N   S E A

LEBANO

Bayrî
(Beîrut)

Saida
(Sidon)

Lambert Conformal Conic Projection

1:3,500,000

© COLOUR LIBRARY BOOKS

0   50   100   150   200   250 KILOMETRES

0   25   50   75   100   125   150 STATUTE MILES

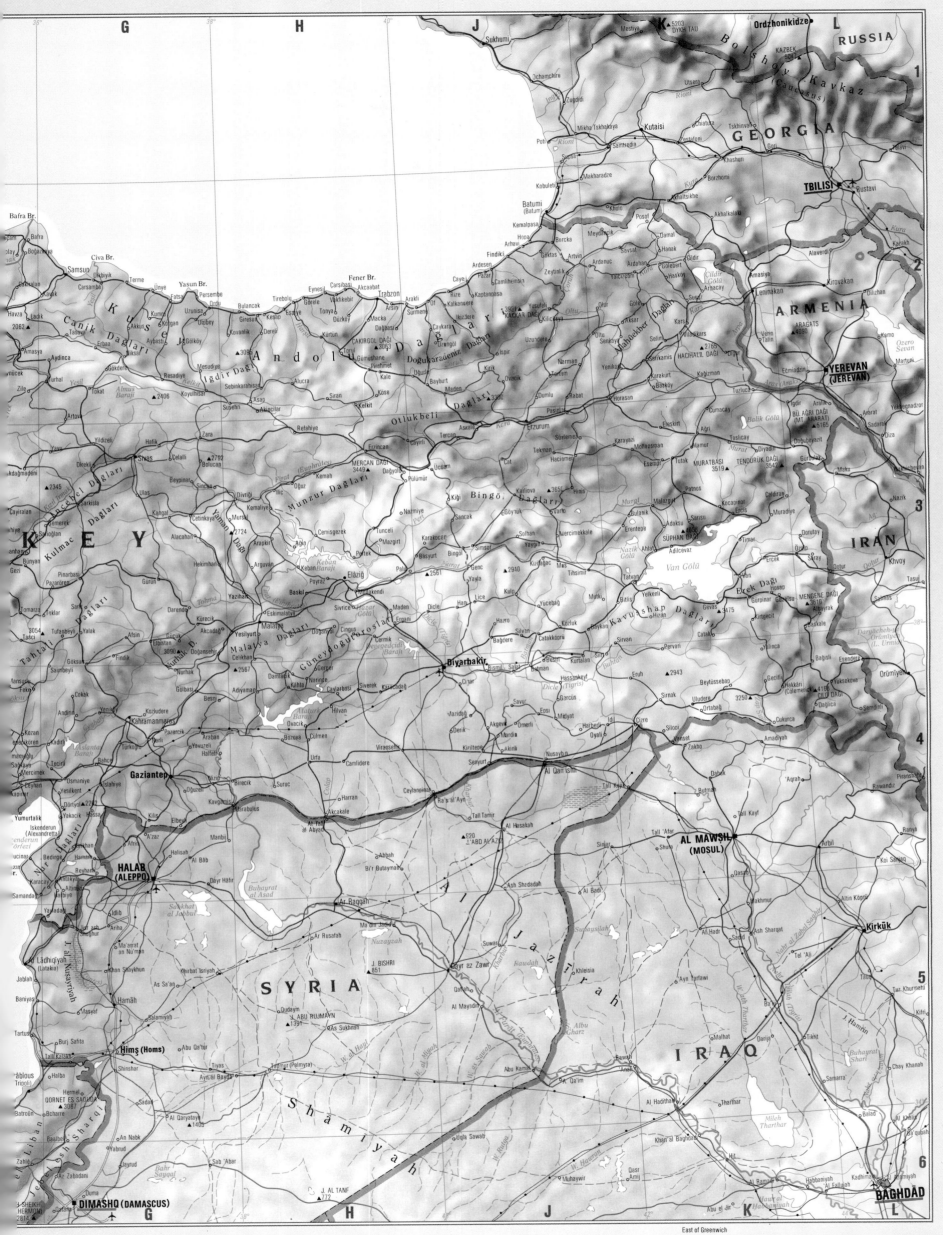

77

Miller Oblated Stereographic Projection

1:8,000,000

© COLOUR LIBRARY BOOKS

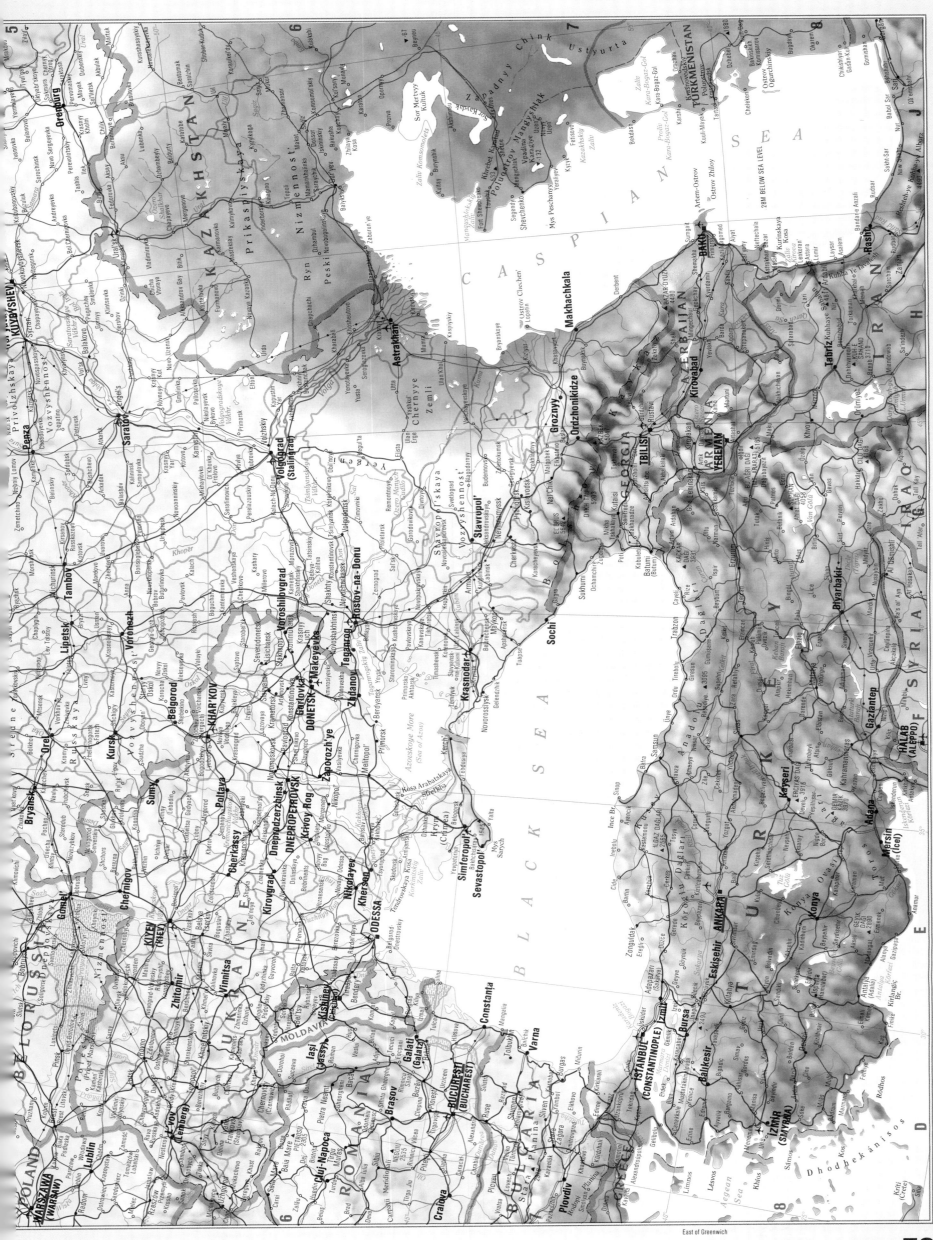

Designed and produced by E.S.R.

Conic Projection

© COLOUR LIBRARY BOOKS

1:17,000,000

| 0 | 100 | 200 | 300 | 400 | 500 | 600 | 700 | 800 KILOMETRES |

| 0 | 100 | 200 | 300 | 400 | 500 STATUTE MILES |

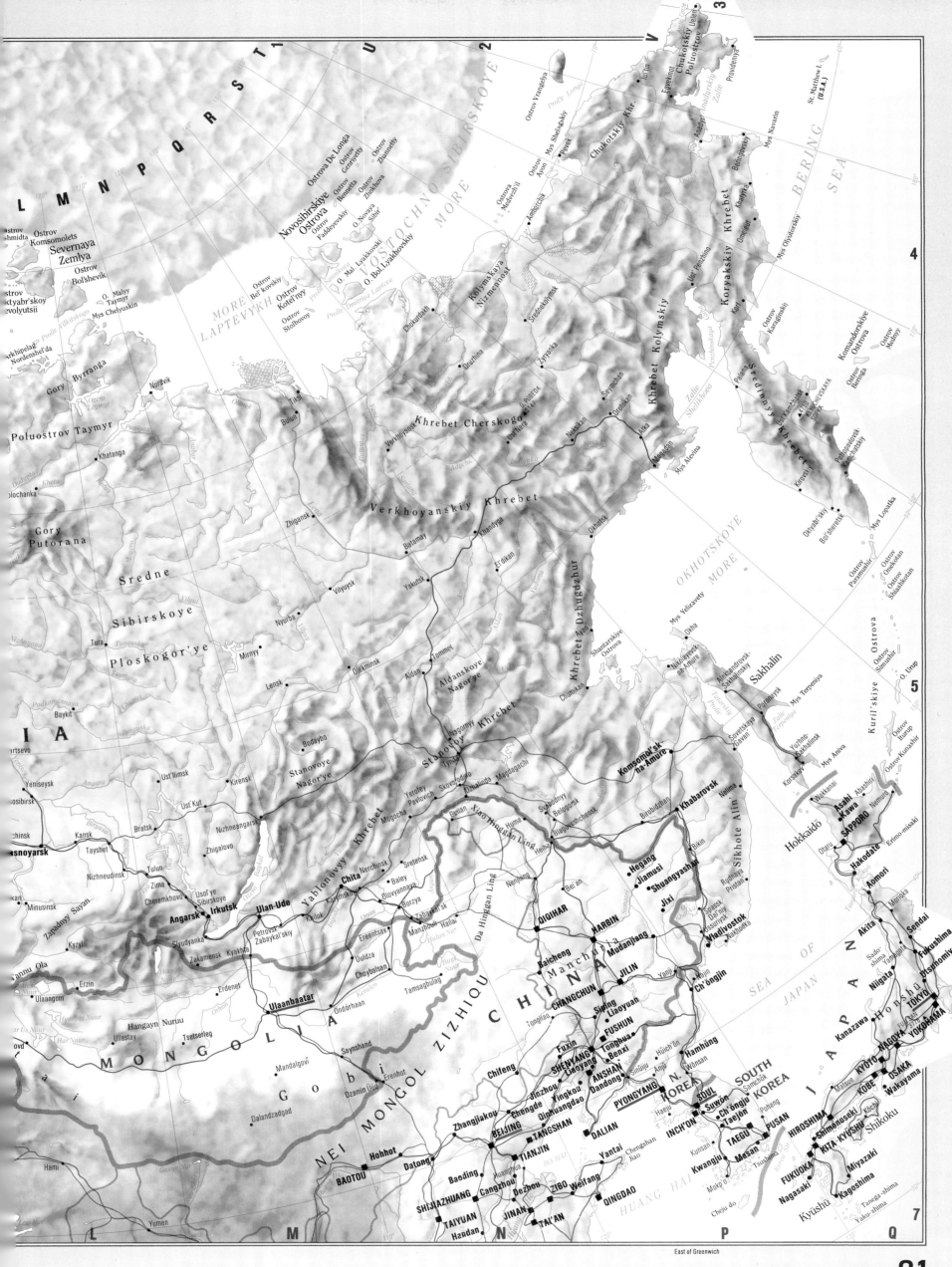

Lambert Azimuthal Equal Area Projection

1:25,000,000

0   200   400   600   800   1000 KILOMETRES

0   100   200   300   400   500   600 STATUTE MILES

© COLOUR LIBRARY BOOKS

Designed and produced by E.S.R.

East of Greenwich

Miller Oblated Stereographic Projection

1:11,500,000

© COLOUR LIBRARY BOOKS

| | 100 | 200 | 300 | 400 | 500 | 600 | 700 | 800 KILOMETRES |
| | 50 | 100 | 150 | 200 | 250 | 300 | 350 | 400 | 450 | 500 STATUTE MILES |

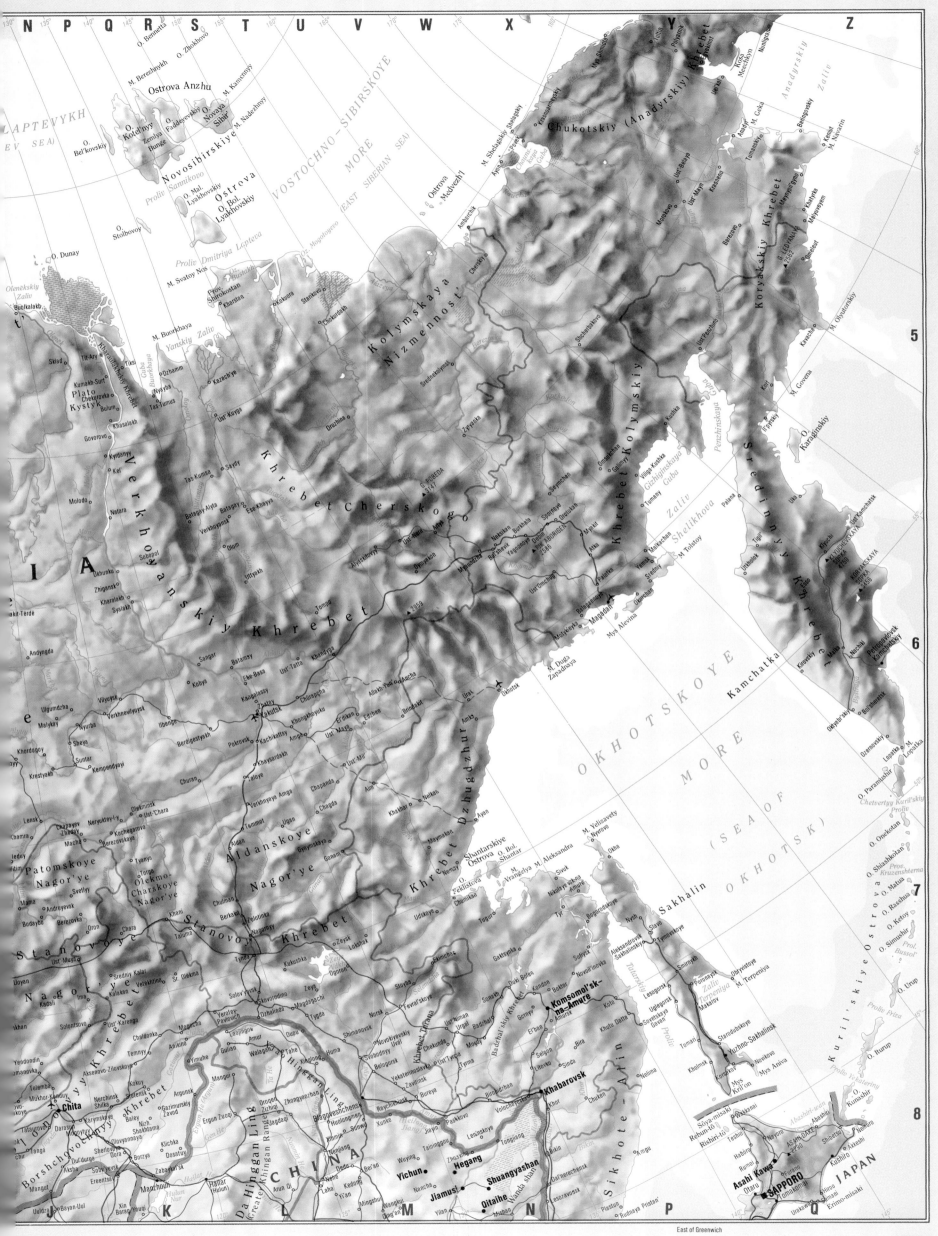

LAPTEVYKH
(EV SEA)

Ostrova Anzhu

O. Bennetta
M. Berezhnykh
O. Zhokhovo
M. Kamennyy
O. Kotel'nyy
Zemlya
Bunge
M. Nadezhny
Novaya
Sibir'
Novosibirskiye
O. Mal.
Lyakhovskiy
Ostrova
O. Bol.
Lyakhovskiy

Proliv Sannikovo

O. Bel'kovskiy

VOSTOCHNO–SIBIRSKOYE

MORE

(EAST SIBERIAN SEA)

Ostrova
Medvezh'i

O. Stolbovoy
Proliv Dmitriya Lapteva

O. Dunay

Chukotskiy (Anadyrskiy) Khrebet

Olenëkskiy
Zaliv

Koryakskiy Khrebet

Anadyrskiy Zaliv

5

Kolymskaya
Nizmennost'

Verkhoyanskiy Khrebet

Khrebet Cherskogo

Khrebet Kolymskiy

Zaliv
Shelikhova

Sredinnyy Khrebet

IA

6

Khrebet Dzhugdzhur

Kamchatka

OKHOTSKOYE

MORE

(SEA OF
OKHOTSK)

Aldanskoye
Nagor'ye

Stanovoy Khrebet

Shantarskiye
Ostrova O. Bol.
Shantar

Patomskoye
Nagor'ye
Olekmo–
Charskoye
Nagor'ye

Sakhalin

7

Stanovoye
Nagor'ye

Kuril'skiye Ostrova

Komsomol'sk-
na-Amure

Yuzhno-Sakhalinsk

Khabarovsk

Sikhote–Alin

8

Chita

CHINA

Da Hinggan Ling
(Greater Khingan Range)

Yichun Hegang

Shuangyashan

JAPAN

Asahi Kawa
SAPPORO

Jiamusi Qitaihe

Miller Oblated Stereographic Projection

1:11,500,000

© COLOUR LIBRARY BOOKS

0	100	200	300	400	500	600	700	800 KILOMETRES
0	50	100	150	200	250	300	350	450	500 STATUTE MILES

SEA OF JAPAN
HUANG HAI
(YELLOW SEA)
DONG HAI
(EAST CHINA SEA)
NAN HAI
(SOUTH CHINA SEA)
PACIFIC OCEAN
Bo Hai
(Gulf of Chihli)
Korea Bay
Luzon Strait
Bashi Haixia
Korea Strait
Taiwan Haixia
Tropic of Cancer
Beibu Wan
NORTH KOREA
SOUTH KOREA
JAPAN
TAIWAN (FORMOSA)
PHILIPPINES
Luzon
VIETNAM
Hokkaidō
Honshū
Shikoku
Kyūshū
Hainan Dao
Nansei-shotō
(Ryukyu Islands)
Okinawa
Amami O-shima
Tanega-shima
Yaku-shima
Batan Is.
Babuyan Is.
HEILONGJIANG
JILIN
LIAONING
HEBEI
SHANXI
SHAANXI
SHANDONG
HENAN
JIANGSU
ANHUI
HUBEI
ZHEJIANG
JIANGXI
HUNAN
FUJIAN
GUANGDONG
GUANGXI
GUIZHOU
SICHUAN
NINGXIA
NEIMONGOL ZIZHIQU
(INNER MONGOLIAN AUT. REGION)
MONGOLIA
Gobi
Da Hinggan Ling
(Greater Khingan Range)
Xiao Hinggan Ling
Sikhote-Alin
Yablonovyy Khrebet
Borshchovochnyy Khrebet
Ozero Baykal
BEIJING (PEKING)
TIANJIN
SHANGHAI
SHENYANG (MUKDEN)
HARBIN
CHANGCHUN
JILIN (KIRIN)
QIQIHAR (TSITSIHAR)
DALIAN (LÜDA)
QINGDAO (TSINGTAO)
JINAN (TSINAN)
SHIJIAZHUANG
TAIYUAN
XI'AN
ZHENGZHOU
NANJING
HANGZHOU
WUHAN
NANCHANG
CHANGSHA
FUZHOU
GUANGZHOU
(CANTON)
KOWLOON
Victoria
HONG KONG
(U.K.)
MACAO
(Port.)
CHONGQING
CHENGDU
GUIYANG
LANZHOU
HANOI
HAIPHONG
PYONGYANG
SOUL (SEOUL)
INCH'ON
PUSAN
TAEGU
T'AI-PEI
KAO-HSIUNG
T'ai-nan
HIROSHIMA
OSAKA
KOBE
KYOTO
SAPPORO
Ulaanbaatar
(Ulan Bator)
Irkutsk
Ulan-Ude
Chita
Khabarovsk
Vladivostok
East of Greenwich
Designed and produced by E.S.R.

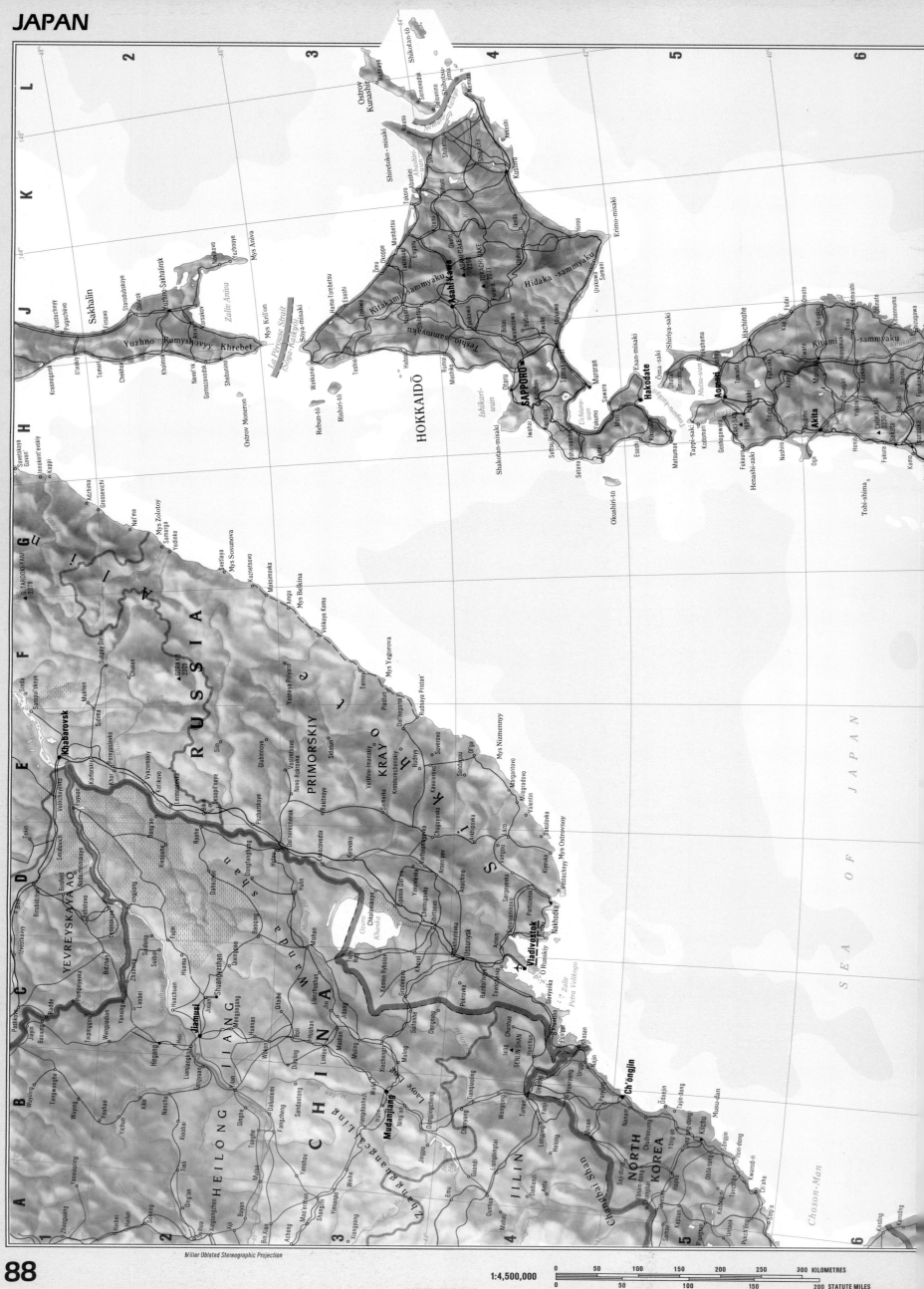

Miller Oblated Stereographic Projection

© COLOUR LIBRARY BOOKS

1:4,500,000

| 0 | 50 | 100 | 150 | 200 | 250 | 300 KILOMETRES |

| 0 | 50 | 100 | 150 | 200 STATUTE MILES |

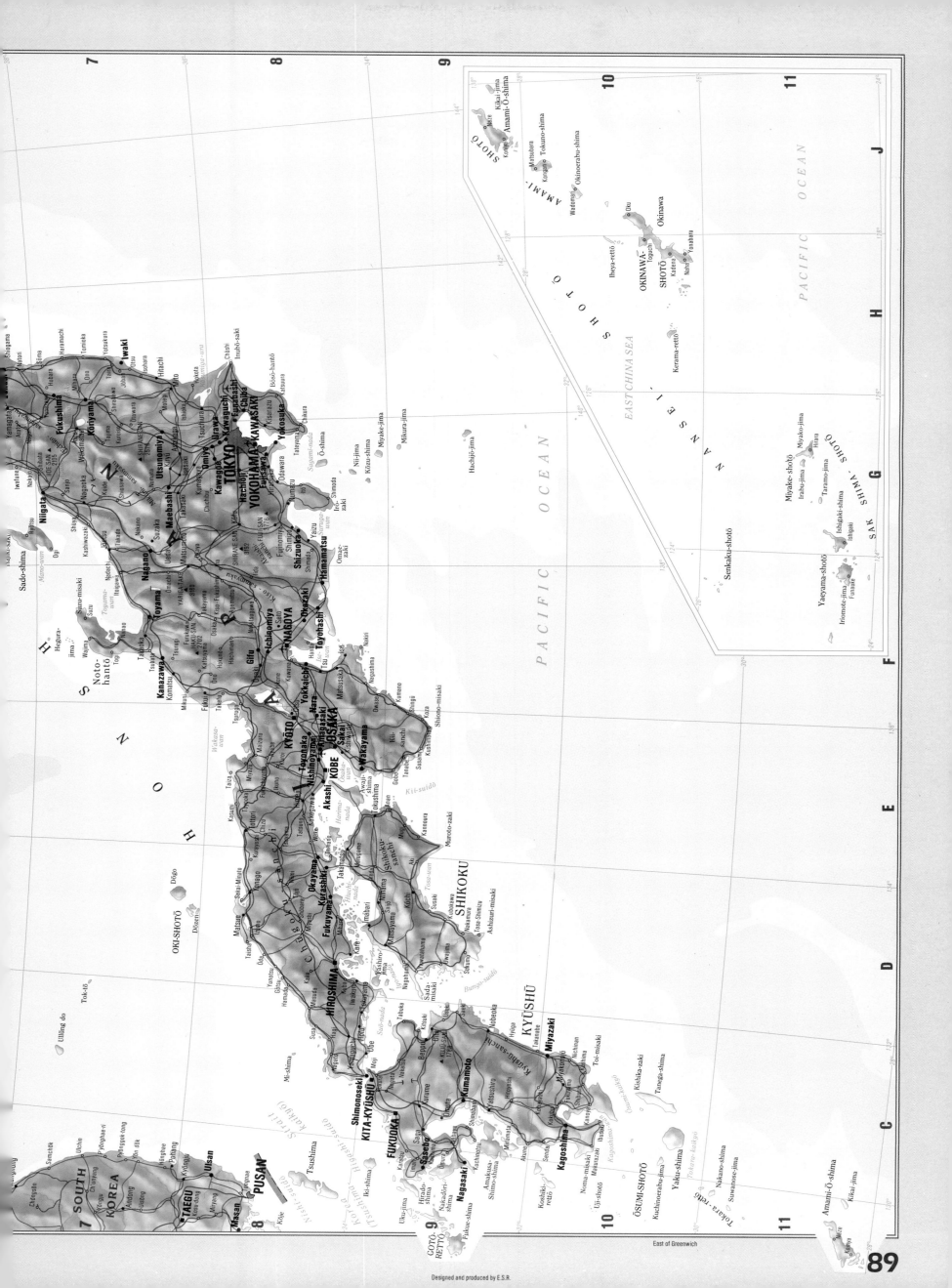

SOUTH-EAST ASIA

Mercator Projection

1:12,000,000

© COLOUR LIBRARY BOOKS

| 0 | 100 | 200 | 300 | 400 | 500 | 600 | 700 | 800 KILOMETRES |

| 0 | 100 | 200 | 300 | 400 | 500 STATUTE MILES |

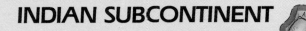

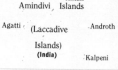

Miller Oblated Stereographic Projection

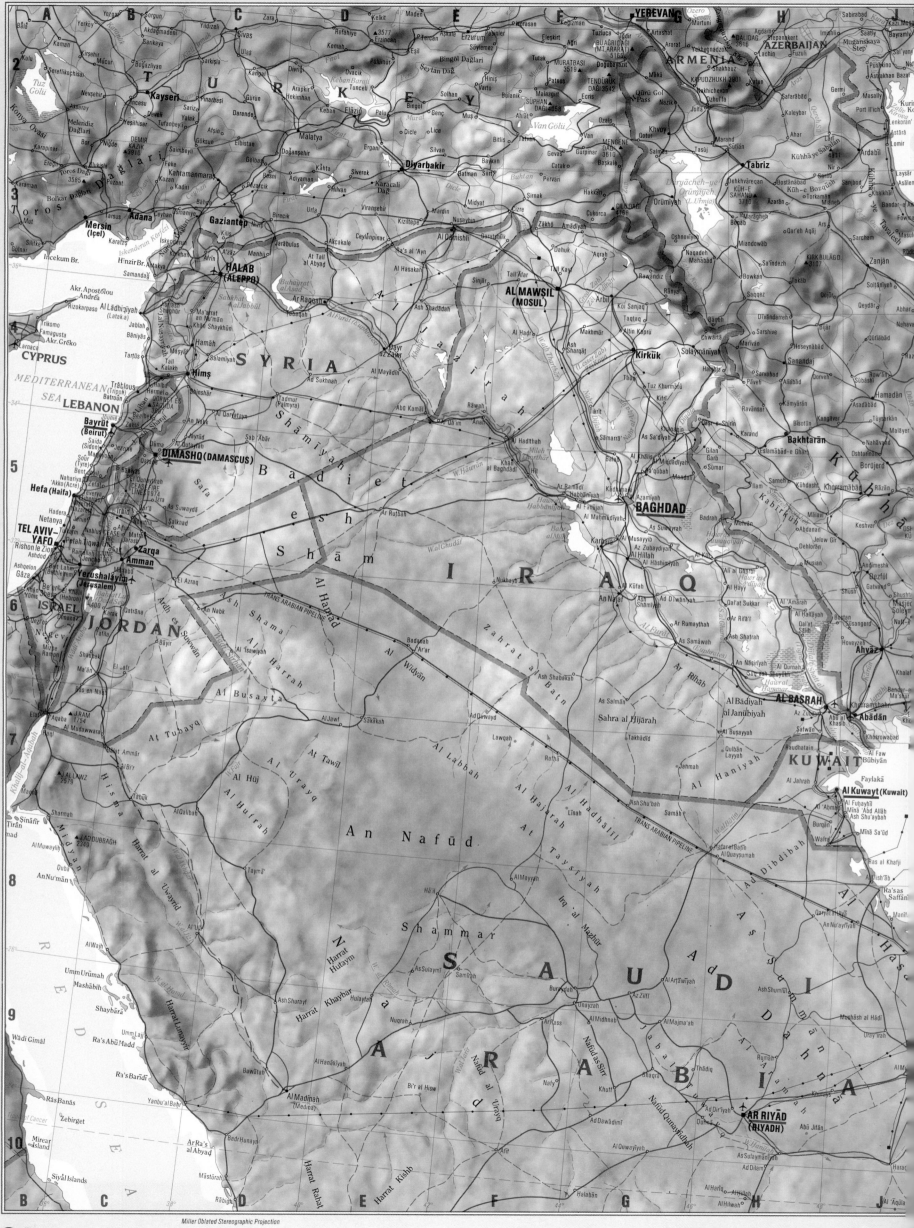

Miller Oblated Stereographic Projection

1:6,000,000

© COLOUR LIBRARY BOOKS

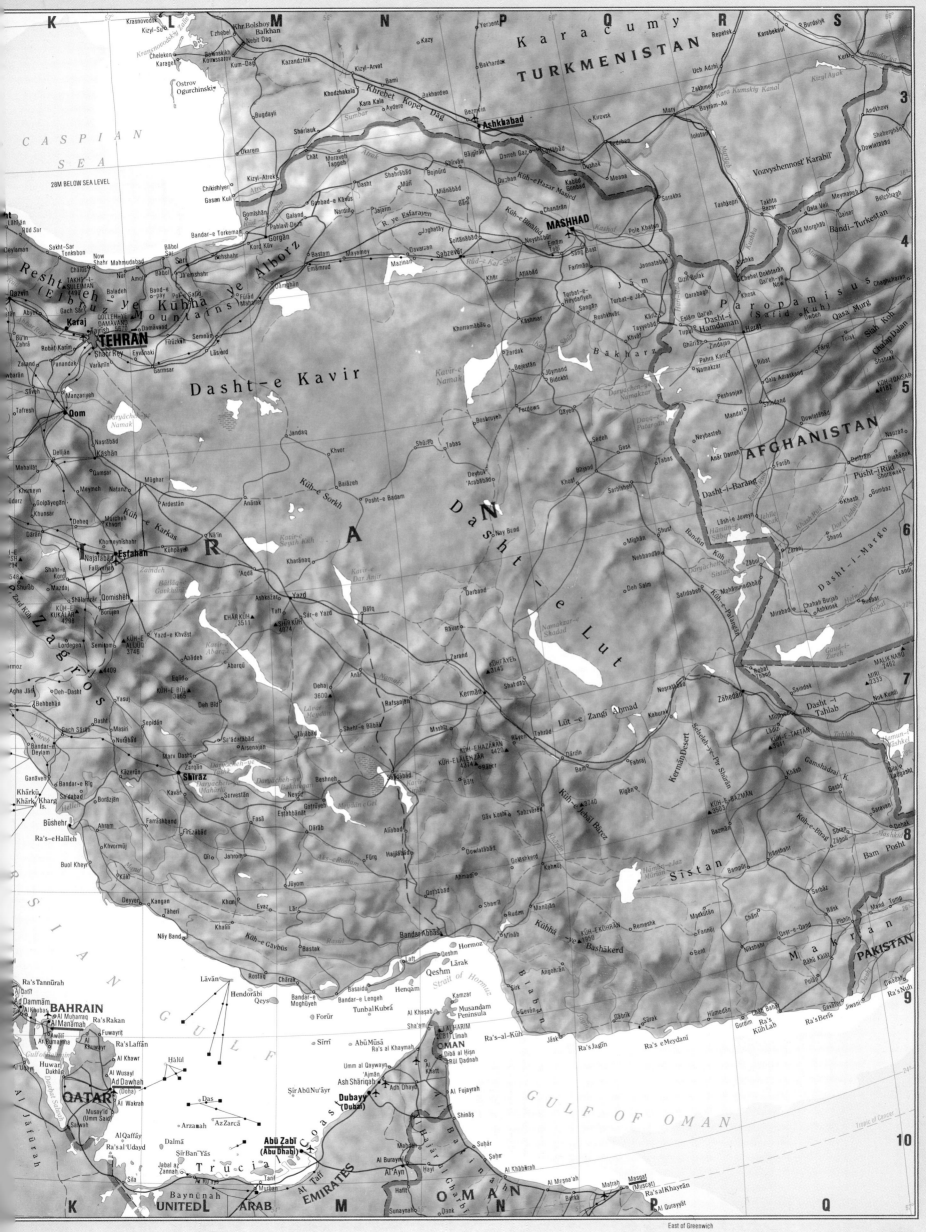

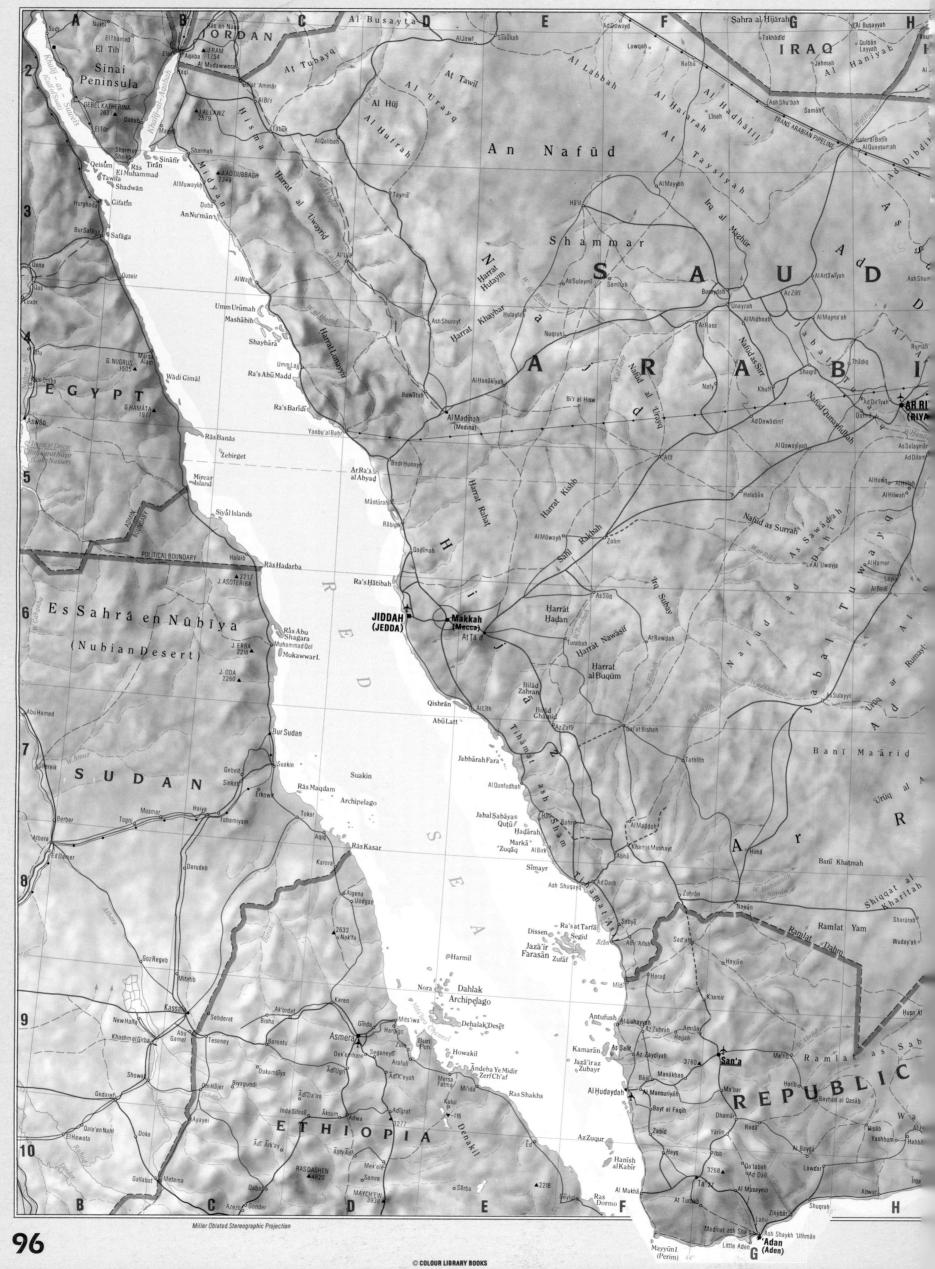

Miller Oblated Stereographic Projection

© COLOUR LIBRARY BOOKS

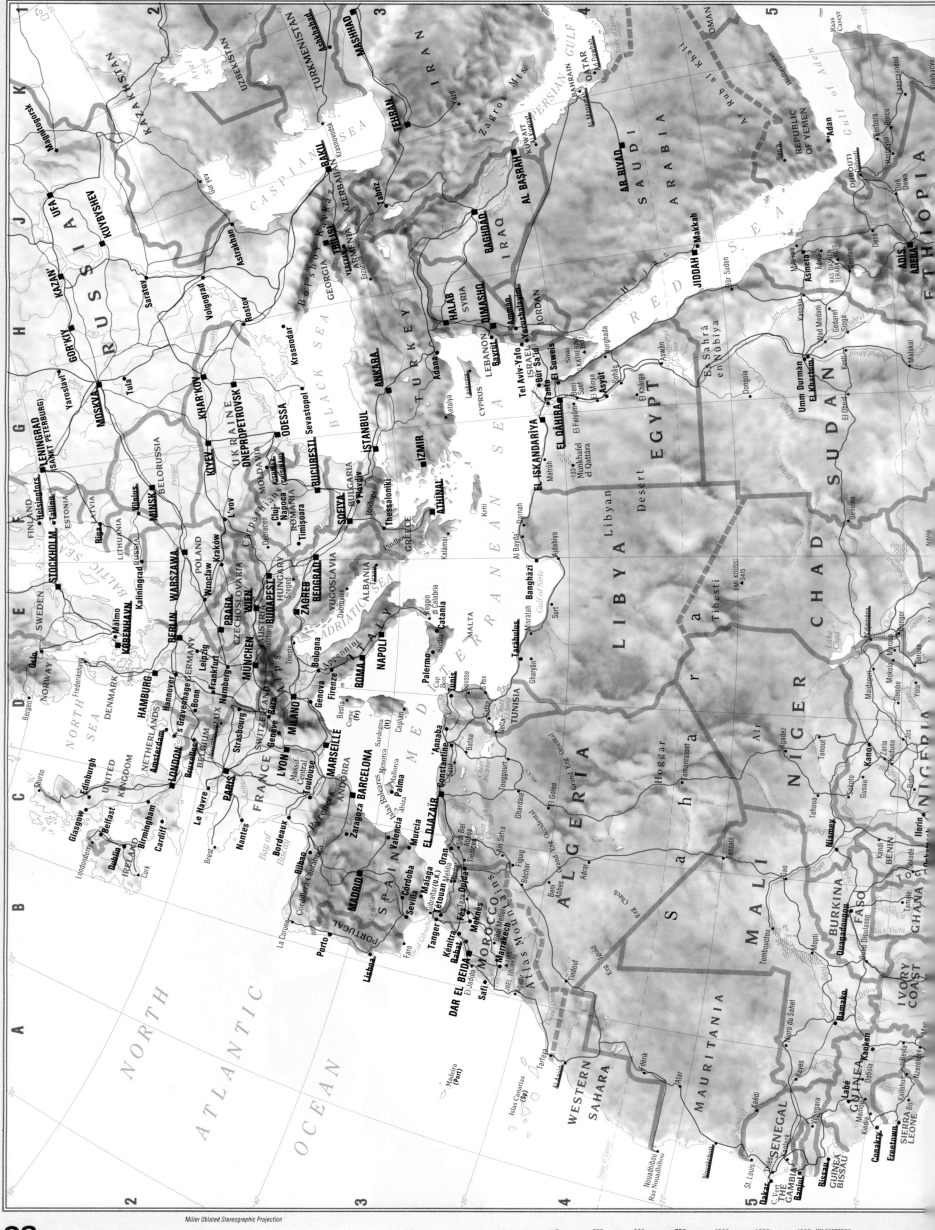

Miller Oblated Stereographic Projection

1:23,000,000

© COLOUR LIBRARY BOOKS

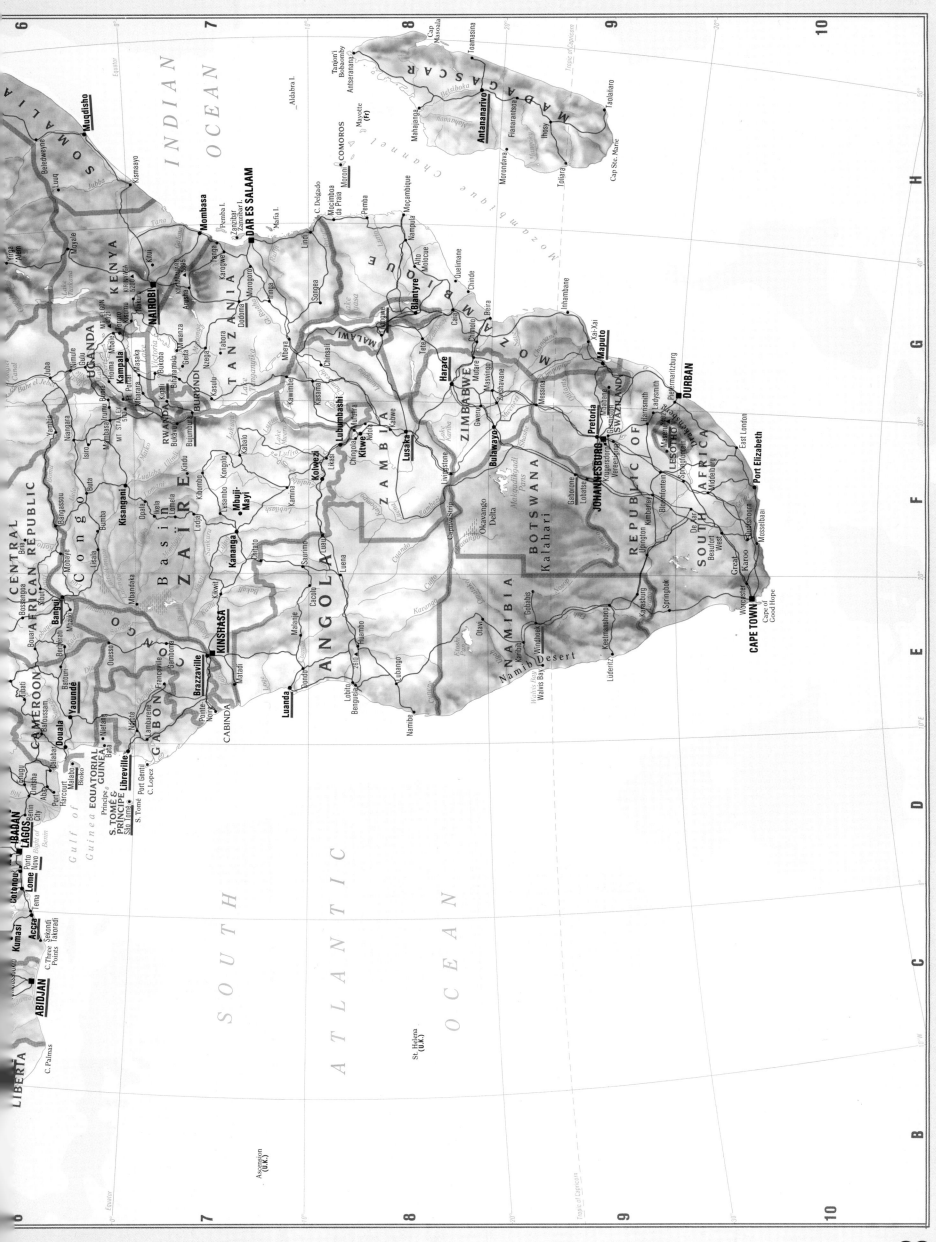

Designed and produced by E.S.R.

North Atlantic Ocean

Madeira (Portugal)
Funchal

Ilhas Selvagens (Portugal)

Islas Canarias (Canary Is.) (Spain)
La Palma
Sta. Cruz de la Palma
Gomera
Valverde
Hierro
Tenerife
Sta. Cruz de Tenerife
Gran Canaria
Las Palmas
Lanzarote
Arrecife
Fuerteventura
Puerto del Rosario

SPAIN
Cádiz
Algeciras
Gibraltar (U.K.)
Strait of Gibraltar
Cap Spartel
Tanger
Asilah
Larache (El Araiche)
Ksar el Kebir
Ceuta (Sp.)
Tétouan
Chaouen
Cap des Trois Fourches
Melilla (Spain)
Nador
Malaga
Almería
Sa. Nevada
Ténès
Mostaganem
Arzew
Oran
Mascara
Hauts Plateau
Beni Saf
Ghazaouet
Tlemcen
Oujda
Jerada
Taza

Kénitra
Salé
Rabat
DAR EL BEIDA (CASABLANCA)
El Jadida
Settat
Khouribga
Oued Zem
Beni Mellal
Kasba Tadla
Safi
Essaouira
Youssoufia
MOROCCO
Demnate
Marrakech (Marrakesh)
JEBEL TOUBKAL 4165
Cap Rhir
Agadir
Taroudannt
Tiznit
Sidi Ifni
Meknès
Sefrou
Fès
Khenifra
Moyen Atlas
El Rachidia
Ksar es Souk
Anti-Atlas
Haut Atlas
Ouarzazate
Zagora
Tagounite
Cap Juby
Tan-Tan
Tarfaya (Villa Bens)
Oued Drâa
Oued Tigzerte
Hamada du Dra
Tindouf
Béchar
Kenadsa
Grand Erg Occidental
Beni Abbès
Timimoun
Ksabi
Adrar
Reggane
ALGERIA

WESTERN SAHARA
Al Aaiún (Laâyoune)
Es Semara
As Saguia al Hamra
Boujdour
Bir Moghrein (Fort Trinquet)
Ad Dakhla (Villa Cisneros)
Baie de Rio de Oro
C. Barbas
Fdérik
Zouerate
Erg Iguidi
Erg Chech
Tanezrouft
Meredoua

Tropic of Cancer
Nouadhibou (Pt. Etienne)
Ras Nouadhibou (C. Blanc)
Makteir
Atari
Chinguetti
Akjoujt
Ouarâne
El Djouf
Taoudeni
Sahara
Tessalit
Adrar des Iforas
Aguelhok
C. Timiris
MAURITANIA
Nouakchott
Beila
Boutilimit
Tidjikdja
Tichitt
Moudjéria
Araouane
Kidal
Mederdra
Aleg
Tamchaket
Aouker
MALI
Oualata
Néma
Kiffa
Aioun el Atrouss
Lac Faguibine
Tombouctou (Timbuktu)
Ras el Ma
Goundam
Niafunké
Gourma-Rharous
Bamba
Bourem
Gao
Ansongo
St. Louis
Dagana
Podor
Bogué
Kaédi
Matam
Timbédra
Diorbivol
Mbout
Sélibabi
Bakel
Kayes
Nioro du Sahel
Balé
Nara
Douentza
Tilla
Louga
Linguère
Senegal
Tivaouane
Thiès
Diourbel
Cape Vert
Dakar
Mbour
Fatick
Kaolack
Kaffrine
Tambacounda
Bafoulabé
Kita
Sokolo
Niono
Mopti
Bandiagara
Ouahigouya
Yako
Djenné
Ségou
SENEGAL
THE GAMBIA
Banjul (Bathurst)
Georgetown
Basse Santa Su
Kédougou
Bafing
Kati
Bamako
Koutiala
Koudougou
Ouagadougou
BURKINA FASO
GUINEA BISSAU
Bissau
Bolama
C. Roxo
Arquipelago dos Bijagos
Ziguinchor
Kolda
Vélingara
Koundara
Gaoual
Boké
GUINEA
Labé
Pita
Dabola
Dinguiraye
Siguiri
Kankan
Bougouni
Sikasso
Bobo Dioulasso
GHANA
Cap Verga

Miller Oblated Stereographic Projection   West of Greenwich   1:9,000,000

© COLOUR LIBRARY BOOKS

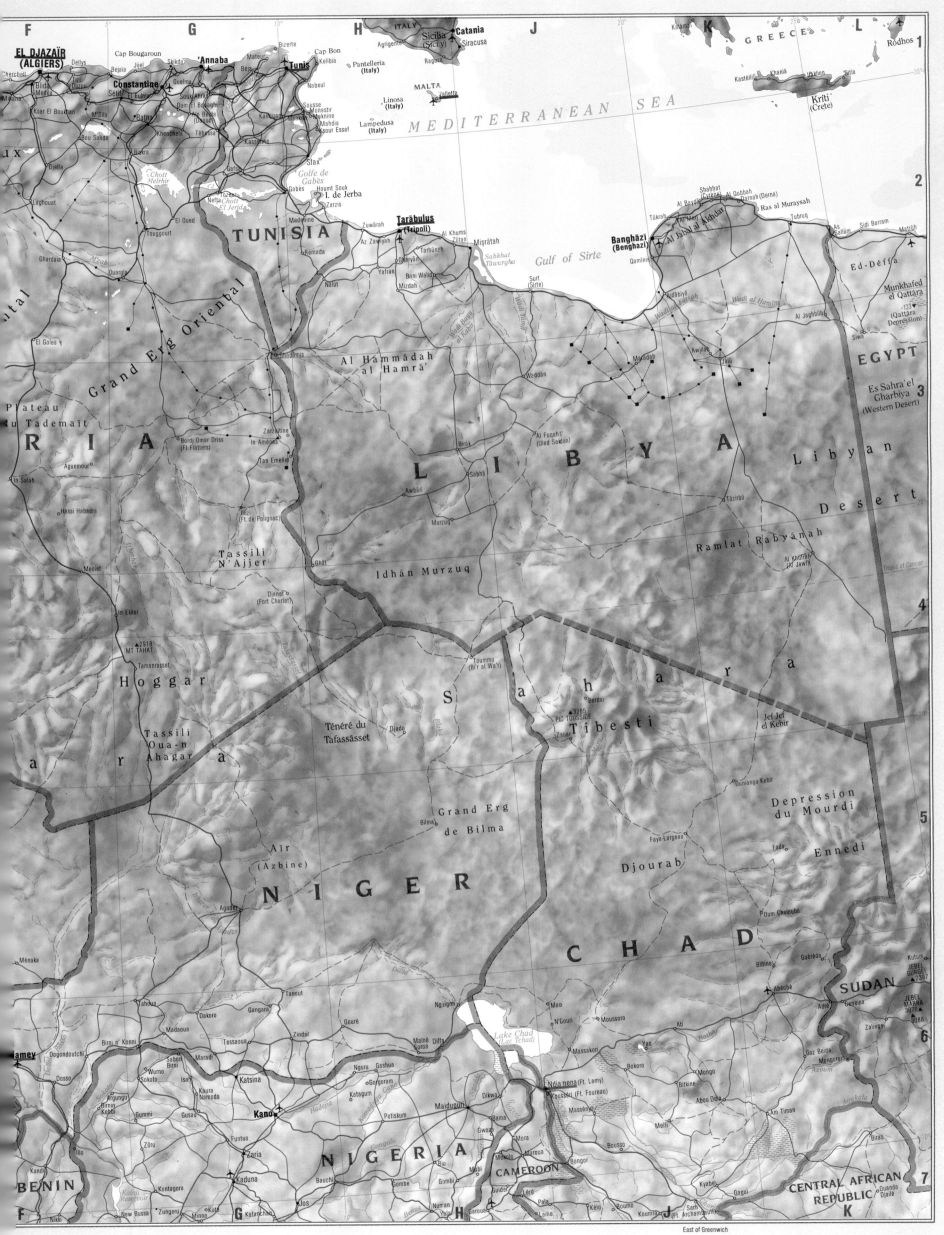

Designed and produced by E.S.R.

EL ISKANDARÎYA (ALEXANDRIA)
El Mansûra
El Mahalla El Kubra
Tanta
Shibîn el Kôm
Benhâ
EL GÎZA
EL QÂ'HIRA (CAIRO)
El Faiyûm
Beni Suef
Bibâ
El Fashn
Maghâgha
Beni Mazâr

EGYPT

Es Sahrâ'el Gharbîya (Western Desert)

Libyan
Desert

El Minya
Mallawi
Dairût
Asyût
Tahta
Sohâg

Dakhla Oasis
Mut
El Qasr
El Khârga
El Wâhat el-Khârga

Ed-Déffa
Munkhafed el Qattâra
-133 (Qattâra Depression)
Siwa

Al Jaghbûb

LIBYA

Ajdâbiya
Wadi al Farîgh
Wadi al Hamîm
Waddân
Marâdah
Awjilah
Jâlû

Al Hammâdah al Hamrâ'
Ghadamis
Wadi Bayy al Kebîr
Wadi Tanezzuft

Birâk
Sabhâ
Murzuq
Awbâri

Idhân Murzuq

Tâzirbû

Ramlat Rabyânah

Al Khufrah (Al Jawf)

ALGERIA
Bordj Omar Driss (Ft. Flatters)
Zarzaïtine
In Amenas
In Ecker
Tan Emellel
Illizi (Ft. de Polignac)
Tassili N'Ajjer
Djanet (Fort Charlet)

Saha ra

Tibesti
PIC TOUSSIDE ▲3265
Zouar
Bardaï

Toummo (Bi'r al Wa'r)

Jef Jef el Kebir

Ténéré du Tafassâsset
Djado
Bilma

Grand Erg de Bilma

Aïr (Azbine)

NIGER

Depression du Mourdi

Djourab
Faya-Largeau
Fada
Ennedi

Ou/nianga Kebir

Nûbîya

Tanout
Gouré
Zindâr
Nguigmi
Mao
N'Gouri
Moussoro
Ati
Biltine
Guéréda

CHAD

SUDA

Kufum
JEBEL GURGEL ▲2397
JEBEL MARRA 3070▲ ▲3088
El Fasher
Dirra
Umm Keddada
Umm Bel
Iyal Bakhit
Bara
Kagmar
El Homra

Nguru
Gashua
Geïgoram
Katagum
Hadejia
Potiskum
Difa
Maïné Soroa
Massakori
Lake Chad (Lac Tchad)
Bokoro
Yao
Batha
Adré
Geneina
Zalingei
Nyala
Taweisha
Ghubeish
El Odaiya
En Nahud
Wad Banda
Abu Zabad
El Obeid
Er Rahad
Sungikai
Delami
J. ED DAIR ▲1413

NIGERIA
Bauchi
Biu
Gombe
Damaturu
Mubi
Maïduguri
Dikwa
Ndjamena (Ft. Lamy)
Kousséri (Ft. Foureau)
Bama
Gwoza
Mora
Maroua
Mongo
Bitkine
Mongororo
Azoum
Goz Beida
Nyala
NUBA MTS ▲1324
Kadugli
Talodi
Rashad

Gombi
Mubi
Mokolo
Guider
Léré
Pala
Lame
Kélo
Moundou
Doba
Sarh (Ft. Archambault)
Koumra
Kyabé
Gagui
Am Timan
Aoukalé
Buram
El Muglad

Shebshi Mts.
Numan
Yola
Jalingo
Ibi
Wukari
Takum
Kontcha
Massif de l'Adoumaoua

Bongor
Massénya
Abou Deïa
Melfi
Ndélé
Ouanda Djalé
Birao
Raga
Aweil
Meshra'er Req
Ayod
Duk Fadiat
Duk Fariwil

Bana
Ngaoundéré
Tibati
Banyo
Bétaré Oya
Bouar
Bozoum
Bocaranga
Batangafo
Kaga Bandoro
Mouka
Ouadda
Deim Zubeir
Wau
Rumbek
Yirol

CENTRAL AFRICAN
REPUBLIC

Nkambé
Mbengwi
Bamenda
Bafoussam
Foumban
Foumbot
Bélabo
Bertoua
Batouri
Berbérati
Carnot
Bossangoa
Bossembélé
Sibut
Bria
Yalinga
Ippy
Bambari
Bakouma
Kouango
Zémio
Obo
Tambura

CAMEROON
Yabassi
Monatélé
Nanga Eboko
Doumé
Abong Mbang
Bafia
Yaoundé
Bibatou
Mbalmayo
Akonolinga
Bertoua
Nola
Yokadouma
Berbérati
Bangui
Mbaïki
Zongo
Bossobolo
Mobaye
Mobayi-Mbongo (Banzyville)
Bangassou
Rafaï
Bambari

Kribi
Ebolowa
Sangmelima
Ebebiyin
Ngoïla
Kunzulu
Libenge
Gemena
Businga
Bondo
Monga
Bili
Ango
Bambesa
Niangara
Faradje
Dungu
Yei

CONGO

ZAÏRE

Miller Oblated Stereographic Projection

1:9,000,000

© COLOUR LIBRARY BOOKS

0 100 200 300 400 500 600 KILOMETRES

0 50 100 150 200 250 300 350 400 STATUTE MILES

Designed and produced by E.S.R.

A   B   C   D   E

1

20°

WESTERN
SAHARA

C. Barbas

Nouadhibou
(Pt. Etienne)
Ras Nouadhibou
(C. Blanc)

C. Timiris

Makteir

Ouarâne

MAURITANIA

El   Djouf

S   a   h

Tropic of Cancer

Fderik Zouerate

Atâr

Chinguetti

Akjoujt

Erg   Chech

Taoudenni

Tessalit

Aguelhok

Tanezrouft

Poste
Weygand

2

20°

15°

Nouakchott

Beila

Mederdra

Boutilimit

Aleg

Moudjéria

Tidjikdja

Tichitt

Aouker

Tamchaket

Kiffa

Aioun el Atrouss

Néma

Timbédra

Oualata

MALI

Araouane

L. Faguibine
Tombouctou
(Timbuktu)

Ras el Ma

Gourma-
Rharous

Bamba

Bourem

Niger

Gao

Ansongo

St. Louis

Louga

Kébémer

Tivaouane

Cape Vert
Dakar

Mbour
Fatick
Foundiougne

Diourbel

Thiès

Kaolack

Kaffrine

Linguère

Dagana

Podor

Bogué

Kaédi

Matam

Diorbivol

Mbout

SENEGAL

Maka

Tambacounda

Bakel

Sélibabi

Ballé

Kayes

Nioro du Sahel

Nara

Niafounké

Goundam

Douentza

Mopti

Bandiagara

Gourma

The Gambia

Banjul
(Bathurst)
Brikama

Georgetown

Basse Santa Su

Kolda
Vélingara

Ziguinchor

Kédougou

Satadougou

Kita

Ségou

Djenné

San

Ouahigouya

Tougan

Yako

3

15°

THE GAMBIA

C. Roxo

Bissau

Bolama

Cacheu

GUINEA
BISSAU

Arquipelago
dos Bijagos

Gabu

Koundara

Foula Mori

Gaoual

Yambering

Boké

Labé

Pita

Dabola

Dalaba

Mamou

Dinguiraye

Siguiri

Kati

Bafoulabé

Bamako

Koutiala

Sikasso

Bobo
Dioulasso

Banfora

Boromo

Koudougou

BURKINA FASO

Ouagadougou

Fada
N'Gourma

Tenkodogo

Dapaong

Cap Verga

Boffa

Kindia

GUINEA

Timbo

Faranah

Kouroussa

Kankan

Bougouni

Massigui

Dédougou

Houndé

Léo

Navrongo

Tumu

Bolgatanga

Hawki

4

10°

Dubréka

Conakry

Forécariah

Kambia

Port Loko

Makeni

Lunsar

Kabala

Falaba

Kissidougou

Guékédou

Macenta

Beyla

Odienné

Boundiali

Korhogo

Ferkessédougou

Kong

Bouna

Gaoua

Lawra

Bole

Wa

Batié

Doboya

White Volta

Tamale

Yendi

SIERRA
LEONE

Freetown

Yawri Bay

Shenge

Sherbro

Moyamba

Magburaka

Sefadu

Kailahun

Pendembu

Segbwema

Wologisi
Mts.

Nzérékoré

Lola

1752
MTS. NIMBA

Biankouma

Man

Touba

Séguéla

Mankono

Katiola

Bouaké

IVORY   COAST

Dabakala

Bondoukou

Kintampo

Damongo

Salaga

Keta

Sokodé

GHANA

TOGO

5

5°

Sherbro Island

Bonthe

Pujehun

Kenema

Gbarnga

Totota

LIBERIA

Monrovia

Robertsport

Buchanan

Timbo

Zwedru

Saint Paul

Guiglo

Daloa

Gagnoa

Soubré

Yamoussoukro

Sinfra

Bouaflé

Toumodi

Dimbokro

Agboville

Abengourou

Sunyani

Kumasi

Aya-Yenhino

Bekwai

Awaso

Obuasi

Dunkwa

Enchi

Mampong

Morees

Nkawkaw

Koforidua

Oda

Akosombo
Dam

Ho

Akuse

Tema

Volta

Lake
Volta

Greenville
(Sinoe)

Sasstown

Harper

C. Palmas

Grand
Lahou

Abidjan

Sassandra

San Pédro

Tabou

Grand-
Bassam

Anyama
Bingerville

Aboisso

Axim

Dixcove

Cape Three Points

Asamankese

Nsuta

Tarkwa

Winneba

Saltpond
Cape Coast

Sekondi Takoradi

Accra

ATLANTIC

6

Miller Oblated Stereographic Projection

West of Greenwich

1:9,000,000

0   100   200   300   400   500   600 KILOMETRES

0   50   100   150   200   250   300   350 400 STATUTE MILES

© COLOUR LIBRARY BOOKS

B

Santo
Antão

Porto Novo
Mindelo

São Vincente

São Nicolau

Sal

CAPE
VERDE

Boa Vista

7

São
Tiago

Fogo

Maio

Brava

Praia

C

L

25°

Equator

15°

East of Greenwich

EQUATORIAL AFRICA

Miller Oblated Stereographic Projection

1:9,000,000

| 0 | 100 | 200 | 300 | 400 | 500 | 600 KILOMETRES |

| 0 | 50 | 100 | 150 | 200 | 250 | 300 | 350 | 400 STATUTE MILES |

© COLOUR LIBRARY BOOKS

SOUTHERN AFRICA

Miller Oblated Stereographic Projection

1:9,000,000

| 0 | 100 | 200 | 300 | 400 | 500 | 600 KILOMETRES |

| 0 | 50 | 100 | 150 | 200 | 250 | 300 | 350 | 400 STATUTE MILES |

© COLOUR LIBRARY BOOKS

Designed and produced by E.S.R.

East of Greenwich

TANZANIA
MALAWI
MOZAMBIQUE
MADAGASCAR
COMOROS
Grande Comore
Mcroni
Moheli
Anjouan
Mayotte (France)
Dzaoudzi
Makondi Plateau
C. Delgado
Lindi
Mikindani
Mtwara
Masasi
Kitangari
Palma
Mocimboa da Praia
Tunduru
Songea
Livingstone Mts.
Chilumba
Chinsali
Mzuzu
Lundazi
Nkhotakota
Kasungu
Chipata (Fort Jameson)
Mchinji (Ft. Manning)
Lilongwe
Dowa
Salima
Chipoka
Mangochi
Ncheu
Balaka
Liwonde
Zomba
Blantyre
Limbe
Chiromo
Nsanje (Port Herald)
Cobue
Lichinga
Mataca
Mecula
Mueda
Ibo
Quissanga
Pemba
Mecufi
Lurio
Ancuabe
Montepuez
Balama
Marrupa
Maua
Namapa
Memba
Nacala-a-Velha
Maaia
Cuamba
Malema
Ribáuè
NAMULI 2419
Moçambique
Nampula
Meconta
Mogincual
Namaponda
Angoche
Gurué
Alto Molócue
Gilé
Moma
Pebane
Namarroi
Errego
Lugela
Mocuba
Namacurra
Quelimane
Mopeia Velha
Chinde
Caia
Mutarara
Chemba
CHIPERONE
Macossa
Furancungo
Ulongué
Fingoe
Cabora Bassa Dam
Magoe
Tete
Moatize
Zambeze
Mutoko
Marondera
Gorongoza
Nova Vanduzi
Muanza
Inchope
Mutare (Umtali)
Chimoio
Chimanimani
Dombe
Buzi
Beira
Nova Sofala
Chipinge
Espungabera
Algueirão
Machanga
Nova Mambone
Save
Jofane
Inhassôro
I. do Bazaruto
I. Benguérua
Vilanculos
P. S. Sebastião
Massangena
Madade
Chicualacuala
Maxaila
Chigubo
Mapai
Limpopo
Massinga
Mabalane
Massingir
Homoine
Inhambane
Panda
Inharrime
Chókwè
Chibuto
Macuácua
Xai-Xai
Manhiça
Maputo
Baía de Maputo
C. de Santa Maria
Bela Vista
Lebombo Mountains
Makatini Flats
Ubombo
Nongoma
Lake St. Lucia
Cape Saint Lucia
Empangeni
C. St. André
Toraka Vestale
Juan de Nova (France)
Bassas da India (France)
I. de l'Europa (France)
INDIAN OCEAN
Tanjon'i Bobaomby
Antseranana (Diégo-Suarez)
Nosy Mitsio
Nosy Bé
Hell-Ville
Ambilobe
Vohimarina (Vohémar)
Ambanja
Massif du Tsaratanana
2876
Sambava
Bealanana
Analalava
Antsohihy
Andapa
Antalaha
Befandriana
Maroantsetra
Mahajanga
Soalala
Port Bergé
Marovoay
C. Masoala
Mananara
Besalampy
Stampiky
Ambato Boeny
Maevatanana
Tsaratanana
Mandritsara
Nosy Boraha (Sainte-Marie)
Ambodifototra
Fenoarivo Atsinanana
Mahabe
Morafenobe
A'tomainty
Maintirano
Vavatenina
Alaotra
A'tondrazaka
Toamasina (Tamatave)
Plateau du Bemaraha
Ankazobe
Anjozorobe
Antsalova
Tsiroanomandidy
Miarinarivo
Arivonimamo
Moramanga
Antananarivo (Tananarive)
Andevoranto
Bekopaka
Manambolo
Soavinandriana
Ambatolampy
Anosibe an Ala
Vatomandry
Belo-Tsiribihina
Betafo
Antsirabe
Fandriana
Marolambo
Morondava
Mahabo
A'tofinandrahana
Ambositra
Nosy-Varika
Massif du Makay
Tsitondroina
A'bimahasoa
Vohilava
Mananjary
Morombe
Manja
Ankiliabo
Mangoky
Bérorohá
Fianarantsoa
Ifanadiana
Ambalavao
Ikongo
Andringitra
Ankazoabo
Ihosy
Manakara
Vohipeno
Farafangana
Fitsitika
Toliara (Tuléar)
Betroka
Vangaindrano
Soalara
Onilahy
Betioky
Midongy Atsimo
Mt. de l'Ivakoany
Bekily
Beampingaratra
1956
Itampolo
Ampanihy
Taolañaro (Fort Dauphin)
Ambovombe
C. Sainte Marie
Faux Cap
Tropic of Capricorn
MAURITIUS
Port Louis
Beau Bassin
Curepipe
Mahébourg
Réunion (France)
St. Denis
St. Benoit
St. Pierre
Mascarene Islands

Bonne Projection

East of Greenwich

1:19,000,000

© COLOUR LIBRARY BOOKS

| 0 | 200 | 400 | 600 | 800 KILOMETRES |
| 0 | 100 | 200 | 300 | 400 | 500 STATUTE MILES |

N P NAURU Q R Gilbert Islands (Kiribati) S T U V W

1

PACIFIC

Kilinailau Is.
Tauu Is.
Nukumanu Is.
Sohano
Bougainville
Kieta

Banaba
Nonouti
Tabiteuea
Beru
Nukunau
Kingsmill Group
Onotoa
Tamana
Arorae

Howland I.
Baker I.
(U.S.A.)

Winslow Reef

Equator

OCEAN

KIRIBATI

2

SOLOMON
Choiseul
Vella Lavella
New Georgia
Santa Isabel
Vangunu
Kolombangara
Russell Is.
Florida Is.
Malaita
Honiara
Maramasike
Guadalcanal
San Cristóbal

Stewart Is.

McKean I.
Birnie I.
Enderbury I.
Rawaki

Nikumaroro
Orona
Manra

Carondelet Reef

Phoenix Islands (Kiribati)

ISLANDS

Nanumea
Niutao
Nanumanga

Nui
Vaitupu

Nukufetau

Funafuti

TUVALU

Nukulaelae

Tokelau
(N.Z.)
Atafu
Nukunono
Fakaofo

3

Rennell I.
Indispensable Reefs

Nupani
Tinaku a
Duff Is.
Swallow Is.
Ndeni
Santa Cruz Is.
Utupua
Vanikoro Is.
Cherry
Mitre
Tikopia

Niulakita

Rotuma
Eaglestone Reef

Swains I.

WESTERN SAMOA

Pukapuka
Nassau

L

Mellish Reef

Torres Is.
Vot Tandé
Uréparapara
Banks Islands
Vanua Lava
Santa Maria
Méré Lava
Cap Nahoi
Espíritu Santo
Aoba
Maéwo
Malo
Pentecost I.
Malakula
Ambrym
VANUATU
Epi
Shepherd Is.

Iles Wallis
(Fr.)
Uvea
Futuna
Iles de Horn
Alofi
(Fr.)

Savaii
Upolu
Apia
Manua
Tau
Rose I.
Tutuila

Suvorov I.

4

A

Iles Chesterfield
(Fr.)
Récifs d'Entrecasteaux
Sable

Efaté
Vila
Erromango
Tanna

Vanua Levu
Yasawá Group
FIJI
Viti Levu
Nadi
Taveuni
Lau Group
Koro
Suva
Lakeba
Kadavu

Niuafo'ou
Tafahi
Niuatoputapu

Cook Islands
(New Zealand)

Mellish Reef
Kenn Reef
Wreck Reef
Cato

MT. PANIÉ
1628
Ouvéa
Lifou
Is. Loyauté
Thio
Maré
Nouméa
Ile des Pins
Walpole
Matthew
Hunter

Ceva-i-Ra

Caye de l'observatoire
Bellona Reefs
Bouraíl
Nouvelle Calédonie (France)

Vatoa
Ono-i-Lau
Tuvana-i-Tholo
Tuvana-i-Ra

Fonualei
Late
Vava'u Group
Kao
Tofua
Ha'apai Group
Nomuka
Nuku'alofa
Tongatapu
Tongatapu Group
Eua
Ata

TONGA

Niue
(N.Z.)

Palmerston I.

5

Aneityum (Anatom)

Minerva Reefs

Tropic of Capricorn

6

Middleton Reef
Elizabeth Reef

Norfolk I.
Philip I.
(Aust.)

7

Lord Howe I.
(Aust.)

Raoul
Kermadec Is.
(N.Z.)
Macauley I.
Curtis I.
L'Esperance Rock

T A S M A N

Three Kings Is.
C. Maria van Diemen
North Cape
Kaitaia
Dargaville
Whangarei
Great Barrier I.
Auckland
Manukau
Thames
Hamilton
Tauranga
North Island
Rotorua
Whakatane
East Cape
New Plymouth
RUAPEHU
Gisborne
Mahia Peninsula
Hawera
Napier
Wanganui
Hastings
Palmerston North
C. Farewell
Picton
Masterton
NEW
Motueka
Nelson
Westport
Blenheim
Cook Strait
Wellington
Greymouth
Kaikoura
South Island
Hokitika
ZEALAND
Rangiora
MT. COOK
3764
Christchurch
Lyttelton
Cascade Pt.
Queenstown
Ashburton
Timaru
L. Wakatipu
Alexandra
Oamaru
L. Te Anau
C. Providence
Gore
Dunedin
C. Saunders
Foveaux Strait
Invercargill
Stewart I.
Snares Is.

Chatham Is.
(N.Z.)
Pitt I.

8

9

S E A

10

Bounty Is.
(N.Z.)

Antipodes Is.
(N.Z.)

Auckland Is.
(N.Z.)

11

Macquarie I.
(Aust.)

Campbell I.
(N.Z.)

N P Q R S T U V W X Y Z

INDIAN

OCEAN

TIMOR SEA

Melville I.   Croker I.
C. Van Diemen
Bathurst I.

Ashmore Reef

Seringapatum Reef

Scott Reef

Joseph
Bonaparte
Gulf

Darwin

Beegle
Reef

C. Lévêque

MT. HANN
854

Dampier
Land

Broome
Roebuck Bay

Derby
Yeeda River
Ellendale

Kimberley
Plateau

MT. ORD
936

MT. LUSH
786
Ord

Wyndham
Kununurra

Fitzroy Crossing   Halls Creek   Antrim
Plateau

Christmas Creek

Eighty Mile Beach
Wallal Downs   Canning Basin

Larrey Pt.
Port Hedland
Goldsworthy

Great Sandy Desert

Tanami

Exmouth
Rise

Dampier
Archipelago

Barrow I.

Dampier
Karratha

Marble Bar

Lake
Waukarlycarly

Percival
Lakes

Lake
Tobin

Lake
Wills

Lake
White

MT. SINGLETON
844
MT. Doreen
Yuendumu

NORT

TERR

North West Cape

Onslow
Paraloola

Hammersley Range

Mulga Downs

Chichester
Range

Roy Hill

Lake
Dora

Thresell Ra.
Broadhurst Ra.

Lake
Mackay

MT. LEISIER
1005

MT. ZIEL
1511
Macdonnell Range

Pt. Cloates

Winning Pool

MT. BROCKMAN
1114

MT. BRUCE
1228

MT. NEWMAN
1228
Newman

Robertson Ra.

Lake
Disappointment

Tropic of Capricorn

Lyndon

Gifford Creek
MT. AUGUSTUS
1106

MT. EGERTON
994

Mitgun

WESTERN

Gibson Desert

MT. METHWIN
908

Lake
Hopkins

Lake
Neale
Lake
Amadeus

MT. DEERING
1220

AYERS ROCK
860

MT. MORRIS
1255

Lake
McLeod
Boologooro

Gascoyne
Carnarvon

Jimba Jimba   Landor
MT. STEER

MT. FRASER
802
Peak Hill

Robinson Ranges

AUSTRALIA

Lake
Carnegie

Barrow
Range

MT. BURT
663

Tomkinson
Ranges

MT. WOODROFFE
1514

MT. ILLBILLE
917

Dirk Hartog I.

Shark
Bay

Woorarmel

Berringarra

Meekatharra

Wiluna
Lake
Way

Musgrave Ranges

Birksgate Ra.

Edel
Land

Meeberrie

Billabalong

Cue
Lake
Austin
Sandstone

MT. SHENTON
595

Great Victoria Desert

Lake Dey-Dey
Lake Maurice

Bluff Pt.

Houtman
Rocks

Geraldton
Dongara

Edah Wagga

Mullewa Wurarga

Morawa Paynes Find

MT. Magnet

Lake
Barlee

Lake
Ballard

Lake Carey

Lake Minigwal

Lake Rason

Laverton

Nullarbor

Ooldea

Wubin

Lake Moore

Bonnie Rock

Lake
Yindarlgooda

Kalgoorlie
Karonie
Zanthus

Rawlinna

Loongana   Forrest
Deakin

Cook

Nullarbor

Watheroo

Moora

Bindin

Northam

Merredin

Southern Cross

Kambalda
Lake Lefroy

Lake Rebecca

Plain

Moopna

Head
of
Bight

Pt. Fowler

Perth
Fremantle
Rockingham
Mandurah

MT. COOKE
582

Cunderdin
Quairading
Beverley
Pingelly
Narrogin
Kondinin

The
Johnston
Lakes

Lake Cowan

Norseman

Lake Dundas

Balladonia

Eyre   Madura

Great   Australian   Bight

Williams
Harvey   Collie

Bunbury

Bridgetown
Kojonup

Narrogin

Newdegate
Lake Grace
Lake King

Ravensthorpe

Esperance
Esperance Bay

C. Pasley

Russel Ra.

Archipelago of
the Recherche

C. Naturaliste

C. Leeuwin   Augusta
Jardee
Northcliffe
Normalup
Pt. D'Entrecasteaux   Pt. Nuyts

BLUFF KNOLL
1110
Pt. Henry
Albany
King George Sound

Miller Oblated Stereographic Projection

1:10,500,000

0   100   200   300   400   500   600   700   800 KILOMETRES

0   100   200   300   400   500 STATUTE MILES

© COLOUR LIBRARY BOOKS

PAPUA NEW GUINEA

Goulburn Is.   Wessel Islands

C. York
Cape
York
Peninsula

C. Arnhem

Groote Eylandt

Gulf of Carpentaria

Arnhem Land

Sir Edward Pellew Group

Mornington I.

Wellesley Is.

CORAL SEA

Osprey Reef

Holmes Reefs

Flinders Reefs

Lihou Reefs

Marion Reefs

Iles Chesterfield

QUEENSLAND

Great Dividing Range

Mount Isa

Simpson Desert

Great Artesian Basin

Lake Eyre (North)

Lake Eyre (South)

SOUTH AUSTRALIA

Coober Pedy

Lake Torrens

Lake Gairdner

Lake Frome

Flinders Ranges

Kenn Reef

Wreck Reef

Tropic of Capricorn

BRISBANE

Fraser Island

Gold Coast

C. Byron

Middleton Reef

Elizabeth Reef

NEW SOUTH WALES

Coff's Harbour

Smoky Cape

Port Macquarie

Lord Howe I.

Newcastle

SYDNEY

Wollongong

Canberra

AUSTRALIAN CAPITAL TERRITORY

Adelaide

Kangaroo I.

VICTORIA

MT. KOSCIUSCO

MELBOURNE

Geelong

Wilson's Promontory

TASMAN SEA

Bass Strait

King I.

Flinders I. Furneaux Group

TASMANIA

Hobart

Designed and produced by E.S.F.

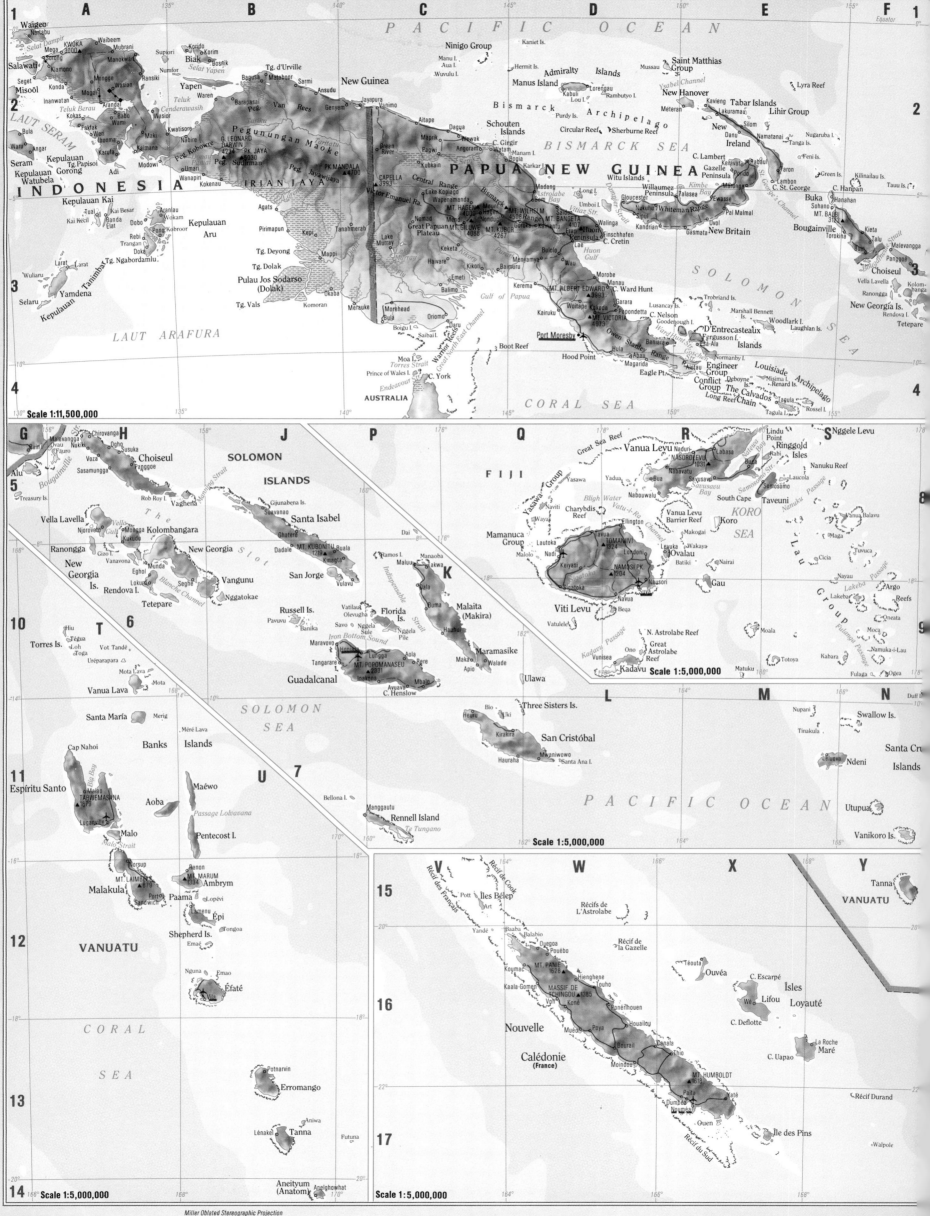

Scale 1:11,500,000

Scale 1:5,000,000

Scale 1:5,000,000

Scale 1:5,000,000

Scale 1:5,000,000

Miller Oblated Stereographic Projection

North Island

South Island

NEW ZEALAND

TASMAN SEA

PACIFIC OCEAN

Auckland

Wellington

Christchurch

Lambert Azimuthal Equal Area Projection

1:20,000,000

| 0 | 100 | 200 | 300 | 400 | 500 | 600 | 700 | 800 | 900 | 1000 KILOMETRES |

| 0 | 100 | 200 | 300 | 400 | 500 | 600 STATUTE MILES |

© COLOUR LIBRARY BOOKS

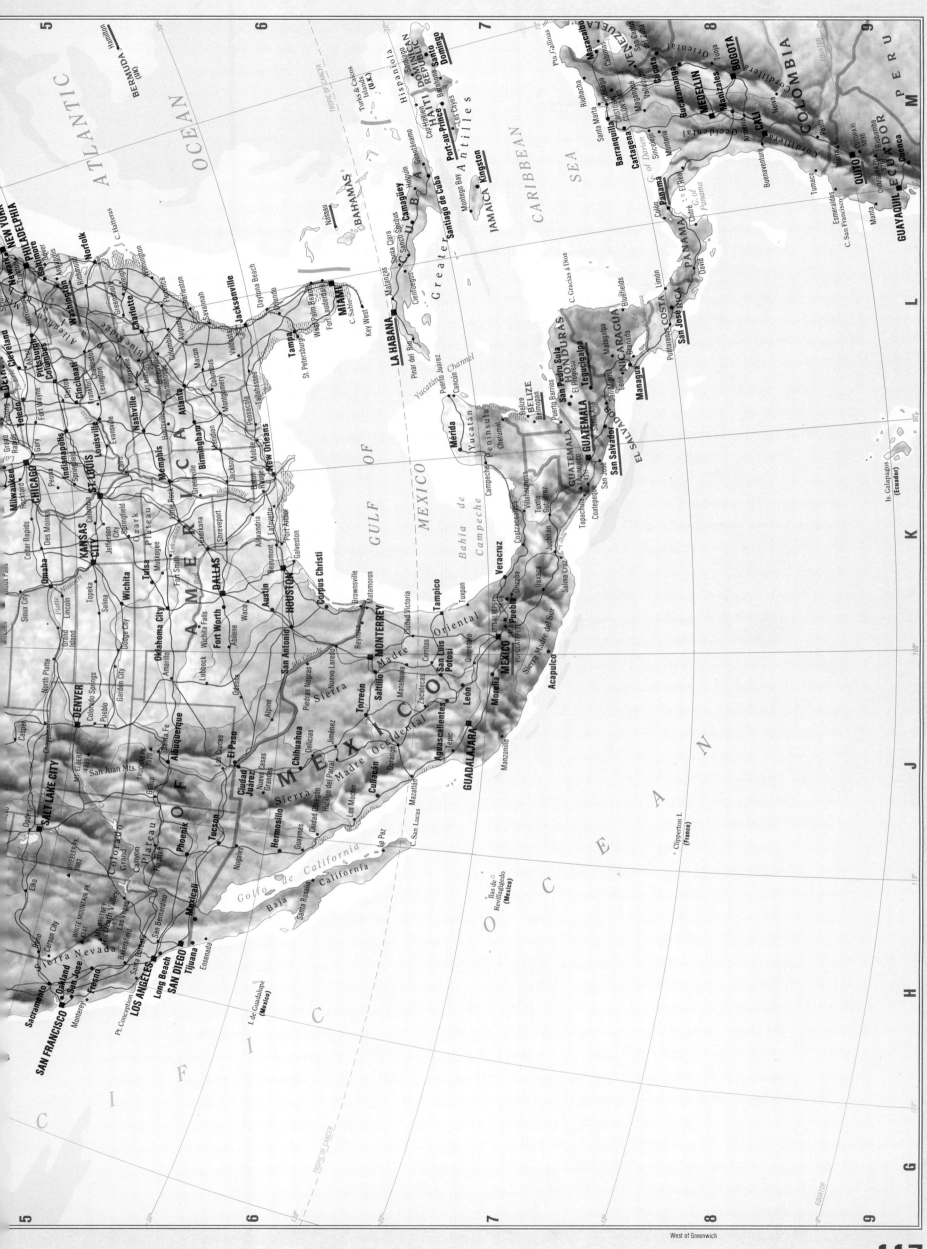

ALASKA

RUSSIA

Chukotskiy
Poluostrov
Michigmen
O. Arakamchechen
Gambell
N. Cape
St. Lawrence I.
Southeast C.

B E R I N G

S E A

Chukchi
Sea
C. Krusenstern
C. Espenberg
C. Prince of Wales
Kotzebue
Port Clarence
Nome
C. Rodney

De Long Mts.

Baird Mountains

Seward
Peninsula

Norton
Sound
C. Darby
Norton B.
C. Denbigh
Stuart I.
St. Michael

C H U K C H I
S E A

Pt. Hope

THUNDER MT.

Noatak

Kobuk

Endicott Range

Ray Mts.

A L A S K A

(U.S.A.)

Kuskokwim Mountains

Kaiyuh Mts.

Yukon

Melozitna

Kilbuck Mts.

A l a s k a Range

MT. McKINLEY
MT. FORAKER

Talkeetna Mts.

Kenai
Peninsula

Cook
Inlet
Anchorage

MT. MARCUS BAKER

Chugach Mts.

Kenai Mts.
Seward

Prince
William
Sound

Valdez
Cordova

Icy C.
Pt. Franklin
Wainwright
Pt. Barrow
Barrow

Smith B.
C. Halkett
Harrison Bay
Prudhoe Bay

B E A U F O R T

S E A

C. Kellett
Sachs Harbour
Bank

C. Lambton

Baillie I.
C. Dalhousie

Martin Pt.
Kaktovik
Herschel I.

Mackenzie
Bay

MT. MICHELSON

Davidson Mts.

Richardson Mts.

I N U V I K

Old Crow

Fort McPherson
Inuvik
Arctic Red River

Fort Yukon

Black

White Mts.

Circle

Eagle

Dawson

Ogilvie Mts.

M a c k e n z i e

Y U K O N

Keno Hill
Mayo

Dawson Range

MT. SANFORD

MT. BONA

St. Elias Mountains

MT. LOGAN

MT. ST. ELIAS

Malaspina
Gl.

Yakutat

Icy B.
Dry B.

MT. FAIRWEATHER

G U L F   O F   A L A S K A

Montague I.
Kayak I.
Hinchinbrook
MT. STELLER
Bering Gl.

Kodiak I.
Afognak I.
MT. DENISON
KATMAI VOL.
Barren Is.
Pt. Banks
Shelikof Str.

Aleutian Range

Bristol
Bay

Kvichak
Iliamna
Lake

C. Newenham

C. Constantine

Hagemeister I.

Togiak

Kuskokwim
Bay

Kilbuck Mts.

Kuskokwim

B E R I N G

S E A

Norway
Junction

Carmacks

Whitehorse

Carcross
Teslin

Skagway
White
Pass
Haines

Chichagof
I.
Admiralty
I.

Baranof
I.
Sitka

Kruzof I.

Alexander

Archipelago

Prince
of
Wales

Ketchikan

Dall I.
C. Muzon

Dixon Entrance

C. Knox
Rose Pt.

Graham
I.

Queen
Charlotte
Islands

Moresby
I.

P A C I F I C

O C E A N

Watson Lake

Dease Lake

Telegraph
Creek

Stikine Mts.

Cassiar Mts.

Polly Mountains

MT. SIR JAMES McBRIEN

M a c k e n z i e   M o u n t a i n s

Virginia
Falls

Fort Good Hope

Norman Wells

Fort Norman

N O

Franklin Mountains

Fort Franklin

R O C K

MT. ROOSEVELT

SIFTON PASS

Terrace
Kitimat
Prince Rupert

B R I T I

C O L U M

MT. WADDINGTON

Vancouver
Island

Bella Bella

Queen Charlotte
Sound

Calvert I.

C. Scott

Port Hardy

Campbell River

VICTORIA PK.

C. Cook

C. Flattery

Amundsen

Melville Hills

Parry Pen.

Franklin
B.

Bipolar Oblique Conic Conformal Projection

1:9,000,000

| 0 | 100 | 200 | 300 | 400 | 500 | 600 KILOMETRES |

| 0 | 50 | 100 | 150 | 200 | 250 | 300 | 350 | 400 STATUTE MILES |

© COLOUR LIBRARY BOOKS

Aa **Ab** **Ac** **Ad** **Ae** **Af** **Ag**

Attu I.
Near Islands
Agattu I.

Buldir I.

Kiska I.
Rat Islands
Amchitka I.

Semisopochnoi I.
Little Sitkin I.

Tanaga I.
Gt. Sitkin I.
Atka I.
Andreanof Islands

Amatignak I.
Kanaga I.
Adak I.

Amlia I.
Seguam I.
Yunaska I.

Islands of the
Four Mts.

Umnak I.
TULIK VOL.
KOROVIN VOL.
Fox
Islands
OKMOK VOL.
MAKUSHIN VOL.
Unalaska I.
Dutch Harbor
Akutan I.
Krenitzin Is.
Unimak I.
SHISHALDIN VOL.

A l e u t i a n   I s l a n d s

Aleutian Trench

Bowers Bank

B E R I N G

S E A

Pribilof Is.
St. Paul I.
St. George I.

Alaska Peninsula

Meshik
Nelson
Lagoon
VENIAMINOF VOL.
Fort Randall
False Pass
PAVLOF VOL.
Kupreanof
Pt.
Sanak I.
Shumagin
Is.
Perryville

Aleutian Trench

1:12,500,000

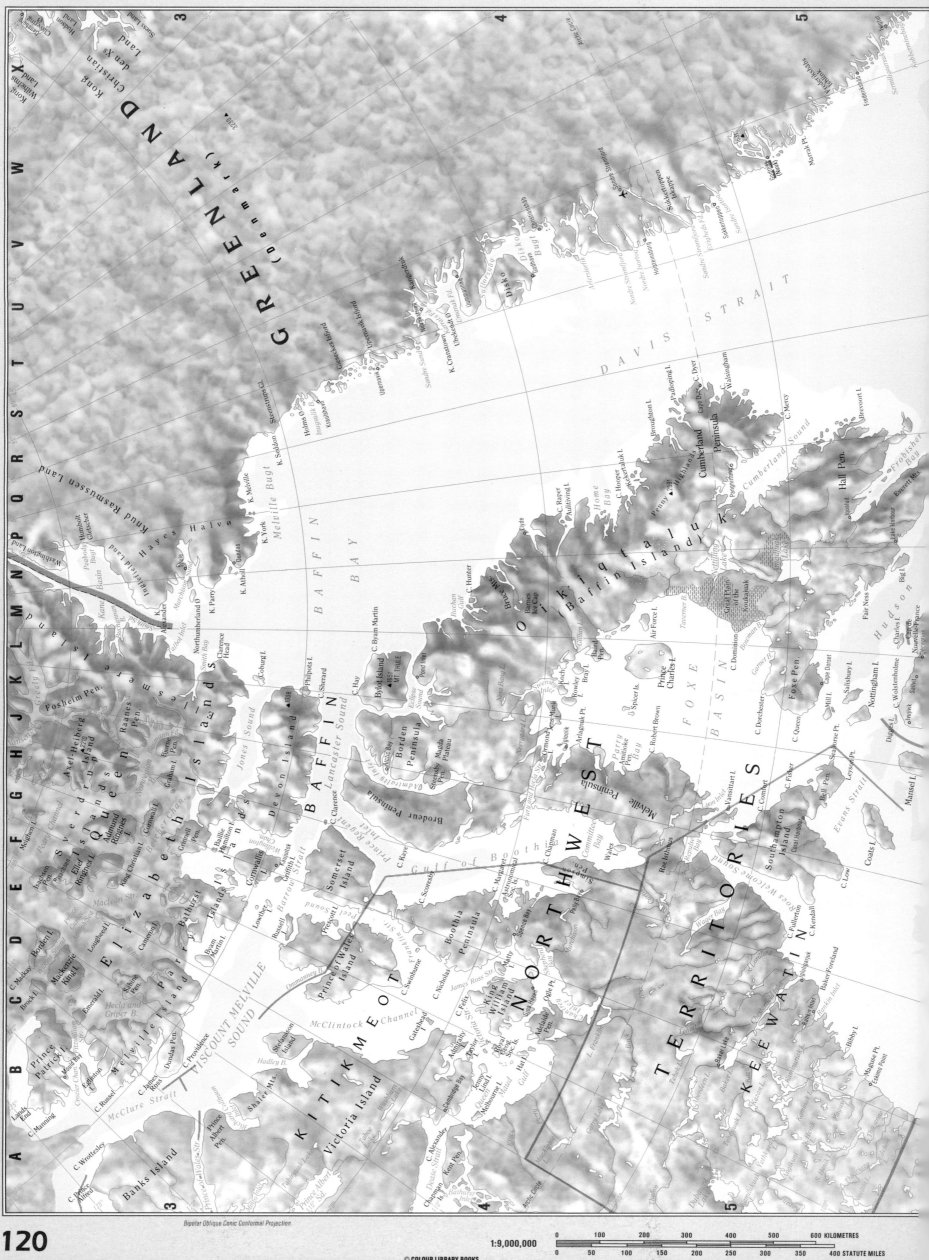

Bipolar Oblique Conic Conformal Projection

1:9,000,000

| 0 | 100 | 200 | 300 | 400 | 500 | 600 KILOMETRES |
| 0 | 50 | 100 | 150 | 200 | 250 | 300 | 350 | 400 STATUTE MILES |

© COLOUR LIBRARY BOOKS

Bipolar Oblique Conic Conformal Projection

1:5,000,000

| 0 | 50 | 100 | 150 | 200 | 250 | 300 | 350 | 400 KILOMETRES |

| 0 | 50 | 100 | 150 | 200 | 250 STATUTE MILE |

© COLOUR LIBRARY BOOKS

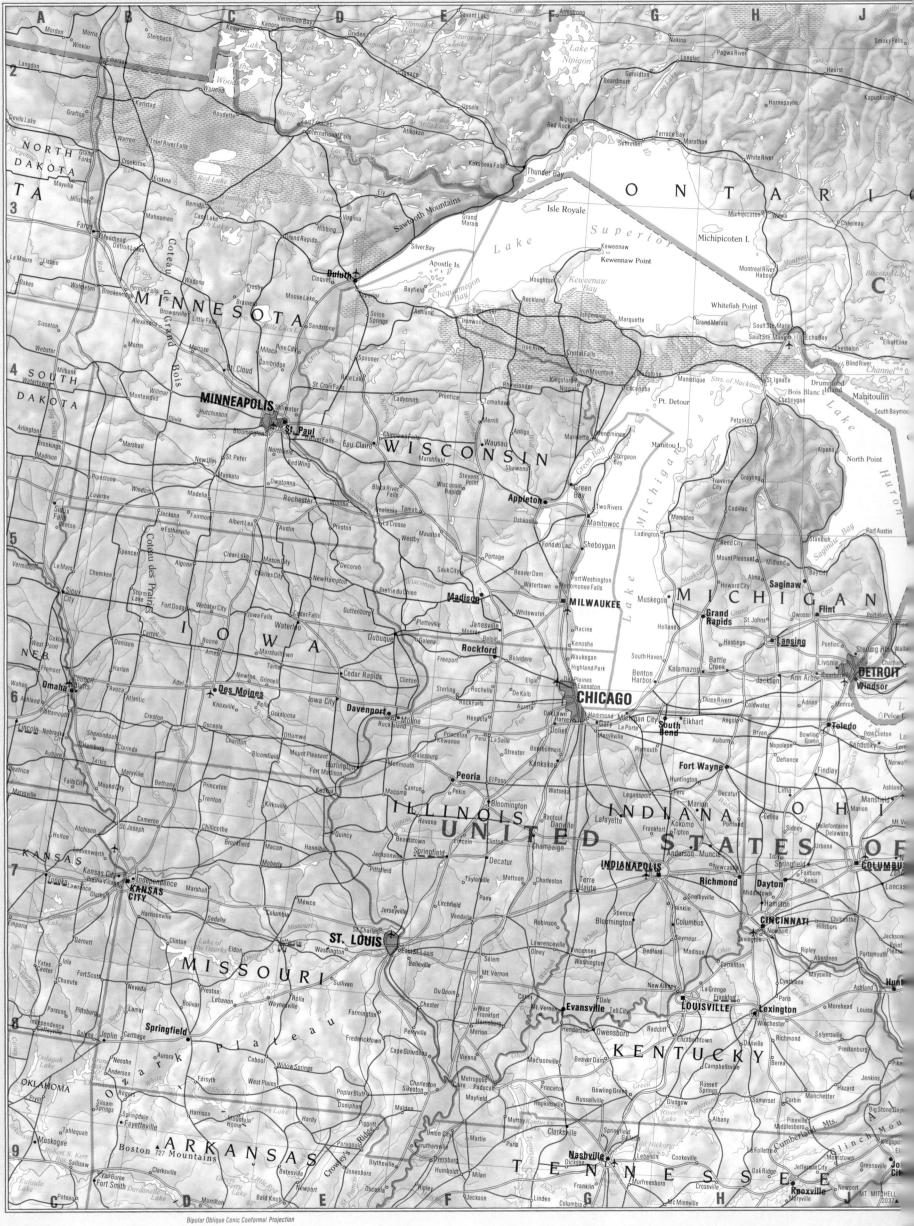

Bipolar Oblique Conic Conformal Projection

1:5,000,000

| 0 | 50 | 100 | 150 | 200 | 250 | 300 | 350 | 400 KILOMETRE |
| 0 | 50 | 100 | 150 | 200 | 250 STATUTE M |

Designed and produced by E & R
West of Greenwich

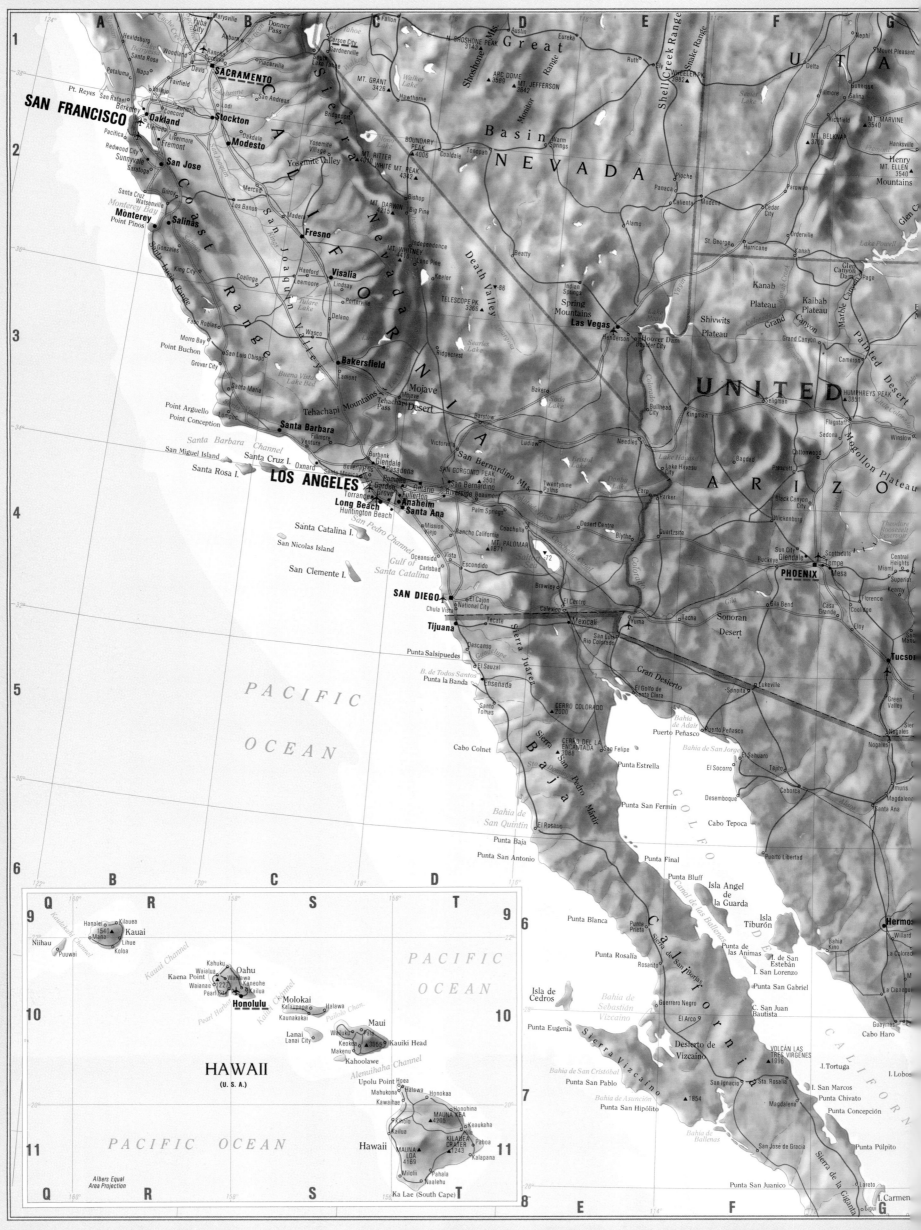

1:5,000,000

| 0 | 50 | 100 | 150 | 200 | 250 | 300 | 350 | 400 KILOMETRES |

| 0 | 50 | 100 | 150 | 200 | 250 STATUTE MILES |

© COLOUR LIBRARY BOOKS

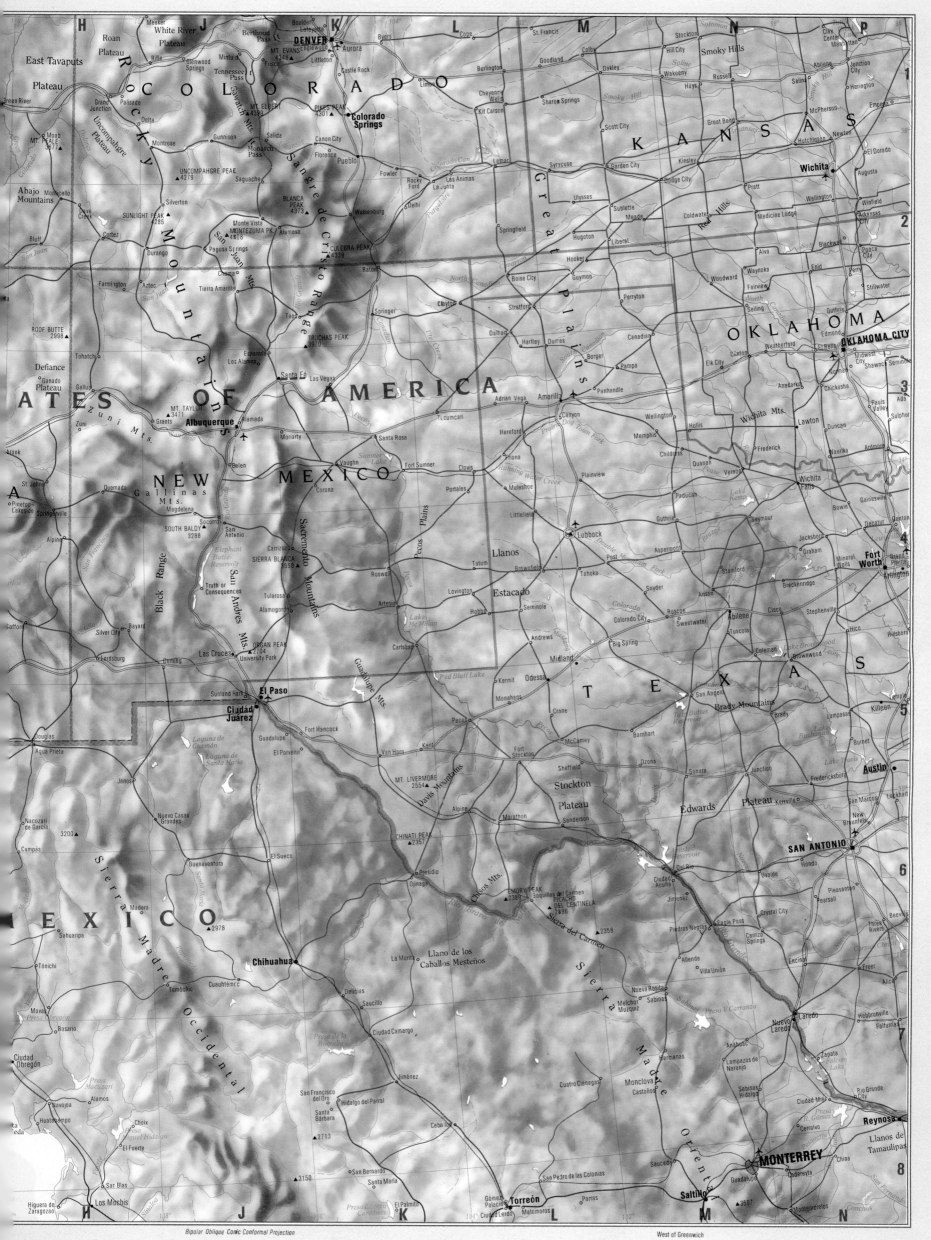

SOUTH-EAST U.S.A.

Bipolar Oblique Conic Conformal Projection

1:5,000,000

© COLOUR LIBRARY BOOKS

| 0 | 50 | 100 | 150 | 200 | 250 | 300 | 350 | 400 KILOMETRES |
| 0 | | 50 | | 100 | | 150 | | 200 | 250 STATUTE MILES |

Bipolar Oblique Conic Conformal Projection

1:6,500,000

© COLOUR LIBRARY BOOKS

GULF OF MEXICO

PACIFIC OCEAN

Tropic of Cancer

Arrecife Alacrán

PTA. Yalkubal
Progreso
Dzilam de Bravo
Tizimín
Río Lagartos
Cabo Catoche
Pta. Morros
Mérida
Celestún
Umán
Motul
Pto. Juárez
C. San Antonio
C. Corrientes

Campeche
Ticul
Valladolid
I. de Cozumel
Peto
Polyuc
Champotón
Felipe Carrillo Puerto
Pta. Herrero

Frontera
Llanos de
Tabasco y Campeche
Ciudad del Carmen
Laguna de Términos
Francisco Escárcega
Xpujil
Chetumal
Banco Chinchorro

MEXICO
Y u c a t á n

Macuspana
Teapa
Tenosique
La Unión
Orange Walk
Ambergris Cay

Comitán
Tikal
La Libertad
Flores
Belmopán
Hicks Cays
Turneffe Is.

2958
BELIZE
1122
Stann Creek
Lighthouse Reef
Glover Reef

GUATEMALA
Ciudad Cuauhtémoc
ALTO CUCHUMATANES
Cobán
3140
San Luis
San Antonio Nuevo
Pta. Gorda
Golfo de Honduras
Islas de la Bahía

VOLCÁN DE TAJUMULCO
Huehuetenango
Sierra de las Minas
Zacapa
Puerto Barrios
Pto. Cortés
Pta. Sal
La Ceiba
Cabo Camarón

Quezaltenango
VOLCÁN DE AGUA 3752
GUATEMALA Antigua Guatemala
Salamá
San Pedro Sula
El Progreso
Yoro
2435
Trujillo
Iriona
Pta. Patuca

Retalhuleu
Escuintla
Masagua
Guazacapán
Sta. Rosa de Copán
Sta. Bárbara
HONDURAS
Catacamas
Huampusirpi
Caratasca
Pta. Cabo Gracias á Dios

San Salvador
Sta. Ana
Metapán
Chalatenango
Comayagua
Juticalpa
Waspán
Pto. Cabezas

SAN SALVADOR
EL SALVADOR
Nueva San Salvador
San Vicente
San Miguel
Colomoncagua
Danlí
Yablis
La Luz
Isabella

Acajutla
Sonsonate
Zacatecoluca
La Unión
Nacaome
2438
Cordillera
Alamicamba

G. de Fonseca
Choluteca
VN. COSIGÜINA
859
Estelí
Matagalpa
Prinzapolca

1745
Merida
NICARAGUA
Chinandega
Chichigalpa
Juigalpa
Rama
Pta. de Perlas

Corinto
León
Tipitapa
Acoyapa
Chilamate
Bluefields

MANAGUA
Masaya
Granada
Lago de Nicaragua
Chontales

Jinotepe
I. de Ometepe
San Carlos
Cord. de Yolaina

Rivas
C. Sta. Elena
La Cruz
San Juan del Norte
Bahía de San Juan del Norte

2020
Liberia
COSTA RICA
Guápiles
Limón

Pen. de Nicoya
Puntarenas
VN IRAZÚ 3432
Cartago
SAN JOSÉ
Alajuela
Heredia

G. de Nicoya
Quepos
CHIRRIPÓ 3820
Dominical
Pta. Manzanilla
Pta. San Blas

Bahía de Coronado
Palmar
Pen. Valiente
Panamá Canal
Colón
San Miguelito
El Llano

Pen. de Osa
Golfito
Pto. Cortés
CERRO SANTIAGO 2826
Santa Fé
Penonomé
La Chorrera
PANAMÁ
Golfo del Darién
Puerto Obaldía

Pta. Burica
Concepción
David
Pedregal
Serranía de Tabasará
Río Hato
2621
Acandí
Monte

PANAMA
Golfo de Chiriquí
Santiago
Golfo de Panamá
Pedasí
I. del Rey
La Palma
El Real
Palo de las Letras

I. Coiba
Península de Azuero
Pta. Mala
Pta. Garachiné
Pavarandocito
395
PARAMI L.
Dabeiba

Pta. Mariato
Tonosí
C. Marzo

Caribbean

U.S.A.
Sarasota
Arcadia
Port Pierce
FLORIDA
Port Charlotte
Belle Glade
West Palm Beach
Fort Myers
Cape Coral
Boca Raton
Grand Bahama
Little Abaco
Great Abaco

Naples
Fort Lauderdale
Hollywood
Hialeah
Mores I.
Cherokee Sound
Great Abaco

C. Romano
MIAMI
Berry Is.
Eleuthera
Governor's Harbour

C. Sable
Key Largo
Nassau
New Providence
Dunmore Town

Florida Keys
Nicholls Town
Andros
Kemps Bay
Great Guana Cay
Great Exuma I.

Key West
Straits of Florida
Anguilla Is.
Snap Pt.

LA HABANA
Matanzas
Arch. de Sabana
Artemisa
Güines
Sagua la Grande
Arch. de Camagüey

Pinar del Río
Colón
Caibarién
Cayo Romano

Ba. de Guadiana
La Fe
Golfo de Batabanó
Pen. de Zapata
Cienfuegos
Santa Clara
Sancti Spíritus
Morón
Cayo Sabinal

Isla de la Juventud
Arch. de los Canarreos
Trinidad
Ciego de Ávila
Nuevitas

CUBA
Golfo de Ana María
Camagüey
Victoria de las Tunas
Holguín
Bayamo

Jardines de la Reina
Golfo de Guacanayabo
Manzanillo
Sierra Maestra
2005

Little Cayman
Cayman Brac
Cabo Cruz

Georgetown
Grand Cayman (U.K.)

Cayman Trench
Montego Bay
St. Ann's Bay
Port Antonio

South Negril Pt.
Lucea
Kingston
JAMAICA
May Pen
Spanish Town
BLUE MOUNTAIN PK.

Portland Pt.
Pedro Cays

Swan Is. (Hond.)
Serranilla Bank (Col.)
Bajo Nuevo (Col.)

Mosquitia
Quita Sueño Bank (Col.)
Serrana Bank (U.S.A. and Col.)

I. de Providencia (Col.)
Casyo Roncador (Col.)
C A R I

Costa de Mosquitos
I. de San Andrés (Col.)
Is. del Maíz (Corn Is.) (Nic. and U.S.A.)

G. de Morrosquillo
Golfo de Darién
Turbo

Bipolar Oblique Conic Conformal Projection

1:7,000,000

| 0 | 50 | 100 | 150 | 200 | 250 | 300 | 350 | 400 KILOMETRES |
| 0 | 50 | 100 | 150 | 200 | 250 STATUTE MILES |

© COLOUR LIBRARY BOOKS

ATLANTIC

OCEAN

Tropic of Cancer

BAHAMAS

Arthur's Town
Cat I.
Hawknest Pt.
Conception I.
San Salvador (Watling I.)
Rum Cay
Long I.
Clarence Town
South Pt.
Ragged Cays
Acklins I.
Samana Cray
Crooked I.
Snug Corner
Abraham's Bay
Mayaguana I.
Kew
Caicos Is. (U.K.)
Hogsty Reef
Little Inagua I.
Matthew Town
Great Inagua
Turks I. (U.K.)
Salt Cay

Cabo Lucrecia
Banes
Moa
Baracoa
Cabo Maisí
Santiago de Cuba
Guantánamo
Palma Soriano
Ile de la Tortue
Port-de-Paix
Cap-Haïtien
Monte Cristi
C. Isabela
Puerto Plata
Santiago
Bahía de Escocesa
C. Samaná
Bahía de Samaná
Gonaïves
Ile de la Gonâve
St-Marc
Hinche
Cordillera
PICO DUARTE 3175
La Vega
San Francisco de Macorís
Sabana de la Mar
Yuna
Golfe de la Gonâve
HAITI
C. Dame Marie
Jérémie
Dame Marie
PORT-AU-PRINCE
Massif de la Hotte 2347
Les Cayes
Ile-à-Vache
Pte-à-Gravois
Jacmel
San Juan
LA SELLE 2680
Lago Enriquillo
Barahona
Baní
SANTO DOMINGO
San Pedro de Macorís
Higüey
La Romana
I. Saona
DOMINICAN REPUBLIC
Pedernales
Isla Beata
Cabo Beata
C. Engaño
Navassa I. (U.S.A.)
Jamaica Channel

Windward Passage

CARIBBEAN SEA

Mona Passage

Puerto Rico Trench

Virgin Islands
Anegada (U.K.)
Aguadilla
Arecibo
Bayamón
SAN JUAN
Caguas
St. Thomas (U.S.A.)
Road Town
Virgin Gorda (U.K.)
Tortola (U.K.)
Anguilla (U.K.)
Saint Martin (Fr.)
Mayagüez
CERRO DE PUNTA 1338
Ponce
Charlotte Amalie
St. John (U.S.A.)
Vieques
Sint Maarten (Neth.)
Saba (Neth.)
St Eustatius (Neth.)
Barbuda
Antigua
St. John's
ANTIGUA AND BARBUDA
I. Mona
C. Rojo
Puerto Rico (U.S.A.)
Frederiksted
St. Croix (U.S.A.)
Basseterre
ST. KITTS-NEVIS (U.K.)
Plymouth
Montserrat (U.K.)
Guadeloupe (France)
La Désirade
Pointe-à-Pitre
Basse Terre
Marie Galante (France)
Iles des Saintes
I. de Aves (Bird I.) (Ven.)
DOMINICA
Roseau
Marigot
Martinique (France)
Fort-de-France
ST. LUCIA
Castries
Kingstown
ST. VINCENT
The Grenadines
GRENADA
St. George's
Carriacou
BARBADOS
Bridgetown

Lesser Antilles

Leeward Islands

Windward Islands

Lesser Antilles

Punta Gallinas
Pto. Estrella
Oranjestad
Aruba (Neth.)
Curaçao (Neth.)
Bonaire (Neth.)
Willemstad
Kralendijk
Is. Las Aves (Ven.)
I. Blanquilla (Ven.)
Tobago
Scarborough
TRINIDAD AND TOBAGO
Carrizal
Península de Guajira
Castilletes
Amuay
Punto Fijo
Paraguaná
Coro
Punta Gallinas
Is. Los Roques (Ven.)
I. Orchila (Ven.)
Isla de Margarita (Ven.)
Los Testigos (Ven.)
Trinidad
Riohacha
Santa Marta
Cabo de la Aguja
Maicao
Golfo de Venezuela
San Rafael
Capatárida
Mirimire
Pto. Cumarebo
La Asunción
Porlamar
I. La Tortuga (Ven.)
Cariaco
Río Caribe
Penín. de Paria
Güiria
Port of Spain
Arima
Río Claro
San Fernando
Galeota Pt.
BARRANQUILLA
Soledad
Sabanalarga
Ciénaga
PICO CRISTÓBAL COLÓN 5775
Valledupar
Maracaibo
Cabimas
Sta. Rita
San Luis
Churuguara
Barbacoa
Maiquetía
CARACAS
Guarenas
Guatire
Cabo Codera
Cumaná
Barcelona
Carúpano
Maturín
CARTAGENA
Turbaco
Calamar
Arjona
Robles La Paz
Ciudad Ojeda
Lagunillas
Machiques
Cabimas
Valencia
Maracay
Villa de Cura
San Juan de los Morros
Los Teques
Pto. Cabello
Pto. La Cruz
San Mateo
Anaco
Carúpano
CERRO BOLÍVAR
Anaco
Pedernales
Carmen
Sincelejo
Plato
El Banco
Mompós
Lago de Maracaibo
Sierra de Perijá
Barquisimeto
Yaritagua
Yaracuy
El Tocuyo
Tinaco
San Carlos
Carora
Acarigua
Ortiz
Aragua de Barcelona
Zaraza
Las Mercedes
Valle de la Pascua
El Tigre
Mata Negra
Tucupita
Caucasia
Sabanalarga
Barranca
Bobures
Valera
Trujillo
La Ceiba
Nueva Florida
Guanare
Calabozo
Pariaguán
Boca del Pao
El Tigre
Anaco
Barrancas
Boca Grande
San José de Amacuro
Port Kaituma
COLOMBIA
Simití
El Banco
San Carlos del Zulia
El Vigía
Mérida
Barinas
Cordillera de Mérida
PICO BOLÍVAR 5007
Ciudad Guayana
Upata
Serranía de Imataca
GUYANA
Planeta Rica
Ayapel
Majagual
ALTO DE TAMAR 2350
Ocaña
Concordias
San Cristóbal
VENEZUELA
Ciudad Bolívar
Represa Raúl Leoni
Guasipati
El Callao
Tumeremo
Zaragoza
Cúcuta
EL VIEJO 4100
Pamplona
La Fría
San Silvestre
Mantecal
San Fernando de Apure
Cabruta
Mapire
Ciudad Piar
CERRO MATO 1863
Maripa
CERRO BOLÍVAR 802
Ciudad Piar
La Paragua
San Pedro de las Bocas
El Dorado
Kartuni
BUCARAMANGA
Barrancabermeja
Piedecuesta
Cúbara
Rubio
San Antonio de Caparo
Guasdualito
Elorza
La Urbana
Las Trincheras
Yarumal
Banadía
Arauca
Apure
Santa María
La Paragua

133

West of Greenwich

Designed and produced by E.S.R.

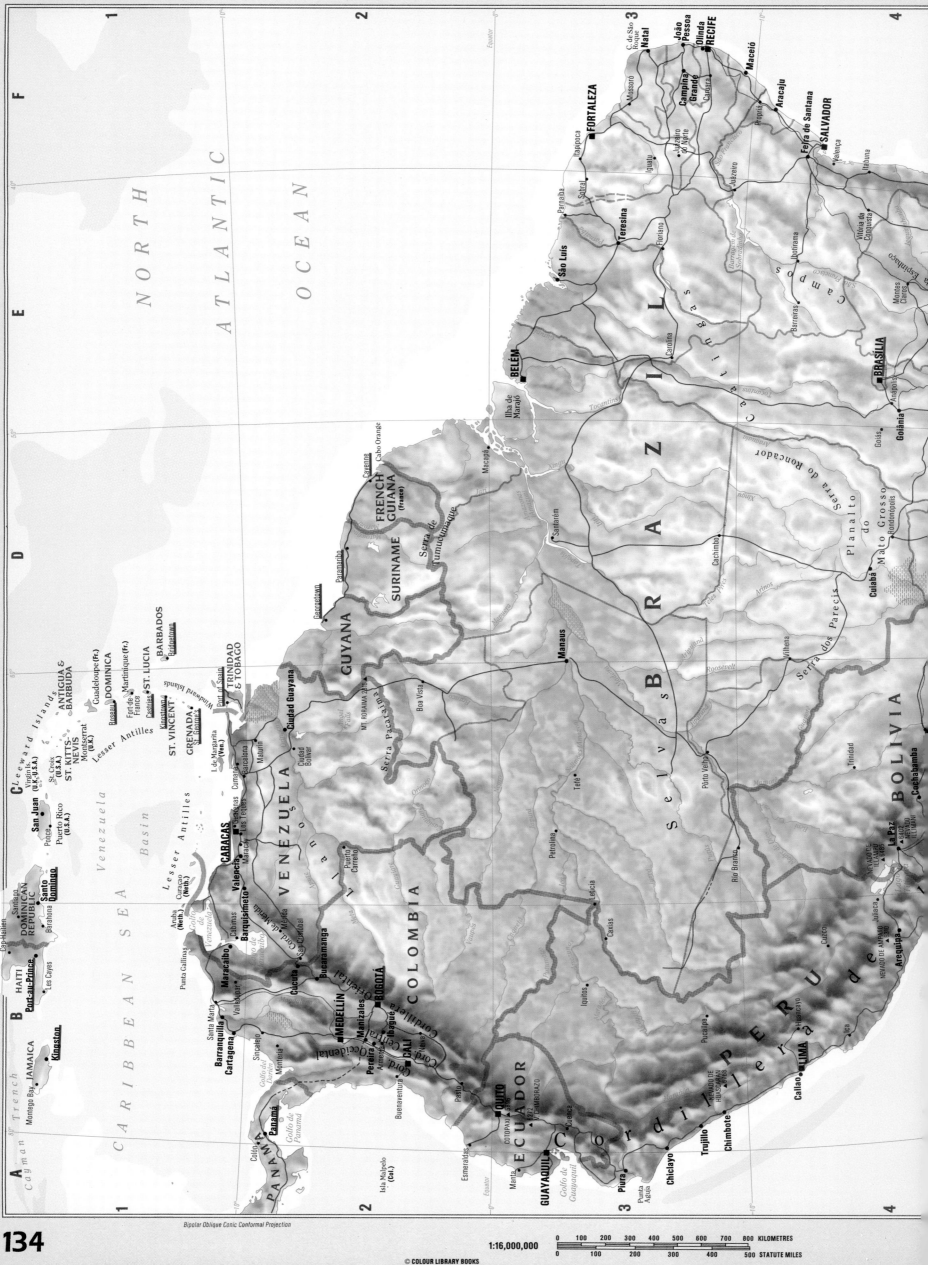

Bipolar Oblique Conic Conformal Projection

1:16,000,000

© COLOUR LIBRARY BOOKS

| 0 | 100 | 200 | 300 | 400 | 500 | 600 | 700 | 800 KILOMETRES |

| 0 | 100 | 200 | 300 | 400 | 500 STATUTE MILES |

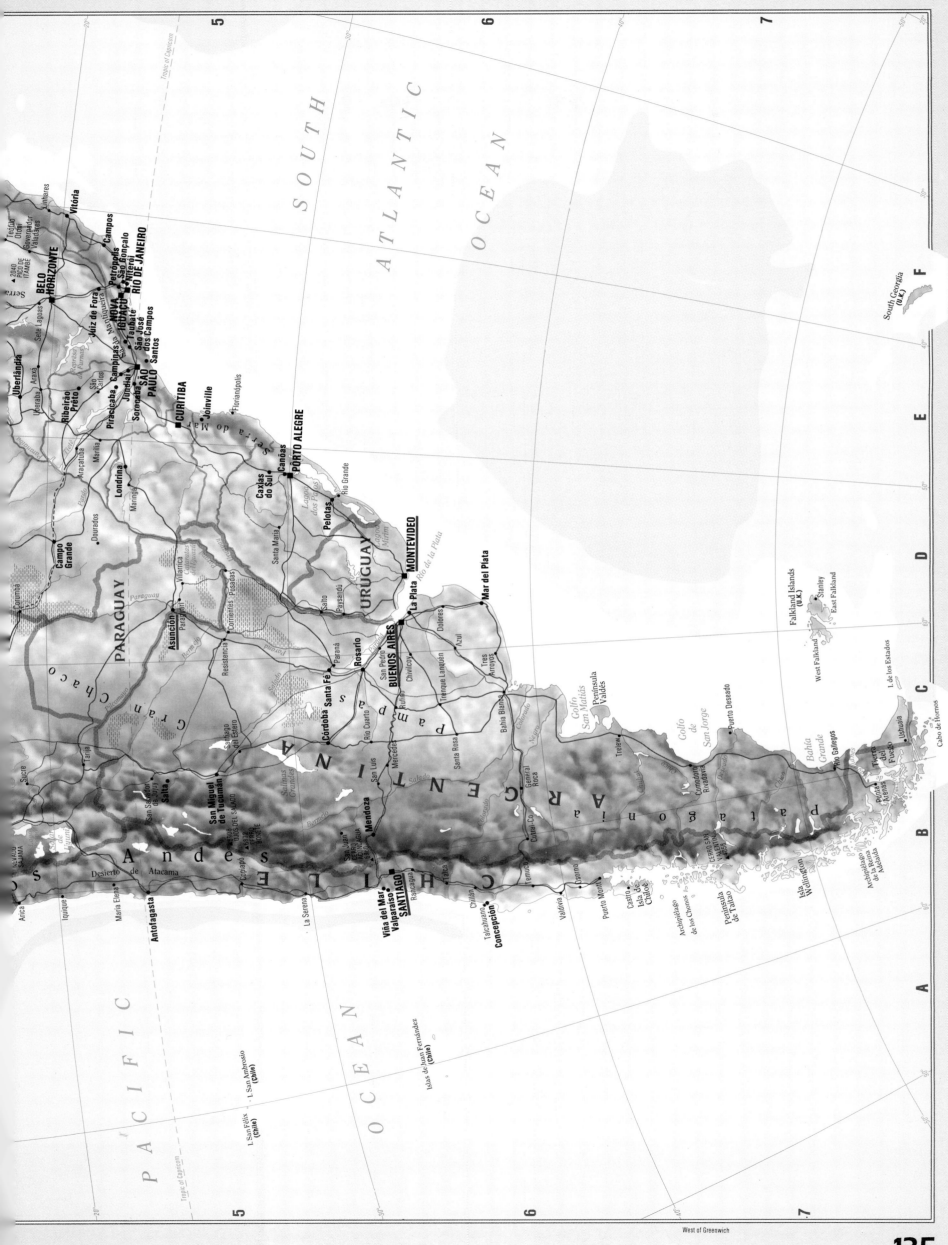

Bipolar Oblique Conic Conformal Projection

1:11,000,000

© COLOUR LIBRARY BOOKS

| 0 | 100 | 200 | 300 | 400 | 500 | 600 | 700 | 800 KILOMETRES |

| 0 | 100 | 200 | 300 | 400 | 500 STATUTE MILES |

Designed and produced by E.S.R.

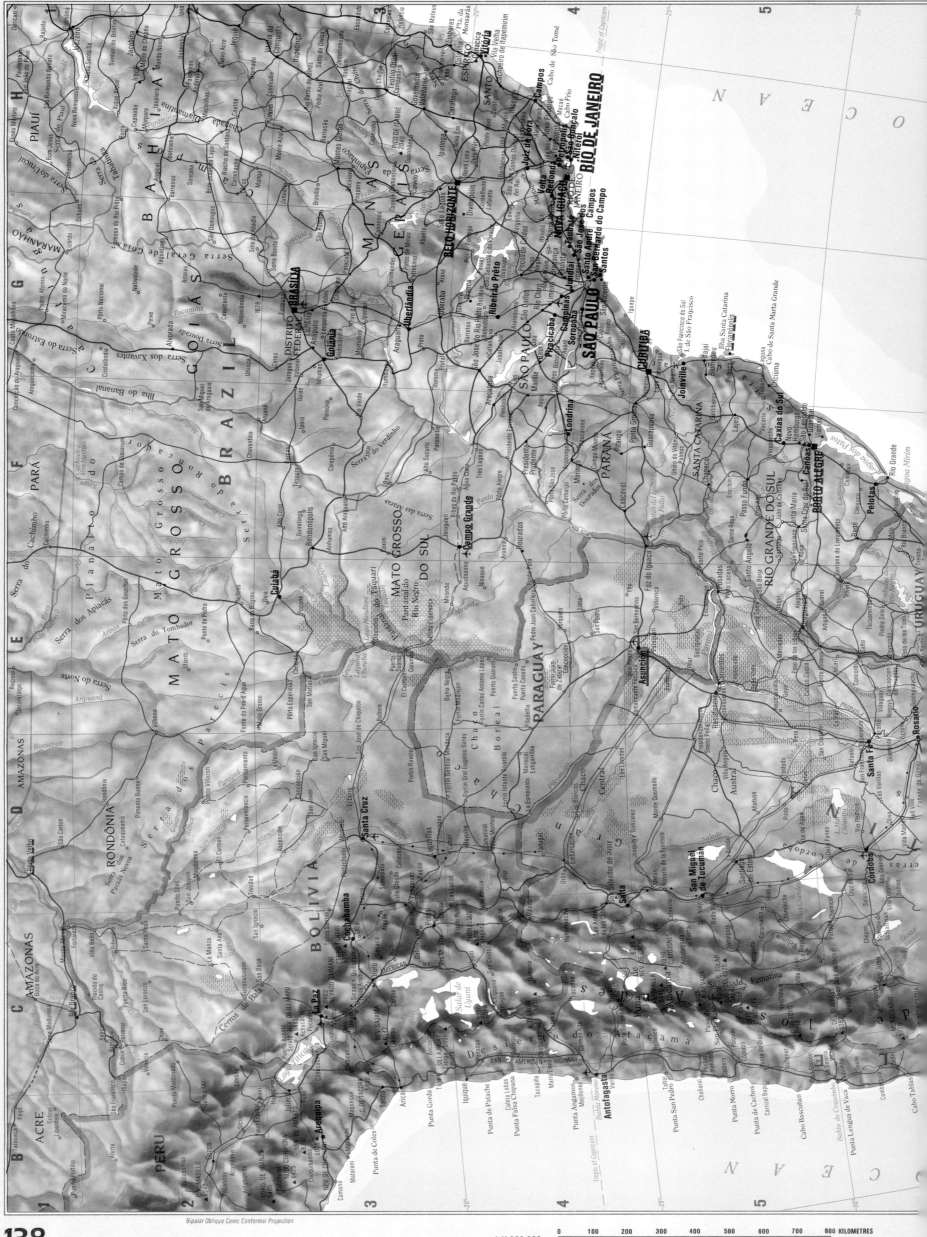

Bipolar Oblique Conic Conformal Projection

1:11,000,000

| 0 | 100 | 200 | 300 | 400 | 500 | 600 | 700 | 800 KILOMETRES |

| 0 | 100 | 200 | 300 | 400 | 500 STATUTE MILES |

© COLOUR LIBRARY BOOKS

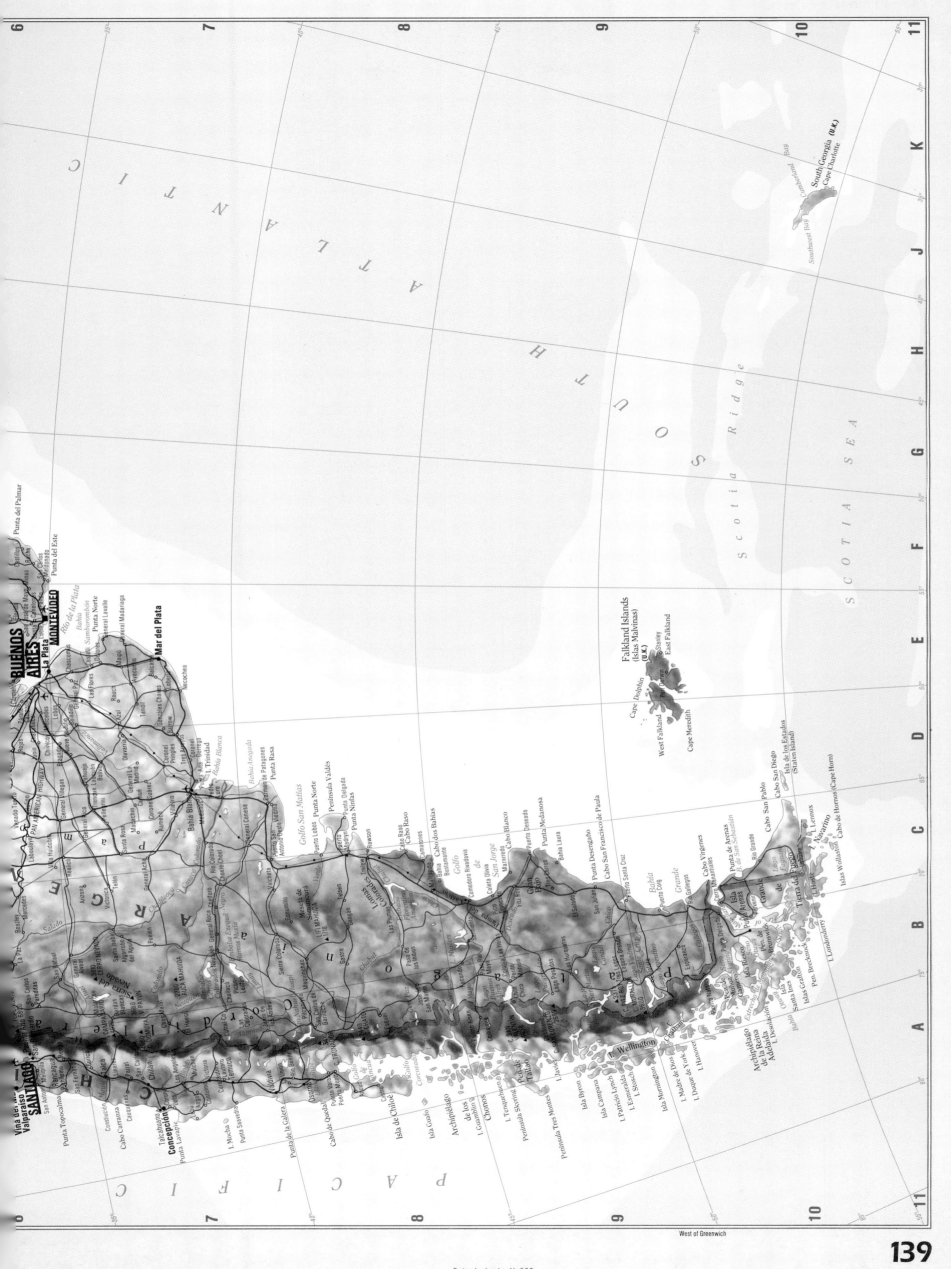

West of Greenwich

Designed and produced by E.S.R.

THE ARCTIC

X 150° Y 165° Z 180° West of Greenwich East of Greenwich A 165° 150° B

PACIFIC OCEAN

Honshu

JAPAN

Andreanof Islands

Aleutian Is.

Near Is.
(U.S.A.)

8

Hokkaido

SAPPORO
Asahi Kawa

Os. Iturup

Kuril'skiye Ostrova

BERING SEA

Komándorskiye Ostrova
(Russia)

KLYUCHEVSKAYA
SOPKA
4750 ▲

Sredinnyy Khrebet

7

Okhotskoye More

Sakhalin

Kodiak I.

Aleutian Range

Nuniyak I.

St. Lawrence I.

Koryakskiy Khrebet

Anadyr

Magadan

Khabarovsk

Komsomol'sk-na-Amure

W

Gulf of Alaska

Nome

Seward Peninsula

Chukotskiy Poluostrov

RUSSIA

Khrebet Dzhugdzhur

6

Nikolayevsk-na-Amure

CHINA

Vancouver Island

Queen Charlotte Is.

Alexander Archipelago

Anchorage

Alaska Range

ALASKA
(U.S.A.)

Bering Strait

Khrebet Kolymskiy

Yakutsk

D

Prince Rupert

▲4670
MT. FAIRWEATHER

MT. MCKINLEY
6194

Fairbanks

Pevek

Ambarchik

Kolyma

Indigirka

5

Coast Mountains

MT. ROBSON
3854 ▲

Rocky Mountains

Dawson

Brooks Range

C. Lisburne

Chukchi Sea

Os. Vrangelya

Vostochno Sibirskoye More

Verkhoyanskiy Khrebet

Tiksi

E

Mackenzie Mts.

Prudhoe Bay

Barrow

Point Barrow

4

Mackenzie

Inuvik

BEAUFORT SEA

Novosibirskiye Ostrova

More Laptevykh

Olenek Zal.

3

Great Slave Lake

Great Bear Lake

C. Bathurst

Amundsen Gulf

Banks Island

McClure Strait

2

M. Chelyuskin

Poluostrov Taymyr

Khatanga

Srednesibirskoye Ploskogor ye

F

Lake Athabasca

NORTH WEST TERRITORIES

Victoria Island

ARCTIC OCEAN

Lomonosov Ridge

Severnaya Zemlya

Reindeer Lake

CANADA

Yellowknife

Prince of Wales I.

Queen
Elizabeth
Islands

North Magnetic Pole (1987) ✕

1

North Pole ✕

Harris Ridge

Angara Ridge

Dikson

Churchill

Boothia Peninsula

Melville Peninsula

Back

Ellesmere Island

M. Zhelaniya

Obskaya Guba

Zapadno Sibirskaya Ravnina

G

Southampton I.

Smith Sound

North Geomagnetic Pole (1985) ✕

Thule

Lincoln Sea

K. Morris Jesup

Zemlya Frantsa-Iosifa
(Russia)

Pol. Yamal

OMSK

Hudson Bay

Foxe Basin

Oikiqtaluk
(Baffin Island)

Melville Bugt

Wandel Sea

Nordaustlandet

Novaya Zemlya

Karskoye More

Vorkuta

GORA NARODNAYA
1894 ▲

Peninsule d' Ungava

▲ 2591

Baffin Bay

Upernavik

Svalbard
(Norway)

Ostrov Kolguyev

Pechora

Ural'skiy Khrebet

CHELYABINSK

C. Chidley

Davis Strait

GREENLAND
(Denmark)

Greenland Sea

Barentsevo More

Ostrov Kolguyev

Ukhta

Scheffervllle

Labrador

Godthåb
(Nuuk)

Scoresbysund

Nordkapp

Murmansk

Kol'skiy Poluostrov

Arkhangel'sk

Beloye More

Kirov

KIRYBYSHEV

Goose Bay

Ammassalik

MT. FOREL
3360 ▲

Murmansk

C. Bauld

Denmark Strait

K. Farvel

Maximum extent of pack ice

NORWEGIAN SEA

Arctic Circle

NORWAY

FINLAND

Onezhskoye Ozero

Kuybyshevskoye Vdkhr.

R

Newfoundland

Reykjavik

ICELAND

Ladozhskoye Ozero

Helsingfors

LENINGRAD
(SANKT PETERBURG)

MOSKVA

KAZAKHSTAN

ATLANTIC OCEAN

Føroyar
(Denmark)

Shetland Is.

SWEDEN

Tallinn

ESTONIA

RUSSIA

KHAR'KOV

Orkney Is.

North Sea

OSLO

STOCKHOLM

Riga

LATVIA

LITHUANIA

Vilnius

MINSK

BELORUSSIA

EL'BRUS
5642 ▲

Edinburgh

UNITED KINGDOM

KØBENHAVN

DENMARK

Baltic Sea

Russia

KIYEV

UKRAINE

GEORG.

Dublin

IRELAND

WARSZAWA

BERLIN

POLAND

ODESSA

AMSTERDAM

NETH.

Rhein

GERMANY

Bonn

PRAHA

CZECH.

Kishinev

MOLD.

Black Sea

LONDON

BELG.

BRUXELLES

LUX.

PARIS

MÜNCHEN

WIEN

AUSTRIA

Donau

HUNG.

BUDAPEST

ROMANIA

BUCURESTI

ANKARA

Loire

FRANCE

Bern

SWITZ.

Alps

ISTANBUL

SYR.

LYON

BEOGRAD

YUGOSLAVIA

SOFIYA

BULG.

TURKEY

Q

MARSEILLE

ITALY

Tirane

ALB.

CYPRUS

LEBAN.

ROMA

GREECE

P

Bilbao

N SPAIN 10 M BARCELONA

ATHINAI

Mediterranean Sea

140

Polar Stereographic Projection

Scale 1:30,000,000 (Approx.)

| 0 | 250 | 500 | 750 | 1000 | 1250 | 1500 KILOMETRES |

| 0 | 250 | 500 | 750 | 1000 STATUTE MILES |

© COLOUR LIBRARY BOOKS

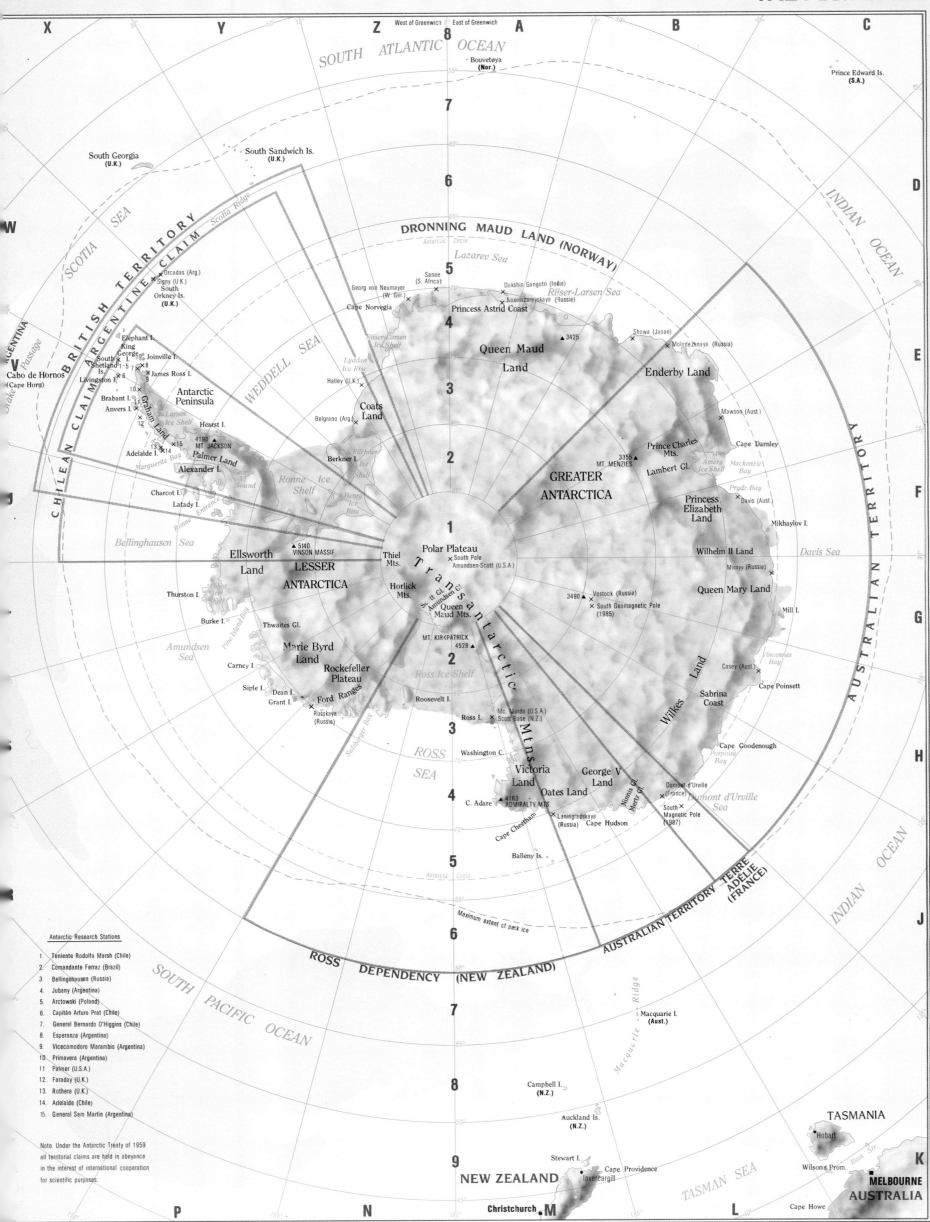

X Y Z 8 *West of Greenwich* *East of Greenwich* A B C

SOUTH ATLANTIC OCEAN

• Bouvetøya
(Nor.)

Prince Edward Is.
(S.A.)

7

South Georgia
(U.K.)

South Sandwich Is.
(U.K.)

W 6 D

SCOTIA SEA

Scotia Ridge

DRONNING MAUD LAND (NORWAY)

Antarctic Circle

Lazarev Sea

5

Sanae (S. Africa)
Dakshin Gangotri (India)
Georg von Neumayer (W. Ger.)
Novolazareyskaya (Russia)
Rüser-Larsen Sea
Showa (Japan)
Cape Norvegia
Princess Astrid Coast
Molodezhnaya (Russia)

BRITISH TERRITORY

ARGENTINE CLAIM

Orcadas (Arg.)
Signy (U.K.)
South Orkney Is.
(U.K.)

4

▲ 3425

Enderby Land

E

ARGENTINA

CHILEAN CLAIM

Elephant I.
King George
South Shetland Is.
Joinville I.
James Ross I.
Livingston I.
Brabant I.
Anvers I.

Riiser-Larsen Ice Shelf

Lyddan Ice Rise

Halley (U.K.)

Queen Maud Land

Mawson (Aust.)

Cape Darnley

Cabo de Hornos
(Cape Horn)

WEDDELL SEA

3

Coats Land

Prince Charles Mts.

Mackenzie Bay

Antarctic Peninsula

Belgrano (Arg.)

MT. MENZIES ▲ 3355

Lambert Gl.

Amery Ice Shelf

Prydz Bay

Davis (Aust.)

J

Graham Land
Hearst I.
4190 MT. JACKSON
13 14
15
Adelaide I.
Palmer Land

Berkner I.

Filchner Ice Shelf

2

Princess Elizabeth Land

Mikhaylov I.

AUSTRALIAN TERRITORY

Marguerite Bay

Alexander I.

Henry Ice Rise

Wilhelm II Land

Davis Sea

Charcot I.
Latady I.

George VI Sound

Ronne Ice Shelf

Mirnyy (Russia)

Bellinghausen Sea

Ellsworth Land

▲ 5140 VINSON MASSIF

Thiel Mts.

Polar Plateau
× South Pole
Amundsen-Scott (U.S.A.)

1

Transantarctic Mts.

Queen Mary Land

F

LESSER ANTARCTICA

Horlick Mts.

3490 ×
Vostock (Russia)
× South Geomagnetic Pole (1985)

Mill I.

Thurston I.

Scott Gl.
Amundsen Gl.
Queen Maud Mts.

Casey (Aust.)

Vincennes Bay

Burke I.

MT. KIRKPATRICK
4528 ▲

Wilkes Land

Cape Poinsett

G

Amundsen Sea

Marie Byrd Land

Rockefeller Plateau

Sabrina Coast

Carney I.

Thwaites Gl.

Cape Goodenough

Siple I.
Dean I.
Grant I.
Ford Ranges

Russkaya (Russia)

Roosevelt I.

Ross Ice Shelf

Mc. Murdo (U.S.A.)
Scott Base (N.Z.)
Ross I.

Porpoise Bay

Dumont d'Urville (France)

Dumont d'Urville Sea

H

ROSS SEA

Washington C.

Victoria Land

George V Land

South Magnetic Pole (1987) ×

Nimrod Gl.
Mertz Gl.

C. Adare
4163 ▲ ADMIRALTY MTS.

Oates Land

Leningradskaya (Russia)
Cape Hudson

4

Cape Cheetham

Balleny Is.

5

Antarctic Circle

J

6

Maximum extent of pack ice

ROSS DEPENDENCY (NEW ZEALAND)

AUSTRALIAN TERRITORY

TERRE ADÉLIE (FRANCE)

INDIAN OCEAN

SOUTH PACIFIC OCEAN

7

Macquarie Ridge

Macquarie I.
(Aust.)

Antarctic Research Stations

1. Teniente Rodolfo Marsh (Chile)
2. Comandante Ferraz (Brazil)
3. Bellingshausen (Russia)
4. Jubany (Argentina)
5. Arctowski (Poland)
6. Capitán Arturo Prat (Chile)
7. General Bernardo O'Higgins (Chile)
8. Esperanza (Argentina)
9. Vicecomodoro Marambio (Argentina)
10. Primavera (Argentina)
11. Palmer (U.S.A.)
12. Faraday (U.K.)
13. Rothera (U.K.)
14. Adelaide (Chile)
15. General Sam Martin (Argentina)

8

Campbell I.
(N.Z.)

TASMANIA

Auckland Is.
(N.Z.)

• Hobart

Note. Under the Antarctic Treaty of 1959 all territorial claims are held in abeyance in the interest of international cooperation for scientific purposes.

9

Stewart I.
Cape Providence
Invercargill

Wilsons Prom.

TASMAN SEA

Bass Str.

NEW ZEALAND

MELBOURNE
AUSTRALIA

Christchurch • M

Cape Howe

L

K

Polar Stereographic Projection

Designed and produced by E.S.R.

THE WORLD

A · West of Greenwich · East of Greenwich · B · C · D · E · F

GREENLAND
(Denmark)

Svalbard
(Norway)

Zemlya Frantsa-Iosifa
(U.S.S.R.)

Severnaya Zemlya

Novosibirskiye Ostrova

Jan Mayen
(Norway)

Novaya
Zemlya

Karskoye
More

More
Laptevykh

Lyakhovskiye
Ostrova

ICELAND

Reykjavik

Føroyar
(Denmark)

Nordkapp

Barentsevo
More

Poluostrov
Yamal

Gydanskiy
Poluostrov

Plato
Putorana

Gory Byrranga

Ozero Taymyr

Kolmskaya
Nizmennost'

Verkhoyanskiy

Khrebet Cherskogo

Arctic Circle

Norwegian
Sea

Shetland Is.
(U.K.)

Lappland

SWEDEN

FINLAND

Helsingfors

Pechora

Ural'skiy Khrebet

Zapadno
Sibirskaya
Ravnina

Sredne
Sibirskoye
Ploskogor'ye

Okhotskoye
More

NORWAY

Oslo Stockholm Tallinn
Helsingfors

Gulf of Bothnia

Beloye
More

RUSSIA

Sakhalin

UNITED
KINGDOM

Dublin

IRELAND

LONDON

North
Sea

København
Amsterdam

Baltic
Sea

ESTONIA

LATVIA
Riga

LITH

LENINGRAD
(Sankt Peterburg)

Ozero
Ladozhskoye

Kuybyshevskoye
Vodokhranilishche

Ozero Baykal

Buril'skiye Ostrova

Kuril

NORTH
ATLANTIC
OCEAN

's-Gravenhage
BEL
Bruxelles

DENMARK

NETH.

Berlin
Warszawa

GERMANY

POLAND

Minsk

BELORUSSIA

Kiyev (Kiev)
UKRAINE

MOSKVA

Kirgiz
Step'

KAZAKHSTAN

Alma-Ata

Tashkent
Kyzylkum

Aral'skoye
More

Ozero Balkhash

MONGOLIA
Gobi

Ulaanbaatar

Sikhote Alin'

BEIJING

N.KOREA
Pyöngyang

Sea of
Japan

JAPAN

LUX.
PARIS
FRANCE

Praha
CZECH

Wien
AUST.

Budapest
HUNG.

ROM.

Kishinev
(Chişinău)

MOLDAVIA

Bucureşti

Prikaspiyskaya
Nizmennost'

UZBEKISTAN
Samarkand
KIRGHIZIA
Bishkek

Tian Shan

Tarim
Pendi

Taklimakan
Shamo

Huang
He

TIANJIN

SÓUL
KOREA

TÓKYÓ

Acores
(Port.)

PORTUGAL

Lisboa

Madeira
(Port.)

Madrid

SPAIN

AND.

SWITZ.
Bern

YUGO.

Roma

Beograd

BULG.
Sofiya

Tirana
ALB.

GREECE

Black Sea

GEORGIA El'Brus
Tbilisi
ARMENIA
Yerevan
AZER. Baku

Caspian
Sea

Karakumy

TURKMENISTAN
Ashkhabad

TAJIKI.
Dushanbe

Kabul

Hindu
Kush

Kunlun
Shan

Xizang
Gaoyuan

Taklimakan
Shamo

Huang Hai

SHANGHAI

Chang Jiang

CHINA

Tai-pei
TAIWAN

Sea of
Japan

Ilas Canarias
(Sp.)

WESTERN
SAHARA

Al Aaiún

Rabat

MOROCCO

Atlas Mountains

TUNISIA

El Djazair

Tunis

MALTA
Valletta

Mediterranean
Sea

CYPRUS

Athinai

TURKEY

Ankara

Levkosia

Bayrut LEB.
Dimashq

SYRIA

Baghdad

IRAQ

ISRAEL
Yerushalayim
Amman
JOR.

Zagros

Kühha-ye

TEHRAN

IRAN

Kabul

AFGHANISTAN

Islamabad

PAKISTAN

Thar
Desert

New
Delhi

DELHI

Himalaya

Kathmandu
NEPAL

EVEREST

BHU.
BANG.
Dhaka

BURMA

Tropic of Cancer

Hoggar

Sahara

ALGERIA

LIBYA

EGYPT

Tibesti

EL QAHIRA

Red
Sea

Al Kuwayt
Al Manamah KUW.
QAT. BAH.
Ar Riyad Ad Dawhah
U.A.E.

SAUDI
ARABIA

OMAN

Masqat

Arabian
Sea

KARACHI

BOMBAY

INDIA

Deccan

MADRAS

CALCUTTA

Bay of
Bengal

Rangoon

Viangchan

LAOS
THAI-
LAND
KRUNG THEP
CAM.

Hanoi

VIETNAM

HONG KONG
(U.K.)

MANILA

Luzon

PHILIPPINES

Mindanao

Marianas
Is.

Guam (U.S.A.)

Caroline Islands

CAPE
VERDE

Praia

Dakar SEN.
THE
GAMBIA
Banjul
GUINEA
BISSAU Bissau
Conakry GUINEA
SIERRA LEONE
Freetown
Monrovia
LIBERIA

MAURITANIA

Nouakchott

MALI

Bamako

BUR.
FASO

Ouagadougou

NIGER

Niamey

N'djaména

CHAD

L. Chad

El Khartum

SUDAN

San'a
YEMEN

Suqutra (S. Yem.)

Lakshadweep
(India)

Andaman
Islands
(India)

Colombo

SRI LANKA

Malé

MALDIVES

BU.
BRU.
Bandar Seri
Begawan

Kuala Lumpur
MALAYSIA
SINGAPORE

Borneo

Maluku

Sulawesi

Nan Hai

Micro

Me

Abidjan

TOGO

IVORY
COAST

NIGERIA

Porto Novo
Lagos

Accra

Lomé

CENTRAL
AFRICAN REP.

Bangui

CAMEROON

Yaoundé

ETHIOPIA

Adis Abeba

SOMALIA

Muqdisho

Equator

SÃO TOMÉ
AND PRÍNCIPE

Malabo
EQ. GUINEA

Libreville

GABON

Congo
Basin

ZAIRE

UGANDA

Kampala

Victoria

KENYA

Nairobi

East Indies

Sumatera

Jawa
JAKARTA

INDONESIA

Timor

New
Guinea

PAPUA
NEW
GUINEA

Port Moresb

Ascension
(U.K.)

Brazzaville

Kinshasa

Luanda

RW.
Kigali

BU.
Bujumbura

Dodoma

TANZANIA

KILIMANJARO

Victoria

SEYCHELLES

Laut Arafura

Laut
Timor

Gt. Barrier Reef

Coral
Sea

St. Helena
(U.K.)

ANGOLA

ZAMBIA

Lusaka

Llongwe
MAL.

Harare

ZIMBABWE

MOZAMBIQUE

Mozambique Channel

COMOROS
Moroni

MADAGASCAR

Antananarivo

Réunion
(Fr.)

MAURITIUS
Port Louis

INDIAN OCEAN

AUSTRALIA

L. Eyre

Gt. Dividing Range

Darling

SOUTH
ATLANTIC
OCEAN

Tropic of Capricorn

Tristan da Cunha
(U.K.)

Gough I.
(U.K.)

NAMIBIA

Windhoek

BOTSWANA

Gaborone

Kalahari

Pretoria

SOUTH
AFRICA

Maseru
LESOTHO

Mbabne SWAZILAND
Maputo

Orange

Cape of Good Hope

Gt. Victoria Desert

C. Leeuwin

Canberra

Tasmania

Iles Crozet
(Fr.)

Prince Edward Is.
(S.A.)

Ile Kerguelen
(Fr.)

Heard I.
(Aus.)

South
Sandwich Is.
(U.K.)

Mercator Projection

1:85,000,000 (Scale at the Equator)

ARCTIC   OCEAN

Vostochno
Sibirskoye
More

Ostrov Vrangelya

Chucki
Sea

Pt. Barrow

Brooks Range

ALASKA
(U.S.A.)

McKINLEY
6194 ▲

Alaska Range

Khrebet Kolymsky

Anadyrsky
Zaliv

Bering Str.

Yukon

Bering
Sea

Gulf of Alaska

Kodiak I.

Aleutian   Islands

Aleutian   Trench

Beaufort Sea

Mackenzie Mts

Banks
Island

Amundsen
Gulf

Victoria Island

Great Bear Lake

Great Slave Lake

L. Athabasca

Reindeer Lake

CANADA

Rocky Mountains

Vancouver I.

Columbia

Great
Plains

UNITED STATES
OF
AMERICA

Gt. Salt Lake

SAN FRANCISCO

LOS ANGELES

Missouri

L. Winnipeg

Great
Lakes

CHICAGO

Ottawa

St. Lawrence

Appalachian   Mts.

NEW YORK
PHILADELPHIA
Washington

Viscount Melville
Sound

Queen

Elizabeth

Islands

Ellesmere
Island

Kane
Basin

Baffin Bay

Oikiqtaluk

Davis Str.

Foxe
Basin

Back

Hudson Str.

Hudson Bay

Labrador Sea

Labrador

Newfoundland

Bermuda
(U.K.)

Lincoln
Sea

GREENLAND
(Denmark)

Reykjavik
ICELAND

Arctic Circle

Kap Farvel

NORTH
ATLANTIC
OCEAN

Açores
(Port.)

NORTH

PACIFIC

OCEAN

Hawaiian

Islands

HAWAII
(U.S.A.)

Isla de Guadalupe
(Mex.)

MEXICO
CIUDAD DE
MÉXICO

Islas de Revillagigedo
(Mex.)

Gulf of Mexico

BAHAMAS
Nassau

La Habana   CUBA   West Indies

Belmopan
BELIZE   Port au Prince   DOMINICAN REP.
HAITI   Santo Domingo
Kingston   JAMAICA   Puerto Rico (U.S.A.)
GUATEMALA   HONDURAS
Guatemala   Tegucigalpa   Caribbean Sea   Leeward Is.
San Salvador   EL SALVADOR
Managua   NICARAGUA   Windward Is.
San José   Caracas   BARBADOS
COSTA RICA   Panamá   TRINIDAD
VENEZUELA   AND TOBAGO
PANAMA   Georgetown   Paramaribo
Bogotá   GUY   SUR   Cayenne
COLOMBIA   FRENCH GUIANA

Tropic of Cancer

CAPE
VERDE
Praia

Trust Territory of
the Pacific Islands

Marshall Is.

POLYNESIA

Line   Islands

Christmas I.

NAURU   Gilbert   Phoenix Is.
Tarawa   Is.

KIRIBATI

SOLOMON ISLANDS   TUVALU
Honiara   Santa Cruz   Fanafuti
Is.

MELANESIA   Iles
Wallice   W.   SAMOA
FIJI   (Fr.)   SAMOA   Apla   (U.S.A.)
VANUATU   Vila
Nouvelle
Calédonie   Suva   TONGA
(Fr.)   Nuku'alofa

Iles Marquises
(Fr.)

French Polynesia
(Fr.)

Iles Tuamotu

Tahiti

Iles de la
Société

Cook Islands
(N.Z.)

Iles Gambier

Pitcairn I.
(U.K.)   Ducie I.
(U.K.)

Isla de Pascua
(Easter I.)
(Chile)

SOUTH

PACIFIC

OCEAN

Islas Galápagos
(Ecuador)

Quito
EQUADOR

PERU

LIMA

Islas Juan
Fernández
(Chile)

Santiago

ACONCAGUA
6960

BRAZIL

Planalto   do
Mato Grosso

La Paz
BOLIVIA

Orinoco

Negro

Amazon

Brasília

PARAGUAY

Asunción

SÃO PAULO   RÍO DE JANEIRO

URUGUAY
Montevideo

BUENOS AIRES

ARGENTINA

Patagonia

Isla Fernando
de Noronha
(Brazil)

Equator

Ilha da Trindade
(Brazil)

Tropic of Capricorn

30°

SOUTH

ATLANTIC

OCEAN

NEW ZEALAND
Wellington

Chatham Is.
(N.Z.)

Tasman Sea

Auckland Is.
(N.Z.)

Macquarie Is.
(Aus.)

Falkland Is.
(U.K.)

Cabo de Hornos

South Georgia
(U.K.)

Scotia Sea

South
Sandwich
Is. (U.K.)

GLOSSARY AND ABBREVIATIONS

Language abbreviations in glossary

Afr	Afrikaans	*Dut*	Dutch	*I-C*	Indo-Chinese	*Mal*	Malay	*S-C*	Serbo-Croat
Alb	Albanian	*Fin*	Finnish	*Ice*	Icelandic	*Mlg*	Malagasy	*Som*	Somali
Ar	Arabic	*Fr*	French	*Ind*	Indonesian	*Mon*	Mongolian	*Sp*	Spanish
Ber	Berber	*Gae*	Gaelic	*It*	Italian	*Nor*	Norwegian	*Swe*	Swedish
Bul	Bulgarian	*Ger*	German	*Jap*	Japanese	*Per*	Persian	*Th*	Thai
Bur	Burmese	*Gr*	Greek	*Khm*	Khmer	*Pol*	Polish	*Tib*	Tibetan
Ch	Chinese	*Heb*	Hebrew	*Kor*	Korean	*Por*	Portuguese	*Tu*	Turkish
Cz	Czechoslovakian	*Hin*	Hindi	*Lao*	Laotian	*Rom*	Romanian	*Vt*	Vietnamese
Dan	Danish	*Hun*	Hungarian	*Lat*	Latvian	*Rus*	Russian	*Wel*	Welsh

Glossary

A

Abar (*Ar*) – wells
Abyar (*Ar*) – wells
Adasi (*Tu*) – island
Adrar (*Ber*) – mountains
Ain (*Ar*) – spring, well
Akra (*Gr*) – cape, point
Alb (*Ger*) – mountains
Alpen (*Ger*) – mountains
Alpes (*Fr*) – mountains
Alpi (*It*) – mountains
Alto (*Por*) – high
-alv (*Swe*) – river
-alven (*Swe*) – river
Appenino (*It*) – mountain range
Aqabat (*Ar*) – pass
Archipielago (*Sp*) – archipelago
Arquipielago (*Por*) – archipelago
Arrecife (*Sp*) – reef
Ayia (*Gr*) – saint
Ayios (*Gr*) – saint
Ayn (*Ar*) – spring, well

B

Bab (*Ar*) – strait
Bad (*Ger*) – spa
Badiyah (*Ar*) – desert
Bælt (*Dan*) – strait
Baharu (*Mal*) – new
Bahia (*Sp*) – bay
Bahr (*Ar*) – bay, canal, lake, stream
Bahrat (*Ar*) – lake
Baia (*Por*) – bay
Baie (*Fr*) – bay
Baja (*Sp*) – lower
Ban (*Khm, Lao, Th*) – village
-bana (*Jap*) – cape, point
Banco (*Sp*) – bank
-bandao (*Ch*) – peninsula
Bandar (*Per*) – bay
Baraji (*Tu*) – reservoir
Barqa (*Ar*) – hill
Barragem (*Por*) – reservoir
Bassin (*Fr*) – basin, bay
Batin (*Ar*) – depression
Beinn (*Gae*) – mountain
Beloyy (*Rus*) – white
Ben (*Gae*) – mountain
Bereg (*Rus*) – bank, shore
Berg (*Ger*) – mountain
Berge (*Afr*) – mountains
Bheinn (*Gae*) – mountain
Biar (*Ar*) – wells
Bir (*Ar*) – well
Bi'r (*Ar*) – well
Birkat (*Ar*) – well
Birket (*Ar*) – well
Boca (*Sp*) – river mouth
Bocche (*It*) – mouths, estuary
Bodden (*Ger*) – bay
Bogazi (*Tu*) – strait
Boka (*S-C*) – gulf, inlet
Bol'shoy (*Rus*) – big
Bol'shoye (*Rus*) – big
Bory (*Pol*) – forest
Bratul (*Rom*) – river channel
Bucht (*Ger*) – bay
Bugt (*Dan*) – bay
Buhayrat (*Ar*) – lagoon, lake
Bukit (*Mal*) – hill, mountain
Bukt (*Nor*) – bay
Bulak (*Rus*) – spring
Burnu (*Tu*) – cape, point
Burun (*Tu*) – cape, point
Busen (*Ger*) – bay
Buyuk (*Tu*) – big

C

Cabo (*Por, Sp*) – cape, point
Cachoeira (*Sp*) – waterfall
Cap (*Fr*) – cape, point
Campos (*Sp*) – upland
Cao Nguyen (*Th*) – plateau, tableland
Cataratas (*Sp*) waterfall
Cayi (*Tu*) – stream
Cayo (*Sp*) – islet, rock
Cerro (*Sp*) – hill
Chaco (*Sp*) – jungle
Chaine (*Fr*) – mountain chain
Chapada (*Por*) – hills
Ch'eng (*Ch*) – town
Chiang (*Ch*) – river
Chiang (*Th*) – town
Chott (*Ar*) – marsh, salt lake
Chute (*Fr*) – waterfall
Cienaga (*Sp*) – marshy lake
Ciudad (*Sp*) – city, town
Co (*Tib*) – lake
Col (*Fr*) – pass
Colinas (*Sp*) – hills
Cordillera (*Sp*) – mountain range
Costa (*Sp*) – coast, shore
Cote (*Fr*) – coast, slope
Coteau (*Fr*) – hill, slope
Coxilha (*Por*) – mountain pasture
Cuchillas (*Sp*) – hills

D

Dag (*Tu*) – mountain
Dagi (*Tu*) – mountain
Daglari (*Tu*) – mountains
-dake (*Jap*) – peak
-dal (*Nor*) – valley
Dao (*Ch*) – island
Darreh (*Per*) – valley
Daryacheh (*Per*) – lake
Dasht (*Per*) – desert
Denizi (*Tu*) – sea
Desierto (*Sp*) – desert
Djebel (*Ar*) – mountain
-djik (*Dut*) – dyke
Do (*Kor, Jap, Vt*) – island
Dolina (*Rus*) – valley
Dolok (*Ind*) – mountain
Dolna (*Bul*) – lower
Dolni (*Cz*) – lower
-dong (*Kor*) – village
-dorp (*Afr*) – village
Dur (*Ar*) – mountains

E

Eiland (*Dut*) – island
Eilanden (*Dut*) – islands
-elva (*Nor*) – river
Embalse (*Sp*) – reservoir
Erg (*Ar*) – sandy desert
Estero (*Sp*) – bay, estuary, inlet
Estrecho (*Sp*) – strait
Etang (*Fr*) – lagoon, pond
Ezers (*Lat*) – lake

F

Feng (*Ch*) – mountain, peak
Fels (*Ger*) – rock
Firth (*Gae*) – estuary
-fjall (*Swe*) – mountains
Fjeld (*Dan*) – mountain
-fjell (*Nor*) – mountain
-floi (*Ice*) – bay
-fjoraur (*Ice*) – fjord
Forde (*Ger*) – inlet
Foret (*Fr*) – forest
-foss (*Ice*) – waterfall

G

-gan (*Jap*) – rock
Gang (*Ch*) – harbour
Ganga (*Hin*) – river
Gata (*Jap*) – inlet, lagoon
Gave (*Fr*) – torrent
Gebel (*Ar*) – mountain
Gebirge (*Ger*) – mountains
Ghat (*Hin*) – range of hills
Ghubbat (*Ar*) – bay
Glen (*Gae*) – valley
Gletscher (*Ger*) – glacier
Gobi (*Mon*) – desert
Golfe (*Fr*) – bay, gulf
Golfo (*It, Sp*) – bay, gulf
Golu (*Tu*) – lake
Gora (*Bul*) – forest
Góra (*Pol, Rus*) – mountain
-gorod (*Rus*) – small town
Gory (*Pol, Rus*) – mountains
Grada (*Rus*) – mountain range
Grad (*Bul, Rus, S-C*) – city, town
Gross (*Ger*) – big
Gryada (*Rus*) – ridge
Guba (*Rus*) – bay
-gunto (*Jap*) – island group
Gunung (*Ind, Mal*) – mountain

H

Hadh (*Ar*) – sand dunes
Hafen (*Ger*) – harbour, port
Haff (*Ger*) – bay, lagoon
Hai (*Ch*) – sea
Haixia (*Ch*) – strait
-holm (*Dan*) – island
Halvo (*Dan*) – peninsula
-hama (*Jap*) – beach
Hamada (*Ar*) – plateau
-hamar (*Ice*) – mountain
Hammadah (*Ar*) – plain, stony desert
Hamun (*Per*) – marsh
-hanto (*Jap*) – peninsula
Harrat (*Ar*) – lava field
Hav (*Swe*) – gulf
Havet (*Nor*) – sea
-havn (*Dan, Nor*) – harbour
Hawr (*Ar*) – lake
He (*Ch*) – river
Heide (*Ger*) – heath, moor
-hisar (*Tu*) – castle
Ho (*Ch*) – river
Hohe (*Ger*) – hills
Horn (*Ger*) – peak, summit
Hu (*Ch*) – lake
-huk (*Swe*) – cape, point

I

Idd (*Ar*) – well
Idhan (*Ar*) – sand dunes
Ile (*Fr*) – island
Iles (*Fr*) – islands
Ilha (*Por*) – island
Ilhas (*Por*) – islands
Insel (*Ger*) – island
Inseln (*Ger*) – islands
Irq (*Ar*) – sand dunes
Irmak (*Tu*) – large river
Isfjord (*Dan*) – glacier
Iskappe (*Dan*) – icecap
Isla (*Sp*) – island
Islas (*Sp*) – islands
Isola (*It*) – island
Isole (*It*) – islands
Istmo (*Sp*) – isthmus

J

Jabal ʿ(*Ar*) – mountain
-jarvi (*Fin*) – lake
Jaza 'ir (*Ar*) – islands
Jazirat (*Ar*) – island
Jazovir (*Bul*) – reservoir
Jbel (*Ar*) – mountain
Jebel (*Ar*) – mountain
Jezero (*Alb, S-C*) – lake
Jezioro (*Pol*) – lagoon, lake
Jezirat (*Ar*) – island
-jiang (*Ch*) – river
Jibal (*Ar*) – mountain
Jiddat (*Ar*) gravel plain
-jima (*Jap*) – island
-joki (*Fin*) – river
-jokull (*Ice*) – glacier

K

Kaap (*Afr*) – cape, point
-kai (*Jap*) – bay, sea
-kaikyo (*Jap*) – strait
Kanaal (*Dut*) – canal
Kap (*Ger*) – cape, point
-kapp (*Nor*) – cape, point
Kas (*Khm*) – island
Kavir (*Per*) – desert
-kawa (*Jap*) – river
Kenet (*Alb*) – inlet
Kep (*Alb*) – cape, point
Kepulauan (*Ind*) – archipelago, islands
Kereb (*Ar*) – hill, ridge
Khalij (*Ar*) – bay, gulf
Khawr (*Ar*) – wadi
Khrebet (*Ru*) – mountain range
Kiang (*Ch*) – river
Klein (*Afr, Ger*) – small
Ko (*Th*) – island
-ko (*Jap*) – inlet, lake
Koh (*Khm*) – island
Kolpos (*Gr*) – gulf
Kolymskoye (*Rus*) – mountain range
Korfezi (*Tu*) – bay, gulf
Kosa (*Rus*) – spit
Kotlina (*Cz, Pol*) – basin, depression
Kraj (*Cz, Pol, S-C*) – region
Krasnyy (*Rus*) – red
Kray (*Rus*) – region
Kreis (*Ger*) – district
Kryazh (*Rus*) – mountains
Kucuk (*Tu*) – small
Kuh (*Per*) – mountain
Kuhha (*Per*) – mountains
Kum (*Rus*) – sandy desert
Kyst (*Dan*) – coast
Kyun (*Bur*) – island
Kyunzu (*Bur*) – islands

L

La (*Tib*) – pass
Lac (*Fr*) – lake
Lacul (*Rom*) – lake
Laem (*Th*) – point
Lago (*It, Por, Sp*) – lake
Lagoa (*Por*) – lagoon
Laguna (*Sp*) – lagoon, lake
Lam (*Th*) – stream
Lande (*Fr*) – heath, sandy moor
Laut (*Ind*) – sea
Ling (*Ch*) – mountain range
Liman (*Rus*) – bay, gulf
Limni (*Gr*) – lagoon, lake
Llano (*Sp*) – plain, prairie
Llanos (*Sp*) – plains, prairies

M

Mae Nam (*Th*) – river
Mala (*S-C*) – small
Malaya (*Rus*) – small
Male (*Cz*) – small
Maloye (*Rus*) – small
Malyy (*Rus*) – small
Mar (*Por, Sp*) – sea
Mare (*It*) – sea
Masirah (*Ar*) – channel
Massif (*Fr*) – mountains
Mato (*Por*) – forest
Meer (*Afr, Dut, Ger*) – lake, sea
Menor (*Por, Sp*) – lesser, smaller
Mer (*Fr*) – sea
Mesa (*Sp*) – tableland
Minami (*Jap*) – south
-misaki (*Jap*) – cape, point
Mont (*Fr*) – mountain
Montagna (*It*) – mountain
Montagne (*Fr*) – mountain
Montagnes (*Fr*) – mountains
Montana (*Sp*) – mountain
Montanas (*Sp*) – mountains
Monte (*It, Por, Sp*) – mountain
Monti (*It*) – mountains
More (*Rus*) – sea
Mull (*Gae*) – cape, point, promontory
Munkhafad (*Ar*) – depression
Muntii (*Rom*) – mountains
Mynydd (*Wel*) – mountain
Mys (*Rus*) – cape, point

N

-nada (*Jap*) – gulf, sea
Nadrz (*Cz*) – reservoir
Nafud (*Ar*) – desert, dune
Nagor'ye (*Rus*) – highland, uplands
Nagy- (*Hun*) – great
Nahr (*Ar*) – river
Namakzar (*Per*) – desert, salt flat
Nei (*Ch*) – inner
Ness (*Gae*) – cape, promontory
Neu (*Ger*) – new
Nevada (*Sp*) – snow capped mountains
Nevado (*Sp*) – mountain
Ngoc (*Vt*) – mountain peak
-nisi (*Gr*) – island
Nisoi (*Gr*) – islands
Nisos (*Gr*) island
Nizhnyaya (*Rus*) – lower
Nizina (*Pol*) – depression, lowland
Nizmennost' (*Rus*) – lowland
Noord (*Dut*) – north
Nord (*Dan, Fr, Ger*) – north
Norte (*Por, Sp*) – north
Nos (*Bul, Rus*) – point, spit
Nosy (*Mlg*) – island
Nova (*Bul*) – new
Nova (*Cz*) – new
Novaya (*Rus*) – new
Nove (*Cz*) – new
Novi (*Bul*) – new
Nudo (*Sp*) – mountain
Nuruu (*Mon*) – mountain range
Nuur (*Mon*) – lake

O

Ø (*Dan*) – island
Oblast' (*Rus*) – province

Llyn (*Wel*) – lake
Loch (*Gae*) – lake
Lough (*Gae*) – lake

Occidental (Fr, Rom, Sp) – western
Oki (Jap) – bay
-oog (Ger) – island
Ojo (Sp) spring
Orasul (Rom) – city
Ori (Gr) – mountains
Oriental (Fr, Rom, Sp) – eastern
Ormos (Gr) – bay
Oros (Gr) – island
Ort (Ger) – cape, point
Ostrov (Rus) – island
Ostrova (Rus) – islands
Otok (S-C) – island
Otoki (S-C) – islands
Ouadi (Ar) – wadi, dry watercourse
Oued (Ar) – dry river bed, wadi
Ovasi (Tu) – plain
Ozero (Rus) – lake

P

Pampa (Sp) – plain
Paṅiai (Ind) – lake
Paso (Sp) – pass
Passage (Fr) – pass
Passo (It) – pass
Pasul (Rom) – pass
Pelagos (Gr) – sea
Pendi (Ch) – basin
Pengunungnan (Ind) – mountain range
Peninsola (It) – peninsula
Peninsule (Fr) – peninsula
Pereval (Rus) – pass
Peski (Rus) – desert, sands
Phnom (Khm) – hill, mountain
Phu (Vt) – mountain
Pic (Fr) – peak
Picacho (Sp) – peak
Pico (Sp) – peak
Pik (Rus) – peak
Pingyuan (Ch) – plain
Pizzo (It) – peak
Planalto (Por) – plateau
Plana (S-C, Sp) – plain
Planina (Bul, S-C) – mountains
Plato (Afr, Bul, Rus) – plateau
Ploskogor'ye (Rus) – plateau
Ploskogorje (Rus) – plateau
Poco (Ind) – peak

Pohorie (Cz) – mountain range
Pointe (Fr) – cape, point
Pojezierze (Pol) – plateau
Poluostrov (Rus) – peninsula
Polwysep (Pol) – peninsula
Ponta (Por) – cape, point
Presa (Sp) – reservoir
Proliv (Rus) – strait
Pueblo (Sp) – village
Puerto (Sp) – harbour, pass
Pulau (Ind, Mal) – island
Puna (Sp) – desert plateau
Puncak (Ind) – peak
Punta (It, Sp) – cape, point
Puy (Fr) – peak

Q

Qalamat (Ar) – well
Qalib (Ar) – well
Qararat (Ar) – depression
Qolleh (Per) – mountain
Qornet (Ar) – peak
Qundao (Ch) – archipelago

R

Ramlat (Ar) – dunes
Ra's (Ar, Per) – cape, point
Ras (Ar) – cape, point
Rass (Som) – cape, point
Ravnina (Rus) – plain
Recife (Por) – reef
Represa (Por) – dam
Reshteh (Per) – mountain range
-retto (Jap) – island chain
Rijeka (S-C) – river
Rio (Por, Sp) – river
Riviere (Fr) – river
Rt (S-C) – cape, point
Rubha (Gae) – cape, point
Ruck (Ger) – mountain
Rucken (Ger) – ridge
Rud (Per) – river
Rudohorie (Cz) – mountains
Rzeka (Pol) – river

S

Sabkhat (Ar) – salt flat
Sagar (Hin) – lake
Sahara (Ar) – desert

Sahl (Ar) – plain
Sahra (Ar) – desert
Sa'id (Ar) – highland
-saki (Jap) – cape, point
Salar (Sp) – salt pan
Salina (Sp) – salt pan
San (Sp) – saint
-san (Jap) – mountain
-sanchi (Jap) – mountainous area
Sankt (Ger, Swe) – saint
-sanmyaku (Jap) – mountain range
Santa (Sp) – saint
Sao (Por) – saint
Sar (Kur) – mountain
Satu (Rom) – village
Sawqirah (Ar) – bay
Se (I-C) – river
See (Ger) – lake
-sehir (Tu) – town
Selat (Ind) – channel, strait
-selka (Fin) – bay
Selva (Sp) – forest
Serra (Por) – mountain range
Serrania (Sp) – mountains
-seto (Jap) – channel, strait
Severnaya (Rus) – southern
Sfintu (Rom) – saint
Shamo (Ch) – desert
Shan (Ch) – mountains
Shandi (Ch) – mountainous area
Shatt (Ar) – river mouth, river
-shima (Jap) – islands
Shiqqat (Ar) – interdune trough
-shoto (Jap) – group of islands
Sierra (Sp) – mountain range
Sint (Afr, Dut) – saint
Slieve (Gae) – range of hills
So (Dan, Nor) – lake
Soder- (Swe) – southern
Sondre (Dan, Nor) – southern
Song (Vt) – river
Spitze (Ger) – peak
Sredne (Rus) – middle
Stadt (Ger) – town
Stara (Cz) – old
Staraya (Rus) – old
Stenon (Gr) – strait, pass
Step' (Rus) – plain, steppe
Strelka (Rus) – spit
Stretto (It) – strait

-suido (Jap) – channel, strait
Sund (Swe) – sound, strait
Szent- (Hun) – saint

T

-take (Jap) – peak
Tall (Ar) – hill
Tallat (Ar) – hills
Tanggula (Tib) – pass
Tanjong (Ind, Mal) – cape, point
Tanjon'i (Mlg) – cape, point
Tanjung (Ind, Mal) – cape, point
Tao (Ch) – island
Taraq (Ar) – hills
Tassili (Ber) – rocky plateau
Tau (Rus) – mountains
Taung (Bur) – mountain, south
Tekojarvi (Fin) – reservoir
Tell (Ar) – hill
Teluk (Ind) – bay
Tenere (Fr) – desert
Terre (Fr) – land
Thale (Th) – lake
Thamad (Ar) – well
Tirat (Ar) – canal
Tjarn (Swe) – lake
Tso (Tib) – lake
Tonle (Khm) – lake
Tutul (Ar) – hills

U

Ujung (Ind) – cape, point
-ura (Jap) – inlet
Urayq (Ar) – sand ridge
Uruq (Ar) – dunes
Ust (Rus) – river mouth
Uul (Mon) – mountain

V

Valea (Rom) – valley
-varos (Hun) – town
-varre (Nor) – mountain
-vatten (Swe) – lake
Vaux (Fr) – valleys
Velika (S-C) – big
Velikaya (Rus) – big
Verkhne (Rus) – upper
-vesi (Fin) – lake, water
Ville (Fr) – town
Vinh (Vt) – bay

Virful (Rom) – peak
Vodokhranilishche (Rus) – reservoir
Volcan (Sp) – volcano
Vorota (Rus) – strait
Vostochnyy (Rus) – eastern
Vozvyshennost' (Rus) hills, upland
Vpadina (Rus) – depression

W

Wadi (Ar) – river, stream
Wahat (Ar) – oasis
Wai (Ch) – outer
Wald (Ger) – forest
Wan (Ch) – bay
Wasser (Ger) – lake, water
Wenz (Ar) – river
Wielka (Pol) – big

X

Xan (Ch) – strait
Xi (Ch) – stream, west
Xia (Ch) – gorge, lower
Xian (Ch) – county
Xiao (Ch) – small
Xu (Ch) – island

Y

Yam (Heb) – lake
-yama (Jap) – mountain
Yarimadasi (Tu) – peninsula
Yazovir (Bul) – reservoir
Ye (Bur) – island
Yoma (Bur) – mountain range
Yugo- (Rus) – southern
Yuzhnyy (Rus) – southern

Z

Zaki (Jap) – cape, point
Zalew (Pol) – bay, inlet
Zaliv (Rus) – bay
-zan (Jap) – mountain
Zapadno (Rus) – western
Zatoka (Pol) – bay
Zee (Dut) – sea
Zemiya (Rus) – island, land
-zhen (Ch) – town

Abbreviations

A

A. – Alp, Alpen, Alpi
Akr. – Akra
And. – Andorra
Arch. – Archipelago
Arr. – Arrecife
Aust. – Australia
Ay. – Ayios

B

B. – Bahia, Baia, Baie, Bay, Bucht, Bukt
Ba. – Bahia
Bang. – Bangladesh
Bah. – Bahrain
Bel. – Belgium
Ben. – Benin
Bg. – Berg
Bhu. – Bhutan
Bk. – Bukit
Bol. – Bol'shoy, Bol'shoye
Br. – Burnu, Burun
Bru. – Brunei
Bt. – Bukit
Bu. – Burundi
Bü. – Büyük
Bulg. – Bulgaria
Bur. Faso – Burkina Faso

C

C. – Cabo, Cap, Cape, Cerro
Can. – Canal, Canale
Cga. – Cienaga
Chan. – Channel
Co. – Cerro
Col. – Columbia
Cord. – Cordillera
Cr. – Creek
Czech. – Czechoslovakia

D

D. – Dag, Dagi, Daglari, Daryacheh
D.C. – District of Columbia
Den. – Denmark
Djib. – Djibouti

E

E. – East
Eq. – Equatorial
Est. – Estrecho

F

Fd. – Fjord
Fk. – Fork
Fr. – France
Ft. – Fort

G

G. – Golfe, Golfo, Guba, Gulf, Gora, Gunung
Gd. – Grand
Gde. – Grande
Geb. – Gebirge
Gen. – General
Geog. – Geographical
Ger. – Germany
Gh. – Ghana
Gl. – Glacier
Gr. – Grande, Gross
Gt. – Great
Guy. – Guyana

H

Har. – Harbour
Hd. – Head
Hung. – Hungary

I

I. – Ile, Ilha, Insel, Isla, Island, Isle, Isola, Isole

Is. – Ilhas, Iles, Islands, Islas, Isles
Isth. – Isthmus

J

J. – Jabal, Jbel, Jebel, Jezioro, Jezero, Jazair
Jor. – Jordan

K

K. – Kap, Kuh, Kuhha, Koh, Kolpos
Kam. – Kampuchea
Kan. – Kanal, Kanaal
Kep. – Kepulauan
Khr. – Khrebet
Kör. – Körfezi
Kuw. – Kuwait

L

L. – Lac, Lacul, Lago, Lake, Limni, Llyn, Loch, Lough
Lag. – Lagoon, Laguna
Leb. – Lebanon
Liech. – Liechtenstein
Lit. – Little
Lux. – Luxembourg

M

M. – Mys
Mal. – Malawi
Mex. – Mexico
Mgne. – Montagne
Mt. – Mont, Mount, Mountain
Mti. – Monti
Mtii. – Muntii
Mts. – Monts, Mounts, Mountains

N

N. – Nord, North, Nos
Neb. – Nebraska

Neth. – Netherlands
Nev. – Nevado
N.H. – New Hampshire
Nizh. – Nizhnyaya
Nizm. – Nizmennost
Nor. – Norway
N.Z. – New Zealand

O

O. – Ost, Ostrov
Os. – Ostova
Oz. – Ozero

P

P. – Point
Pass. – Passage
Penn. – Pennsylvania
Peg. – Peganungan
Pen. – Peninsola, Peninsula, Peninsule
Pk. – Peak, Puncak
Pl. – Planina
Pol. – Poluostrov
Port. – Portugal
Prom. – Promontory
Pt. – Point
Pta. – Ponta, Punta
Pte. – Pointe
Pto. – Puerto, Punto

Q

Qat. – Qatar

R

R. – Reshteh
Ra. – Range
Rep. – Republic
Res. – Reservoir
Rés. – Réservoir
Rom. – Romania
Rw. – Rwanda

S

S. – Shatt, South
Sa. – Serra, Sierra
S.A. – South Africa
Sd. – Sound, Sund
Sp. – Spain
Sprs. – Springs
St. – Saint, Sint
Sta. – Santa
Ste. – Sainte
Str. – Strait
Sur. – Suriname
Switz. – Switzerland

T

Tg. – Tanjong, Tanjung
Tk. – Teluk

U

U.A.E. – United Arab Emirates
U.K. – United Kingdom
U.S.A. – United States of America

V

V. – Volcano
Vdkhr. – Vodokhranilishche
Ven. – Venezuela
Verkh. – Verkhne
Vn. – Volcan
Vol. – Volcan, Volcano

W

W. – Wadi, Wald, West

Y

Y. – Yarimadasi
Yug. – Yugoslavia

Z

Zal. – Zaliv

INDEX

The index includes an alphabetical list of all names appearing in the map section of the atlas. Names on the maps and in the index are generally in the local language. For names in languages not written in the Roman alphabet, the officially accepted transliteration system has been used.

Most features are indexed to the largest scale map on which they appear. Extensive features are usually indexed to maps that show the features completely or show them in their relationship to surrounding areas. For extensive regional features, locations are given for the approximate centre of the feature, those for linear features are given at the position of the name.

Each entry in the index is located by a page number and an alphanumeric grid reference on that particular page. The grid is defined by letters, positioned at the top and at the bottom of the map spread, and numbers, shown at the sides of the spread. For example, Bandung in Indonesia has the reference 90 D7. It can thus be found on page 90 in the grid square D7.

Where two identical names are referenced to the same page and grid square, it should be noted that they relate to different adjacent features. For example, the name Avon appears twice in the index and in both cases it is referenced to 52 E3. These two entries locate firstly the county of Avon and secondly the River Avon.

Name	Page	Grid
Ad Dammam	97	K3
Ad Darb	96	F8
Ad Dawadimi	96	G4
Ad Dawhah	97	K4
Ad Dila	97	K7
Ad Dilam	96	H5
Ad Diriyah	96	H4
Ad Duwaniyah	94	G6
Ad Duwayd	96	F1
Adel	124	C6
Adelaide *Antarctic*	141	V5
Adelaide *Australia*	113	H5
Adelaide *Bahamas*	129	P8
Adelaide Island	141	V5
Adelaide Peninsula	120	G4
Aden	96	G10
Aden, Gulf of	103	J5
Adh Dhayd	97	M4
Adi	114	A2
Adi Ark'ay	96	C10
Adi Dairo	96	D9
Adige	68	C3
Adigrat	96	D9
Adiguzel Baraji	76	C3
Adi Keyah	96	D9
Adilabad	92	E5
Adilcevaz	77	K3
Adin	122	D7
Adirondack Mountains	125	N4
Adis Abeba	103	G6
Adi Ugri	96	D9
Adiyaman	77	H4
Adjud	73	J2
Adjuntas, Presa de las	131	K6
Adka	118	Ac9
Adlington	55	G3
Admello	68	C2
Admiralty Gulf	112	F1
Admiralty Inlet	120	J3
Admiralty Island *Canada*	119	Q2
Admiralty Island *U.S.A.*	118	J4
Admiralty Islands	114	D2
Admund Ringnes Island	120	G2
Ado-Ekiti	105	G4
Adonara	91	G7
Adoni	92	E5
Adorf	70	E3
Adoumaoua, Massif de l'	105	H4
Adour	65	C7
Adra	66	E4
Adrano	69	E7
Adrar	100	E3
Adre	102	D5
Adria	68	D3
Adrian *Michigan, U.S.A.*	124	J6
Adrian *Texas, U.S.A.*	127	L3
Adriatic Sea	68	E4
Adwa	96	D9
Adwick le Street	55	H3
Adycha	85	P3
Adzhima	88	G1
Adzvavom	78	K2
Aegean Sea	75	H3
Afafura, Laut	91	K7
Afanasevo	78	J4
Affobakka	137	F3
Affric	56	C3
Afghanistan	92	B2
Afgooye	107	J2
Afif	96	F5
Afikpo	105	G4
Afmadow	107	H2
Afognak Island	118	E4
Afon Efyrnwy	52	D2
Afrin	77	G4
Afsin	77	G3
Afyon	76	D3
Agadez	101	G5
Agadir	100	D2
Agadyr	86	C2
Agaie	105	G4
Agalta, Sierra de	132	E7
Agano	89	G7
Agapa *Russia*	84	D2
Agapa *Russia*	84	D2
Agapitovo	84	D3
Agartala	93	H4
Agaruut	87	K3
Agats	114	B3
Agatti	92	D6
Agattu Island	118	Aa9
Agbaja	105	G4
Agboville	104	E4
Agdam	94	H2
Agde	65	E7
Agematsu	89	F8
Agen	65	D6
Aghada	59	F9
Agha Jari	95	J6
Agiabampo, Estero de	130	E4
Agin	77	H3
Agira	69	E7
Aglasun	76	D4
Agnanda	75	F4
Agno	68	C3
Agnone	69	E5
Agout	65	D7
Agra	92	E3
Agram	72	C3
Agreda	67	F2
Agri	69	F5
Agri	77	K3
Agrigento	69	D7
Agrinion	75	F3
Agropoli	69	E5
Agua Clara	138	F4
Aguadas	136	B2
Aguadilla	133	P5
Aguanaval	130	H5
Agua Prieta	127	H5
Aguascalientes	130	H7
Agua, Volcan de	132	B7
Aguelhok	100	F5
Aguemour	101	F3
Aguilar de Campoo	66	D1
Aguilas	67	F4
Aguja, Cabo de la	133	K9
Aguja, Punta	136	A5
Agulhas, Kaap	108	D6
Agusan	91	H4
Ahar	94	H2
Aheim	62	A5
Ahimahasoa	109	J4
Ahipara Bay	115	D1
Ahititi	115	E3
Ahlat	77	K3
Ahmadabad	92	D4
Ahmadi	95	N8
Ahmadnagar	92	D5
Ahmadpur	92	D3
Ahmar Mountains	103	H6
Ahoskie	129	P2
Ahram	95	K7
Ahtari	62	L5
Ahtarinjarvi	62	L5
Ahuachapan	132	C8
Ahvaz	94	J6
Ahvenanmaa	63	H6
Ahwar	96	H10
Aiddejavrre	62	K2
Aidhipsos	75	G3
Aigen	68	D1
Aigues	65	F6
Aiken	129	M4
Ailao Shan	93	K4
Ailsa Craig	57	C5
Aim	85	N5
Aimores, Serra dos	138	H3
Ain	65	F5
Ain Beida	101	G1
Ain Bessem	67	H4
Ain Defla	67	G4
Ain El Hadjel	67	H5
Ain Oulmene	67	J5
Ain Sefra	100	E2
Ainsworth	123	Q6
Aioun el Atrouss	100	D5
Aiquile	138	C3
Air	101	G5
Airbangis	90	B5
Airdrie	57	E5
Aire *France*	64	F4
Aire *U.K.*	55	J3
Airedale	55	H3
Aire-sur-l'Adour	65	C7
Air Force Island	120	M4
Airgin Sum	87	L3
Airi-selka	62	L3
Aisne	64	E4
Aitape	114	C2
Aith	56	F1
Aix-en-Provence	65	F7
Aix-les-Bains	65	F6
Aiyina	75	G4
Aiyinion	75	G2
Aiyion	75	G3
Aizawl	93	H4
Aizpute	63	J8
Aizu-Wakamatsu	89	G7
Ajaccio	69	B5
Ajana	112	C4
Ajanta Range	92	E4
Ajdabiya	101	K2
Ajlun	94	B5
Ajman	97	M4
Ajmer	92	D3
Akaishi-sanchi	89	G8
Akalkot	92	E5
Akamkpa	105	G4
Akaroa Head	115	D5
Akbou	67	J4
Akbulak	79	K5
Akcaabat	77	H2
Akcaakale	77	H4
Akcadag	77	G3
Akcakoca	76	D2
Akcaova	76	C4
Akcay	76	C4
Akchatau	86	C2
Ak Daglari	76	C4
Akdagmadeni	77	F3
Ak Dovurak	84	E6
Akershus	63	D6
Akeshir Golu	76	D3
Aketi	106	D2
Akgevir	77	J4
Akhalkalaki	77	K2
Akhaltsikhe	77	K2
Akhdar, Al Jabal al	101	K2
Akhdar, Jabal	97	N5
Akhdar, Wadi	96	C3
Akheloos	75	F3
Akhiok	118	E4
Akhisar	76	B3
Akhmim	103	F2
Akhtubinsk	79	H6
Akhtyrka	79	E5
Aki	89	D9
Akimiski Island	121	K7
Akincilar	77	H2
Akinkeen	59	D9
Akinli	77	J4
Akita	88	H6
Akjoujt	100	C5
Akkavare	62	J3
Akkeshi	88	K4
Akko	94	B5
Akkoy	76	B4
Akkus	77	G2
Aklavik	118	H2
Akniste	63	L8
Akola	92	E4
Akonolinga	105	H5
Akordat	96	C9
Akot	92	E4
Akpatok Island	121	N5
Akpinar	76	E3
Akqi	86	D3
Akranes	62	T12
Akron	125	K6
Aksar	77	K2
Aksaray	76	E3
Aksay *China*	86	G4
Aksay *Kazakhstan*	79	J5
Aksehir	76	D3
Akseki	76	D4
Aksenovo-Zilovskoye	85	K6
Aks-e Rostam	95	M7
Aksha	85	J6
Akshimrau	79	J7
Aksu *China*	86	E3
Aksu *Turkey*	76	D4
Aksu *Kazakhstan*	79	J5
Aksu Cayi	76	D4
Aksum	96	D9
Aksumbe	86	B3
Aktau	84	A6
Akti	75	H2
Aktogay	86	D2
Akulivik	120	L5
Akune	89	C9
Akun Island	118	Ae9
Akure	105	G4
Akureyri	62	V12
Akuse	104	F4
Akutan Island	118	Ae9
Akwanga	105	G4
Akyab	93	H4
Akyatan Golu	76	F4
Akyazi	76	D2
Akyurt	76	E2
Akzhar	86	C3
Al Aaiun	100	C3
Alabama *U.S.A.*	129	J4
Alabama *U.S.A.*	129	J4
Alaca	76	F2
Alacahan	77	G3
Alacam	77	F2
Alacam Daglari	76	C3
Alacran, Arrecife	131	Q6
Alagoas	137	K5
Alagoinhas	137	K6
Alagon *Spain*	66	C2
Alagon *Spain*	67	F2
Al Ahmadi	97	J2
Al Ajaiz	97	N7
Alajarvi	62	K5
Alajuela	132	E9
Alakanuk	118	C3
Alakol, Ozero	86	E2
Alakyla	62	L3
Al Amarah	94	H6
Alameda *California, U.S.A.*	126	A2
Alameda *New Mexico, U.S.A.*	127	J3
Alamicamba	132	E8
Alamo	126	E2
Alamogordo	127	K4
Alamos	127	H7
Alamosa	127	K2
Aland	63	H6
Alands hav	63	M6
Alanya	76	E4
Alaotra, Lake	109	J3
Alapayevsk	84	Ad5
Al Aqulah	97	J5
Alarcon, Embalse de	66	E3
Al Artawiyah	96	G3
Alasehir	76	C3
Al Ashkhirah	97	P6
Alaska	118	E3
Alaska, Gulf of	118	F4
Alaska Peninsula	118	Af8
Alaska Range	118	E3
Alassio	68	B4
Alatna	118	E2
Alatyr	78	H5
Alausi	136	B4
Alaverdi	77	L2
Alavus	62	K5
Al Ayn	97	M4
Alayor	67	J3
Alayskiy Khrebet	86	C4
Al Azamiyah	77	L6
Alazeya	85	S2
Alba	68	B3
Al Bab	77	G4
Albacete	67	F3
Alba de Tormes	66	D2
Al Badi	96	H5
Al Badi	77	J5
Alba Iulia	73	G2
Albak	63	D8
Alba, Mount	115	B6
Albanel, Lake	121	M7
Albania	74	E2
Albano	137	F4
Albany *Australia*	112	D5
Albany *Canada*	121	K7
Albany *Georgia, U.S.A.*	129	K5
Albany *Kentucky, U.S.A.*	124	H8
Albany *New York, U.S.A.*	125	P5
Albany *Oregon, U.S.A.*	122	C5
Albarracin	67	F2
Al Basrah	94	H6
Albatross Bay	113	J1
Albatross Point	115	E3
Al Bayda	96	G10
Albayrak	77	L3
Albemarle	129	M3
Albemarle Island	136	A7
Albemarle Sound	129	P2
Albenga	68	B3
Albentosa	67	F2
Alberche	66	D2
Alberga	113	G4
Albergaria-a-Velha	66	B2
Alberique	67	F3
Albert	64	E3
Alberta	119	M5
Albert Edward, Mount	114	D3
Albert Kanaal	64	F3
Albert, Lake	107	F2
Albert Lea	124	D5
Albert Nile	107	F2
Albertville *France*	65	G6
Albertville *Zaire*	107	E4
Albi	65	E7
Albina	137	G2
Al Bir	96	C2
Al Birk	96	E7
Albocacer	67	G2
Albo, Monti	69	B5
Alboran, Isla de	66	E5
Alborg	63	D8
Alborg Bugt	63	D8
Alborz, Reshteh-ye Kuhta ye	95	K3
Albro	113	K3
Albufeira	66	B4
Albu Gharz, Sabkhat	77	J5
Albuquerque	127	J3
Al Buraymi	97	M4
Albury	113	K6
Al Busayyah	94	H6
Al Buzun	97	K9
Alcacer do Sal	66	B3
Alcala de Henares	66	E2
Alcamo	69	D7
Alcanices	66	C2
Alcaniz	67	F2
Alcantara	66	C3
Alcantara	137	J4
Alcantara, Embalse de	66	C3
Alcaraz	66	E3
Alcaraz, Sierra de	66	E3
Alcaudete	66	D4
Alcazar de San Juan	66	E3
Alcester	53	F2
Alcolea del Pinar	66	E2
Alcoutim	66	C4
Alcoy	67	F3
Alcubierre, Sierra de	67	F2
Alcublas	67	F3
Alcudia	67	H3
Aldabra Islands	82	C7
Aldama	131	K6
Aldan *Russia*	85	M5
Aldan *Russia*	85	N4
Aldanskoye Nagorye	85	M5
Alde	53	J2
Aldeburgh	53	J2
Aldeia Nova	66	C4
Alderley Edge	55	G3
Alderney	53	M6
Aldershot	53	G3
Aldridge	53	F2
Aleg	100	C5
Alegrete	138	E5
Aleksandra, Mys	85	P6
Aleksandriya	79	E6
Aleksandrov	78	F4
Aleksandrovac	73	F4
Aleksandrov Gay	79	H5
Aleksandrovsk	78	K4
Aleksandrovskoye	79	G7
Aleksandrovsk-Sakhalinskiy	85	Q6
Aleksandry, Ostrov	80	F1
Alekseyevka *Kazakhstan*	84	A6
Alekseyevka *Russia*	79	F5
Aleksin	78	F5
Alem Paraiba	138	H4
Alencon	64	D4
Alenquer	137	G4
Alentejo	66	C3
Alenuihaha Channel	126	S10
Aleppo	77	G4
Aleria	69	B4
Alerta	136	C6
Ales	65	F6
Aleshki	78	H2
Alessandria	68	B3
Alessio	74	E2
Alesund	62	B5

Name	Pg	Ref
Aleutian Islands	118	Ab9
Aleutian Range	118	D4
Aleutian Trench	143	H3
Alevina, Mys	85	S5
Alexander Archipelago	118	J4
Alexander Bay	108	C5
Alexander, Cape	119	P2
Alexander City	129	K4
Alexander Island	141	V4
Alexander, Kap	120	M2
Alexandra *Australia*	113	K6
Alexandra *New Zealand*	115	B6
Alexandretta	77	G4
Alexandria *Egypt*	102	E1
Alexandria *Romania*	73	H4
Alexandria *South Africa*	108	E6
Alexandria *U.K.*	57	D5
Alexandria *Louisiana, U.S.A.*	128	F5
Alexandria *Minnesota, U.S.A.*	124	C4
Alexandria *Virginia, U.S.A.*	125	M7
Alexandroupolis	75	H2
Aleysk	84	C6
Al Fallujah	77	K6
Alfambra *Spain*	67	F2
Alfambra *Spain*	67	F2
Alfaro	136	B4
Alfatar	73	J4
Al Faw	94	J7
Alfeld	70	C3
Alfios	75	F4
Alford *Grampian, U.K.*	56	F3
Alford *Lincolnshire, U.K.*	55	K3
Alfreton	55	H3
Al Fuhayhil	97	J2
Al Fujayrah	97	N4
Al Fuqaha	101	J3
Al Furat	77	J5
Algard	63	A7
Algarrobo del Aguila	139	C7
Algarve	66	B4
Algatart	86	C3
Algeciras	66	D4
Algena	96	D8
Alger, Baie d	67	H4
Algeria	101	F3
Al Ghaydah	97	L8
Alghero	69	B5
Algiers	101	F1
Algoa Bay	108	E6
Algodoes	137	K5
Algodonales	66	D4
Algona	124	C5
Algonquin Park	125	L4
Algueirao	109	F4
Al Hadd	97	P5
Al Hadithah	94	F4
Al Hadr	77	K5
Al Halfayah	94	H6
Al Hallaniyah	97	N8
Al Hamar	96	H5
Alhambra	66	E3
Al Hanakiyah	96	E4
Al Hariq	96	H5
Al Hasa	97	J3
Al Hasakah	77	J4
Al Hashimiyah	94	G5
Al Hawtah	96	H9
Al Hayy	94	H5
Al Hillah *Iraq*	94	G5
Al Hillah *Saudi Arabia*	96	H5
Al Hilwah	96	H5
Al Hudaydah	96	F9
Al Hufuf	96	J4
Al Huraydah	97	J9
Aliabad	94	H4
Aliabad	95	M7
Aliaga	76	B3
Aliaga	67	F2
Aliakmon	75	G2
Ali al Gharbi	94	H5
Alibag	92	D5
Alibey, Ozero	73	L3
Alibunar	73	F3
Alicante	67	F3
Alice	128	C7
Alice, Punta	69	F6
Alice Springs	113	G3
Aligarh	92	E3
Aligudarz	95	K6
Alijuq, Kuh-e	95	K6
Al Ikhwan	97	N10
Alima	106	C3
Alindao	102	D6
Alingsas	63	E8
Alipka	84	D5
Al Isawiyah	94	C6
Alisos	126	G5
Alistati	75	G2
Aliwal North	108	E6
Al Jaghbub	101	K2
Al Jahrah	97	H2
Al Jawarah	97	N7
Al Jawf *Libya*	101	K4
Al Jawf *Saudi Arabia*	96	D2
Al Jazirah	77	J4
Al Jubayl	97	J3
Aljustrel	66	B4
Al Kalban	97	P6
Al Kamil	97	P5
Al Khaburah	97	N5
Al Khalis	94	G5
Al Khaluf	97	P6
Al Khasab	97	N3
Al Khatt	97	N4
Al Khawr	97	K4
Al Khubar	97	K3
Al Khufrah	101	K4
Al Khums	101	H2
Al Khuraybah	97	J9
Al Khuwayr	97	K3
Alkmaar	64	F2
Al Kufah	94	G5
Al Kut	94	G5
Al Kuwayt	97	H2
Allada	105	F4
Al Ladhiqiyah	77	F5
Allahabad	92	F3
Allahuekber Daglari	77	K2
Allakh-Yun	85	P4
Allanmyo	93	J5
Allanridge	108	E5
Allaqi, Wadi	103	F3
Allariz	66	C1
Alldays	108	E4
Allegheny	125	L6
Allegheny Mountains	124	J8
Allegheny Plateau	125	K7
Allen *Philippines*	91	G3
Allen *U.K.*	52	C4
Allen, Bog of	59	H6
Allendale	129	M4
Allende	127	M6
Allen, Lough	58	F4
Allenstein	71	J2
Allentown	125	N6
Alleppey	92	E7
Aller	70	D2
Allerston	55	J2
Allevard	65	G6
Allgauer Alpen	68	C2
Alliance *Nebraska, U.S.A.*	123	N6
Alliance *Ohio, U.S.A.*	125	K6
Allier	65	E5
Allik	121	Q6
Al Lith	96	E6
Alloa	57	E4
Al Luhayyah	96	F9
Allur	92	F6
Alma *Canada*	125	Q2
Alma *Michigan, U.S.A.*	124	H5
Alma *Nebraska, U.S.A.*	123	Q7
Alma-Ata	86	D3
Almaciles	66	E4
Almada	66	B3
Al Maddah	96	F7
Almaden	66	D3
Al Madinah	96	D4
Almagro	66	E3
Al Mahmudiyah	94	G5
Al Majmaah	96	G4
Almalyk	86	B3
Al Manamah	97	K3
Almanor, Lake	122	D7
Almansa	67	F3
Al Mansuriyah	96	F9
Almanzor, Pic de	66	D2
Al Mariyah	97	L5
Al Marj	101	K2
Al Masnaah	97	N5
Al Mawsil	77	K4
Al Mayadin	77	J5
Al Mayyah	96	F3
Almazan	66	E2
Almeirim	137	G4
Almelo	64	G2
Almendra, Embalse de	66	C2
Almeria	66	E4
Almeria, Golfo de	66	E4
Almetyevsk	78	J5
Almhult	63	F8
Al Midhnab	96	G4
Almina, Punta	66	D5
Al Miqdadiyah	94	G5
Almiropotamos	75	H3
Almiros	75	G3
Almirou, Kolpos	75	H5
Al Mishab	96	J3
Almodovar	66	B4
Almond	57	E4
Almonte	66	D3
Almora	92	E3
Al Mubarraz	97	J4
Al Mudawwara	94	B7
Al Mudaybi	97	P5
Al Mudayrib	97	P5
Al Muharraq	97	K3
Al Mukalla	97	J9
Al Mukha	96	F10
Almuradiel	66	E3
Al Musaymir	96	G10
Al Musayyib	94	G5
Almus Baraji	77	G2
Al Muwayh	96	E5
Al Muwaylih	96	B3
Aln	57	G5
Alness	56	D3
Alnwick	55	H1
Alofi	111	T4
Alor	91	G7
Alora	66	D4
Alor, Kepulauan	91	G7
Alotau	114	E4
Alpe-d'Huez	65	G6
Alpena	124	J4
Alpercatas, Serra das	137	J5
Alpine *Arizona, U.S.A.*	127	H4
Alpine *Texas, U.S.A.*	127	L5
Alps	50	J6
Alpu	76	D3
Al Qaffay	97	K4
Al Qaim	77	J5
Al Qalibah	96	C2
Al Qamishli	94	E3
Al Qaryatayn	77	G5
Al Qatif	97	J3
Al Qatn	97	J9
Al Qaysumah	96	H2
Al Qubbah	101	K2
Alqueva, Barragem de	66	C3
Alquippa	125	K6
Al Qunfudhah	96	E7
Al Qurayni	97	L6
Al Qurayyat	97	P5
Al Qurnah	94	H6
Al Qutayfah	94	C5
Al Quwayiyah	96	G4
Al Quzah	97	J9
Al Ramadi	77	K6
Als	70	C1
Alsace	64	G4
Alsask	123	K2
Alsasua	67	E1
Alsek	118	H4
Alsfeld	70	C3
Alsh, Loch	56	C3
Alsten	62	E4
Alstermo	63	F8
Alston	55	G2
Alta	62	P2
Altaelv	62	K2
Altafjord	62	K1
Alta Gracia	138	D6
Altagracia	133	M9
Altai	86	G2
Altamaha	129	M5
Altamira	137	G4
Altamira	69	F5
Altamura	69	F5
Altamura, Isla de	130	E5
Alta, Sierra	67	C2
Altay *Russia*	84	Ae4
Altay *China*	86	F2
Altay *Mongolia*	86	H2
Altdorf	68	B2
Altenburg	70	E3
Altinekin	76	E3
Altinhisar	76	F3
Altinkaya	76	D4
Altin Kopru	77	L5
Altinova	76	B3
Altinozu	77	G4
Altintas	76	D3
Altkirche	65	G5
Altmark	70	D2
Altmuhl	70	D4
Altnaharra	56	D2
Alto Araguaia	138	F3
Alto Coite	138	F3
Alto Molocue	109	G3
Alton *Hampshire, U.K.*	53	G3
Alton *Staffordshire, U.K.*	53	F2
Altoona	125	L6
Alto Sucuriu	138	F3
Altrincham	55	G3
Altun Shan	92	F1
Alturas	122	D7
Al Ubaylah	97	K6
Alucra	77	H2
Aluksne	63	M8
Al Ula	96	C3
Alumine	139	B7
Al Uqayr	97	K4
Alur Setar	90	C4
Al Uwayja	96	G5
Alva	128	C2
Alvarado	131	M8
Alvaro Obregon	131	N8
Alvdal	63	H5
Alvdalen	63	F6
Alvito	66	C3
Alvorada	137	H6
Alvsborg	63	E8
Alvsbyn	62	J4
Al Wajh	96	C3
Al Wakrah	97	K4
Alwar	92	E3
Alwen Reservoir	55	F3
Alwinton	57	F5
Al Wusayl	97	K4
Alyaskitovyy	85	Q4
Alyat	94	J2
Alyth, Forest of	57	E4
Alytus	71	L1
Alzamay	84	F5
Amadeus, Lake	112	G3
Amadiyah	77	K4
Amadjuak Lake	120	M5
Amagasaki	89	E8
Amager	63	E9
Amahai	91	H6
Amakusa-Shimo-shima	89	C9
Amal	63	E7
Amalfi	69	E5
Amalias	75	F4
Amalner	92	E4
Amami-O-shima	89	B11
Amami-shoto	89	J10
Amandola	69	D4
Amantea	69	F6
Amanzimtoti	108	F6
Amapa	137	G3
Amapa	137	G3
Amarante	66	B2
Amarapura	93	J4
Amargosa	126	D3
Amarillo	127	M3
Amaro	69	E4
Amasiya	77	K2
Amasra	76	E2
Amasya	77	F2
Amatignak Island	118	Ac9
Amatrice	69	D4
Amazon	137	G4
Amazonas	137	G4
Amazon, Mouths of the	137	G4
Ambala	92	E2
Ambalavao	109	J4
Ambanja	109	J2
Ambar	84	E3
Ambarchik	85	U3
Ambarnyy	78	E2
Ambato	136	B4
Ambato-Boeny	109	J3
Ambatolampy	109	J3
Amberg	70	D4
Ambergris Cay	132	D5
Amberieu-en-Bugey	65	F6
Ambert	65	E6
Ambikapur	92	F4
Ambilobe	109	J2
Amble-by-the-Sea	55	H1
Ambleside	55	G2
Ambodifototra	109	J3
Amboise	65	D5
Ambon *Indonesia*	91	H6
Ambon *Indonesia*	91	H6
Ambositra	109	J4
Ambovombe	109	J5
Ambriz	106	B4
Ambrym	114	U12
Amchitka Island	118	Ab9
Amchitka Pass	118	Ab9
Amdassa	91	J7
Amderma	84	Ad3
Amdo	93	H2
Ameca	130	G7
Amecameca	131	K8
Amendolara	69	F6
Ameralik	120	R5
American	122	D8
American Falls Reservoir	122	H6
American Samoa	111	U4
Americus	129	K4
Amersham	53	G3
Amery Ice Shelf	141	E5
Ames	124	D5
Amesbury	53	F3
Amfiklia	75	G3
Amfilokhia	75	F3
Amfipolis	75	G2
Amfissa	75	G3
Amga *Russia*	85	N4
Amga *Russia*	85	N4
Amgu	88	F3
Amguema	85	Y3
Amgun	85	P6
Amherst *Canada*	121	P8
Amherst *U.S.A.*	125	L8
Amiata, Monte	69	C4
Amiens	64	E4
Amikino	85	L6
Amilhayt, Wadi al	97	L7
Amindivi Islands	92	D6
Amirante Islands	82	D7
Amistad Reservoir	127	M6
Amitioke Peninsula	120	K4
Amka	85	Q5
Amland	64	F2
Amlia Island	118	Ad9
Amlwch	55	E3
Amman	94	B6
Ammanford	52	C3
Ammer	70	D4
Ammersee	70	D5
Amol	95	L3
Amorgos *Greece*	75	H4
Amorgos *Greece*	75	J4
Amos	125	L2
Amot *Buskerud, Norway*	63	C7
Amot *Telemark, Norway*	63	C7
Amotfors	63	E7
Ampana	91	G6
Ampanihy	109	H4
Ampato, Nevado de	138	B3
Amposta	67	G2
Ampthill	53	G2
Amqui	125	S2
Amran	96	F9
Amravati	92	E4
Amritsar	92	D2
Amroha	92	E3
Amrum	70	C1
Amsterdam *Netherlands*	64	F2
Amsterdam *U.S.A.*	125	N5
Am Timan	102	D5
Amuay	133	M9
Amundsen Glacier	141	P1
Amundsen-Scott	141	A1
Amundsen Sea	141	S5
Amuntai	90	F6
Amur *China*	87	N1
Amur *Russia*	85	Q6
Amuri Pass	115	D5
Amursk	85	P6
Amurskaya Oblast	85	M6
Amur, Wadi	103	F4

Name	Page	Ref
Auburn *Indiana, U.S.A.*	124	H6
Auburn *Maine, U.S.A.*	125	Q4
Auburn *Nebraska, U.S.A.*	124	C6
Auburn *New York, U.S.A.*	125	M5
Aubusson	65	E6
Auca Mahuida	139	C7
Auce	63	K8
Auch	65	D7
Auchavan	57	E4
Auchengray	57	E5
Auchterarder	57	E4
Auckland	115	E2
Auckland Islands	141	M8
Aude	65	E7
Auderville	64	C4
Audierne, Baie 'd	65	A5
Aue	70	E3
Augher	58	H4
Aughnacloy	58	J4
Aughrim *Galway, Ireland*	59	F6
Aughrim *Wicklow, Ireland*	59	K7
Aughton	55	H3
Augsburg	70	D4
Augusta *Australia*	112	D5
Augusta *Georgia, U.S.A.*	129	M4
Augusta *Italy*	69	E7
Augusta *Kansas, U.S.A.*	128	D2
Augusta *Maine, U.S.A.*	125	R4
Augusta *Montana, U.S.A.*	122	H4
Augustine Island	118	E4
Augustow	71	K2
Augustus, Mount	112	D3
Auletta	69	E5
Aulia	103	F4
Aulitiving Island	120	N4
Aulne	64	B4
Aultbea	56	C3
Aumont	65	E6
Aupalak	121	N6
Aurangabad	92	E5
Auray	65	B5
Aurdal	63	C6
Aure *Norway*	62	B5
Aure *Norway*	62	C5
Aurich	70	B2
Aurillac	65	E6
Aurkuning	90	E6
Aurora *Colorado, U.S.A.*	123	M8
Aurora *Illinois, U.S.A.*	124	F6
Aurora *Missouri, U.S.A.*	124	D8
Aurora *Nebraska, U.S.A.*	123	R7
Au Sable	124	J4
Auskerry Sound	56	F1
Aust-Agder	63	D7
Austin *Minnesota, U.S.A.*	124	D5
Austin *Nevada, U.S.A.*	126	D1
Austin *Texas, U.S.A.*	128	D5
Austin, Lake	112	D4
Australia	110	F6
Australian Capital Territory	113	K6
Austria	68	D2
Austurhorn	62	X12
Autazes	136	F4
Authie	64	D3
Autlan	130	G8
Autun	65	F5
Auvergne *Australia*	112	G2
Auvergne *France*	65	E6
Auxerre	65	E5
Avallon	65	E5
Avanos	76	F3
Avare	138	G4
Avas	75	H2
Avcilar	76	C2
Avebury	53	F3
Aveiro *Portugal*	66	B2
Aveiro *Portugal*	66	B2
Avellino	69	E5
Avelon Peninsula	121	R8
Aversa	69	E5
Aves, Isla de	133	R7
Avesnes	64	E3
Avesta	63	G6
Aveyron	65	E6
Avezzano	69	D4
Avgo	75	H5
Aviemore	57	E3
Aviemore, Lake	115	C6
Avigliano	69	E5
Avignon	65	F7
Avila	66	D2
Avila, Sierra de	66	D2
Aviles	66	D1
Avisio	68	C2
Aviz	66	C3
Avlum	63	C8
Avoca *Australia*	113	J6
Avoca *Iowa, U.S.A.*	124	C6
Avola	69	E7
Avon *Devon, U.K.*	52	D4
Avon *Hampshire, U.K.*	53	F4
Avon *U.K.*	52	E3
Avon *U.K.*	52	E3
Avonmouth	52	E3
Avon Park	129	M7
Avon Water	57	D5
Avranches	64	C4
Avrig	73	H3
Avuavu	114	K6
Awaji-shima	89	E8
Awali	97	K3
Awanui	115	D1
Awarik, Uruq al	96	H7
Awarua Point	115	A6
Awa-shima	89	G6
Awash Wenz	103	H5
Awaso	104	E4
Awatere	115	D4
Awbari	101	H3
Aweil	102	E6
Awe, Loch	57	C4
Awful, Mount	115	B6
Awgu	105	G4
Awjilah	101	K2
Axbridge	52	E3
Axe *Dorset, U.K.*	52	E4
Axe *Somerset, U.K.*	52	E3
Axel-Heiberg Island	120	H2
Axim	104	E5
Axios	75	G2
Ax-les-Thermes	65	D7
Axminster	52	D4
Ayabe	89	E8
Ayacucho *Argentina*	139	E7
Ayacucho *Peru*	136	C6
Ayaguz	86	F2
Ayamonte	66	C4
Ayan *Russia*	84	H5
Ayan *Russia*	85	P5
Ayancik	76	F2
Ayas	76	E3
Ayaviri	136	C6
Ayayei	96	C10
Aya-Yenahin	104	E4
Aybasti	77	G2
Aydarkul , Ozero	86	B3
Aydere	95	N2
Aydin	76	B4
Aydinca	77	G2
Aydincik	76	E4
Aydin Daglari	76	C3
Ayerbe	67	F1
Ayers Rock	112	G4
Ayeshka	84	E6
Ayia Anna	75	G3
Ayia Marina	75	J5
Ayios	75	G4
Ayios Andreas	75	G4
Ayios Evstratios	75	H3
Ayios Kirikos	75	J4
Ayios Nikolaos *Greece*	75	F3
Ayios Nikolaos *Greece*	75	H5
Ayios Petros	75	F3
Aykathonisi	75	J4
Aykhal	84	J3
Aylesbury	53	G3
Ayllon	66	E2
Aylmer, Lake	119	P3
Aylsham	53	J2
Ayn al Bayda	77	G5
Ayni	86	B4
Ayn Tarfawi	77	K5
Ayn, Wadi al	97	M5
Ayod	102	F6
Ayon	85	V3
Ayon, Ostrov	85	V3
Ayora	67	F3
Ayr *U.K.*	57	D5
Ayr *U.K.*	57	D5
Ayranci	76	E4
Ayre, Point of	54	E2
Aysgarth	55	H2
Ayshirak	86	C2
Aytos	73	J4
Ayun	97	L8
Ayutthaya	93	K6
Ayvacik	76	B3
Ayvali	76	D4
Azambuja	66	B3
Azamgarh	92	F3
Azaran	94	H3
Azaz	77	G4
Azazga	67	J4
Azbine	101	G5
Azerbaijan	79	H7
Azezo	96	C10
Azogues	136	B4
Azoum	102	D5
Azov, Sea of	79	F6
Azovskoye More	79	F6
Azpeitia	66	E1
Azraq, Bahr el	103	F5
Azrou	100	D2
Aztec	127	H2
Azuaga	66	D3
Azuari	137	G3
Azuero, Peninsula de	132	G11
Azul *Argentina*	139	E7
Azul *Mexico*	131	Q9
Azul, Cordillera	136	B5
Azur, Cote d'	65	G7
Azvaday	76	E2
Az Zabadani	77	G6
Az Zafir	96	E7
Az Zahran	97	K3
Az Zarqa	97	L4
Az Zawiyah	101	H2
Az Zaydiyah	96	F9
Az Zilfi	96	G3
Az Zubaydiyah	94	G5
Az Zubayr	94	H6
Az Zuhrah	96	F9
Az Zuqur	96	F9

B

Name	Page	Ref
Baaba	114	W16
Baalbek	77	G5
Baamonde	66	C1
Baardheere	107	H2
Babadag	73	K3
Babaeski	76	B2
Babahoyo	136	B4
Babai Gaxun	87	J3
Baba, Koh-i-	92	C2
Babar	91	H7
Babar, Kepulauan	91	H7
Babayevo	78	F4
Babbacombe Bay	52	D4
Babelthuap	91	J4
Babine Lake	118	K5
Babo	114	A2
Babol	95	L3
Babol Sar	95	L3
Baboua	102	B6
Babstovo	88	D1
Babushkin	84	H6
Babuyan *Philippines*	91	F4
Babuyan *Philippines*	91	G2
Babuyan Channel	91	G2
Babuyan Islands	91	G2
Bacabal	137	J4
Bacan	91	H6
Bacau	73	J2
Baccegalhaldde	62	J2
Back	119	R2
Backa	63	E6
Backaland	56	F1
Backa Topola	72	E3
Backe	62	G5
Bac Ninh	93	L4
Bacolod	91	G3
Bacup	55	G3
Badagara	92	E6
Badajoz	66	C3
Badalona	67	H2
Badanah	94	E6
Bad Aussee	68	D2
Badby	53	F2
Bad Doberan	70	D1
Bad Ems	70	B3
Baden	68	B2
Baden-Baden	70	C4
Badenoch	57	D4
Badgastein	68	D2
Bad Homburg	70	C3
Badiet esh Sham	94	D5
Bad Ischl	68	D2
Bad Kissingen	70	D3
Bad Kreuznach	70	B4
Bad Lands	123	N4
Bad Mergentheim	70	C4
Badminton	52	E3
Bad Neustadt	70	D3
Bad Oldesloe	70	D2
Ba Don	93	L5
Badong	93	M2
Badrah	94	G5
Badr Hunayn	96	D5
Bad Segeberg	70	D2
Bad Tolz	70	D5
Badulla	92	F7
Bad Wildungen	70	C3
Badzhal	85	N6
Badzhalskiy Khrebet	85	N6
Bae Can	93	L4
Baena	66	D4
Baeza	136	B4
Bafa Golu	76	B4
Bafang	105	H4
Bafata	104	C3
Baffin Bay *Canada*	120	N3
Baffin Bay *U.S.A.*	128	D7
Baffin Island	120	L3
Bafia	105	H5
Bafing Makana	100	C6
Bafoulabe	100	C6
Bafoussam	105	H4
Bafq	95	M6
Bafra	77	F2
Bafra Burun	77	F2
Baft	95	N7
Bafwasende	106	E2
Bagamoya	107	G4
Bagan Datuk	90	C5
Bagansiapiapi	90	C5
Baganyuvam	78	K2
Bagaryak	84	Ad5
Bagdad	126	F3
Bagdere	77	J3
Bage	138	F6
Bagenalstown	59	J7
Baggs	123	L7
Baghdad	77	L6
Bagherhat	93	G4
Bagheria	69	D6
Baghlan	92	C1
Bagh nam Faoileann	56	A3
Bagneres-de-Bigorre	65	D7
Bagneres-de-Luchon	65	D7
Bagnoles-de-l'Orne	64	C4
Bagnolo Mella	68	C3
Bagoe	104	D3
Bagrationovsk	71	J1
Bagshot	53	G3
Baguio	91	G2
Bagusa	114	B2
Bahamas	132	J2
Baharampur	93	G4
Bahau	90	C5
Bahaur	90	E6
Bahawalpur	92	D3
Bahce	77	G4
Bahia	137	J6
Bahia Blanca	139	D7
Bahia Bustamante	139	C9
Bahia, Islas de la	132	D6
Bahia Kino	126	G6
Bahia Laura	139	C9
Bahia Negra	138	E4
Bahias, Cabo dos	139	C8
Bahr	96	E7
Bahr, Abu	97	J6
Bahraich	92	F3
Bahrain	97	K3
Bahrain, Gulf of	97	K4
Bahr Sayqal	77	G6
Bahu Kalat	95	Q9
Baia de Maputo	109	F5
Baia Mare	73	G2
Baian, Band-i-	92	C2
Baiao	137	H4
Baiazeh	95	M5
Baicheng *Jilin, China*	87	N2
Baicheng *Xinjiang Uygur Zizhiqu, China*	86	E3
Baie Comeau	125	R2
Baie-du-Poste	121	M7
Baiji	77	K5
Baiju	87	N5
Baikal, Lake	84	H6
Baile Atha Cliath	59	K6
Baile Herculane	73	G3
Bailieborough	58	J5
Baillie Hamilton Island	120	H2
Baillie Island	118	K1
Bailundo	106	C5
Baimuru	114	C3
Bainbridge	129	K5
Bain-de-Bretagne	65	C5
Baing	91	G8
Bains-les-Bains	65	G4
Baird Inlet	118	C3
Baird Mountains	118	C2
Baird Peninsula	120	L4
Bairin Youqi	87	M3
Bairin Zuoqi	87	M3
Bairnsdale	113	K6
Baise	65	D7
Baixingt	87	N3
Baiyanghe	86	F3
Baja	72	E2
Baja, Punta	126	E6
Bajgiran	95	P3
Bajil	96	F9
Bajmok	72	E3
Bakchar	84	C5
Bakel	104	C3
Baker *Chile*	139	B9
Baker *California, U.S.A.*	126	E3
Baker *Montana, U.S.A.*	123	M4
Baker *Oregon, U.S.A.*	122	F5
Baker Foreland	119	S3
Baker Island	111	T1
Baker Lake	119	R3
Baker, Mount	122	D3
Bakersfield	126	C3
Bakewell	55	H3
Bakharden	95	N2
Bakhardok	95	P2
Bakharz	95	P4
Bakhchisaray	79	E7
Bakhmach	79	E5
Bakhta	84	D4
Bakhtaran	94	H4
Bakhtegan, Daryacheh-ye	95	L7
Bakhty	86	F2
Bakinskikh Komissarov	95	M2
Bakir	76	B3
Bakkafjordur	62	X11
Bakkafloi	62	X11
Bakkagerdi	62	Y12
Baklan	76	C4
Bako	103	G6
Bakongan	90	B5
Bakony	72	D2
Bakouma	102	D6
Baku	79	H7
Bakwanga	106	D4
Bala	52	D2
Bala	76	E3
Balabac	91	F4
Balabac Strait	90	F4
Balabio	114	W16
Bala, Cerros de	136	D6
Balacita	73	G3
Balad	77	L6
Baladch	95	K3
Balagannoye	85	R5
Balaghat	92	F4
Balaghat Range	92	E5
Balaguer	67	G2
Balaikarangan	90	E5
Balaka	107	F5
Balakhta	84	E5
Balakleya	79	F6
Balakovo	79	H5
Bala Lake	52	D2
Balama	109	G2
Balambangan	91	F4
Bala Morghab	95	R4
Balangir	92	F4

Name	Page	Grid
Basel	68	A2
Basento	69	F5
Bashakerd, Kuhha-ye	95	P8
Bashi Haixia	87	N7
Basht	95	K6
Basilan *Philippines*	91	G4
Basilan *Philippines*	91	G4
Basildon	53	H3
Basingstoke	53	F3
Baskale	77	L3
Baskatong, Reservoir	125	N3
Baskil	77	H3
Baskoy	77	K2
Basle	68	A2
Basoko	106	D2
Bassano del Grappa	68	C3
Bassar	104	F4
Bassas da India	109	G4
Bassein	93	H5
Bassenthwaite	55	F2
Bassenthwaite Lake	55	F2
Basse Santa Su	104	C3
Basseterre	133	R6
Basse Terre	133	S6
Bassett	123	Q6
Bassila	105	F4
Bass Strait	113	K6
Bastad	63	E8
Bastak	95	M8
Bastam	95	M3
Basti	92	F3
Bastia	69	B4
Bastogne	64	F4
Bastrop *Louisiana, U.S.A.*	128	G4
Bastrop *Texas, U.S.A.*	128	D5
Basyurt	77	J3
Bata	105	G5
Batabano, Golfo de	132	F3
Batagay	85	N3
Batagay-Alyta	85	N3
Batakan	90	E6
Bataklik Golu	76	E4
Batala	92	E2
Batalha	66	B3
Batamay	85	M4
Batan	91	G1
Batang	93	J2
Batangafo	102	C6
Batangas	91	G3
Batanghari	90	C6
Batan Islands	91	G1
Batatais	138	G4
Batavia	125	L5
Bataysk	79	F6
Batchelor	112	G1
Batesville	128	G3
Bath *U.K.*	52	E3
Bath *U.S.A.*	125	M5
Batha	102	C5
Bathgate	57	E5
Bathurst *Australia*	113	K5
Bathurst *Canada*	125	T3
Bathurst *The Gambia*	104	B3
Bathurst Inlet	119	P2
Bathurst Island	112	G1
Bathurst Islands	120	F2
Batie	104	E4
Batiki	114	R8
Batinah, Al	97	N4
Batin, Wadi al	96	H2
Batiscan	125	P3
Batitoroslar	76	D4
Batlaq-e Gavkhuni	95	L5
Batley	55	H3
Batman *Turkey*	77	J4
Batman *Turkey*	77	J4
Batna	101	G1
Baton Rouge	128	G5
Batouri	105	H5
Batroun	77	F5
Batsfjord	62	N1
Battambang	93	K6
Batticaloa	92	F7
Battle *Canada*	119	N5
Battle *U.K.*	53	H4
Battle Creek	124	H5
Battle Harbour	121	Q7
Battle Mountain	122	F7
Batu	103	G6
Batubetumbang	90	D6
Batum	77	J2
Batumi	77	J2
Batu Pahat	90	C5
Batuputih	91	F5
Baturaja	90	D6
Baturite	137	K4
Baubau	91	G7
Bauchi	105	G3
Bauda	92	F4
Baudette	124	C2
Baudo	136	B2
Baudouinville	107	E4
Bauge	65	C5
Bauhinia Downs	113	K3
Baukau	91	H7
Bauld, Cape	121	Q7
Baumann Fjord	120	J2
Baunie	113	L4
Baurtregaum	59	C8
Bauru	138	G4
Baus	138	F3
Bautzen	70	F3
Bawdeswell	53	J2
Bawdsey	53	J2
Bawean	90	E7
Bawiti	102	E2
Bawku	104	E3
Bawtry	55	H3
Baxley	129	L5
Bayamo	132	J4
Bayamon	133	P5
Bayan	88	A2
Bayan-Aul	84	B6
Bayandalay	87	J3
Bayanday	84	H6
Bayan Harshan	93	J2
Bayanhongor	86	J2
Bayan Mod	87	J3
Bayan Obo	87	K3
Bayano, Laguna	132	H10
Bayan-Ondor	86	H3
Bayantsagaan	86	H3
Bayantsogt	87	K2
Bayan-Uul	87	L2
Bayard *Nebraska, U.S.A.*	123	N7
Bayard *New Mexico, U.S.A.*	127	H4
Bayat *Turkey*	76	D3
Bayat *Turkey*	76	F2
Bayburt	77	J2
Bay City *Michigan, U.S.A.*	124	J5
Bay City *Texas, U.S.A.*	128	E6
Baydaratskaya Guba	84	Ae3
Baydhabo	107	H2
Baydon	53	F3
Bayerischer Wald	70	E4
Bayeux	64	C4
Bayfield	124	E3
Bayhan al Qasab	96	G9
Bayindir	76	B3
Baykadam	86	B3
Baykal	84	G6
Baykalovo	84	Ae5
Baykal, Ozero	84	H6
Baykan	77	J3
Bay-Khak	84	E6
Baykit	84	F4
Baynunah	97	L5
Bayombong	91	G2
Bayona	66	B1
Bayonne	65	C7
Bayo Point	91	G3
Bayram-Ali	95	R3
Bayramic	76	B3
Bayramiy	94	J2
Bayramtepe	76	C2
Bayreuth	70	D4
Bayrut	76	F6
Bay Saint Louis	128	H5
Bayt al Faqih	96	F9
Baytown	128	E6
Bayy al Kabir, Wadi	101	H2
Baza	66	E4
Bazaliya	71	M4
Bazar-Dyuzi	79	H7
Bazaruto, Ilha do	109	G4
Bazas	65	C6
Bazman	95	Q8
Bazman, Kuh-e-	95	Q7
Bcharre	77	F5
Beach	123	N4
Beachy Head	53	H4
Beaconsfield	53	G3
Beadnell Bay	55	H1
Beagh, Lough	58	G2
Beagle Gulf	112	G1
Beagle Reef	112	E2
Beal	57	G5
Bealanana	109	J2
Beaminster	52	E4
Beampingaratra	109	J4
Bear	122	J6
Beara Peninsula	59	C9
Beardmore	124	G2
Beardstown	124	E6
Bear Island *Canada*	121	K7
Bear Island *Ireland*	59	C9
Bear Lake	122	J7
Bearley	53	F2
Bearn	65	C7
Bear Paw Mount	122	K3
Bearsden	57	D5
Beartooth Range	123	K5
Beata, Cabo	133	M6
Beata, Isla	133	M6
Beatrice	123	R7
Beatty	126	D2
Beattyville	125	M2
Beau Basin	109	L7
Beaucaire	65	F7
Beaufort *Malaysia*	90	F4
Beaufort *U.S.A.*	129	M4
Beaufort Sea	118	H1
Beaufort West	108	D6
Beaugency	65	D5
Beauly *U.K.*	56	D3
Beauly *U.K.*	56	D3
Beauly Firth	56	D3
Beaumaris	54	E3
Beaumont *France*	64	E4
Beaumont *California, U.S.A.*	126	D4
Beaumont *Texas, U.S.A.*	128	E5
Beaune	65	F5
Beaurepaire	65	F6
Beauvais	64	E4
Beauvoir-sur-Mer	65	B5
Beaver *Saskatchewan, Canada*	119	P5
Beaver *Yukon, Canada*	118	K3
Beaver Dam *Kentucky, U.S.A.*	124	G8
Beaver Dam *Wisconsin, U.S.A.*	124	F5
Beaverhill Lake	119	N5
Beawar	92	D3
Beazley	139	C6
Bebedouro	138	G4
Bebington	55	F3
Beccles	53	J2
Becej	72	F3
Becerrea	66	C1
Bechar	100	E2
Becharof Lake	118	D4
Bechet	73	G4
Beckingham	55	J3
Beckley	125	K8
Beclean	73	H2
Bedale	55	H2
Bedarieux	65	E7
Bede, Point	118	E4
Bedford *U.K.*	124	G7
Bedford *U.K.*	53	G2
Bedford Level	53	H2
Bedfordshire	53	G2
Bedlington	55	H1
Bedwas	52	D3
Bedworth	53	F2
Beer Sheva	94	B6
Beeston	53	F2
Beeswing	57	E5
Beeville	128	D6
Befale	106	D2
Befandriana	109	J3
Begejska Kanal	72	F3
Begoml	63	N10
Behbehan	95	K6
Behraamkale	76	B3
Behshahr	95	L3
Beian	87	P2
Beibu Wan	93	L4
Beihai	93	L4
Beijing	87	M4
Beila	100	B5
Beinn a' Ghlo	57	E4
Beinn Bheigier	57	B5
Beinn Dearg *Highland, U.K.*	56	D3
Beinn Dearg *Tayside, U.K.*	57	E4
Beinn Dorain	57	D4
Beinn Eighe	56	C3
Beinn Fhada	57	D4
Beinn Ime	57	D4
Beinn Mhor	56	A3
Beinn na Caillich	57	C3
Beinn Resipol	57	C4
Beinn Sgritheall	57	C3
Beipiao	87	N3
Beira	109	F3
Beirut	76	F6
Bei Shan	86	H3
Beit Lahm	94	B6
Beius	73	G2
Beja	66	C3
Beja	101	G1
Bejaia	101	G1
Bejaia, Golfe de	67	J4
Bejar	66	D2
Bejestan	95	P4
Beji	92	C3
Bekdast	79	J7
Bekescsaba	73	F2
Bekily	109	J4
Bekopaka	109	H3
Bekwai	104	E4
Bela *India*	92	F3
Bela *Pakistan*	92	C3
Belabo	105	H5
Belaga	90	E5
Belang	91	G5
Bela Palanka	73	G4
Bela Vista	109	F5
Belawan	90	B5
Belaya *Russia*	78	K4
Belaya *Russia*	85	W3
Belaya-Kalitva	79	G6
Belaya Kholunitsa	78	J4
Belayan	90	F5
Belaya Tserkov	79	E6
Belcher Channel	120	G2
Belcher Islands	121	L6
Belchiragh	94	S4
Belchite	67	F2
Belcoo	58	G4
Belderg	58	C4
Belebey	78	J5
Beledweyne	103	J7
Belem	137	H4
Belen *Turkey*	76	E4
Belen *U.S.A.*	127	J3
Belep, Iles	114	V15
Belesar, Embalse de	66	C1
Belev	79	F5
Belfast *New Zealand*	115	D5
Belfast *U.K.*	58	L3
Belfast Lough	58	L3
Belfield	123	N4
Belford	57	G5
Belfort	65	G5
Belgaum	92	D5
Belgium	64	E3
Belgorod	79	F5
Belgorod-Dnestrovskiy	79	E6
Belgrade	72	F3
Belgrano	141	X3
Belica	71	L2
Beli Lom	73	J4
Beli Manastir	72	E3
Belimbing	90	C7
Belin	65	C6
Belinskiy	79	G5
Belinyu	90	D6
Belitsa	73	G3
Belitung	90	D6
Belize	132	C6
Belkina, Mys	88	F3
Belknap, Mount	122	H8
Belkovskiy, Ostrov	85	P1
Bella Bella	118	K5
Bellac	65	D5
Bella Coola	118	K5
Bellaire	128	E6
Bellary	92	E5
Bella Vista *Argentina*	138	C5
Bella Vista *Argentina*	138	E5
Belleek	58	F4
Bellefontaine	124	J6
Belle Fourche *South Dakota, U.S.A.*	123	N5
Belle Fourche *Wyoming, U.S.A.*	123	M5
Belle Glade	129	M7
Belle Ile	65	B5
Belle Isle	121	Q7
Belleme	64	D4
Belleville *Canada*	125	M4
Belleville *Illinois, U.S.A.*	124	F7
Belleville *Kansas, U.S.A.*	123	R8
Bellevue *Idaho, U.S.A.*	122	G6
Bellevue *Washington, U.S.A.*	122	C4
Belley	65	F6
Bellingham *U.K.*	57	F5
Bellingham *U.S.A.*	122	C3
Bellinghaussen Sea	141	U5
Bellingshaussen	141	W6
Bellinzona	68	B2
Bello	136	B2
Bellona Island	114	J7
Bellona Reefs	111	N6
Bellpuig	67	G2
Bellshill	57	D5
Belluno	68	D2
Bell Ville	138	D6
Belly	122	H3
Belmont	56	A1
Belmonte *Portugal*	66	C2
Belmonte *Spain*	66	E3
Belmopan	132	C6
Belmullet	58	B4
Belogorsk	79	E6
Belogorye	71	M4
Belogradchik	73	G4
Belo Horizonte	138	K4
Beloit	124	F5
Belokorovichi	79	D5
Belomorsk	78	E3
Belorado	66	E1
Belorechensk	79	F7
Beloren	76	E4
Belorussia	71	L2
Belorusskaya Gryada	71	L2
Belot, Lac	118	K2
Belo-Tsiribihina	109	H3
Belousovka	84	C6
Belovo	84	D6
Beloye More	78	F2
Beloye Ozero	78	F3
Belozersk	78	F4
Belozerskoye	84	Ae5
Belper	55	H3
Belsay	57	G5
Belterra	137	F4
Belton	55	J3
Beltsy	73	J2
Belturbet	58	H4
Belukha, Gora	86	F2
Belvedere Marittimo	69	E6
Belvidere	124	F5
Belvoir, Vale of	53	G2
Belyando, River	113	K3
Belyayevka	73	L2
Belyy, Ostrov	85	A2
Belyy Yar	84	D5
Belzyce	71	K3
Bemaraha, Plateau du	109	J3
Bembridge	53	F4
Bemidji	124	C3
Benabarre	67	G1
Ben Alder	57	D4
Benalla	113	K6
Benares	92	F3
Ben Avon	57	E3
Benbaun	59	C5
Ben Chonzie	57	E4
Bencorr	59	C5
Ben Cruachan	57	C4
Bend	122	D5
Bende	105	G4
Bender Qaasim	103	J5
Bendery	79	D6
Bendigo	113	J6
Benesov	70	F4
Benevento	69	E5
Bengbu	87	M5
Benghazi	101	K2
Bengkalis	90	C5
Bengkulu	90	C6
Bengo, Baia do	106	B4
Bengoi	91	J6
Bengtsfors	63	E7

Benguela 106 B5
Benguerua, Ilha 109 G4
Benha 102 F1
Ben Hope 56 D2
Beni *Bolivia* 136 D4
Beni *Zaire* 107 E2
Beni Abbes 100 E2
Benicarlo 67 G2
Benidorm 67 F3
Beni Mazar 102 F2
Beni Mellal 100 D2
Benin 105 F4
Benin, Bight of 105 F4
Benin City 105 G4
Beni Saf 100 E1
Beni Suef 102 F2
Ben Klibreck 56 D2
Ben Lawers 57 D4
Ben Ledi 57 D4
Ben Lomond 57 D4
Ben Loyal 56 D2
Ben Lui 57 D4
Ben Macdui 57 E3
Ben MorCoigach 56 C3
Ben More *Central, U.K.* 57 D4
Ben More *Strathclyde, U.K.* 56 B4
Ben More Assynt 56 D2
Benmore, Lake 115 C6
Bennachie 56 F3
Benn Cleuch 57 E4
Bennetta, Ostrov 85 R1
Ben Nevis 57 C4
Bennington 125 P5
Benoni 108 E5
Be, Nosy 109 J2
Ben Rinnes 56 E3
Bensheim 70 C4
Benson *U.K.* 53 F3
Benson *U.K.* 126 G5
Ben Starav 57 C4
Bent 95 P8
Bentinck Island 93 J6
Bent Jbail 94 B5
Bentley 55 H3
Benton 128 F3
Benton Harbor 124 G5
Bentung 90 C5
Benue 105 G4
Ben Venue 57 D4
Ben Vorlich 57 D4
Benwee 58 C5
Benwee Head 58 C4
Ben Wyvis 56 D3
Benxi 87 N3
Beo 91 H5
Beograd 72 F3
Beppu 89 C9
Beqa 114 R9
Berat 74 E2
Berau, Teluk 114 A2
Berber 103 F4
Berbera 103 J5
Berberati 102 C7
Berck 64 D3
Berdichev 79 D6
Berdigestyakh 85 M4
Berdyansk 79 F6
Berea 124 H8
Bereeda 103 K5
Beregovo 79 C6
Berens 119 R5
Berens River 119 R5
Bere Regis 52 E4
Berettyo 73 F2
Berettyoujfalu 73 F2
Bereza 71 L2
Berezhany 71 L4
Berezhnykh, Mys 85 Q1
Berezina 78 D5
Berezino 78 D5
Berezna 79 E5
Berezniki 78 K4
Berezno 71 M3
Berezovka *Russia* 78 K3
Berezovka *Russia* 85 K5
Berezovka *Russia* 85 T3
Berezovka *Ukraine* 79 E6
Berezovo *Russia* 84 Ae4
Berezovo *Russia* 85 W4
Berezovskaya 85 K5
Berg 108 C6
Berga 67 G1
Bergama 76 B3
Bergamo 68 B3
Bergeforsen 62 G5
Bergen *E. Germany* 70 E1
Bergen *Norway* 63 J6
Bergen op Zoom 64 F3
Bergerac 65 D6
Bergfors 62 H2
Bergisch-Gladbach 70 B3
Bergsviken 62 J4
Berhala, Selat 90 C6
Beringa, Ostrov 81 T4
Bering Glacier 118 G3
Beringovskiy 85 X4
Bering Sea 143 H3
Bering Strait 118 B2
Berislav 79 E6
Beris, Ra's 95 Q9
Berja 66 E4
Berkak 62 C5
Berkakit 85 L5
Berkeley *U.K.* 52 E3

Berkeley *U.S.A.* 126 A2
Berkhamsted 53 G3
Berkner Island 141 W3
Berkovitsa 73 G4
Berkshire 53 F3
Berkshire Downs 53 F3
Berkshire Mountains 125 P5
Berlevag 62 N2
Berlin *E. Germany* 70 E2
Berlin *U.S.A.* 125 Q4
Bermeja, Sierra 66 D4
Bermejo *Argentina* 138 C6
Bermejo *Argentina* 138 D4
Bermeo 66 E1
Bermillo de Sayago 66 C2
Bermuda 117 N5
Bern 68 A2
Bernau 70 E2
Bernay 64 D4
Bernburg 70 D3
Berne 68 A2
Berner Alpen 68 A2
Berneray *U.K.* 57 A4
Berneray *U.K.* 56 A3
Bernina, Piz 68 B2
Beroroha 109 J4
Berounka 70 E4
Berre, Etang de 65 F7
Berriedale 56 E2
Berriedale Water 56 E2
Berrigan 113 K6
Berringarra 112 D4
Berrouaghia 67 H4
Berry *Australia* 113 L5
Berry *France* 65 E5
Berryessa, Lake 122 C8
Berry Head 52 D4
Berry Islands 132 J1
Bershad 73 K1
Berthoud Pass 123 L8
Bertoua 105 H5
Beru 111 S2
Beruri 136 E4
Berwick 125 M6
Berwick-upon-Tweed 57 F5
Berwyn Mountains 52 D2
Berzence 72 D2
Besalampy 109 H3
Besancon 65 G5
Besar, Kai 91 J7
Besbre 65 E5
Beshneh 95 M7
Besiri 77 J4
Beskidy Zachodnie 71 H4
Beslan 79 G7
Besni 77 G4
Bessarabia 73 K2
Bessarabka 73 K2
Bessbrook 58 K4
Bessemer *Alabama, U.S.A.* 129 J4
Bessemer *Winconsin, U.S.A.* 124 F3
Bestamak *Kazakhstan* 86 D2
Bestamak *Kazakhstan* 79 K6
Bestobe 84 A6
Bestuzhevo 78 G3
Betafo 109 J3
Betanzos 66 B1
Betare Oya 105 H4
Bethal 108 E5
Bethanie 108 C5
Bethany 124 C6
Bethel 118 C3
Bethel Park 125 L6
Bethesda *U.K.* 54 E3
Bethesda *U.S.A.* 125 M7
Bethlehem *Israel* 94 B6
Bethlehem *South Africa* 108 E5
Bethulie 108 E6
Bethune *France* 64 D4
Bethune *France* 64 E3
Betioky 109 H4
Betpak-Dala 86 B2
Bet-Pak-Data 86 B2
Betroka 109 J4
Betsiamites 125 R2
Betsiboka 109 J3
Bettiah 92 F3
Bettyhill 56 D2
Betul 92 E4
Betwa 92 E4
Betws-y-coed 54 F3
Beuvron 65 D5
Beverley *Australia* 112 D5
Beverley *U.K.* 55 J3
Beverly Hills 126 C3
Bexhill 53 H4
Beykoz 76 C2
Beyla 104 D4
Beylul 96 F10
Beyneu 79 K6
Beypazari 76 D2
Beypinar 77 G3
Beysehir 76 D4
Beysehir Golu 76 D4
Beyton 53 H2
Beytussebap 77 K4
Bezhetsk 78 F4
Beziers 65 E7
Bezmein 95 P2
Bhadgaon 92 G3
Bhadrachalam 92 F5
Bhadrakh 92 G4
Bhadravati 92 E6
Bhagalpur 92 G3

Bhakkar 92 D2
Bhamo 93 J4
Bhandara 92 E4
Bhanrer Range 92 F4
Bharatpur *Pradesh, India* 92 F4
Bharatpur *Rajasthan, India* 92 E3
Bharuch 92 D4
Bhatinda 92 D2
Bhatpara 93 G4
Bhavnagar 92 D4
Bhawanipatna 92 F5
Bhilwara 92 D3
Bhima 92 E5
Bhiwani 92 E3
Bhopal 92 E4
Bhopalpatnam 92 F5
Bhor 92 D5
Bhubaneshwar 92 G4
Bhuj 92 C4
Bhumiphol Dam 93 J5
Bhusawal 92 E4
Bhutan 93 G3
Bia 136 D4
Biaban 95 N8
Biabanak 95 S5
Biak 114 B2
Biala Podlaska 71 K2
Bialobrzegi 71 J3
Bialowieza 71 K2
Bialystok 71 K2
Bianco 69 F6
Biankouma 104 D4
Biaro 91 H5
Biarritz 65 C7
Biasca 68 B2
Biba 102 F2
Bibai 88 H4
Bibala 106 B5
Bibby Island 119 S3
Biberach 70 C4
Bibury 53 F3
Bicester 53 F3
Bicheno 113 K7
Bickle Knob 125 L7
Bida 105 G4
Bidar 92 E5
Biddeford 125 Q5
Biddulph 55 G3
Bidean Nam Bian 57 C4
Bideford 52 C3
Bideford Bay 52 C3
Bidford-on-Avon 53 F2
Bidokht 95 P4
Bidzhan *Russia* 88 C1
Bidzhan *Russia* 88 C2
Biebrza 71 K2
Biel 68 A2
Bielefeld 70 C2
Biella 68 B3
Bielsko-Biala 71 H4
Bielsk Podlaski 71 K2
Bien Hoa 93 L6
Bienne 68 A2
Bienveneu 137 G3
Bienville, Lac 121 M6
Biferno 69 E5
Biga 76 B2
Bigadic 76 C3
Big Bay 114 T11
Big Belt Mountains 122 J4
Big Blue 123 R7
Bigbury Bay 52 D4
Biggar *Canada* 123 K1
Biggar *U.K.* 57 E5
Biggleswade 53 G2
Big Horn 123 K5
Big Horn Mountains 123 L5
Big Island 120 M5
Big Pine 126 C2
Big Piney 123 J6
Big Sheep Mountains 123 L4
Big Sioux 123 R5
Big Snowy Mount 122 K4
Big Spring 127 M4
Big Stone Gap 124 J8
Big Timber 123 J5
Big Trout Lake 119 T4
Bihac 72 C3
Bihar 92 G4
Bihar 92 G3
Biharamulo 107 F3
Bihoro 88 K4
Bihu 87 M6
Bijagos, Arquipelago dos 104 B3
Bijapur 92 E5
Bijar 94 H4
Bijeljina 72 E3
Bijelo Polje 72 E4
Bijie 93 L3
Bijnor 92 E3
Bikaner 92 D3
Bikin *Russia* 88 E2
Bikin *Russia* 88 F2
Bikoro 106 C3
Bilad Bani Bu Ali 97 P5
Bilad Ghamid 96 E6
Bilad Zahran 96 E6
Bilaspur 92 F4
Bilauktaung Range 93 J6
Bilbao 66 E1
Bilchir 85 J6
Bilecik 76 C2
Biled 73 F3
Bile Karpaty 71 G4

Bilesha Plain 107 H2
Bilgoraj 71 K3
Bili 106 E2
Bilin 93 J5
Billabalong 112 D4
Billericay 53 H3
Billingham 55 H2
Billings 123 K5
Billingshurst 53 G3
Bilma 101 H5
Bilma, Grand Erg de 101 H5
Biloela 113 L3
Bilo Gora 72 D3
Biloxi 128 H5
Biltine 102 D5
Bilugyun 93 J5
Binalud, Kuh-e 95 P3
Binatang 90 E5
Binder 87 L2
Bindloe Island 136 A7
Bindura 108 F3
Binefar 67 G2
Binga 108 E3
Bingara 113 L4
Bingerville 104 E4
Bingham 125 R4
Binghamton 125 N5
Bingley 55 H3
Bingol 77 J3
Bingol Daglari 77 J3
Binjai *Indonesia* 90 B5
Binjai *Indonesia* 90 D5
Binongko 91 G7
Bintan 90 C5
Bintuhan 90 C6
Bintulu 90 E5
Bin Xian *Heilongjiang, China* 88 A3
Bin Xian *Shaanxi, China* 93 L2
Binyang 93 L4
Bio 114 K7
Biobio 139 B7
Biograd 72 C4
Bioko 105 G5
Bir 92 E5
Bira *Russia* 88 D1
Bira *Russia* 88 D1
Bira *Russia* 85 P7
Birag, Kuh-e 95 Q8
Birak 101 H3
Bir al Hisw 96 E4
Bir al War 101 H4
Birao 102 D5
Biratnagar 93 G3
Bir Butayman 77 H4
Birca 73 G4
Birch Island 122 D2
Birch Mountains 119 N4
Bird 119 S4
Bird Island 133 R7
Birdlip 53 E3
Birdum 113 G2
Birecik 77 G4
Bireun 90 B4
Bir Fardan 97 J5
Bir Ghabalou 67 H4
Bir Hadi 97 K7
Birhan 103 G5
Birikchul 84 D6
Birjand 95 P5
Birkenhead *New Zealand* 115 E2
Birkenhead *U.K.* 55 F3
Birksgate Range 112 F4
Birlad *Romania* 73 J2
Birlad *Romania* 73 J2
Birlestik 86 B2
Birmingham *U.K.* 53 F2
Birmingham *U.S.A.* 129 J4
Bir Moghrein 100 C3
Birnie Island 111 U2
Birnin Kebbi 105 F3
Birni nKonni 101 G6
Birobidzhan 88 D1
Birofeld 88 D1
Birr 59 G6
Bir, Ras el 103 H5
Birreencorragh 58 C5
Birrimbah 112 G2
Birsk 78 K4
Birtle 123 P2
Birtley 55 H2
Biryusa 84 F5
Birzai 63 L8
Biscay, Bay of 65 B6
Bischofshofen 68 D2
Biscotasi Lake 124 J3
Bisert 78 K4
Bisevo 72 D4
Bisha 96 C9
Bishah, Wadi 96 F6
Bishkek 86 C3
Bishnupur 93 G4
Bishop 126 C2
Bishop Auckland 55 H2
Bishop Burton 55 J3
Bishop's Castle 52 D2
Bishops Falls 121 Q8
Bishop's Stortford 53 H3
Bishri, Jbel 77 H5
Biskra 101 G2
Biskupiec 71 J2
Bislig 91 H4
Bismarck Archipelago 114 D2
Bismarck Range 114 D3
Bismark 123 P4

Name	Page	Grid
Bismil	77	J4
Bismo	63	C6
Bisotun	94	H4
Bispfors	62	G5
Bissau	104	B3
Bissett	123	S2
Bistcho Lake	119	M4
Bistretu	73	G4
Bistrita *Romania*	73	H2
Bistrita *Romania*	73	J2
Bistritei, Muntii	73	H2
Bitburg	70	B3
Bitche	64	G4
Bitik	79	J5
Bitkine	102	C5
Bitlis	77	K3
Bitola	73	F5
Bitonto	69	F5
Bitterfontein	108	C6
Bitterroot	122	G4
Bitterroot Range	122	G4
Bitti	69	B5
Biu	105	H3
Bivolu	73	H2
Biwa-ko	89	E8
Biyad, Al	96	H5
Biyagundi	96	C9
Biysk	84	D6
Bizerta	69	B7
Bizerte	101	G1
Bjargtangar	62	S12
Bjelovar	72	D3
Bjerkvik	62	L2
Bjorklinge	63	G6
Bjorksele	62	H4
Bjorna	62	H5
Bjorneborg *Finland*	63	J6
Bjorneborg *Sweden*	63	F7
Bjornevatn	62	N2
Bjornoya	80	C2
Bjurholm	62	H5
Bjursas	63	F6
Bla Bheinn	56	B3
Black *Alaska, U.S.A.*	118	G2
Black *Arizona, U.S.A.*	127	H4
Black *Arkansas, U.S.A.*	128	G3
Black *New York, U.S.A.*	125	N5
Blackadder Water	57	F5
Blackall	113	K3
Black Bay	124	F2
Black Belt	129	J4
Blackburn	55	G3
Black Canyon City	126	F3
Blackdown Hills	52	D4
Blackfoot	122	H6
Blackford	57	E4
Black Head	59	D6
Blackhead Bay	59	D6
Blackhill	55	H3
Black Hills	123	N5
Black Isle	56	D3
Black Mesa	126	G2
Blackmill	52	D3
Black Mountain	52	D3
Black Mountains	52	D3
Blackpool	55	F3
Black Range	127	J4
Black River Falls	124	E4
Blackrock	58	K5
Black Rock Desert	122	E7
Black Sea	51	P7
Blacksod Bay	58	B4
Blackstairs Mount	59	J7
Blackstairs Mountains	59	J7
Blackthorn	53	F3
Black Volta	104	E4
Black Water	57	E4
Blackwater *Australia*	113	K3
Blackwater *Meath, Ireland*	58	J5
Blackwater *Waterford, Ireland*	59	F8
Blackwater *Essex, U.K.*	53	H3
Blackwater *Hampshire, U.K.*	53	G3
Blackwaterfoot	57	C5
Blackwater Lake	119	L3
Blackwater Reservoir *Highland, U.K.*	57	D4
Blackwater Reservoir *Tayside, U.K.*	57	E4
Blackwell	128	D2
Blackwood	112	D5
Blaenavon	52	D3
Blafjall	62	W12
Blagodarnyy	79	G6
Blagoevgrad	73	G4
Blagoveshchensk *Russia*	78	K4
Blagoveshchensk *Russia*	85	M6
Blagoyevo	78	H3
Blair Atholl	57	E4
Blairgowrie	57	E4
Blaka	101	H4
Blakely	129	K5
Blakeney	53	J2
Blakesley	53	F2
Blanca, Bahia	139	D7
Blanca, Costa	67	F3
Blanca Peak	127	K2
Blanca, Punta	126	E6
Blanca, Sierra	127	K4
Blanc, Cap	69	B7
Blanche Channel	114	H6
Blanche, Lake	113	H4
Blanchland	55	G2
Blanc, Mont	65	G6
Blanco	136	E7
Blanco, Cabo	139	C9
Blanco, Cape	122	B6
Blanda	62	V12
Blandford Forum	53	E4
Blanes	67	H2
Blangy	64	D4
Blankenberge	64	E3
Blanquilla, Isla	136	E1
Blantyre	107	G6
Blarney	59	E9
Blasket Islands	59	A8
Blavet	65	B5
Blaydon	55	H2
Blaye	65	C6
Bleadon	52	E3
Bleaklow Hill	55	H3
Bled	72	C2
Blekinge	63	F8
Bletchley	53	G3
Bleus, Monts	107	F2
Blida	101	F1
Bligh Water	114	R8
Blind River	124	J3
Blisworth	53	G2
Block Island	125	Q6
Bloemfontein	108	E5
Blois	65	D5
Blonduos	62	U12
Bloodvein	123	R2
Bloody Foreland	58	F2
Bloomfield	124	D6
Bloomington *Illinois, U.S.A.*	124	F6
Bloomington *Indiana, U.S.A.*	124	G7
Bloomington *Minnesota, U.S.A.*	124	D4
Bloomsbury	113	K3
Blouberg	108	E4
Blubberhouses	55	H3
Bludenz	68	B2
Bluefield	125	K8
Bluefields	132	F9
Blue Mountain Lake	125	N5
Blue Mountain Peak	132	J5
Blue Mountains	122	E5
Bluemull Sound	56	A1
Blue Ridge	129	K3
Blue Ridge Mountains	129	L3
Blue Stack	53	F3
Blue Stack Mountains	53	F3
Bluff *New Zealand*	115	B7
Bluff *U.S.A.*	127	H2
Bluff Knoll	112	D5
Bluff Point	112	C4
Bluff, Punta	126	F6
Blumenau	138	G5
Blunt	123	Q5
Blyth *Northumberland, U.K.*	55	H1
Blyth *Nottinghamshire, U.K.*	55	H3
Blyth *Suffolk, U.K.*	53	J2
Blythe	126	E4
Blythe Bridge	53	E2
Blytheville	128	H3
Bo	104	C4
Boac	91	G3
Boa Fe	136	C5
Boa Vista *Cape Verde*	104	L7
Boa Vista *Amazonas, Brazil*	136	D4
Boa Vista *Roraima, Brazil*	136	E3
Bobai	93	M4
Bobaomby, Tanjoni	109	J2
Bobbili	92	F5
Bobbio	68	B3
Bobo Dioulasso	104	E3
Bobolice	71	G2
Bobr	70	F3
Bobrinents	79	E6
Bobrka	71	L4
Bobrov	79	G5
Bobruysk	79	D5
Bobures	133	M10
Boca del Pao	136	E2
Boca do Acre	136	D5
Boca Grande	136	E2
Bocaiuva	138	H3
Boca Mavaca	136	D3
Bocaranga	102	C5
Boca Raton	129	M7
Bochnia	71	J4
Bocholt	70	B3
Bochum	70	B3
Bodalla	113	L6
Bodaybo	85	J5
Boddam	56	A2
Boden	62	J4
Bodensee	70	C5
Bodhan	92	E5
Bodmin	52	C4
Bodmin Moor	52	C4
Bodo	62	F3
Bodrum	76	B4
Bodva	71	J4
Bodza, Pasul	73	J3
Boen	65	F6
Boende	106	D3
Boffa	104	C3
Bogalusa	128	H5
Bogan	113	K5
Bogaz	76	E2
Bogazkale	76	F2
Bogazkaya	77	F2
Bogazkopru	76	F3
Bogaziyan	76	F3
Bogbonga	106	C2
Bogen	62	L2
Boggeragh Mountains	59	E8
Boghar	67	H5
Bogia	114	D2
Bognes	62	G2
Bognor Regis	53	G4
Bogo	91	G3
Bogodukhov	79	F5
Bogong, Mount	113	K6
Bogor	90	D7
Bogorodchany	71	L4
Bogorodskoye *Russia*	78	J4
Bogorodskoye *Russia*	85	Q6
Bogota	136	C3
Bogotol	84	D5
Bogra	93	G4
Boguchany	84	F5
Boguchar	79	G6
Bogue	100	C5
Bogue Chitto	128	G5
Boguslav	79	E6
Bo Hai	87	K4
Bohemia	70	E4
Bohmer Wald	70	E4
Bohol	91	G4
Bohol Sea	91	G4
Boiano	69	E5
Boipeba, Ilha	137	K6
Bois Blanc Island	124	H4
Boisdale, Loch	57	A3
Boise *U.S.A.*	122	F6
Boise *U.S.A.*	122	F6
Boise City	127	L2
Bois, Lac des	118	K2
Boissevain	123	P3
Boizenburg	70	D2
Bojana	74	E2
Bojnurd	95	N3
Boka	73	F3
Boka Kotorska	72	E4
Boke	104	C3
Bokhara	113	K4
Boknafjord	63	A7
Bokol	107	G2
Bokoro	102	C5
Boksitogorsk	78	E4
Boktor	85	P6
Bokungu	106	D3
Bolama	104	B3
Bolanos	130	H7
Bolan Pass	92	C3
Bolbec	64	D4
Bolchary	84	Ae5
Bole	104	E4
Boleslawiec	70	F3
Bolgatanga	104	E3
Bolgrad	79	D6
Boli	88	C3
Bolia	106	C3
Boliden	62	J4
Bolinao	91	F2
Bol Irgiz	79	H5
Bolivar	139	D7
Bolivar *Missouri, U.S.A.*	124	D8
Bolivar *Tennessee, U.S.A.*	128	H3
Bolivar, Cerro	133	R11
Bolivar, Pico	133	M10
Bolivia	138	C3
Boljevac	73	F4
Belkhov	79	F5
Bellington	55	G3
Bollnas	63	G6
Bollon	113	K4
Bollstabruk	62	G5
Bolmen	63	E8
Bolobo	106	C3
Bologna	68	C3
Bologoye	78	E4
Bolotnoye	84	C5
Boloven, Cao Nguyen	93	L5
Bolsena, Lago di	69	C4
Bolsherechye	84	A5
Bolsheretsk	85	T6
Bolshevik	85	R4
Bolshevik, Ostrov	81	M2
Bolshezemelskaya Tundra	78	K2
Bolshoy Anyuy	85	U3
Bolshoy Atlym	84	Ae4
Bolshoy Balkhan, Khrebet	95	M2
Bolshoy Begichev, Ostrov	84	J2
Bolshoy Chernigovka	79	J5
Bolshoy Kavkaz	77	L1
Bolshoy Kunyak	84	A5
Bolshoy Lyakhovskiy, Ostrov	85	Q2
Bolshoy Murta	84	E5
Bolshoy Pit	84	E5
Bolshoy Porog	84	E3
Bolshoy Shantar, Ostrov	85	P5
Bolshoy Usa	78	K4
Bolshoy Yenisey	84	E6
Bolshoy Yugan	84	A5
Bolsover	55	H3
Boltana	67	G1
Bolt Head	52	D4
Bolton *Greater Manchester, U.K.*	55	G3
Bolton *Northumberland, U.K.*	57	G5
Bolu	76	D2
Bolucan	77	G3
Bolus Head	59	B9
Bolvadin	76	D3
Bolyarovo	73	J4
Bolzano	68	C2
Bom	114	D3
Boma	106	B4
Bombala	113	K6
Bombay	92	D5
Bomili	106	E2
Bom Jesus	137	J5
Bom Jesus da Lapa	137	J6
Bomlafjord	63	A7
Bomlo	63	A7
Bomongo	106	C2
Bonab	94	H3
Bonaire	133	N8
Bonaire Trench	133	N9
Bona, Mount	118	G3
Bonar Bridge	56	D3
Bonavista	121	R8
Bonavista Bay	121	R8
Bon, Cap	101	H1
Bondo	106	D2
Bondokodi	91	F7
Bondoukou	104	E4
Bone	69	A7
Bo'ness	57	E4
Bonete, Cerro	138	C5
Bone, Teluk	91	G6
Bongabong	91	G3
Bongor	102	C5
Bonham	128	D4
Bonifacio	69	B5
Bonifacio, Strait of	69	B5
Bonn	70	B3
Bonners Ferry	122	F3
Bonnetable	64	D4
Bonneval	64	D4
Bonneville	65	G5
Bonneville Salt Flats	122	H7
Bonnie Rock	112	D5
Bonny *France*	65	E5
Bonny *Nigeria*	105	G5
Bonnyrigg	57	E5
Bono	69	B5
Bonobono	91	F4
Bonorva	69	B5
Bonthe	104	C4
Bontoc	91	G2
Booligal	113	J5
Boologooro	112	C3
Boone *Iowa, U.S.A.*	124	D5
Boone *N. Carolina, U.S.A.*	129	M2
Booneville *Mississippi, U.S.A.*	128	H3
Booneville *New York, U.S.A.*	125	N5
Booroorban	113	J5
Boosaaso	103	J5
Boothia, Gulf of	120	J4
Boothia Peninsula	120	H3
Bootle	55	F3
Boot Reefs	114	C3
Bopeechee	113	H4
Boquilla, Presa de la	127	K7
Boquilas del Carmen	127	L6
Bor *Sudan*	102	F6
Bor *Turkey*	76	F4
Bor *Yugoslavia*	73	G3
Boraha, Nosy	109	J3
Borah Peak	122	H5
Boras	63	E8
Borasambar	92	F4
Borazjan	95	K7
Borba	136	F4
Borborema, Planalto da	137	K5
Borca	73	H2
Borcka	77	J2
Bordeaux	65	C6
Borden Island	120	D2
Borden Peninsula	120	K3
Borders	57	F5
Bordertown	113	J6
Bordeyri	62	U12
Bordj-Bou-Arreridj	67	J4
Bordj Bounaama	67	G5
Bordj Omar Driss	101	G3
Borensberg	63	F7
Boreray	56	A3
Borga	63	L6
Borgarnes	62	U12
Borgefjellet	62	E4
Borger	127	M3
Borgholm	63	G8
Borgo San Lorenzo	68	C4
Borgosesia	68	B3
Borgo Val di Taro	68	B3
Borgo Valsugana	68	C2
Borislav	71	K4
Borisoglebsk	79	G5
Borisov	63	Q9
Borispol	79	E5
Borja	67	F2
Borkovskaya	78	H2
Borkum	70	B2
Borlange	63	F6
Borlu	76	C3
Bormida	68	B3
Bormio	68	C2
Borneo	90	E5
Bornholm	70	F1
Bornholmsgattet	63	F9
Bornova	76	B3
Borohoro Shan	86	E3
Boroko	91	G5
Boromo	104	E3
Boronga Islands	93	H5
Borongan	91	H3
Borovichi	78	E4
Borovlyanka	84	C6
Borovsk	78	K4
Borovskoye	84	Ad6

Name	Page	Grid
Borrika	113	J6
Borris	59	J7
Borrisokane	59	F7
Borrisoleigh	59	G7
Borroloola	113	H2
Borrowdale	55	F2
Borshchev	73	J1
Borshchovochnyy Khrebet	85	J6
Borth	52	C2
Borujen	95	K6
Borujerd	94	J5
Borve	57	A4
Borzhomi	77	K2
Borzya	85	K7
Bosa	69	B5
Bosanski Brod	72	E3
Bosanski Novi	72	D3
Bosanski Petrovac	72	D3
Boscastle	52	C4
Bose	93	L4
Bos Gradiska	72	D3
Boshruyeh	95	N5
Bosilegrad	73	G4
Boskovice	71	G4
Bosna	72	E3
Bosnia-Herzegovina	72	D3
Bosnik	114	B2
Bosobolo	106	C2
Boso-hanto	89	H8
Bosphorus	76	C2
Bossambele	102	C6
Bossangoa	102	C6
Bossier City	128	F4
Bostan *Iran*	94	H6
Bostan *Pakistan*	92	C2
Bostanabad	94	H3
Bosten Bagrax Hu	86	F3
Boston *U.S.A.*	53	G2
Boston *U.S.A.*	125	Q5
Boston Mountains	128	E3
Botesdale	53	J2
Botev	73	H4
Botevgrad	73	G4
Bothel	55	F2
Bothnia, Gulf of	62	J5
Botna	73	K2
Botosani	73	J2
Botsmark	62	J4
Botswana	108	D4
Botte Donato	69	F6
Bottenhavet	63	H6
Bottenviken	62	K4
Bottesford	53	G2
Bottineau	123	P3
Bottisham	53	H2
Bottrop	70	B3
Botucatu	138	G4
Bouafle	104	D4
Bouake	104	D4
Bouar	102	C6
Bouarfa	100	E2
Boucant Bay	113	G1
Bouchegouf	69	A7
Bougainville	114	E3
Bougainville, Cape	112	F1
Bougainville Reef	113	K2
Bougainville Strait	114	J5
Bougaroun, Cap	101	G1
Bougie	67	J4
Bougouni	100	D6
Bougzdul	67	H5
Bouhalloufa	67	G4
Bouillon	64	F4
Bouira	67	H4
Bou Ismail	67	H4
Boujdour	100	C3
Bou Kadir	67	G4
Boulay	64	G4
Boulder	123	M8
Boulder City	126	D3
Boulogne-sur-Mer	64	D3
Boumbe I	102	C7
Boumbe II	102	C7
Boumo	102	C6
Bouna	104	E4
Boundiali	104	D4
Boung Long	93	L6
Boun Tai	93	K4
Bountiful	122	J7
Bounty Islands	111	S11
Bourail	114	W16
Bourbon-l'Archambault	65	E5
Bourbonnais *France*	65	E5
Bourbonnais *U.S.A.*	124	G6
Bourbonne-les-Bains	65	F5
Bourem	100	E5
Bourganeuf	65	D6
Bourg-en-Bresse	65	F5
Bourges	65	E5
Bourgogne	65	E5
Bourgogne, Canal de	65	E5
Bourg-Saint-Andeol	65	F6
Bourke	113	K5
Bourne	53	G2
Bournemouth	53	F4
Bou Saada	101	F1
Boussac	65	E5
Bousso	102	C5
Boutilimit	100	C5
Boves	68	A3
Bovey	52	D4
Bovey Tracy	52	D4
Bovingdon	53	G3
Bovino	69	E5
Bow	122	H2
Bowbells	123	N3
Bowen	113	K3
Bowers Bank	118	Ab9
Bowes	55	G2
Bowfell	55	F2
Bowie	128	D4
Bow Island	122	J3
Bowkan	94	H3
Bowland, Forest of	55	G2
Bowling Green *Kentucky, U.S.A.*	124	G8
Bowling Green *Ohio, U.S.A.*	124	J6
Bowman	123	N4
Bowman Bay	120	M4
Bowness	55	G2
Bowness-on-Solway	55	F2
Bowraville	113	L5
Boxford	53	H2
Bo Xian	93	N2
Boxing	87	M4
Box Tank	113	J5
Boyabat	76	F2
Boyang	87	M6
Boyarka	84	F2
Boyd Lake	119	Q3
Boyer	124	C6
Boyle	58	F5
Boyne	58	K5
Boynton Beach	129	M7
Boyuibe	138	D4
Bozburun	76	C4
Bozcaada	75	H3
Bozdogan	76	C4
Bozeman	122	J5
Bozen	68	C2
Boze Pole	71	G1
Bozkir	76	E4
Bozkurt	76	E2
Bozoum	102	C6
Bozova	77	H4
Bozqush, Kuh-e	94	H3
Bozuyuk	76	D3
Bra	68	A3
Brabant Island	141	V6
Brabourne	53	H3
Brac	72	D4
Bracadale	56	B3
Bracadale, Loch	56	B3
Bracciano	69	D4
Bracke	62	F5
Brackley	53	F2
Bracknell	53	G3
Brad	73	G2
Bradano	69	F5
Bradda Head	54	E2
Bradenton	129	L7
Bradford *U.K.*	55	H3
Bradford *U.S.A.*	125	L6
Bradford-on-Avon	52	E3
Bradwell Waterside	53	H3
Brady	127	N5
Brady Mountains	127	N5
Brae	56	A1
Braemar	57	E3
Braemore	56	E2
Braeswick	56	F1
Braga	66	B2
Bragado	139	D7
Braganca	66	C2
Braganca Paulista	138	G4
Bragar	56	B2
Brahman Baria	93	H4
Brahmani	92	G4
Brahmapur	92	F5
Brahmaputra	93	H3
Braidwood	113	K6
Braila	73	J3
Brailsford	53	F2
Brainerd	124	C3
Braintree	53	H3
Braishfield	53	F3
Brake	70	C2
Brakel	70	C3
Brallos	75	G3
Bramdean	53	F3
Bramham	55	H3
Bramming	63	C9
Brampton *Canada*	125	L5
Brampton *U.K.*	55	G2
Bramsche	70	B2
Brancaster	53	H2
Brancaster Bay	53	H2
Branco	136	E3
Branco, Cabo	137	L5
Brandberg	108	B4
Brandbu	63	D6
Brande	63	C9
Brandenburg	70	E2
Brandesburton	55	J3
Brandon *Canada*	123	Q3
Brandon *U.S.A.*	125	P5
Brandon Bay	59	B8
Brandon Mount	59	B8
Brandon Point	59	B8
Brandval	63	E6
Branesti	73	J3
Braniewo	71	H1
Bran, Pasul	73	H3
Brantford	125	K5
Brantley	129	J5
Brantome	65	D6
Brasileia	136	D6
Brasilia *Distrito Federal, Brazil*	138	F3
Brasilia *Minas Gerais, Brazil*	138	H3
Braslav	63	M9
Brasov	73	H3
Brassey Range	91	F5
Brates, Lacul	73	K3
Bratislava	71	G4
Bratsk	84	G5
Bratslav	73	K1
Braunau	68	D1
Braunsberg	71	H1
Braunschweig	70	D2
Braunton	52	C3
Brava	104	L7
Brava, Costa	67	H2
Bravo del Norte, Rio	127	L6
Brawley	126	E4
Bray	59	K6
Bray Head	59	B9
Bray Island	120	L4
Brazil	137	G5
Brazos	128	D5
Brazzaville	106	C3
Brcko	72	E3
Brda	71	G2
Breadalbane	57	D4
Breaksea Sound	115	A6
Brean	52	D3
Brebes	90	D7
Brechfa	52	C3
Brechin	57	F4
Breckenridge *Texas, U.S.A.*	128	C4
Breckenridge *Minnesota, U.S.A.*	124	B3
Breckland	53	H2
Brecknock, Peninsula	139	B10
Breclav	71	G4
Brecon	52	D3
Brecon Beacons	52	D3
Breda	64	F3
Bredon Hill	53	F3
Bredstedt	70	C1
Breezewood	125	L7
Bregenz	68	B2
Bregovo	73	G3
Breidafjordur	62	T12
Brejo	137	J4
Brekken	62	D5
Brekstad	62	C5
Bremen *U.S.A.*	129	K4
Bremen *W. Germany*	70	C2
Bremerhaven	70	C2
Bremer Range	112	E5
Bremerton	122	C4
Bremervorde	70	C2
Brendon Hills	52	D3
Brenham	128	D5
Brenig, Llyn	55	F3
Brenish	56	A2
Brenner Pass	68	C2
Breno	68	C3
Brenta	68	C3
Brentford	53	G2
Brentwood *U.K.*	53	H3
Brentwood *U.S.A.*	125	P6
Brescia	68	C3
Breskens	64	E3
Breslau	71	G3
Bressanone	68	C2
Bressay	56	A2
Bressay Sound	56	A2
Bressuire	65	C5
Brest *France*	64	A4
Brest *Belorussia*	71	K2
Brestlitovsk	79	E5
Brest Litovsk	71	K2
Bretagne	64	B4
Bretcu	73	J2
Breteuil *France*	64	D4
Breteuil *France*	64	E4
Breton, Cape	121	Q8
Breton Sound	128	H6
Brett	53	H2
Brett, Cape	115	E1
Breueh	90	B4
Brevoort Island	120	P5
Brewer	125	R4
Brewster	122	E3
Brewton	129	J5
Brezhnev	78	J4
Breznice	70	E4
Brezo, Sierra del	66	D1
Bria	102	D6
Briancon	65	G6
Brianne, Llyn	52	D2
Briare	65	E5
Bribie Island	113	L4
Brichany	73	J1
Bricquebe	53	N7
Bride	54	E2
Bridestowe	52	C4
Bridgend *Mid Glamorgan, U.K.*	52	D3
Bridgend *Strathclyde, U.K.*	57	B5
Bridge of Allan	57	E4
Bridge of Gaur	57	D4
Bridge of Orchy	57	D4
Bridge of Weir	57	D4
Bridgeport *Alabama, U.S.A.*	129	K3
Bridgeport *California, U.S.A.*	126	C1
Bridgeport *Connecticut, U.S.A.*	125	P6
Bridgeport *Nebraska, U.S.A.*	123	N7
Bridgeton	125	N7
Bridgetown *Australia*	112	D5
Bridgetown *Barbados*	133	T8
Bridgetown *Canada*	121	N9
Bridgewater	121	P9
Bridgnorth	52	E2
Bridgwater	52	D3
Bridgwater Bay	52	D3
Bridlington	55	J2
Bridlington Bay	55	J2
Bridport	52	E4
Brieg	71	G3
Brienne-le-Chateau	64	F4
Brier Island	125	S4
Briey	64	F4
Brig	68	A2
Brigg	55	J3
Brighouse	55	H3
Brightlingsea	53	J3
Brighton	53	G4
Brignoles	65	G7
Brihuega	66	E2
Brikama	104	B3
Brindakit	85	P4
Brindisi	69	F5
Brinian	56	F1
Brinkley	128	G3
Brioude	65	E6
Brisbane	113	L4
Bristol *U.K.*	52	E3
Bristol *U.S.A.*	125	P6
Bristol Bay	118	D4
Bristol Channel	52	D2
Bristol Lake	126	E3
Bristow	128	D3
British Columbia	118	L4
Brits	108	E5
Britstown	108	D6
Brittle, Lake	57	B3
Brive-la-Gaillarde	65	D6
Briviesca	66	E1
Brixham	52	D4
Brlik	86	C3
Brno	71	G4
Broad	129	M3
Broadback	121	L7
Broad Bay	56	B2
Broad Cairn	57	E4
Broad Haven	58	C4
Broad Hinton	53	F3
Broadhurst Range	112	E3
Broad Sound *Australia*	113	K3
Broad Sound *U.K.*	52	B3
Broadstairs	53	J3
Broads, The	53	J2
Broadus	123	M5
Broadway	53	F2
Brochel	56	B3
Brocken	70	D3
Brockenhurst	53	F4
Brock Island	120	D2
Brockman, Mount	112	D3
Brockton	125	Q5
Brod	73	F5
Broddanes	62	U12
Brodeur Peninsula	120	J3
Brodick	57	C5
Brodick Bay	57	C5
Brodnica	71	H2
Brodokalmak	84	Ad5
Brody	79	D5
Brok	71	J2
Broken Bay	113	L5
Broken Bow *Nebraska, U.S.A.*	123	Q7
Broken Bow *Oklahoma, U.S.A.*	128	E3
Broken Bow Lake	128	E3
Broken Hill *Australia*	113	J5
Broken Hill *Zambia*	107	E5
Bromberg	71	G2
Bromley	53	H3
Bromsgrove	53	E2
Bromyard	52	E2
Bronderslev	63	C8
Bronnoysund	62	E4
Bronte	69	E7
Brookfield	124	D7
Brookhaven	128	G5
Brookings *Oregon, U.S.A.*	122	B6
Brookings *S. Dakota, U.S.A.*	123	R5
Brookneal	125	L8
Brooks	122	H2
Brooks Range	118	D2
Brooksville	129	L6
Broome	112	E2
Broom, Loch	56	C3
Brora *U.K.*	56	D2
Brora *U.K.*	56	E2
Brosteni	73	G3
Broto	67	F1
Brotton	55	J2
Brou	64	D4
Brough	55	G2
Brough Head	56	E1
Brough Ness	56	F2
Broughshane	58	K3
Broughton	57	E5
Broughton in Furness	55	F2
Broughton Island	120	P4
Broughton Poggs	53	F3
Browerville	124	C3
Brow Head	59	C10
Brownfield	127	L4
Brownhills	53	F2
Browning	122	H3
Brownsville	128	D8
Brownwood	128	C5
Brownwood, Lake	127	N5
Bru	62	Y12

C

Chaplygin 79 F5
Chapman 112 F2
Chapman, Cape 120 J4
Chapman Islands 119 P2
Chaqui 138 C3
Chara *Russia* 85 K5
Chara *Russia* 85 K5
Charagua 138 D3
Charak 95 M8
Charambira, Punta 136 B3
Charcot Island 141 U5
Chard 52 E4
Chardzhou 80 H6
Charente 65 C6
Chari 102 C5
Charikar 92 C1
Chariton *U.S.A.* 124 D6
Chariton *U.S.A.* 124 D6
Charkhari 92 E3
Charlemount 58 J4
Charleroi 64 F3
Charlesbourg 125 Q3
Charles, Cape 125 N8
Charles City 124 D5
Charles Island *Canada* 120 M5
Charles Island *Ecuador* 136 A7
Charleston *Illinois, U.S.A.* 124 F7
Charleston *Missouri, U.S.A.* 124 F8
Charleston *S. Carolina, U.S.A.* 129 N4
Charleston *W. Virginia, U.S.A.* 125 K7
Charlestown 58 E5
Charlestown of Aberlour 56 E3
Charleville 113 K4
Charleville-Mezieres 64 F4
Charlotte 129 M3
Charlotte Amalie 133 Q5
Charlotte, Cape 139 J10
Charlotte Harbour 129 L7
Charlottesville 125 L7
Charlottetown 121 P8
Charlton 113 J6
Charlton Island 121 L7
Charmes 64 G4
Charnley 112 F2
Charolles 65 F5
Charters Towers 113 K3
Chartres 64 D4
Charwelton 53 F2
Charybdis Reef 114 Q8
Charyn 86 D3
Chascomus 139 E7
Chaselka 84 C3
Chaslands Mistake 115 B7
Chasong 87 P3
Chasovo 78 J3
Chasseneuil 65 D6
Chat 95 M3
Chateaubriant 65 C5
Chateau Chinon 65 E5
Chateaudun 65 D4
Chateau-Gontier 65 C5
Chateau-la-Valliere 65 D5
Chateaulin 64 A4
Chateauneuf-en-Thimerais 64 D4
Chateauneuf-sur-Loire 65 E5
Chateaurenault 65 D5
Chateauroux 65 D5
Chateau-Salins 64 G4
Chateau-Thierry 64 E4
Chatellerault 65 D5
Chatham *New Brunswick, Canada* 125 T3
Chatham *Ontario, Canada* 124 J5
Chatham *U.K.* 53 H3
Chatham, Isla 139 B10
Chatham Island *Ecuador* 136 A7
Chatham Island *New Zealand* 115 F7
Chatham Islands 115 G7
Chatillon 68 A3
Chatillon-sur-Indre 65 D5
Chatillon-sur-Seine 65 F5
Chato, Cerro 139 B8
Chattahoochee 129 K5
Chattanooga 129 K3
Chatteris 53 H2
Chatyrtash 86 D3
Chaudiere 125 Q3
Chaumont 64 F4
Chaunskaya Guba 85 V3
Chauny 64 E4
Chautauqua Lake 125 L5
Chavantina 138 G6
Chaves *Brazil* 137 H4
Chaves *Portugal* 66 C2
Chaviva 136 C3
Chay Khanah 77 L5
Chaykovskiy 78 J4
Chazhegovo 78 J3
Cheadle 55 G3
Cheb 70 E3
Cheboksary 78 H4
Cheboygan 124 H4
Chechen , Ostrov 79 H7
Chech, Erg 100 E3
Chechuysk 84 H5
Checiny 71 J3
Chedabucto Bay 121 P8
Cheddar 52 E3
Cheduba 93 H5
Cheetham, Cape 141 L4
Chef-Boutonne 65 C5
Chehalis 122 C4
Chehel Dokhtaran 95 R4
Cheju 87 P5
Cheju do 87 P5
Chekhov 88 H2
Chekunda 85 N6
Chekurovka 85 M2
Chekuyevo 78 F3
Chelan 122 D4
Chelan, Lake 122 D3
Chela, Serra da 106 B6
Cheleken 95 L2
Chelforo 139 C7
Cheliff, Oued 100 F1
Chelkar 51 U6
Chelm 71 K3
Chelmsford 53 H3
Chelmuzhi 78 F3
Chelosh 84 D6
Cheltenham 53 E3
Chelva 67 F3
Chelyabinsk 84 Ad5
Chelyuskin 84 G1
Chelyuskin, Mys 81 M2
Chemba 109 F3
Chemille 65 C5
Chemnitz 70 E3
Chenab 92 D2
Cheney 122 F4
Chengde 87 M3
Chengdu 93 K2
Chenghai 87 M7
Chengjiang 93 K4
Chengshan Jiao 87 N4
Chenonceaux 65 D5
Chen Xian 93 M3
Chepen 136 B5
Chepes 139 C6
Chepstow 52 E3
Chequamegon Bay 124 E3
Cher 65 E5
Cherangany Hills 107 G2
Cheraw 129 N3
Cherbourg 64 C4
Cherchell 101 F1
Cherdyn 78 K3
Cheremkhovo 84 G6
Cheremosh 71 L4
Cherepovets 78 F4
Cherevkovo 78 H3
Cherkashina 84 H5
Cherkassy 79 E6
Cherkessk 79 G7
Cherlak 84 A6
Cherlakskiy 84 A6
Cherlmno 71 H2
Chermoz 78 K4
Chernaya *Russia* 78 K2
Chernaya *Russia* 78 K2
Cherni 73 G4
Chernigov 79 E5
Chernigovka *Russia* 88 D3
Chernigovka *Ukraine* 79 F6
Chernikovsk 78 K5
Cherni Lom 73 J4
Chernobyl 79 E5
Chernoostrovskoye 84 D4
Chernousovka 84 A6
Chernovtsy 73 H1
Chernushka 78 K4
Chernutyevo 78 H3
Chernyakhovsk 71 J1
Chernyshevskiy 85 J4
Chernyye Zemli 79 H6
Chernyy Mys 84 C5
Chernyy Otrog 79 K5
Cherokee 124 C5
Cherokee Sound 129 P7
Cherry 111 Q4
Cherskiy 85 U3
Cherskogo, Khrebet 85 Q3
Chertkovo 79 G6
Chertsey *New Zealand* 115 C5
Chertsey *U.K.* 53 G3
Chervonograd 79 C5
Chervonoznamenka 73 L2
Cherwell 53 F3
Chesapeake 125 M8
Chesapeake Bay 125 M8
Chesham 53 G3
Cheshire 55 G3
Cheshkaya Guba 78 H2
Cheshunt 53 G3
Chesil Beach 52 E4
Chester *U.K.* 55 G3
Chester *Illinois, U.S.A.* 124 F8
Chester *Montana, U.S.A.* 122 J3
Chester *S. Carolina, U.S.A.* 129 M3
Chesterfield 55 H3
Chesterfield, Iles 113 M2
Chesterfield Inlet 119 S3
Chester-le-Street 55 H2
Chesters 57 F5
Chesterton Range 113 K4
Chesuncook Lake 125 R3
Chetlat 92 D6
Chetumal 131 Q8
Chetvertyy Kurilskiy Proliv 85 S7
Chetwynd 119 L4
Cheviot Hills 57 F5
Cheviot, The 57 F5
Chew 52 E3
Chew Valley Lake 52 E3
Cheyenne *S. Dakota, U.S.A.* 123 P5
Cheyenne *Wyoming, U.S.A.* 123 M7
Cheyenne Wells 127 L1
Chhapra 92 F3
Chhatarpur 92 E4
Chhindwara 92 E4
Chia-i 87 N7
Chiange 106 B6
Chiani 69 D4
Chiari 68 B3
Chiatura 77 K1
Chiautla 131 K8
Chiavari 68 B3
Chiavenna 68 B2
Chiba 89 H8
Chibia 106 B6
Chibit 84 D6
Chibizhek 84 E6
Chibougamau 125 N2
Chibougamau Lake 125 N2
Chibuto 109 F4
Chicago 124 G6
Chicama 136 B5
Chicapa 106 D4
Chichagof Island 118 H4
Chichester 53 G4
Chichester Range 112 D3
Chichibu 89 G8
Chichigalpa 132 D8
Chickasha 128 D3
Chicko 119 L5
Chiclayo 136 B5
Chico *Argentina* 139 C10
Chico *Argentina* 139 C8
Chico *U.S.A.* 122 D8
Chicoutimi 125 Q2
Chicualacuala 109 F4
Chidambaram 92 E6
Chiddingfold 53 G3
Chidley, Cape 121 P5
Chiefland 129 L6
Chiemsee 70 E5
Chieng-Mai 93 J5
Chienti 68 D4
Chieti 69 E4
Chifeng 87 M3
Chifre, Serra do 138 H3
Chiguana 138 C4
Chigubo 109 F4
Chigwell 53 H3
Chihli, Gulf of 87 K4
Chihuahua 127 J6
Chihuatlan 130 G8
Chiili 86 B3
Chijinpu 86 H3
Chik Ballapur 92 E6
Chikishlyer 95 L3
Chikmagalur 92 E6
Chikura 89 G8
Chi, Lam 93 K5
Chilamate 132 E8
Chilapa 131 K9
Chilas 92 D1
Chilca 136 B6
Chilca, Punta 136 B6
Childers 113 L4
Childress 127 M[illegible]
Chile 139 B7
Chile Chico 139 B9
Chilete 136 B5
Chilham 53 H3
Chilia, Bratul 73 K3
Chilik *Kazakhstan* 86 D3
Chilik *Kazakhstan* 79 J5
Chililabombwe 107 E5
Chillagoe 113 J2
Chillan 139 B7
Chillicothe *Missouri, U.S.A.* 124 D7
Chillicothe *Ohio, U.S.A.* 124 J7
Chilliculco 138 C3
Chiloe, Isla de 139 B8
Chilpancingo 131 K9
Chiltern Hills 53 G3
Chilumba 107 F5
Chi-lung 87 N6
Chilwa, Lake 107 G6
Chimanimani 109 F3
Chimay 64 F3
Chimborazo, Volcan 136 B4
Chimbote 136 B5
Chimishliya 73 K2
Chimkent 86 B3
Chimoio 109 F3
China 128 C8
Chinandega 132 D8
Chinati Peak 127 K6
Chinchilla 113 L4
Chinchilla de Monte Aragon 67 F3
Chinchon 66 E2
Chinchorro, Banco 131 R8
Chindagatuy 86 F2
Chinde 109 G3
Chindwin 93 H4
Chingola 107 E5
Chinguetti 100 C4
Chin Hills 93 H4
Chiniot 92 D2
Chinju 87 P4
Chinon 65 D5
Chinsali 107 F5
Chintalnar 92 F5
Chioggia 68 D3
Chios 75 H3
Chipata 107 F5
Chiperone 109 G3
Chipinge 109 F4
Chiplun 92 D5
Chipoka 107 F5
Chi Pou 93 L6
Chippenham 53 E3
Chippewa 124 E4
Chippewa Falls 124 E4
Chipping 55 G3
Chipping Norton 53 F3
Chipping Ongar 53 H3
Chipping Sodbury 52 E3
Chiputneticook Lakes 125 S4
Chiquinquira 136 C2
Chirchik 86 B3
Chiredzi 109 F4
Chirikof Island 118 D4
Chirimba 84 E5
Chirinda 84 G3
Chirique, Golfo de 132 F11
Chirk 52 D2
Chiromo 107 G6
Chirovanga 114 H5
Chirpan 73 H4
Chirripo 132 F10
Chishmy 78 K5
Chisinau 79 D6
Chisinau 73 K2
Chiskovo 84 F4
Chisone 68 A3
Chisos Mountains 127 L6
Chistopol 78 J4
Chita 85 J6
Chitato 106 D4
Chitembo 106 C5
Chitina 118 G3
Chitinskaya Oblast 85 K6
Chitradurga 92 E6
Chitral 92 D1
Chittagong 93 H4
Chittaurgarh 92 D4
Chittoor 92 E6
Chitungwiza 108 F3
Chiume 106 D6
Chiusi 69 C4
Chiva 67 F3
Chivasso 68 A3
Chivato, Punta 126 G7
Chive 136 D6
Chivhu 108 F3
Chivilcoy 139 D6
Chizha 78 G2
Chizha Vtoraya 79 H5
Chizu 89 E8
Chkalovskoye 88 D3
Chmielnik 71 J3
Choctawhatchee 129 K5
Chodziez 71 G2
Choele-Choel 139 C7
Choire, Loch 56 D2
Choiseul 114 H5
Choix 127 H7
Chojnice 71 G2
Chokai-san 88 H6
Chokurdakh 85 R2
Chokwe 109 F4
Cholderton 53 F3
Cholet 65 C5
Chollerton 57 F5
Choluteca 132 D8
Choma 106 E6
Chomutov 70 E3
Chona 84 H4
Chon Buri 93 K6
Chongan 87 M6
Chongjin 88 B5
Chongju 87 P4
Chongli 87 M3
Chongming Dao 87 M5
Chongqing 93 L3
Chongren 87 M6
Chongson 89 B7
Chongyang 93 M3
Chonos, Archipielago de los 139 B8
Chon Thanh 93 L6
Chop 79 C6
Chorley 55 G3
Chorolque 138 C4
Chortkov 79 D6
Chorzele 71 J2
Choshi 89 H8
Chosica 136 B6
Chos-Malal 139 B7
Choson-Man 87 P4
Choszczno 70 F2
Chota 136 B5
Choteau 122 H4
Choybalsan 87 L2
Christchurch *New Zealand* 115 D5
Christchurch *U.K.* 53 F4
Christiansfeld 63 C9
Christianshab 120 R4
Christie Bay 119 N3
Christmas Creekq 112 F2
Christmas Island *Australia* 83 J8
Christmas Island *Kiribati* 143 H4
Chrzanow 71 H3
Chu 86 C3
Chubartau 86 D2
Chubut 139 C8
Chudleigh 52 D4
Chudovo 78 E4
Chudskoye Ozero 63 M7
Chugach Mountains 118 G3
Chugoku-sanchi 89 D8
Chugunash 84 D6
Chuguyevka 88 D3
Chukchi Sea 118 B2

Name	Page	Grid
Chuken	88	F2
Chukhloma	78	G4
Chukotat	121	L5
Chukotskiy Khrebet	85	W3
Chukotskiy Poluostrov	81	V3
Chulak-Kurgan	86	B3
Chula Vista	126	D4
Chulman	85	L5
Chulmleigh	52	D4
Chulym *Russia*	84	C5
Chulym *Russia*	84	C5
Chum	78	L2
Chumbicha	138	C5
Chumek	86	F2
Chumikan	85	P6
Chumphon	93	J6
Chuna	84	F5
Chunchon	87	P4
Chungju	87	P4
Chunhua	88	C4
Chunoyar	84	F5
Chunya	107	F4
Chunyang	88	B4
Chunyang	89	B7
Chuquibamba	138	B3
Chuquicamata	138	B4
Chur	68	B2
Churan	85	L4
Churapcha	85	N4
Churchill *Canada*	119	S4
Churchill *Canada*	119	S4
Churchill *Newfoundland, Canada*	121	P7
Churchill, Cape	119	S4
Churchill Falls	121	P7
Churchill Peak	118	L4
Church Stretton	52	E2
Churia Ghati Hills	92	G3
Churin	136	B6
Churu	92	D3
Churuguara	136	D1
Chushevitsy	78	G3
Chushul	92	E2
Chusovaya	78	K4
Chusovov	78	K4
Chust	86	C3
Chute des Passes	125	Q2
Chuuronjang	88	B5
Chuxiong	93	K4
Chu Yang Sin	93	L6
Chwarta	94	G4
Chyulu Range	107	G3
Cianjur	90	D7
Cicekdagi	76	F3
Cicia	114	S8
Cide	76	E2
Cidones	66	E2
Ciechanow	71	J2
Ciego de Avila	132	H4
Cienaga	136	C1
Cienfuegos	132	G3
Cieszyn	71	H4
Cieza	67	F3
Ciftehan	76	F4
Cifteler	76	D3
Cifuentes	66	E2
Cihanbeyli	76	E3
Cijara, Embalse de	66	D3
Cilacap	90	D7
Cildir	77	K2
Cildir Golu	77	K2
Cilo Dagi	77	L4
Cimarron	128	A2
Cimone, Monte	68	C3
Cimpeni	73	G2
Cimpina	73	H3
Cimpulung	73	H3
Cimpuri	73	J2
Cinar	77	J4
Cinaruco	136	D2
Cina, Tanjung	90	C7
Cinca	67	G2
Cincer	72	D4
Cincinnati	124	H7
Cinderford	52	E3
Cine	76	C4
Cingus	77	H3
Cinto, Monte	69	B4
Circeo, Capo	69	D5
Circle *Alaska, U.S.A.*	118	C2
Circle *Montana, U.S.A.*	123	M4
Circular Reef	114	D2
Cirebon	90	D7
Cirencester	53	F3
Ciri	136	E5
Ciria	67	E2
Ciro	69	F6
Cisco	128	C4
Cislau	73	J3
Cisna	71	K4
Cisneros	136	B2
Cistierna	66	D1
Citac, Nevado	136	C6
Citlaltepetl, Volcan	131	L8
Citt a di Castello	68	D4
Cittanova	69	F6
Ciucului, Muntii	73	H2
Ciudad Acuna	127	M6
Ciudad Bolivar	136	E2
Ciudad Camargo	127	K7
Ciudad Cuauhtemoc	131	P10
Ciudad del Carmen	131	P8
Ciudad del Maiz	131	K6
Ciudad de Mexico	131	K8
Ciudadela	67	H3
Ciudad Guayana	136	E2
Ciudad Guzman	130	H8
Ciudad Ixtepec	131	M9
Ciudad Juarez	127	J5
Ciudad Lerdo	127	L8
Ciudad Madero	131	L6
Ciudad Mante	131	K6
Ciudad Mier	128	C7
Ciudad Obregon	127	H7
Ciudad Ojeda	133	M9
Ciudad Piar	133	R11
Ciudad Real	66	E3
Ciudad Rodrigo	66	C2
Ciudad Valles	131	K7
Ciudad Victoria	131	K6
Civa Burun	77	G2
Cividale del Friuli	68	D2
Civita Castellana	69	D4
Civitanova Marche	68	D4
Civitavecchia	69	C4
Civray	65	D5
Civril	76	C3
Cizre	77	K4
Clach Leathad	57	D4
Clacton-on-Sea	53	J3
Cladich	57	C4
Claerwen Reservoir	52	D2
Clain	65	D5
Claire, Lac a lEau	121	M6
Claire, Lake	119	N4
Clamecy	65	E5
Clane	59	J6
Clanton	129	J4
Clanwilliam	108	C6
Claonaig	57	C5
Clare *Australia*	113	H5
Clare *Ireland*	59	D7
Clare Island	58	B5
Claremont	125	P5
Claremorris	58	D5
Clarence *New Zealand*	115	D5
Clarence *New Zealand*	115	D5
Clarence, Cape	120	H3
Clarence Head	120	L2
Clarence Strait *Australia*	112	G1
Clarence Strait *U.S.A.*	118	J4
Clarence Town	133	K3
Clarinda	124	C6
Clarion	125	L6
Clark	123	K5
Clarke River	113	K2
Clark Fork *Montana, U.S.A*	122	H4
Clark Fork *Washington, U.S.A.*	122	F3
Clark, Lake	118	E3
Clarksburg	125	K7
Clarksdale	128	G3
Clarks Hill Lake	129	L4
Clarkston	122	F4
Clarksville *Arkansas, U.S.A.*	128	F3
Clarksville *Tennessee, U.S.A.*	129	J2
Clar, Loch nan	56	D2
Clatteringshaws Loch	57	D5
Claughton	55	G2
Clavering O	120	X3
Claxton	129	M4
Clay Center	123	R8
Clay Cross	55	H3
Claydon	53	J2
Clayton *Georgia, U.S.A.*	129	L3
Clayton *New Mexico, U.S.A.*	127	L2
Clear, Cape	59	C10
Clearfield *Pennsylvania, U.S.A.*	125	L6
Clearfield *Utah, U.S.A.*	122	J7
Clear Fork	127	N4
Clear Hills	119	M4
Clear Island	59	D10
Clear Lake *California, U.S.A.*	122	C8
Clear Lake *Iowa, U.S.A.*	124	D5
Clear Lake Reservoir	122	D7
Clearwater *Canada*	122	G2
Clearwater *Canada*	119	P4
Clearwater *Florida, U.S.A.*	129	L7
Clearwater *Idaho, U.S.A.*	122	F4
Clearwater Mountains	122	G4
Cleethorpes	55	J3
Clerke Reef	112	D2
Clermont *Australia*	113	K3
Clermont *France*	64	E4
Clermont-Ferrand	65	E6
Clermont-l'Herault	65	E7
Clervaux	64	G3
Cleve	113	H5
Clevedon	52	E3
Cleveland *U.K.*	55	H2
Cleveland *Mississippi, U.S.A.*	128	G4
Cleveland *Ohio, U.S.A.*	125	K5
Cleveland *Tennessee, U.S.A.*	129	K3
Cleveland *Texas, U.S.A.*	128	E5
Cleveland, Cape	113	K2
Cleveland Hills	55	H2
Cleveland, Mount	122	H3
Cleveleys	55	F3
Clew Bay	58	C5
Clifden *Ireland*	59	B5
Clifden *New Zealand*	115	A7
Cliffe	53	F3
Cliffs of Moher	59	C7
Clifton	55	C2
Clincha Alta	136	B6
Clinch Mountains	129	L2
Clingmans Dome	129	L3
Clinton *Canada*	122	D2
Clinton *Illinois, U.S.A.*	124	F6
Clinton *Iowa, U.S.A.*	124	E6
Clinton *Mississippi, U.S.A.*	128	G4
Clinton *Missouri, U.S.A.*	124	D7
Clinton *N. Carolina, U.S.A.*	129	N3
Clinton *Oklahoma, U.S.A.*	128	C3
Clinton-Colden Lake	119	P3
Clipperton Island	117	J7
Clisham	56	B3
Clisson	65	C5
Clitheroe	55	G3
Cliza	138	C3
Cloates, Point	112	C3
Clogheen	59	G8
Clogherhead	58	K5
Clogher Head	58	K5
Clogh Mills	58	K3
Clonakilty	59	E9
Clonakilty Bay	59	E9
Cloncurry *Australia*	113	J3
Cloncurry *Australia*	113	J3
Clonmel	59	G8
Clonmult	59	F9
Clophill	53	G2
Cloppenburg	70	C2
Cloquet	124	D3
Cloud Peak	123	L5
Cloudy Bay	115	E4
Clough	58	L4
Cloughton	55	J2
Clovelly	52	C3
Clovis	127	L3
Cloyes	65	D4
Cluanie, Loch	57	C3
Cluj-Napoca	73	G2
Clun	52	E2
Cluny	65	F5
Cluses	65	G5
Clusone	68	B3
Clutha	115	B7
Clwyd *U.K.*	55	F3
Clwyd *U.K.*	55	F3
Clwydian Range	55	F3
Clyde *Canada*	120	N3
Clyde *U.K.*	57	E5
Clydebank	57	D5
Clyde, Firth of	57	D5
Clydesdale	57	E5
Clynnog-fawr	54	E3
Clywedog, Llyn	52	D2
Coa	66	C2
Coachella	126	D4
Coachella Canal	126	E4
Coaldale	126	D2
Coalinga	126	B2
Coalisland	58	J3
Coal River	118	K4
Coalville	53	F2
Coan, Cerro	136	B5
Coari *Brazil*	136	E4
Coari *Brazil*	136	E4
Coast Mountains	122	B2
Coast Range	122	C5
Coatbridge	57	D5
Coaticook	125	Q4
Coats Island	120	K5
Coats Land	141	Y3
Coatzacoalcos *Mexico*	131	M8
Coatzacoalcos *Mexico*	131	M9
Coban	132	B7
Cobar	113	K5
Cobh	59	F9
Cobija	136	D6
Cobourg	125	L5
Cobram	113	K6
Cobue	109	F2
Coburg	70	D3
Coburg Island	120	L2
Cochabamba	138	C3
Cochem	70	B3
Cochin	92	E7
Cochrane *Canada*	122	G2
Cochrane *Chile*	139	B9
Cock Bridge	57	E3
Cockburn	113	J5
Cockburnspath	57	F5
Cockenzie	57	F4
Cockerham	55	G3
Cockermouth	55	F2
Cockfield *Durham, U.K.*	55	H2
Cockfield *Suffolk, U.K.*	53	H2
Coco	132	E7
Cocoa	129	M6
Coco Channel	93	H6
Coco Islands	93	H6
Cocoparra Range	113	K5
Cocos	137	J6
Cocula	130	H7
Codajas	136	E4
Cod, Cape	125	R6
Codera, Cabo	136	D1
Codfish Island	115	A7
Codford	53	E3
Codigoro	68	D3
Cod Island	121	P6
Codo	137	J4
Codogno	68	B3
Cod's Head	59	B9
Coen	113	J1
Coeroeni	137	F3
Coesfeld	70	B3
Coeur d'Alene	122	F4
Coeur d'Alene Lake	122	F4
Coevorden	64	G2
Coffeyville	128	E2
Coffin Bay	113	H5
Coff's Harbour	113	L5
Cogealac	73	K3
Coghinas	69	B5
Cognac	65	C6
Cogo	105	G5
Cogolludo	66	E2
Cohuna	113	J6
Coiba, Isla	132	G11
Coigach	56	C2
Coigeach, Rubha	56	C2
Coihaique	139	B9
Coimbatore	92	E6
Coimbra	66	B2
Coipasa, Salar de	138	C3
Cokak	77	G4
Colac	113	J6
Colap	77	H4
Colatina	138	E3
Colby	123	P8
Colchester	53	H3
Cold Ashton	52	E3
Coldstream	57	F5
Coldwater *Kansas, U.S.A.*	127	N2
Coldwater *Michigan, U.S.A.*	124	H6
Colebrook	125	Q4
Coleman *Australia*	113	J1
Coleman *U.S.A.*	127	N5
Colemerick	77	K4
Coleraine *Australia*	113	J6
Coleraine *U.K.*	58	J2
Colesberg	108	E6
Coleshill	53	F2
Coles, Punta de	139	B3
Colfax	122	F4
Colgrave Sound	56	B1
Colhue Huapi, Lago	139	C9
Colima	130	H8
Colima, Nevado de	130	H8
Colinas	137	J5
Colintraive	57	C5
Coll	57	C4
Collatto	68	D2
College Park	129	K4
Collie	112	D5
Collier Bay	112	E2
Colliford Lake Reservoir	52	C4
Collingbourne Kingston	53	F3
Collingham	55	J3
Collingwood *Canada*	125	K4
Collingwood *New Zealand*	115	D4
Collins	128	H5
Collin Top	58	K3
Collooney	58	F4
Colmar	64	G4
Colmars	65	G6
Colmenar	66	D4
Colmenar Viejo	66	E2
Colne *Essex, U.K.*	53	H3
Colne *Lancashire, U.K.*	55	G3
Cologne	70	B3
Colombia	136	C3
Colombo	92	E7
Colomoncagua	132	C7
Colon *Cuba*	132	G3
Colon *Panama*	132	H10
Colonia Las Heras	139	C9
Colonna, Capo	69	F6
Colonsay	57	B4
Colorado *Argentina*	139	D7
Colorado *Arizona, U.S.A.*	126	E4
Colorado *Texas, U.S.A.*	127	M4
Colorado *U.S.A.*	123	L8
Colorado Canal	123	N8
Colorado, Cerro	126	E5
Colorado City	127	M4
Colorado River Aqueduct	126	D4
Colorado Springs	127	K1
Colsterworth	53	G2
Coluene	137	G6
Columbia *Missouri, U.S.A.*	124	D7
Columbia *Pennsylvania, U.S.A.*	125	M7
Columbia *S. Carolina, U.S.A.*	129	M4
Columbia *Tennessee, U.S.A.*	129	J3
Columbia *Washington, U.S.A.*	122	D5
Columbia, District of	125	M7
Columbia Falls	122	G3
Columbia, Mount	119	M5
Columbine, Cape	108	C6
Columbus *Georgia, U.S.A.*	129	K4
Columbus *Indiana, U.S.A.*	124	H7
Columbus *Mississippi, U.S.A.*	128	H4
Columbus *Montana, U.S.A.*	123	K5
Columbus *Nebraska, U.S.A.*	123	R7
Columbus *Ohio, U.S.A.*	124	J7
Columbus *Texas, U.S.A.*	128	D6
Colville *Alaska, U.S.A.*	118	D2
Colville *Washington, U.S.A.*	122	F3
Colville, Cape	115	E2
Colville Channel	115	E2
Colville Lake	118	K2
Colwyn Bay	54	F3
Comacchio	68	D3
Comana	73	J3
Comandante Ferraz	141	W6
Comandante Fontana	138	E5
Comayagua	132	D7
Combarbala	138	B6
Combe Martin	52	C3
Comber	58	L3
Combermere Bay	93	H5
Combourg	64	C4
Comeragh Mountains	59	G8
Comfort, Cape	120	K4

Comilla 93 H4
Comitan 131 N9
Committee Bay 120 J4
Como 68 B3
Comodoro Rivadavia 139 C9
Como, Lago di 68 B3
Comorin, Cape 92 E7
Comoros 109 H2
Compiegne 64 E4
Comporta 66 B3
Compostela 130 G7
Conakry 104 C4
Conara Junction 113 K7
Concarneau 65 B5
Conceicao do Araguaia 137 H5
Concepcion *Bolivia* 138 D3
Concepcion *Chile* 138 B7
Concepcion *Panama* 132 F10
Concepcion *Paraguay* 138 E4
Concepcion del Oro 130 J5
Concepcion del Uruguay 138 E6
Concepcion, Punta 126 G7
Conception Bay 121 R8
Conception Island 133 K3
Conception, Point 126 B3
Concho 127 M5
Conchos *Mexico* 128 C8
Conchos *Mexico* 127 K6
Concord *California, U.S.A.* 126 A2
Concord *N. Carolina, U.S.A.* 129 M3
Concord *New Hampshire, U.S.A.* 125 Q5
Concordia *Argentina* 138 E6
Concordia *U.S.A.* 123 R8
Condamine 113 L4
Condeuba 138 J6
Condolobin 113 K5
Condom 65 D7
Conecuh 129 J5
Conegliano 68 D3
Conflict Group 114 E4
Confolens 65 D5
Congjiang 93 L3
Congleton 55 G3
Congo 106 B3
Congo 106 D2
Congo Basin 99 E6
Conisbrough 55 H3
Coniston 55 F2
Coniston Water 54 E2
Connah's Quay 55 F3
Connaught 58 D5
Conneaut 125 K6
Connecticut *U.S.A.* 125 P6
Connecticut *U.S.A.* 125 P6
Connellsville 125 L6
Conn, Lough 58 D4
Connors Range 113 K3
Conon 56 D3
Conon Bridge 56 D3
Conrad 122 J3
Conselheiro Lafaiete 138 H4
Conselheiro Pena 138 H3
Consett 55 H2
Con Son 93 L7
Constance, Lake 70 C5
Constancia dos Baetas 136 E5
Constanta 73 K3
Constantina 66 D4
Constantine 101 G1
Constantine Bay 52 B4
Constantine, Cape 118 D4
Constantinople 76 C2
Constitucion 139 B7
Contamana 136 C5
Contas 137 J6
Contratacion 136 C2
Contrexeville 64 F4
Contulmo 139 B7
Contwoyto Lake 119 N2
Conway *Arkansas, U.S.A.* 128 F3
Conway *New Hampshire, U.S.A.* 125 Q5
Conway *S. Carolina, U.S.A.* 129 N4
Conway Bay 54 F3
Conwy 54 F3
Coober Pedy 113 G4
Cook 112 G5
Cook, Cape 122 A2
Cookeville 129 K2
Cook Inlet 118 E3
Cook Islands 143 H5
Cook, Mount 115 C5
Cook, Recif de 114 W15
Cookstown 58 J3
Cook Strait 115 E4
Cooktown 113 K2
Coolibah 112 G2
Coolidge 126 G4
Cooma 113 K6
Coomnadiha 59 C9
Coomscarrea 59 B9
Coonamble 113 K5
Coondapoor 92 D6
Coongan 112 D3
Coopers Creek 113 H4
Cooroy 113 L4
Coosa 129 J4
Coos Bay *U.S.A.* 122 B6
Coos Bay *U.S.A.* 122 B6
Cootamundra 113 K5
Cootehill 58 H4
Copacabana 138 C3
Copa, Cerro 138 C4
Cope 123 N8
Copenhagen 63 E9
Copiapo 138 B5
Copinsay 56 F2
Copkoy 76 B2
Copper 118 G3
Copper Center 118 F3
Coppermine *Canada* 119 M2
Coppermine *Canada* 119 N2
Copper Mount 122 F2
Copplestone 52 D4
Copsa Mica 73 H2
Coquet 57 G5
Coquimbo 138 B5
Coquimbo, Bahia de 138 B5
Corabia 73 H4
Coracora 136 C7
Coral Harbour 120 K5
Coral Sea Plateau 113 K2
Corantijn 136 F3
Corbeil-Essonnes 64 E4
Corbiere 53 M7
Corbieres 65 E7
Corbigny 65 E5
Corbin 124 H8
Corbones 66 D4
Corbridge 55 G2
Corby 53 G2
Corby Glen 53 G2
Corcaigh 59 E9
Corcovado, Golfo 139 B8
Corcubion 66 B1
Cordele 129 L5
Cordoba 131 L8
Cordoba *Argentina* 138 D6
Cordoba *Spain* 66 D4
Cordoba, Sierras de 138 D6
Cordova 136 B6
Cordova 118 F3
Corfe 52 D4
Corfu *Greece* 74 E3
Corfu *Greece* 74 E3
Coria 66 C2
Corigliano Calabro 69 F6
Corinda 113 H2
Corinth *Greece* 75 G4
Corinth *U.S.A.* 128 H3
Corinth, Gulf of 75 G3
Corinto *Brazil* 138 H3
Corinto *Nicaragua* 132 D8
Corixa Grande 138 E3
Cork *Ireland* 59 E9
Cork *Ireland* 59 E9
Corlay 64 B4
Corleone 69 D7
Corlu 76 B2
Cornafulla 59 F6
Corner Brook 121 Q8
Cornhill-on-Tweed 57 F4
Corning 125 M5
Corn Islands 132 F8
Cornudilla 66 E1
Cornwall *U.K.* 52 C4
Cornwall *U.K.* 125 N4
Cornwallis Island 120 H2
Cornwall Island 120 H2
Coro 136 D1
Coroata 137 J4
Corocoro 138 C3
Coromandel *Brazil* 138 G3
Coromandel *New Zealand* 115 E2
Coromandel Coast 92 F6
Coromandel Peninsula 115 E2
Corona 127 K3
Coronado, Bahia de 132 E10
Coronation Gulf 119 N2
Coronel 139 B7
Coronel Dorrego 139 D7
Coronel Pringles 139 D7
Coronel Suarez 139 D7
Corovode 75 F2
Corps 65 F6
Corpus Christi 128 D7
Corpus Christi Bay 128 D7
Corpus Christi, Lake 128 D6
Corque 138 C3
Corran 57 C4
Corraun Peninsula 58 C5
Corrib, Lough 59 D6
Corrientes *Argentina* 138 E5
Corrientes *Peru* 136 B4
Corrientes, Cabo *Colombia* 136 B2
Corrientes, Cabo *Cuba* 132 E4
Corrientes, Cabo *Mexico* 130 G7
Corrigan 128 E5
Corrigin 112 D5
Corry 125 L6
Corryvreckan, Gulf of 57 C4
Corse 69 B4
Corse, Cap 68 B4
Corsewall Point 57 C5
Corsica 69 B4
Corsicana 128 D4
Corte 69 B4
Cortegana 66 C4
Cortez 127 H2
Cortina d'Ampezzo 68 D2
Cortland 125 M5
Cortona 68 C4
Corubal 104 C3
Coruche 66 B3
Coruh 77 J2
Corum 76 F2
Corumba 138 E3
Corumba 138 G3
Corunna 66 B1
Corvallis 122 C5
Corve 52 E2
Corwen 52 D2
Cos 75 J4
Cosamaloapan 131 M8
Cosamozza 69 B4
Cosenza 69 F6
Cosiguina, Volcan 132 D8
Cosmoledo Islands 82 C7
Cosne 65 E5
Costa, Cordillera de la 133 N9
Costa Rica 132 E9
Costesti 73 H3
Cotabato 91 G4
Cotacachi 136 B3
Cotagaita 138 C4
Cotahuasi 138 B3
Cotentin 64 C4
Cotiella 67 G1
Cotonou 105 F4
Cotopaxi 136 B4
Cottage Grove 122 C6
Cottbus 70 F3
Cottingham 55 J3
Cottonwood 126 F3
Coubre, Pointe de la 65 C6
Coulommiers 64 E4
Coulonge 125 M3
Council Bluffs 124 C6
Coupar Angus 57 E4
Courantyne 136 F3
Courchevel 65 G6
Couronne, Cap 65 F7
Courtenay 122 B3
Courtmacsherry Bay 59 E9
Coutances 64 C4
Couto Magalhaes 137 H5
Coutras 65 C6
Cove 56 C3
Coventry 53 F2
Covilha 66 C2
Covington *Kentucky, U.S.A.* 124 H7
Covington *Virginia, U.S.A.* 125 L8
Cowal 57 C4
Cowan, Lake 112 E5
Cowbit 53 G2
Cowbridge 52 D3
Cowdenbeath 57 E4
Cowes 53 F4
Cowfold 53 G4
Cowlitz 122 C4
Cowra 113 K5
Coxim 138 F3
Coxs Bazar 93 H4
Coxwold 55 H2
Cozumel 131 R7
Cozumel, Isla de 131 R7
Cracow 71 H3
Cradock 108 E6
Craig 123 L7
Craigavon 58 K4
Craignure 57 C4
Crail 57 F4
Crailsheim 70 D4
Craiova 73 G3
Cramlington 55 H1
Cranborne 53 F4
Cranbrook 122 G3
Crane 127 L5
Cranleigh 53 G3
Cranstown, Kap 120 Q3
Craponne-sur-Arzon 65 E6
Crasna *Romania* 73 G2
Crasna *Romania* 73 J2
Crater Lake 122 C6
Crateus 137 J5
Crati 69 F6
Crato 137 K5
Cravo Norte 136 C2
Crawford 123 N6
Crawford Point 91 F3
Crawfordville 129 K5
Crawley 53 G3
Crazy Mountains 123 J4
Creach Bheinn 57 C4
Creag Meagaidh 57 D3
Creagorry 56 A3
Crediton 52 D4
Cree *Canada* 119 P4
Cree *U.K.* 57 D5
Cree Lake 119 P4
Creeslough 58 G2
Creetown 54 E2
Creggan 58 H3
Creggs 58 F5
Crema 68 B3
Cremona 68 B3
Crepaja 72 F3
Creran, Loch 57 C4
Cres *Yugoslavia* 72 C3
Cres *Yugoslavia* 72 C3
Crescent 122 D6
Crescent City 122 B7
Crest 65 F6
Creston 124 C6
Crestview 129 J5
Crete 75 H5
Cretin, Cape 114 D3
Creus, Cap 67 H1
Creuse 65 D5
Crevillente 67 F3
Crewe 55 G3
Crewkerne 52 E4
Crianlarich 57 D4
Criccieth 52 C2
Criciuma 138 G5
Crick 53 F2
Crickhowell 52 D3
Cricklade 53 F3
Crieff 57 E4
Criffel 55 F2
Crikvenica 72 C3
Crimea 79 E6
Cristalandia 137 H6
Cristalina 138 G3
Cristobal Colon, Pico 136 C1
Crisu Alb 73 F2
Crisu Negru 73 F2
Crisu Repede 73 G2
Crna Reka 73 F5
Crni Drim 72 F5
Croaghgorm Mountains 58 F3
Croagh Patrick 58 C5
Croatia 72 C3
Crocketford 57 E5
Crockett 128 E5
Croggan 57 C4
Crohy Head 58 F3
Croick 56 D3
Croisette, Cap 65 F7
Croke, Mount 112 D5
Croker Island 112 G1
Cromalt Hills 56 C2
Cromar 57 F3
Cromarty 56 D3
Cromarty Firth 56 D3
Cromdale, Hills of 56 E3
Cromer 53 J2
Cromwell 115 B6
Crook 55 H2
Crooked *Canada* 122 D5
Crooked *U.S.A.* 119 L4
Crooked Island 133 K3
Crooked Island Passage 133 K3
Crookham 57 F4
Crookhaven 59 C10
Crookston 124 B3
Croom 59 E7
Crosby *Isle of Man, U.K.* 54 E2
Crosby *Merseyside, U.K.* 55 F3
Crosby *U.S.A.* 124 D3
Cross 105 G4
Crossett 128 G4
Cross Fell 55 G2
Crossgar 58 L4
Cross Hands 52 C3
Crosshaven 59 F9
Cross Lake 119 R5
Crossmaglen 58 J4
Crossmolina 58 D4
Cross Sound 118 H4
Crossville 129 K3
Crotone 69 F6
Crouch 53 H3
Crowborough 53 H3
Crowle 55 J3
Crowley's Ridge 128 G3
Crowsnest Pass 119 N6
Croxton Kerrial 53 G2
Croydon *Australia* 113 J2
Croydon *U.K.* 53 G2
Crozet, Iles 142 C6
Crozier Channel 120 C2
Cruces, Punta 136 B2
Crudgington 52 E2
Crumlin 58 K3
Cruz Alta 138 F5
Cruz, Cabo 132 J5
Cruz del Eje 138 C6
Cruzeiro do Sul 136 C5
Cruz Grande *Chile* 138 B5
Cruz Grande *Mexico* 131 K9
Crymych 52 C3
Crystal City 127 N6
Crystal Falls 124 F3
Csongrad 72 F2
Csorna 72 D2
Cuamba 109 G2
Cuando 106 D6
Cuangar 106 C6
Cuango 106 C4
Cuanza 106 C4
Cuatro Cienegas 127 L7
Cuauhtemoc 127 J6
Cuautla 131 K8
Cuba 132 G4
Cubango 106 C6
Cubara 133 L11
Cubuk 76 E2
Cuchi 106 C5
Cuchilla Grande 138 E6
Cuchivero 136 D2
Cuchumatanes, Alto 132 B7
Cuckfield 53 G3
Cucuta 136 C2
Cuddalore 92 E6
Cuddapah 92 E6
Cudgwa 113 K6
Cue 112 D4
Cuellar 66 D2
Cuenca 136 B4
Cuencame 130 H5
Cuenca, Serrania de 66 E2
Cuernavaca 131 K8
Cuero 128 D6
Cuiaba *Brazil* 138 E3

x

F

Name	Page	Grid
Garachine, Punta	132	H10
Gara, Lough	58	F5
Garanhuns	137	K5
Garara	114	D3
Garberville	122	C7
Garboldisham	53	H2
Garbosh, Kuh-e	95	K5
Garcas	138	F3
Gard	65	F7
Garda, Lago di	68	C3
Gardelegen	70	D2
Garden City	127	M2
Garden Grove	126	C4
Gardez	92	C2
Gardhiki	75	F3
Gardiner	123	J5
Gardnerville	126	C1
Gardno, Jezioro	71	G1
Garelochhead	57	D4
Gareloi Island	118	Ac9
Garessio	68	B3
Garforth	55	H3
Gargalianoi	75	F4
Gargunnock	57	D4
Garies	108	C6
Garissa	107	G3
Garland	128	D4
Garmish-Partenkirchen	70	D5
Garmsar	95	L4
Garnet Bay	120	L4
Garnett	128	E1
Garonne	65	C6
Garoua	105	H4
Garrison Dam	123	P4
Garron Point	58	L2
Garrovillas	66	C3
Garry Lake	119	R2
Garry, Loch	57	D3
Garstang	55	G3
Gartempe	65	D5
Gartocharn	57	D4
Garton Lough	58	G3
Garton-on-the-Wolds	55	J2
Garut	90	D7
Garvagh	58	J3
Garve	56	D3
Garvie Mountains	115	B6
Garwa	92	F4
Garwolin	71	J3
Gary	124	G6
Gar Zangbo	92	F2
Garze	93	J2
Garzon	136	B3
Gasan Kuli	95	L3
Gascogne	65	D7
Gascogne, Golfe de	65	C7
Gasconade	124	D8
Gascoyne	112	C3
Gascuna, Golfo de	67	F1
Gasht	95	Q8
Gashua	105	H3
Gask	95	P5
Gasmata	114	E3
Gaspar, Selat	90	D6
Gaspe	121	P8
Gaspe, Cape	121	P8
Gaspe Peninsula	121	N8
Gastonia	129	M3
Gaston, Lake	129	N2
Gastouni	75	F4
Gastre	139	C8
Gata, Cabo de	66	E4
Gatas, Akra	76	E5
Gata, Sierra de	66	C2
Gatchina	63	P7
Gatehouse of Fleet	54	E2
Gateshead	55	H2
Gateshead Island	119	Q1
Gatineau	125	N3
Gatooma	108	E3
Gatruyeh	95	M7
Gatun Lake	132	H10
Gatvand	94	J5
Gatwick	53	G3
Gaud-i-Zureh	95	R7
Gauer Lake	119	R4
Gauhati	93	H3
Gauja	63	L8
Gauldalen	62	D5
Gausta	63	C7
Gavater	95	Q9
Gavbus, Kuh-e	95	L8
Gavdhopoula	75	G5
Gavdhos	75	H5
Gaviao	66	C3
Gav Koshi	95	N7
Gavle	63	G6
Gavleborg	63	G6
Gavrilov-Yam	78	F4
Gawler	113	H5
Gawler Ranges	113	H5
Gaxun Nur	86	J3
Gaya	92	G4
Gaya La	92	F3
Gaydon	53	F2
Gayndah	113	L4
Gaysin	73	K1
Gayvoron	79	D6
Gaza	94	B6
Gazelle Peninsula	114	E2
Gazelle, Recif de la	114	W16
Gaziantep	77	G4
Gazimur	85	K6
Gazimurskiy Zavod	85	K6
Gazipasa	76	E4
Gbarnga	104	D4
Gboko	105	G4
Gdansk	71	H1
Gdov	63	M7
Geary	56	B3
Gebeit	96	C7
Gebze	76	C2
Gecitli	77	K4
Gedaref	103	G5
Gediz Turkey	76	B3
Gediz Turkey	76	C3
Gedney Hill	53	G2
Gedser	70	D1
Gee	64	F3
Geelong	113	J6
Geelvink Channel	112	C4
Geeveston	113	K7
Gegyai	92	F2
Geikie	119	Q4
Geilo	63	C6
Geita	107	F3
Geitlandsjokull	62	U12
Gejiu	93	K4
Geka, Mys	85	X4
Gela	69	E7
Geladi	103	J6
Gelendost	76	D3
Gelendzhik	79	F7
Gelibolu	76	B2
Gelibolu Yarimadasi	75	J2
Gelligaer	52	D3
Gelnhausen	70	C3
Gelsenkirchen	70	B3
Gemena	106	C2
Gemerek	77	G3
Gemlik	76	C2
Gemlik Korfezi	75	K2
Gemona del Friuli	68	D2
Gemund	70	B3
Genale Wenz	103	H6
Genc	77	J3
Geneina	102	D5
General Acha	139	D7
General Alvear	139	C7
General Bernardo O'Higgins	141	W6
General Conesa	139	D8
General La Madrid	139	D7
General Lavalle	139	E7
General Madariaga	139	E7
General Paz	139	E7
General Paz, Lago	139	B8
General Pico	139	D7
General Roca	139	C7
General Sam Martin	141	V5
General Santos	91	H4
General Villegas	139	D7
Geneseo	125	M5
Genessee	125	L5
Geneva Switzerland	68	A2
Geneva U.S.A.	125	M5
Geneva, Lake of	68	A2
Geneve	68	A2
Gen He	87	N1
Genichesk	79	E6
Genil	66	D4
Gennargentu, Monti del	69	B6
Genoa Australia	113	K6
Genoa Italy	68	B3
Genova	68	B3
Genova, Golfo di	68	B3
Genovesa, Isla	136	B7
Genriyetty, Ostrov	81	S2
Gent	64	E3
Genteng	90	D7
Genyem	91	L6
Geographe Bay	112	D5
Geographe Channel	112	C3
Geokchay	79	H7
George Canada	121	N6
George South Africa	108	D6
Georgeham	52	C3
George Island	139	E10
George, Lake	129	M6
George Sound	115	A6
Georgetown Australia	113	H5
George Town Australia	113	K7
Georgetown Gambia	104	C3
Georgetown Grand Cayman, U.K.	132	G5
Georgetown Guyana	136	F2
George Town Malaysia	90	C4
Georgetown U.S.A.	129	N4
George V Land	141	K4
George VI Sound	141	V4
Georgia	77	K1
Georgia	129	K4
Georgian Bay	125	K4
Georgia, Strait of	122	C3
Georgina	113	H3
Georgina Bay	121	K8
Georgiu-Dezh	79	F5
Georgiyevka	86	E2
Georgiyevsk	79	G7
Georg von Neumayer	141	Z4
Gera	70	E3
Geral de Goias, Serra	137	H6
Geraldine	115	C6
Geraldton Australia	112	C4
Geraldton U.S.A.	124	G2
Gerardmer	64	G4
Gerasimovka	84	A5
Gercus	77	J4
Gerede Turkey	76	E2
Gerede Turkey	76	E2
Gereshk	92	B2
Gergal	66	E4
Gerger	77	H4
Gerik	90	C4
Geris	76	D4
Gerlachovsky	71	J4
Germany	70	C3
Germencik	76	B4
Germi	94	J2
Germiston	108	E5
Gerona	67	H2
Gerrards Cross	53	G3
Gerze	76	F2
Geseke	70	C3
Geta	63	G6
Getafe	66	E2
Gettysburg Pennsylvania, U.S.A.	125	M7
Gettysburg S. Dakota, U.S.A.	123	Q5
Geumapang	90	B5
Gevan	95	N8
Gevas	77	K3
Geyik Dagi	76	E4
Geyik Daglari	76	E4
Geyve	76	D2
Gezi	77	F3
Ghadamis	101	G2
Ghaghara	92	F3
Ghana	104	E4
Ghanzi	108	D4
Gharah, Wadi	97	L8
Gharbi, Al Hajar al	97	N4
Gharbiya, Es Sahra el	103	E2
Ghardaia	101	F2
Ghardimaou	69	B7
Gharrat, Shatt al	94	H6
Gharyan	101	H2
Ghat	101	H3
Ghatampur	92	F3
Ghatere	114	J5
Ghayl Ba Wazir	97	J9
Ghayl Bin Yumayn	97	J9
Ghazaouet	100	E1
Ghaziabad	92	E3
Ghazipur	92	F3
Ghazni	92	C2
Gheorgheni	73	H2
Ghimes-Faget	73	J2
Ghisonaccia	69	B4
Ghisoni	69	B4
Ghubbah	97	P10
Ghubeish	102	E5
Ghudaf, Wadi al	94	E5
Ghurian	95	Q4
Giant's Causeway Head	58	J2
Giarre	69	E7
Gibostad	62	H2
Gibraltar	66	D4
Gibraltar Point	55	K3
Gibraltar, Strait of	66	D5
Gibson Desert	112	E3
Gichgeniyn Nuruu	86	H2
Gidole	103	G6
Gien	65	E5
Giesseckes Isfjord	120	Q3
Giessen	70	C3
Gifatin	96	A3
Gifford Creek	112	D3
Gifhorn	70	D2
Gifu	89	F8
Giganta, Sierra de la	130	D5
Gigha Island	57	C5
Gigha, Sound of	57	C5
Giglio, Isola di	69	C4
Gijon	66	D1
Gijunabena Islands	114	J5
Gila	126	F4
Gila Bend	126	F4
Gilan Garb	94	G4
Gilbert	113	J2
Gilbert Islands	111	R2
Gilbert, Mount	122	B2
Gilbues	137	H5
Gile	109	G3
Gilford	58	K4
Gilgandra	113	K5
Gilgit	92	D1
Gillam	119	S4
Gillen, Mount	113	G3
Gillesnuole	62	G4
Gillespie Point	115	B5
Gillette	123	M5
Gillian Lake	120	L4
Gillingham	53	H3
Gill, Lough	58	F4
Gilroy	126	B2
Giluwe, Mount	114	C3
Gimli	123	R2
Gimo	63	H6
Gimone	65	D7
Ginda	96	D9
Gingin	112	D5
Ginir	103	H6
Gioia del Colle	69	F5
Gioia, Golfo di	69	E6
Giona	75	G3
Girardot	136	C3
Girdle Ness	57	F3
Giresun	77	H2
Girga	103	F2
Girgir, Cape	114	C2
Giridih	92	G4
Girifalco	69	F6
Gironde	65	C6
Girvan	57	D5
Gisborne	115	G3
Gisenye	107	E3
Gislaved	63	E8
Gisors	64	D4
Gitega	107	E3
Giurgeni	73	J3
Giurgiu	73	H4
Givet	64	F3
Givors	65	F6
Gizhiginskaya Guba	85	T4
Gizol	114	H6
Gizycko	71	J1
Gjesvar	62	L1
Gjirokaster	75	F2
Gjoa Haven	120	G4
Gjovik	63	D6
Gjuhezes, Kep i	74	E2
Glace Bay	121	Q8
Glacier Bay	118	H4
Glacier Peak	122	D3
Gladstone Australia	113	L3
Gladstone U.S.A.	124	G4
Glama	63	D6
Glamis	57	E4
Glamoc	72	D3
Glarus	68	B2
Glasdrumman	58	L4
Glasgow U.K.	57	D5
Glasgow Kentucky, U.S.A.	124	H8
Glasgow Montana, U.S.A.	123	L3
Glas Maol	57	E4
Glass	56	D3
Glass, Loch	56	D3
Glastonbury	52	E3
Glatz	71	G3
Glauchau	70	E3
Glazov	78	J4
Glda	71	G2
Gleiwitz	71	H3
Glen Affric	56	D3
Glenan, Iles de	65	B5
Glenavy	115	C6
Glen Cannich	56	D3
Glen Canyon	126	G2
Glen Canyon Dam	126	G2
Glencarse	57	E4
Glen Coe	57	D4
Glencoe	108	F5
Glen Cove	125	P6
Glendale Arizona, U.S.A.	126	F4
Glendale California, U.S.A.	126	C3
Glendive	123	M4
Glenelg Australia	113	J6
Glenelg U.K.	56	C3
Glen Esk	57	F4
Glenfinnan	57	C4
Glengad Head	58	H2
Glen Garry Highland, U.K.	57	C3
Glen Garry Tayside, U.K.	57	D4
Glen Innes	113	L4
Glen Mor	57	D3
Glen Moriston	57	D3
Glennallen	118	F3
Glen Orrin	56	D3
Glenrothes	57	E4
Glens Falls	125	P5
Glenshee	57	E4
Glentham	55	J3
Glenwood	128	F3
Glenwood Springs	123	L8
Glin	59	D7
Glina	72	D3
Glittertind	63	C6
Glomach, Falls of	56	C3
Glomfjord	62	E3
Glommerstrask	62	H4
Glossop	55	H3
Glottof, Mount	118	E4
Gloucester Australia	113	L5
Gloucester Papua New Guinea	114	D3
Gloucester U.K.	52	E3
Gloucester U.S.A.	125	Q5
Gloucestershire	52	E3
Gloup	56	A1
Glover Reef	132	D6
Glowno	71	H3
Glubczyce	71	G3
Glubinnoye	88	E2
Glubokoye Belorussia	63	M9
Glubokoye Kazakhstan	84	C6
Gluckstadt	70	C2
Glukhov	79	E5
Glyadyanskoye	84	Ae6
Glybokaya	73	H1
Glyder Fawr	54	E3
Gmelinka	79	H5
Gmund	68	D2
Gmunden	68	D2
Gnalta	113	J5
Gnarp	63	G5
Gniezno	71	G2
Gnoien	70	E2
Gnosall	52	E2
Goa	92	D5
Goalpara	93	H3
Goatfell	57	C5

Goba	103	H6	Goose Lake	122	D7	Gracac	72	C3	Granville	64	C4

Goba 103 H6
Gobabis 108 C4
Gobi 87 K3
Gobo 89 E9
Gochas 108 C4
Godafoss 62 W12
Godalming 53 G3
Godavari 92 F5
Godbout 125 S2
Goderich 125 K5
Godhavn 120 R4
Godhra 92 D4
Godollo 72 E2
Gods 119 S4
Godshill 53 F4
Gods Lake 119 S5
Godthab 120 R5
Godwin Austen 92 E1
Goeland, Lac au 121 L8
Goes 64 E3
Gogama 125 K3
Goginan 52 D2
Gogland, Ostrov 63 M6
Gogolin 71 H3
Goiana 137 L5
Goiania 138 G3
Goias *Brazil* 138 F3
Goias *Brazil* 137 H6
Gojome 88 H6
Gokceada 76 A2
Gokcekaya Baraji 76 D2
Gokdere 77 G2
Gokirmak 76 F2
Gokova Korfezi 76 B4
Goksu *Turkey* 76 E4
Goksu *Turkey* 77 F4
Goksun 77 G3
Goktas 77 J2
Goktepe 76 E4
Gol 63 C6
Golaghat 93 H3
Golam Head 59 C6
Golashkerd 95 N8
Golbasi *Turkey* 76 E3
Golbasi *Turkey* 77 G4
Golcar 55 H3
Golchikha 84 C2
Golconda 122 F7
Golcuk 76 C2
Golcuk Daglari 76 B3
Goldap 71 K1
Gold Coast 113 L4
Golden 122 F2
Golden Bay 115 D4
Goldendale 122 D5
Golden Hinde 122 B3
Goldsboro 129 P3
Goldsworthy 112 D3
Gole 77 K2
Golebert 77 K2
Goleniow 70 F2
Golfito 132 F10
Golfo Aranci 69 B5
Golgeli Daglari 76 C4
Golhisar 76 C4
Golija Planina 72 F4
Golkoy 77 G2
Golmarmara 76 B3
Golmud 93 H1
Golo 69 B4
Golova 76 D4
Golovanevsk 73 L1
Golovnino 88 K4
Golpayegan 95 K5
Golpazari 76 D2
Goma 107 E3
Gombe 105 H3
Gombi 105 H3
Gomel 79 E5
Gomera 100 B3
Gomez Palacio 127 L8
Gomishan 95 M3
Gonaives 133 L5
Gonam *Russia* 85 M5
Gonam *Russia* 85 N5
Gonave, Golfe de la 133 L5
Gonave, Ile de la 133 L5
Gonbad-e Kavus 95 M3
Gonda 92 F3
Gondal 92 D4
Gonder 103 G5
Gondia 92 F4
Gonen *Turkey* 76 B2
Gonen *Turkey* 76 B3
Gongbogyamda 93 H3
Gongolo 105 H3
Gongpoquan 86 H3
Goniadz 71 K2
Gonumillo 139 C8
Gonzales *California, U.S.A.* 126 B2
Gonzales *Texas, U.S.A.* 128 D6
Gonzales Chaves 139 D7
Goob Weyn 107 H3
Goodenough, Cape 141 J5
Goodenough Island 114 E3
Good Hope, Cape of 108 C6
Gooding 122 G6
Goodland 123 P8
Goole 55 J3
Goolgowi 113 K5
Goomen 113 L4
Goondiwindi 113 L4
Goose Bay 121 P7
Goose Creek 129 M4

Goose Lake 122 D7
Goplo, Jezioro 71 H2
Goppingen 70 C4
Gora Kalwaria 71 J3
Gorakhpur 92 F3
Gorazde 72 E4
Gorda, Punta 138 B3
Gordes 76 C3
Gordonsville 125 L7
Gore 115 B7
Gore 103 G6
Gorele 77 H2
Goresbridge 59 J7
Gorey *Ireland* 59 K7
Gorey *U.K.* 53 M7
Gorgan 95 M3
Gorgan, Rud-e 95 M3
Gorgona, Isola di 68 B4
Gorgoram 105 H3
Gori 77 L1
Gorice 75 F2
Gorinchem 64 F3
Goris 94 H2
Gorizia 68 D3
Gorka 78 H3
Gorkha 92 F3
Gorki *Belorussia* 78 E5
Gorki *Russia* 84 Ae3
Gorki *Russia* 78 H4
Gorkiy 78 G4
Gorkovskoye Vodokhranilishche 78 G4
Gorlev 63 D9
Gorlice 71 J4
Gorlitz 70 F3
Gorlovka 79 F6
Gornji Milanovac 72 F3
Gornji Vakuf 72 D4
Gorno-Altaysk 84 D6
Gornozavodsk 88 H2
Gornyak 84 C6
Gornyy *Russia* 79 H5
Gornyy *Russia* 85 P6
Gorodenka 73 H1
Gorodets 78 G4
Gorodok 71 K4
Gorodovikovsk 79 G6
Goroka 114 D3
Gorokhov 71 L3
Gorong, Kepulauan 91 J6
Gorongoza 109 F3
Gorontalo 91 G5
Goroshikha 84 D3
Gorran Haven 52 C4
Gorseinon 52 C3
Gort 59 E6
Gortaclare 58 H3
Gortahork 58 F2
Gorumna Island 59 C6
Goryn 79 D5
Gorzow Wielkopolski 70 F2
Goschen Strait 114 E4
Gosforth 55 H1
Goshogawara 88 H5
Gospic 72 C2
Gosport 53 F4
Gostivar 73 F5
Gota 62 Z14
Gota Kanal 63 G7
Gotaland 63 E8
Goteborg 63 H8
Goteborg Och Bohus 63 D7
Gotene 63 E7
Gotha 70 D3
Gothenburg 63 D8
Gotland 63 H8
Goto-retto 89 B9
Gotse Delchev 73 G5
Gotska Sandon 63 H7
Gotsu 89 D8
Gottingen 70 C3
Gottwaldov 71 G4
Gouda 64 F2
Goudhurst 53 H3
Gough Island 48 F6
Gouin, Reservoir 125 N2
Goulais 124 J3
Goulburn 113 K5
Goulburn Islands 113 G1
Goundam 100 E5
Gourdon 65 D6
Goure 101 H6
Gourma-Rharous 100 E5
Gournay 64 D4
Gourock 57 D5
Govena, Mys 85 V5
Goverla 71 L4
Governador Valadares 138 H3
Governor's Harbour 132 J2
Govind Pant Sagar 92 F4
Govorovo 85 M2
Gowanbridge 115 D4
Gowanda 125 L5
Gower 52 C3
Gowna, Lough 58 G5
Goya 138 E5
Goynucek 77 D2
Goynuk *Turkey* 76 D2
Goynuk *Turkey* 77 J3
Goz Beida 102 D5
Gozne 76 F4
Gozo 74 C4
Goz Regeb 96 B8
Graaff Reinet 108 D6

Gracac 72 C3
Gradaus, Serra dos 137 G5
Grado *Italy* 68 D3
Grado *Spain* 66 C1
Gradoli 69 C4
Gradsko 73 F5
Grafham Water 53 G2
Grafton *Australia* 113 L4
Grafton *N. Dakota, U.S.A.* 123 R3
Grafton *W. Virginia, U.S.A.* 125 K7
Grafton, Islas 139 B10
Graham 128 C4
Graham Island *British Columbia, Canada* 118 J5
Graham Island *N.W. Territories, Canada* 120 H2
Graham Land 141 V5
Grahamstown 108 E6
Graie, Alpi 68 A3
Graiguenamanagh 59 J7
Grain 53 H3
Grajau 137 H4
Grajewo 71 K2
Grampian 56 E3
Grampian Mountains 57 D4
Grampound 52 C4
Gramsh 75 F2
Gran 137 F3
Granada *Nicaragua* 132 E9
Granada *Spain* 66 E4
Granard 58 H5
Gran Bajo 139 C9
Granby *Canada* 125 P4
Granby *U.S.A.* 123 L7
Gran Canaria 100 B3
Gran Chaco 138 D4
Grand *Canada* 125 K5
Grand *Michigan, U.S.A.* 124 H5
Grand *Missouri, U.S.A.* 124 C6
Grand *S. Dakota, U.S.A.* 123 P5
Grand Bahama 132 H1
Grand Bois, Coteau de 124 C3
Grand Canal *China* 87 M5
Grand Canal *Ireland* 59 H6
Grand Canyon *U.S.A* 126 F2
Grand Canyon *U.S.A* 126 F2
Grand Cayman 132 G5
Grand Coulee 122 E4
Grand Coulee Dam 122 E4
Grande *Brazil* 138 G4
Grande *Mexico* 131 L9
Grande *Nicaragua* 132 E8
Grande, Bahia 139 C10
Grande Cache 119 M5
Grande, Cienaga 133 K10
Grande Comore 109 H2
Grande Miquelon 121 Q8
Grande O'Guapay 138 D3
Grande Prairie 119 M4
Grande, Punta 137 G3
Grande, Rio 127 M6
Grande Ronde 122 F5
Gran Desierto 126 E5
Grandes Rocques 53 M7
Grand Falls *New Brunswick, Canada* 125 S3
Grand Falls *Newfoundland, Canada* 121 Q8
Grand Forks 123 R4
Grand Island 123 Q7
Grand Isle 128 H6
Grand Junction 127 H1
Grand Lahou 104 E4
Grand Lake *New Brunswick, Canada* 128 G6
Grand Lake *Newfoundland, Canada* 121 Q8
Grand Lake *U.S.A.* 125 S3
Grand Lake O' the Cherokees 128 E2
Grand-Lieu, Lac de 65 C5
Grand Manan Island 125 S4
Grand Marais *Michigan, U.S.A.* 124 H3
Grand Marais *Minnesota, U.S.A.* 124 E3
Grand-Mere 125 P3
Grandola 66 B3
Grand Popo 105 F4
Grand Prairie 128 D4
Grand Rapids *Canada* 119 R5
Grand Rapids *Michigan, U.S.A.* 124 H5
Grand Rapids *Minnesota, U.S.A.* 124 D3
Grandrieu 65 E6
Grand Saint Bernard, Col du 68 A3
Grand Santi 137 G3
Graney, Lough 59 E7
Grangemouth 57 E4
Grange-over-Sands 55 G2
Grangesberg 63 F6
Grangeville 122 F5
Granite Peak 123 K5
Granitola, Capo 69 D7
Granna 63 F7
Granollers 67 H2
Gran Pajonal 136 C6
Gran Paradiso 68 A3
Grantham 53 G2
Grant Island 141 R4
Grant, Mount 122 E8
Grantown-on-Spey 56 E3
Grants 127 J3
Grantshouse 57 F4

Granville 64 C4
Granville Lake 119 Q4
Grasby 55 J3
Gras, Lac de 119 N3
Grasmere 55 F2
Graso 63 H6
Grasse 65 G7
Grassrange 123 K4
Grass Valley 122 D8
Grassy 113 J7
Grassy Knob 125 K7
Gratens 65 D7
Graus 67 G1
Gravatai 138 F5
Gravdal 62 E2
Gravelines 64 E3
Grave, Pointe de 65 C6
Gravesend 53 H3
Gravois, Pointe-a- 133 L5
Gray 65 F5
Grayling 124 H4
Grays 53 H3
Grays Harbor 122 B4
Graz 68 E2
Great Abaco 132 J1
Great Artesian Basin 113 J4
Great Astrolabe Reef 114 R9
Great Australian Bight 112 F5
Great Ayton 55 H2
Great Baddow 53 H3
Great Bahama Bank 132 H2
Great Bardfield 53 H3
Great Barrier Island 115 E2
Great Barrier Reef 113 K2
Great Basin 122 F7
Great Bear Lake 119 L2
Great Bend 127 N1
Great Blasket Island 59 A8
Great Budworth 55 G3
Great Cumbrae 57 D5
Great Dividing Range 113 K3
Great Driffield 55 J2
Great Dunmow 53 H3
Greater Antarctica 141 D2
Greater Antilles 132 G4
Greater Khingan Range 87 N2
Greater London 53 G3
Greater Manchester 55 G3
Great Exuma Island 132 K3
Great Falls 122 J4
Great Fish 108 E6
Great Gable 55 F2
Great Guana Cay 132 J2
Great Harwood 55 G3
Great Inagua 133 L4
Great Indian Desert 92 D3
Great Island 59 F9
Great Karas Berg 108 C5
Great Karoo 108 D6
Great Lakes 143 L3
Great Longton 55 H2
Great Malvern 52 E2
Great Mercury Island 115 E2
Great Nicobar 93 H7
Great North East Channel 114 C3
Great Ormes Head 54 F3
Great Ouse 53 H2
Great Papuan Plateau 114 C3
Great Plains 123 J2
Great Ruaha 107 G4
Great Sacandaga Lake 125 N5
Great Salt Lake 122 H7
Great Salt Lake Desert 122 H7
Great Sand Hills 123 K2
Great Sandy Desert 112 E3
Great Sankey 55 G3
Great Sea Reef 114 R8
Great Sitkin Island 118 Ac9
Great Slave Lake 119 N2
Great Smeaton 55 H2
Great Stour 53 J3
Great Sugar Loaf 59 K6
Great Torrington 52 C4
Great Victoria Desert 112 F4
Great Wall of China, The 87 L4
Great Whernside 55 H2
Great Witley 52 E2
Great Yarmouth 53 J2
Great Yeldham 53 H2
Great Zab 94 F3
Gredos, Sierra de 66 D2
Greece 75 F3
Greeley 123 M7
Greely Fjord 120 K1
Green *Kentucky, U.S.A.* 124 G8
Green *Wyoming, U.S.A.* 123 J6
Green Bay *Canada* 124 G4
Green Bay *U.S.A.* 124 G4
Green Bell, Ostrov 80 H1
Greenbrier 125 K8
Greencastle 58 K4
Greeneville 129 L2
Greenfield 125 P5
Green Hammerton 55 H2
Greenhead 55 G2
Green Island 115 C6
Greenisland 58 L3
Green Islands 114 E2
Greenland 116 Q1
Greenlaw 57 F4
Greenlough 112 D4
Greenlowther 57 D5
Green Mountains 125 P5

Name	Page	Grid
Greenock	57	D5
Green River *Papua New Guinea*	114	C2
Green River *Utah, U.S.A.*	127	G1
Green River *Wyoming, U.S.A.*	123	K7
Greensboro	129	N2
Greensburg	125	L6
Greenstone Point	56	C3
Green Valley	126	G5
Greenville *Liberia*	104	D4
Greenville *Alabama, U.S.A.*	129	J5
Greenville *Mississippi, U.S.A.*	128	G4
Greenville *N. Carolina, U.S.A.*	129	P3
Greenville *S. Carolina, U.S.A.*	129	L3
Greenville *Texas, U.S.A.*	128	D4
Greenwood *Mississippi, U.S.A.*	128	G4
Greenwood *S. Carolina, U.S.A.*	129	L3
Greers Ferry Lake	128	F3
Gregorio	136	C5
Gregory, Lake	113	H4
Gregory Range	113	J2
Greian Head	57	A3
Greifswald	70	E1
Grein	68	E1
Greipstad	62	H2
Greiz	70	E3
Gremikha	78	F2
Gremyachinsk	78	K4
Grena	63	D8
Grenada	133	S8
Grenada *U.S.A.*	128	H4
Grenadines, The	133	S8
Grenen	63	D8
Grenfell	123	N2
Grenivik	62	V12
Grenoble	65	F6
Grenville, Cape	113	J1
Gresford	55	G3
Gresham	122	C5
Gresik	90	E7
Greta	55	H1
Gretna	55	F2
Grevena	75	F2
Greybull	123	K5
Grey Island	121	Q7
Grey Mare's Tail	57	E5
Greymouth	115	C5
Grey Range	113	J4
Greysteel	58	H2
Greystones	59	K6
Greytown	115	E4
Griefswald Bodden	70	E1
Griffin	129	K4
Griffith	113	K5
Griffith Island	120	G3
Grigoriopol	73	K2
Grimailov	71	M4
Grim, Cape	113	J7
Grimsby	55	J3
Grimsey	62	**W11**
Grimshaw	119	M4
Grimstad	63	C7
Grindavik	62	T13
Grindsted	63	C9
Gringley on the Hill	55	J3
Grinnell	124	D6
Grinnell Peninsula	120	G2
Grintavec	68	E2
Gris-Nez, Cap	64	D3
Griva	78	J3
Grmec Planina	72	D3
Grobming	68	D2
Grodekovo	88	C3
Grodno	71	K2
Groix, Ile de	65	B5
Grombalia	69	C7
Grong	62	E4
Groningen *Netherlands*	64	G2
Groningen *Suriname*	137	F2
Groot	108	D6
Groote Eylandt	113	H1
Grootfontein	108	C3
Grossa, Ponta	137	H3
Grosseto	69	C4
Grossevichi	88	G1
Gros Ventre Mountains	123	J6
Grottaglie	69	F5
Groundhog	124	J2
Grove	53	J3
Grove City	125	K6
Grove Hill	129	J5
Grover City	126	B3
Groznyy	79	H7
Grudovo	73	J4
Grudziadz	71	H2
Gruinard Bay	56	C3
Gruinart, Loch	57	B5
Grums	63	E7
Grunaw	108	C5
Grunberg	70	F3
Grund	62	U12
Grundarfjordur	62	T12
Grundy	124	J8
Gruznovka	84	H5
Gryazi	79	F5
Gryazovets	78	G4
Gryfice	70	F2
Gryfino	70	F2
Guabito	136	A2
Guacanayabo, Golfo de	132	J4
Guadajoz	66	D4
Guadalajara *Mexico*	130	H7
Guadalajara *Spain*	66	E2
Guadalcanal *Solomon Is.*	114	J6
Guadalcanal *Spain*	66	D3
Guadalete	66	D4
Guadalimar	66	E3
Guadalmez	66	D3
Guadalope	67	F2
Guadalquivir	66	D4
Guadalupe *Mexico*	128	B8
Guadalupe *Mexico*	127	J5
Guadalupe *Spain*	66	D3
Guadalupe *Texas, U.S.A.*	128	D6
Guadalupe Mountains	127	K5
Guadalupe, Sierra de	66	D3
Guadalupe Victoria	130	G5
Guadarrama *Spain*	66	D2
Guadarrama *Spain*	66	D2
Guadarrama, Sierra de	66	E2
Guadeloupe	133	S6
Guadeloupe Passage	133	S6
Guadelupe	126	D4
Guadiana	66	C4
Guadiana, Bahia de	132	E3
Guadiana Menor	66	E4
Guadix	66	E4
Guafo, Isla	139	B8
Guainia	136	D3
Guaiquinima, Cerro	136	E2
Guajira, Peninsula de	136	C1
Gualachulian	57	C4
Gualaquiza	136	B4
Gualeguay *Argentina*	138	E6
Gualeguay *Argentina*	138	E6
Gualeguaychu	138	E6
Guam	83	N5
Guama	137	H4
Guamblin, Isla	139	A8
Guampi, Sierra de	136	D2
Guamuchil	130	E5
Gua Musang	90	C5
Guanare *Venezuela*	136	D2
Guanare *Venezuela*	136	D2
Guanay, Sierra	136	D2
Guandi	88	B4
Guangan	93	L2
Guangdong	93	M4
Guanghua	93	M2
Guangnan	93	L4
Guangning	93	M4
Guangping	87	M4
Guangxi	93	L4
Guangyuan	93	L2
Guangze	87	M6
Guangzhou	93	M4
Guanhaes	138	H3
Guanipa	133	R10
Guanoca	136	E1
Guantanamo	133	K4
Guan Xian	93	K2
Guapi	136	B3
Guapiles	132	F9
Guapore	136	E6
Guaqui	138	C3
Guarabira	137	K5
Guarapuava	138	F5
Guara, Sierra de	67	F1
Guarda *Portugal*	66	C2
Guarda *Portugal*	66	C2
Guardo	66	D1
Guarenas	136	D1
Guaribas, Cachoeira	137	G4
Guarico	136	D2
Guasave	130	E5
Guasdualito	136	C2
Guasipati	136	E2
Guastalla	68	C3
Guatemala	132	B7
Guatemala	132	B7
Guaviare	136	D3
Guaxupe	138	G4
Guayaquil	136	B4
Guayaquil, Golfo de	136	A4
Guaymas	126	G7
Guazacapan	132	B7
Guba	103	G5
Guba Dolgaya	84	Ac2
Gubakha	78	K4
Gubbio	68	D4
Gubdor	78	K3
Guben	70	F3
Gucuk	77	G3
Gudar, Sierra de	67	F2
Gudbrandsdalen	63	D6
Gudena	63	C8
Gudur	92	E6
Gudvangen	62	B6
Guekedou	104	C4
Guelma	101	G1
Guelph	125	K5
Guereda	102	D5
Gueret	65	D5
Guernsey *U.K.*	53	M7
Guernsey *U.S.A.*	123	M6
Guerrero Negro	126	E6
Gugu	73	G3
Guhakolak, Tanjung	90	D7
Guia	93	K1
Guide	93	K1
Guider	105	H4
Guidong	93	M3
Guiglo	104	D4
Gui Jiang	93	M4
Guildford	53	G3
Guildtown	57	E4
Guilin	93	M3
Guillestre	65	G6
Guimaraes	66	B2
Guinea	104	C3
Guinea Bissau	104	C3
Guinea, Gulf of	105	F5
Guines	132	F3
Guingamp	64	B4
Guiratinga	138	F3
Guiria	136	E1
Guisanbourg	137	G3
Guisborough	55	H2
Guise	64	E4
Guiseley	55	H3
Guiting Power	53	F3
Guiuan	91	H3
Guixi	87	M6
Gui Xian	93	L4
Guiyang	93	L3
Guizhou	93	L3
Gujarat	92	D4
Gujranwala	92	D2
Gujrat	92	D2
Gulbarga	92	E5
Gulbene	63	M8
Gulcayir	76	D3
Gulcha	86	C3
Gulfport	128	H5
Gulian	87	N1
Gullane	57	F4
Gullfoss	62	V12
Gull Lake	123	K2
Gullspang	63	F7
Gulluk	76	B4
Gulnar	76	E4
Gulpinar	76	B3
Gulsehir	76	F3
Gulyantsi	73	H4
Gumbaz	95	R6
Gummi	105	G3
Gumushacikoy	76	F2
Gumushane	77	H2
Guna	92	E4
Gundagi	113	K6
Gundogmus	76	E4
Gunedidalem	91	H6
Guney	76	C3
Guneydogutoroslar	77	H3
Gungu	106	C4
Gunnedah	113	L5
Gunning	113	K5
Gunnison *Colorado, U.S.A.*	127	J1
Gunnison *Colorado, U.S.A.*	123	K8
Gunnison *Utah, U.S.A*	126	G1
Guntakal	92	E5
Guntersville	129	J3
Guntersville Lake	129	J3
Guntur	92	F5
Gunungsitoli	90	B5
Gunungsugih	90	D6
Gunzenhausen	70	D4
Gurban Obo	87	L3
Gurbulak	77	L3
Gurdim	95	Q9
Gurdzhaani	79	H7
Gure	76	C3
Gurgaon	92	E3
Gurgei, Jebel	102	D5
Gurghiului, Muntii	73	H2
Gurgueia	137	J5
Gur I Topit	75	F2
Gurpinar	77	K3
Gurue	109	G3
Gurun	77	G3
Gurupa	137	G4
Gurupa, Ilha Grande do	137	G4
Gurupi	137	H4
Gurupi, Serra do	137	H4
Guruzala	92	E5
Guryev	79	J6
Gusau	105	G3
Gusev	71	K1
Gusinoozersk	84	H6
Gus-Khrustalnyy	78	G4
Gustrow	70	E2
Gusyatin	73	J1
Gutcher	56	A1
Guthrie *Oklahoma, U.S.A.*	128	D3
Guthrie *Texas, U.S.A.*	127	M4
Gutian	87	M6
Guttenberg	124	E5
Guvem	76	E2
Guyana	136	F2
Guyenne	65	D6
Guymon	127	M2
Guyuan	93	L1
Guzelbag	76	D4
Guzeloluk	76	F4
Guzelsu	77	K3
Guzelyurt	76	F3
Guzman, Laguna de	127	J5
Gvardeysk	71	J1
Gvardeyskoye	73	J1
Gwa	93	H5
Gwabegar	113	K5
Gwadar	92	B3
Gwalior	92	E3
Gwanda	108	E4
Gweebarra Bay	58	F3
Gwelo	108	E3
Gwent	52	E3
Gweru	108	E3
Gwoza	105	H3
Gwydir,	113	K4
Gwynedd	52	D2
Gyangze	93	G3
Gyaring Hu	93	J2
Gydanskaya Guba	84	B2
Gydanskiy Poluostrov	84	B2
Gydnia	71	H1
Gympie	113	L4
Gynymskaya	85	N5
Gyongyos	72	E2
Gyonk	72	E2
Gyor	72	D2
Gypsumville	123	Q2
Gyueshevo	73	G4
Gyula	73	F2

H

Name	Page	Grid
Haabunga	62	W12
Haapai Group	111	U5
Haapajarvi	62	L5
Haapamaki	63	L5
Haapsalu	63	K7
Haardt	70	B4
Haarlem	64	F2
Haast *New Zealand*	115	B5
Haast *New Zealand*	115	B5
Haast Passage	115	B6
Hab	92	C3
Habawnah, Wadi	96	G8
Habban	96	H9
Habbaniyah	94	F5
Habbaniyah, Hawr al	94	F5
Haberli	77	J4
Habirag	87	M3
Haboro	88	H3
Hachenburg	70	B3
Hachijo-jima	89	G9
Hachiman	89	F8
Hachinohe	88	H5
Hachioji	89	G8
Hacibektas	76	F3
Hacihalil Dagi	77	K2
Haciomer	77	J3
Hackas	62	F5
Hadan, Harrat	96	E6
Hadarah	96	E7
Hadarba, Ras	96	C5
Haddenham	53	H2
Haddington	57	F5
Hadd, Ra's al	97	P5
Hadejia	105	G3
Hadera	94	B5
Haderslev	63	E9
Hadhalil, Al	96	G2
Hadhramawt	97	J9
Hadiboh	97	P10
Hadim	76	E4
Hadleigh	53	H2
Hadley Bay	119	P1
Hadong	93	L4
Hadrian's Wall	57	F5
Hadsund	63	D8
Haeju	87	P4
Hafar al Batin	96	H2
Hafik	77	G3
Hafit	97	M5
Hafnarfjordur	62	U12
Hafratindur	62	U12
Haft Gel	94	J6
Haftqala	95	R4
Hag Abdullah	103	F5
Hagemeister Island	118	A3
Hagen	70	B3
Hagen, Mount	114	C3
Hagerstown	125	M7
Hagfors	63	E6
Haggenas	62	F5
Hagi	89	C8
Ha Giang	93	K4
Hagimas	73	H2
Hagley	53	E2
Hagondange	64	G4
Hags Head	59	D7
Hague, Cap de la	64	C4
Haguenau	64	G4
Haian	93	M4
Haibei	88	A2
Haicheng	87	N3
Hai Duong	93	L4
Haifa	94	B5
Haifeng	87	M7
Haikang	93	M4
Haikou	93	M5
Hail	96	E3
Hailar	87	M2
Hailar He	87	M2
Hailsham	53	H4
Hailun	88	A2
Hailuoto *Finland*	62	L4
Hailuoto *Finland*	63	L2
Hainan Dao	93	M5
Haines	118	H4
Haines City	129	M6
Haiphong	93	L4
Haiti	133	L5
Haivare	114	C3
Haiya	96	C7
Hajarah, Al	96	F2
Hajduboszormeny	73	F2
Hajdunanas	73	F2
Hajiki-saki	89	G6
Hajipur	92	G3
Hajjah	96	P9
Hajjiabad	95	M7

Name	Page	Ref
Helsingfors	63	L6
Helsingor	63	E8
Helsinki	63	K6
Helston	52	B4
Helvecia	137	K7
Helvellyn	55	F2
Hemel Hempstead	53	G3
Hempstead	128	D5
Hemsworth	55	H3
Henan	93	M2
Henares	66	E2
Henashi-zaki	88	G5
Henbury	113	G3
Hendek	76	D2
Henderson *Kentucky, U.S.A.*	124	G8
Henderson *N. Carolina, U.S.A.*	129	N2
Henderson *Nevada, U.S.A.*	126	E3
Henderson *Texas, U.S.A.*	128	E4
Hendersonville	129	L3
Hendorabi	95	L8
Hendota	124	F6
Hendrik Verwoerd Dam	108	E6
Hengdaohezi	88	B3
Hengduan Shan	93	J3
Hengelo	64	G2
Hengshan *Hunan, China*	93	M3
Hengshan *Shanxi, China*	87	K4
Hengshui	87	M4
Heng Xian	93	L4
Hengyang	93	M3
Henley-on-Thames	53	G3
Hennebont	65	B5
Henqam	95	M8
Henrietta Maria, Cape	121	K6
Henryetta	128	E3
Henry Ice Rise	141	W2
Henry Mountains	126	G1
Henry Point	112	D5
Henslow, Cape	114	K6
Hentiyn Nuruu	87	K2
Henty	113	K6
Henzada	93	J5
Heppner	122	E5
Hepu	93	L4
Hequ	87	L4
Heradsfloi	62	X12
Herat	95	R4
Herault	65	E7
Herbertville	115	F4
Herby	71	H3
Heredia	132	E9
Hereford *U.K.*	52	E2
Hereford *U.S.A.*	127	L3
Hereford and Worcester	52	E2
Hereke	76	C2
Heretaniwha Point	115	B5
Herford	70	C2
Herington	123	R8
Herisau	68	B2
Herlen Gol	87	L2
Herm	53	M7
Hermanas	127	M7
Herma Ness	56	B1
Hermanus	108	C6
Hermel	94	C4
Hermiston	122	E5
Hermitage	53	F3
Hermitage Bay	121	Q8
Hermit Islands	114	D2
Hermon, Mount	77	G6
Hermosillo	126	G6
Hernad	73	F1
Herne	70	B3
Herne Bay	53	J3
Herning	63	C8
Herrera del Duque	66	D3
Herriard	53	F3
Herrick	113	K7
Herroro, Punta	131	R8
Hersbruck	70	D4
Herschel Island	118	H2
Hertford	53	G3
Hertfordshire	53	G3
Hervey Bay	113	L3
Herzberg	70	D3
Hesdin	64	E3
Hessfjord	62	M2
Hesteyri	63	T11
Hestra	63	E8
Heswall	55	F3
Hethersett	53	J2
Hetton-le-Hole	55	H2
Heuru	114	K7
Heversham	55	G2
Hexham	55	G2
He Xian *Anhui, China*	87	M5
He Xian *Guangxi, China*	93	M4
Heydalir	62	X12
Heysham	55	G2
Heyuan	87	L7
Heywood	55	G3
Heze	93	N1
Hialeah	129	M8
Hibak, Al	97	L6
Hibaldstow	55	J3
Hibbing	124	D3
Hibernia Reef	110	F4
Hickory	129	M3
Hicks Cays	132	C6
Hico	128	C4
Hidaka-sammyaku	88	J4
Hidalgo del Parral	127	K7
Hiddensee	70	E1
Hidrolandia	138	G3
Hieflau	68	E2
Hienghene	114	W16
Hierro	100	B3
Higashi-suido	89	B8
Higham Ferrers	53	G2
Highampton	52	C4
Highbury	113	J2
Highclere	53	F3
High Force	55	G2
High Hesket	55	G2
Highland	56	C3
Highland Park	124	G5
High Level	119	M4
High Point	129	N3
High River	122	H2
High Street	55	G2
High Wycombe	53	G3
Higuera de Zaragozoa	127	H8
Higuey	133	N5
Hiiumaa	63	K7
Hijar	67	F2
Hijaz	96	E6
Hikman, Barr al	97	P6
Hikone	89	F8
Hikurangi	115	E1
Hildesheim	70	C2
Hill City	123	Q8
Hillingdon	53	G3
Hillington	53	H2
Hill Island Lake	119	N3
Hillsboro *N. Dakota, U.S.A.*	123	R4
Hillsboro *Ohio, U.S.A.*	124	J7
Hillsboro *Texas, U.S.A.*	128	D5
Hillsborough	58	K4
Hilo	126	T11
Hilpsford Point	55	F2
Hilton Head Island	129	M4
Hilvan	77	H4
Hilversum	64	F2
Hima	96	G7
Himachal Pradesh	92	E2
Himalaya	92	E3
Himare	74	E2
Himatnagar	92	D4
Himeji	89	E8
Himmerland	63	C8
Himmetdede	76	F3
Hims	94	C4
Hinche	133	L5
Hinchinbrook Island	118	F3
Hinckley	53	F2
Hinderwell	55	J2
Hindhead	53	G3
Hindley	55	G3
Hindmarsh, Lake	113	J6
Hindon	53	E3
Hindubagh	92	C2
Hindu Kush	92	D1
Hindupur	92	E6
Hinganghat	92	E4
Hingoli	92	E5
Hinis	77	J3
Hinnoya	62	F2
Hinojosa del Duque	66	D3
Hintlesham	53	J2
Hinton	119	M5
Hinzir Burun	77	F4
Hirado-shima	89	B9
Hirakud Reservoir	92	F4
Hirara	89	G11
Hiratsuka	89	G8
Hirfanli Baraji	76	E3
Hirlau	73	J2
Hiroo	88	J4
Hirosaki	88	H5
Hiroshima	89	D8
Hirschberg	70	F3
Hirsova	73	J3
Hirtshals	63	C8
Hirwaun	52	D3
Hisar	92	E3
Hisma	96	C2
Hissjon	62	J5
Hit	94	F5
Hitachi	89	H7
Hitchin	53	G3
Hitoyoshi	89	C9
Hitra	62	C5
Hiu	114	T10
Hiuchi-nada	89	D8
Hiz	53	G2
Hizan	77	K3
Hjalmaren	63	G7
Hjalmar Lake	119	P3
Hjelmeland	63	B7
Hjorring	63	C8
Ho	104	F4
Hoa Binh	93	L4
Hobara	89	H7
Hobart	113	K7
Hobbs	127	L4
Hoboksar	86	F2
Hobro	63	C8
Hobyo	103	J6
Hocalar	76	C3
Hochalm Spitze	68	D2
Ho Chi Minh	93	L6
Hochstadt	70	D4
Hockley	53	H3
Hockley Heath	53	F2
Hodal	92	E3
Hodder	55	G3
Hoddesdon	53	G3
Hodge Beck	55	H2
Hodmezovasarhely	72	F2
Hodna, Monts du	67	J5
Hodnet	52	E2
Hodonin	71	G4
Hoea	126	T10
Hoeryong	88	B4
Hof	70	D3
Hofdakaupstadur	62	U12
Hofmeyr	108	E6
Hofn *Iceland*	62	T11
Hofn *Iceland*	62	X12
Hofors	63	G6
Hofsjokull	62	V12
Hofu	89	C8
Hoganas	63	E8
Hoggar	101	G4
Hogsby	63	G8
Hogsty Reef	133	L4
Hohe Rhon	70	C3
Hohe Tauern	68	D2
Hohhot	87	L3
Hoh Xil Shan	92	G1
Hoi An	93	L5
Hoima	107	F2
Hokensas	63	F7
Hokianga Harbour	115	D1
Hokitika	115	C5
Hokkaido	88	H3
Hokksund	63	C7
Hokota	89	H7
Hokou	93	K4
Hokuno	89	F8
Holarfjall	62	V12
Holbeach	53	H2
Holborn Head	56	E2
Holbrook	127	G3
Holdenville	128	D3
Holderness	55	J3
Holdrege	123	Q7
Holguin	132	J4
Holic	71	G4
Holitna	118	D3
Holjes	63	E6
Hollabrunn	68	F1
Holland	124	G5
Hollandstoun	56	F1
Hollis	128	C3
Hollywood	129	M7
Holm	62	E4
Holman Island	119	M1
Holmavik	62	U12
Holme-on-Spalding-Moor	55	J3
Holmes Chapel	55	G3
Holmes Reef	113	K2
Holmfirth	55	H3
Holms O	120	Q3
Holmsund	62	J5
Holoin Gun	86	J3
Holstebro	63	C8
Holsteinsborg	120	R4
Holsworthy	52	C4
Holt	53	J2
Holton *Canada*	121	Q7
Holton *U.S.A.*	124	C7
Holy Cross	118	D3
Holyhead	54	E3
Holyhead Bay	55	E3
Holy Island *Gwynedd, U.K.*	54	E3
Holy Island *Northumberland, U.K.*	55	H1
Holy Island *Strathclyde, U.K.*	57	C5
Holyoke *Colorado, U.S.A.*	123	N7
Holyoke *Massachusetts, U.S.A.*	125	P5
Holywell	55	F3
Holywood *Dumfries and Galloway, U.K.*	57	E5
Holywood *Down, U.K.*	58	L3
Homalin	93	H4
Hombre Muerto, Salar de	138	C5
Home Bay	120	N4
Home Hill	113	K2
Home Point	115	E1
Homer	128	F4
Homer Tunnel	115	A6
Hommelvik	62	D5
Hommersak	63	D6
Homoine	109	G4
Homs	77	G5
Honavar	92	D6
Honaz Dagi	76	C4
Hon Chong	93	K6
Hondo *Mexico*	131	Q8
Hondo *U.S.A.*	128	C6
Honduras	132	C7
Honduras, Golfo de	132	C6
Honefoss	63	D6
Honesdale	125	N6
Honey Lake	122	D7
Hong Kong	87	L7
Hongliuyuan	86	H3
Hongo	86	G2
Hongor *Mongolia*	87	L2
Hongor *Mongolia*	87	L2
Hongshui He	93	L4
Hong, Song	93	K4
Hongsong	87	P4
Honguedo Strait	121	P8
Hongxing Sichang	86	F3
Hongze	87	M5
Hongze Hu	87	M5
Honiara	114	J4
Honingham	53	J2
Honiton	52	D4
Honjo	88	G6
Hon Khoai	93	K7
Honningsvag	62	L1
Honohina	126	T11
Honokaa	126	T10
Honolulu	126	S10
Honshu	89	E7
Hood	119	N2
Hood Canal	122	C4
Hood Island	136	A7
Hood, Mount	122	D5
Hood Point	114	D4
Hood River	122	D5
Hoogeveen	64	G2
Hooghly	93	G4
Hook	53	G3
Hooker	127	M2
Hook Head	59	J8
Hook Norton	53	F3
Hooper, Cape	120	N4
Hoor	63	E9
Hoorn	64	F2
Hoover Dam	126	E2
Hopa	77	J2
Hope *Canada*	122	D3
Hope *U.K.*	55	H3
Hope *U.S.A.*	128	F4
Hopedale	121	P6
Hopelchen	131	Q8
Hope, Loch	56	D2
Hopen	80	D2
Hope Pass	115	C5
Hope, Point	118	B2
Hopes Advance, Cape	121	N5
Hopetown	108	D5
Hopewell	125	M8
Hopkins Lake	112	F3
Hopkinsville	124	G8
Hoquiam	122	C4
Horasan	77	K2
Horby	63	E9
Hordaland	63	B6
Horezu	73	G3
Horley	53	G3
Horlick Mountains	141	R1
Hormoz	95	N8
Hormuz, Strait of	95	N8
Horn *Austria*	68	E1
Horn *Iceland*	62	T11
Hornavan	62	G3
Horn, Cape	139	C10
Horncastle	55	J3
Horndal	63	G6
Horndean	53	F4
Hornefors	62	H5
Hornepayne	124	H2
Horn Head	58	G2
Horn, Iles de	111	T4
Horningsham	52	E3
Horn Mountains	119	L3
Hornos, Cabo de	139	C11
Hornsea	55	J3
Horovice	70	E4
Horqin Youyi Qianqi	87	N2
Horqin Zuoyi Houqi	87	N3
Horqueta	138	E4
Horsehoe Bend	122	F6
Horsens	63	C9
Horsey	53	J2
Horsforth	55	H3
Horsham *Australia*	113	J6
Horsham *U.K.*	53	G3
Horsham Saint Faith	53	J2
Horsley	53	G3
Horsovsky Tyn	70	E4
Horten	63	D7
Horton	118	L2
Horwich	55	G3
Hosaina	103	G6
Hosap	77	K3
Hose Mountains	90	E5
Hoseynabad	94	H4
Hoshangabad	92	E4
Hoshiarpur	92	E2
Hospet	92	E5
Hospitalet	67	H2
Hossegor	65	C7
Hoste, Isla	139	C11
Hotamis	76	E4
Hotan	92	F1
Hotazel	108	D5
Hoti	91	J6
Hoting	62	G4
Hot Springs *Arkansas, U.S.A.*	128	F3
Hot Springs *S. Dakota, U.S.A.*	123	N6
Hottah Lake	119	M2
Hotte, Massif de la	133	K5
Houailou	114	W16
Houdan	64	D4
Houghton	124	F3
Houghton-le-Spring	55	H2
Houlton	125	S3
Houma *China*	93	M1
Houma *U.S.A.*	128	G6
Houmt Souk	101	H2
Hounde	104	E3
Hounslow	53	G3
Houston *Mississippi, U.S.A.*	128	H4
Houston *Texas, U.S.A.*	128	E6
Houtman Rocks	112	C4
Hova	63	F7
Hovd	86	G2
Hovd Gol	86	G2
Hove	53	G4
Hoveyzeh	94	J6

Hovingham 55 J2
Hovlya 79 G6
Hovsgol 87 K3
Hovsgol Nuur 86 J1
Howa 102 E4
Howakil 96 E9
Howard City 124 H5
Howard Lake 119 P3
Howden Moor 55 H3
Howden Reservoir 55 H3
Howe, Cape 113 K6
Howe of the Mearns 57 F4
Howitt, Mount 113 K6
Howland Island 111 T1
Howrah 93 G4
Hoxtolgay 86 F2
Hoxud 86 F3
Hoy 56 E2
Hoyanger 63 B6
Hoyerswerda 70 F3
Hoylake 55 F3
Hoyos 66 C2
Hoy Sound 56 E2
Hradeckralove 70 F3
Hron 71 H4
Hrubieszow 71 K3
Hsin-cheng 87 N7
Hsin-chu 87 N7
Hsipaw 93 J4
Huab 108 B4
Huacho 136 B6
Huachuan 88 C2
Huacrachuco 136 B5
Huade 87 L3
Huadian 87 P3
Huaibei 93 N2
Huaide 87 N3
Huai He 93 M2
Huaihua 93 M3
Huaiji 93 M4
Huainan 87 M5
Huairou 87 M3
Huaiyin 87 M5
Huajuapan de Leon 131 L9
Huallaga 136 B5
Huallanca 136 B5
Huama 88 C2
Huamachuco 136 B5
Huambo 106 C5
Huampusirpi 132 E7
Huanan 88 C2
Huancane 138 C3
Huancavelica 136 B6
Huancayo 136 B6
Huangehuan 93 N2
Huang Hai 87 N4
Huang He 87 L4
Huanghua 87 M4
Huangling 93 L1
Huangpi 93 M2
Huangshi 93 M2
Huang Xian 87 N4
Huangyan 87 N6
Huangyuan 93 K1
Huanren 87 P3
Huanta 136 C6
Huanuco 136 B5
Huan Xian 93 L1
Huanzo, Cordillera 136 C6
Huara 138 C3
Huaral 136 B6
Huaraz 136 B5
Huarmey 136 B6
Huascaran, Nevado 136 B5
Huatabampo 127 H7
Huayin 93 M2
Huayuan 93 L3
Hubei 93 M2
Hubli 92 E5
Hucknall 55 H3
Huddersfield 55 H3
Hudiksvall 63 G6
Hudson Florida, U.S.A. 129 L6
Hudson New York, U.S.A. 125 P5
Hudson New York, U.S.A. 125 P5
Hudson Bay 116 L3
Hudson, Cape 141 L5
Hudson Land 120 X3
Hudson Strait 120 M5
Hue 93 L5
Huebra 66 C2
Huedin 73 G2
Huehuento, Cerro 130 G5
Huehuetenango 132 B7
Huelgoat 64 B4
Huelva Spain 66 C4
Huelva Spain 66 C4
Huercal Overa 67 F4
Huesca 67 F1
Huescar 66 E4
Huetamo 131 J8
Huete 66 E2
Hufrah, Al 96 D2
Hughenden 113 J3
Hugh Town 52 K5
Hugo 128 E4
Hugo Reservoir 128 E3
Hugoton 127 M2
Huhehot 87 L3
Huiarau Range 115 F3
Huichapan 131 K7
Huicholes, Sierra de los 130 G6
Huichon 87 P3
Huila, Nevado del 136 B3

Huimin 87 M4
Huisne 65 D4
Huitong 93 L3
Huittinen 63 K6
Huixtla 131 N10
Huize 93 K3
Huizhou 87 L7
Huj, Al 96 D2
Huka Falls 115 E3
Hukou 87 M6
Hula 114 D4
Hulan He 88 A2
Hulayfah 96 E4
Huld 87 K3
Hulin 88 D3
Hull Canada 125 N4
Hull U.K. 55 J3
Hultsfred 63 F8
Hulun 87 M2
Hulun Nur 87 M2
Huma 87 P1
Humahuaca 138 B4
Humaita 136 E5
Humarklo 62 X12
Humaya 130 F5
Humber 55 J3
Humber, Mouth of the 55 K3
Humberside 55 J3
Humboldt Canada 123 M1
Humboldt Nevada, U.S.A. 122 E7
Humboldt Tennessee, U.S.A. 128 H3
Humboldt, Mount 114 X16
Humbolt Gletscher 120 P2
Humedan 95 P9
Humphreys Peak 126 G3
Humpolec 70 F4
Hunafloi 62 U12
Hunan 93 M3
Hunchun 88 C4
Hunfeld 70 C3
Hungary 72 D2
Hungerford 53 F3
Hunghae 89 B7
Hungnam 87 P4
Hungry Hill 59 C9
Hunjiang 87 P3
Huns Mountains 108 C5
Hunsruck 70 B4
Hunstanton 53 H2
Hunsur 92 E6
Hunte 70 C2
Hunter 113 L5
Hunter, Cape 120 M3
Hunter Islands 113 J7
Huntingdon U.K. 53 G2
Huntingdon U.S.A. 125 M6
Huntington Indiana, U.S.A. 124 H6
Huntington W. Virginia, U.S.A. 124 J7
Huntington Beach 126 C4
Huntley 52 E3
Huntly New Zealand 115 E2
Huntly U.K. 56 F3
Huntsville Canada 125 L4
Huntsville Alabama, U.S.A. 129 J3
Huntsville Texas, U.S.A. 128 E5
Huolongmen 87 P2
Huon Gulf 114 D3
Huon Peninsula 114 D3
Hurd, Cape 125 K4
Hurdiyo 103 K5
Hure Qi 87 N3
Hurghada 103 F2
Hurimta 87 K2
Hurliness 56 E2
Hurn 53 F4
Huron 123 Q5
Huron, Lake 124 J4
Hurricane 126 F2
Hurrungane 63 B6
Hurunui 115 D5
Husavik Denmark 62 Z14
Husavik Iceland 62 W11
Husbands Bosworth 53 F2
Husbondliden 62 H4
Hushan 88 C3
Hushinish 56 A3
Husi 73 K2
Huskvarna 63 F8
Husn Al Abr 96 H8
Husum Sweden 62 H5
Husum W. Germany 70 C1
Hutag 86 J2
Hutaym, Harrat 96 E3
Hutchinson Kansas, U.S.A. 128 D1
Hutchinson Minnesota, U.S.A. 124 C4
Hutou 88 D2
Huttenberg 68 E2
Huttoft 55 K3
Hutton, Mount 113 K4
Hutubi 86 F3
Huwar 97 K4
Huxley, Mount 115 B6
Huyuk 76 D4
Huzhou 87 N5
Hvallatur 62 S12
Hvammstangi 62 U12
Hvar 72 D4
Hveragerdi 62 U13
Hvita 62 U12
Hwange 108 E3
Hwlffordd 52 C2
Hyannis Massachusetts, U.S.A. 125 Q6
Hyannis Nebraska, U.S.A. 123 P7

Hyargas Nuur 86 G2
Hyde New Zealand 115 C6
Hyde U.K. 55 G3
Hyderabad India 92 E5
Hyderabad Pakistan 92 C3
Hyeres 65 G7
Hyeres, Iles d' 65 G7
Hyesan 88 B5
Hyltebruk 63 E8
Hyndman Peak 122 G6
Hynish Bay 57 B4
Hyrynsalmi 62 N4
Hythe Hampshire, U.K. 53 F4
Hythe Kent, U.K. 53 J3
Hyuga 89 C9
Hyvinkaa 63 L6

I

Iaco 136 D5
Iacobeni 73 H2
Ialomita 73 J3
Iapala 109 G2
Iar Connaught 59 D6
Iasi 73 J2
Ib 78 J3
Iba 91 F2
Ibadan 105 F4
Ibague 136 B3
Ibarra 136 B3
Ibb 96 G10
Ibiapaba, Serra da 137 J4
Ibiza Spain 67 G3
Ibiza Spain 67 G3
Ibn Suaydan, Ramlat 97 M6
Ibo 109 H2
Ibonma 91 J6
Ibotirama 138 J6
Ibra 97 P5
Ibra, Wadi 102 D5
Ibri 97 N5
Ibriktepe 76 B2
Ibsley 53 F4
Ibusuki 89 C10
Ica 136 B6
Ica 136 D4
Icana Brazil 136 E3
Icana Brazil 136 D3
Icel 76 F4
Iceland 62 V12
Ichalkaranji 92 D5
Ichchapuram 92 F5
Ichera 84 H5
Ichilo 138 D3
Ichinomiya 89 F8
Ichinoseki 88 H6
Ichnya 79 E5
Ichoa 138 C3
Icy Bay 118 G4
Icy Cape 118 C1
Icy Strait 118 H4
Idabel 128 E4
Idah 105 G4
Idaho 122 G5
Idaho Falls 122 H6
Idanha-a-Nova 66 C3
Idar-Oberstein 70 B4
Ider 86 H2
Idfu 103 F3
Idhi Oros 75 H5
Idhra 75 G4
Idil 77 J4
Idiofa 106 C3
Idiouia 67 G5
Idlib 94 C4
Idre 63 E6
Idrigill Point 56 B3
Ieper 64 E3
Ierapetra 75 H5
Ierissos 75 G2
Iesi 68 D4
Ifanadiana 109 J4
Ife 105 F4
Iforas, Adrar des 100 F5
Igara Parana 136 C4
Igarape Miri 137 H4
Igarka 84 D3
Igdir 76 E2
Igdir 77 L3
Igdir Dagi 77 H2
Iggesund 63 G6
Iglesia 139 C6
Iglesias 69 B6
Igloolik 120 K4
Igluligarjuk 119 S3
Ignace 124 E2
Igneada 76 B2
Igneada Burun 76 C2
Igoumenitsa 75 J4
Igra 78 J4
Iguala 131 K8
Igualada 67 G2
Iguape 138 G4
Iguatu 137 K5
Iguazu, Cataratas del 138 F5
Iguazu Falls 138 F5
Iguidi, Erg 100 D3
Iheya-retto 89 H10
Ih-Hayrhaan 87 K2
Ihlara 76 F3
Ihosy 109 J4

Ihsaniye 76 D3
Iida 89 F8
Iide-san 89 G7
Iisalmi 62 M5
Ijebu Ode 105 F4
IJmuiden 64 F2
IJssel 64 F2
IJsselmeer 64 E3
Ijzer 64 E3
Ik 78 J4
Ika 84 H5
Ikaalinen 63 K6
Ikaria 75 J4
Ikast 63 C8
Iked 89 D8
Ikeda 88 J4
Ikela 106 D3
Iki-shima 89 B9
Ikizce 76 E3
Ikizdere 77 J2
Ikom 105 G4
Ikomba 107 F4
Ikongo 109 J4
Ikpikpuk 118 E1
Ikuno 89 E8
Ila 105 F4
Ilagan 91 G2
Ilam 94 H5
Ilanskiy 84 F5
Ilaro 105 F4
Ilawa 71 H2
Ilbenge 85 L4
Ileanda 73 G2
Ilebo 106 D3
Ilek 79 J5
Ilesha 105 F4
Ilfracombe 52 C3
Ilgaz 76 E2
Ilgaz Daglari 76 F2
Ilgin 76 D3
Ilheus 137 K6
Ili 86 D3
Ilia 73 G3
Iliamna Lake 118 D4
Ilic 77 H3
Iligan 91 G2
Ilikurangi 115 G2
Ilinskiy 88 J1
Ilintsy 73 K1
Iliodhromia 75 G3
Iliomar 91 H7
Ilja 71 M1
Ilkeston 53 F2
Ilkley 55 H3
Ilkley Moor 55 H3
Illampu, Nevado de 138 C3
Illapel 138 B6
Illbille, Mount 112 G4
Iller 70 D4
Illescas 66 E2
Illimani, Nevado 138 C3
Illinois U.S.A. 124 E6
Illinois U.S.A. 124 E6
Illizi 101 G3
Illo 105 F3
Illote, Punta 136 A4
Ilm 70 D3
Ilmen, Ozero 78 E4
Ilminster 52 E4
Iloilo 91 G3
Ilorin 105 F4
Ilpyrskiy 85 U5
Ilsin-dong 88 B5
Ilwaki 91 H7
Ilych 78 K3
Ilza 71 J3
Ilzanka 71 J3
Ima 85 K5
Imabari 89 D8
Imamoglu 77 F4
Iman 88 E3
Imandra, Ozero 62 Q3
Imari 89 B9
Imataca, Serrania de 136 E2
Imatra 63 N6
Imese 106 C2
Imishli 94 J2
Immenstadt 70 D5
Immingham 55 J3
Imola 68 C3
Imotski 72 D4
Imperatriz 137 H5
Imperia 68 A4
Imperial 123 P7
Imperieuse Reef 112 C2
Impfondo 106 C2
Imphal 93 H4
Imrali 76 C2
Imst 68 C2
Imundsen Gulf 118 L1
Imuris 126 G5
Ina 89 F8
Inagh 59 D7
Inakona 114 K6
In Amenas 101 G3
Inangahua Junction 115 C4
Inanwatan 91 J6
Inapari 136 D6
Inari 62 M2
Inarijarvi 62 M2
Inawashiro-ko 89 H7
Inca 67 H3
Incebel Daglari 77 G3
Ince Burun 76 F1

Name	Page	Grid
Jagin	95	P9
Jagin, Ra's	95	P9
Jagst	70	C4
Jagtial	92	E5
Jaguarao	138	F6
Jaguariaiva	138	G4
Jaguaribe *Brazil*	137	K5
Jaguaribe *Brazil*	137	K5
Jague	138	C5
Jahmah	94	G7
Jahrom	95	L7
Jaicos	137	J5
Jailolo	91	H5
Jailolo, Selat	91	H5
Jaipur	92	E3
Jaisalmer	92	D3
Jajarm	95	N3
Jajce	72	D3
Jajpur	92	G4
Jakarta	90	D7
Jakhau	92	C4
Jakobstad	62	K5
Jakupica	73	F5
Jalaid Qi	87	N2
Jalalabad	92	D2
Jalalpur Pirwala	92	D3
Jalapa *Mexico*	131	L8
Jalapa *Mexico*	131	N9
Jalasjarvi	62	K5
Jalgaon	92	E4
Jalingo	105	H4
Jalna	92	E5
Jalon	67	F2
Jalor	92	D3
Jalostotitlan	130	H7
Jalpa	130	H7
Jalpaiguri	93	G3
Jalpan	131	K7
Jalu	101	K2
Jam	95	Q4
Jamaica	132	J5
Jamaica Channel	133	K5
Jamalpur *Bangladesh*	93	G4
Jamalpur *India*	92	G3
Jamanxim	137	F5
Jamari	136	E5
Jambi	90	C6
James	123	R6
James Bay	121	K7
James Island	136	A7
James Ross, Cape	120	D3
James Ross Island	141	W6
James Ross Strait	120	G4
Jamestown *South Africa*	108	E6
Jamestown *N. Dakota, U.S.A.*	123	Q4
Jamestown *New York, U.S.A.*	125	L5
Jamjo	63	F8
Jamkhandi	92	E5
Jamkhed	92	E5
Jammerbugten	63	C8
Jammu	92	D2
Jammu and Kashmir	92	E2
Jamnagar	92	D4
Jampur	92	D3
Jamsa	63	L6
Jamshedpur	92	G4
Jamtland	62	F5
Jamuna	93	G3
Janda, Laguna de la	66	D4
Jandaq	95	M4
Jandiatuba	136	D4
Janesville	124	F5
Janjira	92	D5
Jan Mayen	48	F2
Jannatabad	95	Q4
Janos	127	H5
Januaria	138	H3
Janubiyah, Al Badiyah al	94	H6
Jaora	92	E4
Japan	89	G7
Japan, Sea of	88	D6
Japan Trench	142	F3
Japaratuba	137	K6
Japura	136	D4
Jarabulus	94	D3
Jaragua	138	G3
Jaraguari	138	F4
Jarama	66	E2
Jarandilla	66	D2
Jarash	94	B5
Jardee	112	D5
Jardines de la Reina	132	H4
Jari	137	G3
Jarir, Wadi al	96	F4
Jarna	63	G7
Jarnac	65	C6
Jaromer	70	F3
Jaroslaw	71	K3
Jarpen	62	E5
Jarrow	55	H2
Jarruhi	94	J6
Jartai	87	K4
Jarvso	63	G6
Jashpurnagar	92	F4
Jask	95	N9
Jasper *Canada*	119	M5
Jasper *Alabama, U.S.A.*	129	J4
Jasper *Florida, U.S.A.*	129	L5
Jasper *Texas, U.S.A.*	128	F5
Jassy	73	J2
Jastrebarsko	72	C3
Jastrowie	71	G2
Jastrzebie-Zdroj	71	H4
Jaszbereny	72	E2
Jatai	138	F3
Jatapu	136	F4
Jath	92	E5
Jativa	67	F3
Jatoba	137	G6
Jau	136	E4
Jau	138	G4
Jauaperi	136	E4
Jauja	136	B6
Jaunpur	92	F3
Java	90	E7
Java Trench	142	E5
Javier, Isla	139	B9
Javor	72	E3
Javorniky	71	H4
Jawa	90	D7
Jawa, Laut	90	E7
Jawb, Al	97	K5
Jawhar	107	J2
Jawor	71	G3
Jayanca	136	B5
Jaya, Puncak	91	K6
Jayapura	91	L6
Jayawijaya, Pegunungan	91	K6
Jayena	66	E4
Jaypur	92	F5
Jayrud	94	C5
Jazirah, Al	94	E4
Jaz Murian, Hamun-e	95	P8
Jebal Barez, Kuh-e	95	P7
Jebba	105	F4
Jebel, Bahr el	102	F6
Jech Doab	92	D2
Jedburgh	57	F5
Jedeida	69	B7
Jefferson	122	H5
Jefferson City *Missouri, U.S.A.*	124	D7
Jefferson City *Tennessee, U.S.A.*	129	L2
Jefferson, Mount *Nevada, U.S.A.*	122	F8
Jefferson, Mount *Oregon, U.S.A.*	122	D5
Jef Jef el Kebir	102	D3
Jehile Puzak	95	Q6
Jekabpils	63	L8
Jeldesa	103	H6
Jelenia Gora	70	F3
Jelgava	63	K8
Jelow Gir	94	H5
Jemaja	90	D5
Jember	90	E7
Jeminay	86	F2
Jemnice	70	F4
Jena	70	D3
Jendouba	69	B7
Jenin	94	B5
Jenkins	124	J8
Jennings	128	F5
Jenny Lind Island	119	Q2
Jens Munk Island	120	L4
Jequie	137	J6
Jequitinhonha *Brazil*	138	H3
Jequitinhonha *Brazil*	138	H3
Jerada	100	E2
Jerba, Ile de	101	H2
Jeremie	133	K5
Jeremoabo	137	K6
Jerevan	77	L2
Jerez	130	H6
Jerez de la Frontera	66	C4
Jericho *Australia*	113	K3
Jericho *Israel*	94	B6
Jerome	122	G6
Jersey	53	M7
Jersey City	125	N6
Jerseyville	124	E7
Jerusalem	94	B6
Jervis Inlet	122	C2
Jeseniky	71	G3
Jessheim	63	D6
Jessore	92	G4
Jesup	129	M5
Jevnaker	63	D6
Jezerce	74	E1
Jeziorak, Jezioro	71	H2
Jeznas	71	L1
Jezzine	94	B5
Jhang Maghiana	92	D2
Jhansi	92	E3
Jhelum *Pakistan*	92	D2
Jhelum *Pakistan*	92	D2
Jialing Jiang	93	L2
Jiamusi	88	C2
Jian	93	N3
Jianchuan	93	J3
Jiande	87	M6
Jiange	93	L2
Jiangjin	93	L3
Jiangjunmiao	86	F3
Jiangmen	93	M4
Jiangsu	87	M5
Jiangxi	93	M3
Jianning	87	M6
Jianou	87	M6
Jianquanzi	86	H3
Jianshi	93	L2
Jiaohe	87	P3
Jiaoling	87	M7
Jiaozuo	93	M1
Jia Xian	87	L4
Jiaxing	87	N5
Jiayin	88	C1
Jiayuguan	86	H4
Jiboia	136	D3
Jibou	73	G2
Jibsh, Ra's	97	P6
Jicatuyo	132	C7
Jiddah	96	D6
Jidong	88	C3
Jiekkevarre	62	H2
Jieknaffo	62	G3
Jiesavrre	62	L2
Jihlava *Czechoslovakia*	70	F4
Jihlava *Czechoslovakia*	71	G4
Jijel	101	G1
Jijia	73	J2
Jijiga	103	H6
Jijihu	86	F3
Jilava	73	J3
Jiloca	67	F2
Jilove	70	F4
Jima	103	G6
Jimba Jimba	112	D4
Jimena de la Frontera	66	D4
Jimenez	127	M6
Jimenez *Mexico*	128	C8
Jimenez *Mexico*	127	K7
Jimo	87	N4
Jinan	87	M4
Jincheng	93	M1
Jinchuan	93	L1
Jingbian	87	K4
Jingchuan	93	L1
Jingdezhen	87	M6
Jinghai	87	M4
Jinghe	86	E3
Jinghong	93	K4
Jingle	87	L4
Jingmen	93	M2
Jingpo	88	B3
Jingpo Hu	88	B4
Jingtai	93	K1
Jingxi	93	L4
Jing Xian	93	L3
Jinhua	87	M6
Jining *Nei Mongol Zizhiqu, China*	87	L3
Jining *Shandong, China*	87	M4
Jinja	107	F2
Jinkou	87	N4
Jinning	93	K4
Jinotepe	132	D9
Jinsha Jiang	93	J3
Jinta	86	H4
Jinxi	87	N3
Jinxi	87	N4
Jin Xian	87	N4
Jinzhou	87	N3
Jinzhou Wan	87	N4
Jiparana	136	E5
Jipijapa	136	A4
Jiquilpan	130	H8
Jirriiban	103	J6
Jirueque	66	E2
Jirwan	97	K5
Jishou	93	L3
Jisr ash Shughur	94	C4
Jiu	73	G3
Jiujiang	93	N3
Jiuling Shan	93	M3
Jiutai	87	P3
Jiwa , Al	97	M5
Jiwani	92	B3
Jiwani, Ras	92	B4
Jixi *Anhui, China*	87	M5
Jixi *Heilongjiang, China*	87	Q2
Jixian	88	C2
Jizan	96	F8
Jizl, Wadi	96	C3
Jiz, Wadi al	97	K8
Joao Pessoa	137	L5
Joaquin V. Gonzalez	138	D5
Joban	89	H7
Jodar	66	E4
Jodhpur	92	D3
Joensuu	62	N5
Joetsu	89	G7
Jofane	109	F4
Joffre, Mount	122	G2
Jogeva	63	M7
Joghatay	95	N3
Johannesburg	108	E5
John Day *U.S.A.*	122	D5
John Day *U.S.A.*	122	E5
John H. Kerr Reservoir	129	N2
John O'Groats	56	E2
Johnshaven	57	F4
Johnson City	129	L2
Johnston *U.K.*	52	B3
Johnston *U.S.A.*	129	M4
Johnstone	57	D5
Johnston Lakes, The	112	E5
Johnstown	125	L6
Johor Baharu	90	C5
Joigny	65	E5
Joinville *Brazil*	138	G5
Joinville *France*	64	F4
Joinville Island	141	W6
Jokkmokk	62	H3
Jokulbunga	62	T11
Jokulsa a Bru	62	X12
Jokulsa-a Fjollum	62	W12
Jolfa	94	G2
Joliet	124	G6
Joliette	125	P3
Jolo *Philippines*	91	G4
Jolo *Philippines*	91	G4
Jonava	63	N9
Jonesboro	128	G3
Jones Sound	120	J2
Jonglei Canal	102	F6
Joniskis	63	K8
Jonkoping *Sweden*	63	F8
Jonkoping *Sweden*	63	F8
Jonquiere	125	Q2
Jonzac	65	C6
Joplin	124	C8
Jordan	94	B6
Jordan	94	B5
Jordan *U.S.A.*	123	L4
Jordanow	71	H4
Jordan Valley	122	F6
Jorhat	93	H3
Jorn	62	J4
Jorong	90	E6
Jorpeland	63	B7
Jos	105	G3
Jose de San Martin	139	B8
Joseph Bonaparte Gulf	112	F1
Joseph, Lac	121	N7
Josselin	65	B5
Jos Sodarso, Pulau	91	K7
Jostedalsbreen	63	B6
Jotunheimen	63	C6
Jounie	94	B5
Joutsa	63	M6
Joyces Country	59	C5
J. Percy Priest Lake	129	J2
Juan Aldama	130	H5
Juan de Fuca Strait	122	B3
Juan de Nova	109	H3
Juan Fernandez, Islas de	135	A6
Juanjui	136	B5
Juarez, Sierra	126	D4
Juazeiro	137	J5
Juazeiro do Norte	137	K5
Juba	103	F7
Jubany	141	W6
Jubba	107	H2
Juby, Cap	100	C3
Jucar	67	F3
Juchitan	131	M9
Judenburg	68	E2
Juigalpa	132	E8
Juist	70	B2
Juiz de Fora	138	H4
Juklegga	63	E6
Julia	136	D4
Juliaca	138	B3
Julia Creek	113	J3
Julianhab	116	Q2
Julijske Alpe	72	B2
Julio de Castilhos	138	F5
Jullundur	92	E2
Jumilla	67	F3
Jumla	92	F3
Junagadh	92	D4
Junction	127	N5
Junction City	123	R8
Jundiai	138	G4
Juneau	118	J4
Junee	113	K5
Jungfrau	68	A2
Junggar Pendi	86	F2
Junin	139	D6
Junin de los Andes	139	B7
Junosuando	62	K3
Junsele	62	G5
Jun Xian	93	M2
Jura *France*	65	G5
Jura *U.K.*	57	C5
Jura, Sound of	57	C5
Juratishki	71	L1
Juriti	137	F4
Jurua *Brazil*	136	D4
Jurua *Brazil*	136	D4
Juruena	136	F6
Jussey	65	F5
Jutai *Brazil*	136	D4
Jutai *Brazil*	136	D5
Juterbog	70	E3
Juticalpa	132	D7
Jutland	63	C8
Juuka	62	N5
Juva	63	M6
Juventud, Isla de la	132	F4
Ju Xian	87	M4
Juymand	95	P4
Juyom	95	M7
Juzna Morava	73	F4
Jylland	63	C8
Jyvaskyla	62	L5

K

Name	Page	Grid
Kaala-Gomen	114	W16
Kaamanen	62	M2
Kaavi	62	N5
Kaba	104	C4
Kabaena	91	G7
Kabala	104	C4
Kabale	107	E3
Kabalega Falls	107	F2
Kabalo	106	E4
Kabambare	107	E3
Kabara	114	S9
Kabba	105	G4
Kabinatagami	124	H1
Kabinda	106	D4
Kabirkuh	94	H5
Kabompo	106	D5
Kabongo	106	E4
Kabud Gonbad	95	P3

Kabul *Afghanistan*	92	C2
Kabuli	114	D2
Kaburuang	91	H5
Kabwe	107	E5
Kabyrdak	84	A5
Kachchh, Gulf of	92	C4
Kachchh, Rann of	92	C4
Kachemak Bay	118	E4
Kachikattsy	85	M4
Kachug	84	H6
Kackar Dagi	77	J2
Kadali	85	J5
Kadan Kyun	93	J6
Kadavu	114	R9
Kadavu Passage	114	R9
Kadena	89	H10
Kadhimain	94	G5
Kadikoy	76	B2
Kadina	113	H5
Kadinhani	76	E3
Kadiri	92	E6
Kadirli	77	G4
Kadoma	108	E3
Kadrifakovo	73	G5
Kadugli	102	E5
Kaduna *Nigeria*	105	G3
Kaduna *Nigeria*	105	G4
Kadzherom	78	K3
Kaedi	100	C5
Kaena Point	126	R10
Kaeo	115	D1
Kaesong	87	P4
Kafan	94	H2
Kafanchan	105	G4
Kaffrine	104	B3
Kafirevs, Akra	75	H3
Kafue *Zambia*	106	E6
Kafue *Zambia*	107	E6
Kafue Dam	108	E3
Kaga Bandoro	102	C6
Kagizman	77	K2
Kagmar	102	F5
Kagoshima	89	C10
Kagoshima-wan	89	C10
Kagul	79	D6
Kahama	107	F3
Kahan	92	C3
Kahayan	90	E6
Kahnuj	95	N8
Kahoku	89	H6
Kahoolawe	126	S10
Kahramanmaras	77	G4
Kahta	77	H4
Kahuku	126	R10
Kahurak	95	P7
Kahurangi Point	115	D4
Kaiama	105	F4
Kaiapoi	115	D5
Kaibab Plateau	126	F2
Kai Besar	114	A3
Kaifeng	93	M2
Kaihu	115	D1
Kai Kecil	114	A3
Kai, Kepulauan	91	J7
Kaikohe	115	D1
Kaikoura	115	D5
Kaikoura Range	115	D5
Kailahun	104	C4
Kailu	87	N3
Kailua *U.S.A.*	126	S10
Kaimana	91	J6
Kaimanawa Mountains	115	F3
Kaimur Range	92	F4
Kainantu	114	D3
Kainji Reservoir	105	F3
Kaipara Harbour	115	E2
Kaiping	93	M4
Kairouan	101	H1
Kairuku	114	D3
Kaiserslautern	70	B4
Kaisiadorys	71	L1
Kaitaia	115	D1
Kaitangata	115	B7
Kaiteur Falls	136	F3
Kaitumalven	62	J3
Kaiwaka	115	E2
Kaiwi Channel	126	S10
Kaiyuan *Liaoning, China*	87	N3
Kaiyuan *Yunnan, China*	93	K4
Kaiyuh Mountains	118	D3
Kajaani	62	M4
Kajo Kaji	102	F7
Kaka	103	F5
Kakabeka Falls	124	F2
Kakamari	107	F2
Kakamas	108	D5
Kakamega	107	F2
Kakapotahi	115	C5
Kake	89	D8
Kakhovskoye Vodokhranilishche	79	E6
Kaki	95	K7
Kakinada	92	F5
Kakisa Lake	119	M3
Kakogawa	89	E8
Kaktovik	118	G1
Kalabagh	92	D2
Kalabahi	91	G7
Kalabaka	75	F3
Kalabakan	91	F5
Kalabo	106	D6
Kalach	79	G5
Kalachinsk	84	A5
Kalach-Na-Donu	79	G6

Kaladar	125	M4
Ka Lae	126	T11
Kalahari	108	D4
Kalai-Khumb	86	C4
Kalajoki *Finland*	62	K4
Kalajoki *Finland*	62	L5
Kalakan	85	K5
Kalamai	75	G4
Kalamata	75	G4
Kalamazoo *U.S.A.*	124	H5
Kalamazoo *U.S.A.*	124	H5
Kalao	91	G7
Kalaotoa	91	G7
Kalapana	126	T11
Kalar	85	K5
Kalarash	73	K2
Kalarne	62	G5
Kalat	92	C3
Kalaupapa	126	S10
Kalavardha	75	J4
Kalavrita	75	G3
Kalb, Ra's	97	J9
Kalce	72	C3
Kaldakvisl	62	V12
Kaldungborg	63	D9
Kale *Turkey*	76	C4
Kale *Turkey*	76	C4
Kale *Turkey*	77	H2
Kalecik	76	E2
Kalemie	107	E4
Kal-e-Shur	95	P4
Kalety	71	H3
Kalevala	62	P4
Kalewa	93	H4
Kaleybar	94	H2
Kalfafell	62	W13
Kalgoorlie	112	E5
Kaliakra, Nos	73	K4
Kalianda	90	D7
Kalima	106	E3
Kalimantan	90	E5
Kalimnos *Greece*	75	J4
Kalimnos *Greece*	75	J4
Kalinin	78	F4
Kalininabad	86	B4
Kaliningrad	71	J1
Kalinino	78	K4
Kalininsk	79	G5
Kalinkovichi	79	D5
Kalinovka	79	D6
Kalis	103	J6
Kali Sindh	92	E4
Kalispell	122	G3
Kalisz *Poland*	70	F2
Kalisz *Poland*	71	H3
Kaliua	107	F4
Kalix	62	K4
Kalixalven	62	K3
Kalkan	76	C4
Kalkandere	77	J2
Kall	62	E5
Kallavesi	62	M5
Kalloni	75	J3
Kallsjon	62	E5
Kalmar *Sweden*	63	G8
Kalmar *Sweden*	63	G8
Kalmarsund	63	G8
Kalmykovo	79	J6
Kalni	93	H4
Kalomo	106	E6
Kalon	75	G2
Kalpeni	92	D6
Kalpi	92	E3
Kalpin	86	D3
Kal-Shur, Rud-e	95	P3
Kaluga	78	F5
Kaluku	91	F6
Kalush	79	C6
Kalutara	92	E7
Kalvarija	71	K1
Kalya	78	K3
Kalyan	92	D5
Kalyazin	78	F4
Kama	84	Ad4
Kamaishi	88	H6
Kamalia	92	D2
Kaman	76	E3
Kamaran	96	F9
Kamaria Falls	136	F2
Kamativi	108	E3
Kambalda	112	E5
Kambarka	78	J4
Kambia	104	C4
Kamchatka *Russia*	85	T5
Kamchatka Oblast	85	U5
Kamchiya	73	J4
Kamen	63	N9
Kamenets Podolskiy	73	J1
Kamen, Gora	84	F3
Kamenjak, Rt	72	B3
Kamenka *Kazakhstan*	79	J5
Kamenka *Moldavia*	73	K1
Kamenka *Russia*	84	F5
Kamenka *Russia*	79	G5
Kamenka *Russia*	78	G2
Kamen Kashirskiy	79	D5
Kamen-na-Obi	84	C6
Kamennyy, Mys	85	S1
Kamen Rybolov	88	C3
Kamensk-Shakhtinskiy	79	G6
Kamensk-Uralskiy	84	Ad5
Kamenyuki	71	K2
Kamenz	70	F3
Kames	57	C5

Kameshkovo	78	G4
Kamienna Gora	70	F3
Kamien Pombrski	70	F2
Kamiensk	71	H3
Kamilukuak Lake	119	Q3
Kamina	106	E4
Kaminak Lake	119	R3
Kaminuriak Lake	119	R3
Kamishak Bay	118	E4
Kamisli	76	F4
Kamkaly	86	C3
Kamla	93	G3
Kamloops	122	D2
Kamloops Lake	122	D2
Kammenoye, Ozero	62	P4
Kamnik	72	C2
Kamo *Japan*	88	G6
Kamo *Armenia*	77	L2
Kamp	68	E1
Kampala	107	F2
Kampar	90	C5
Kampen	64	F2
Kamphaeng Phet	93	J5
Kampot	93	K6
Kamsack	123	P2
Kamskiy	78	J3
Kamskoye Vodokhranilishche	78	K4
Kamyaran	94	H4
Kamyshin	79	H5
Kamzar	97	N3
Kan	84	E5
Kana	84	H4
Kanab	126	F2
Kanab Creek	126	F2
Kanab Plateau	126	F2
Kanaga Island	118	Ac9
Kanairiktok	121	P7
Kananda	84	G4
Kananga	106	D4
Kanash	78	H4
Kanastraion, Akra	75	G3
Kanawha	124	K7
Kanazawa	89	F7
Kanchanaburi	93	J6
Kanchenjunga	93	G3
Kanchipuram	92	E6
Kandahar	92	C2
Kandalaksha	62	Q3
Kandalakshskaya Guba	78	E2
Kandang	90	B5
Kandangan	90	F6
Kandanos	75	G5
Kandat	84	D5
Kandi	105	F3
Kandira	76	D2
Kandrian	114	D3
Kandukur	92	E5
Kandy	92	F7
Kane	125	L6
Kane Basin	120	M2
Kaneohe	126	S10
Kanevskaya	79	F6
Kangal	77	G3
Kangalassy	85	M4
Kangan	95	L8
Kangar	90	C4
Kangaroo Island	113	H6
Kangavar	94	H4
Kangaz	73	K2
Kangding	93	K2
Kangean	90	F7
Kangerdtuk	120	R3
Kanggye	87	P3
Kangiqsualujjuaq	121	N6
Kangiqsujuaq	121	M5
Kangirsuk	121	N5
Kangnung	89	B7
Kangping	87	N3
Kangri Karpo Pass	93	J3
Kani	93	H4
Kaniama	106	D4
Kanibadam	86	B3
Kaniet Islands	114	D2
Kanigigsualujak	121	L7
Kanin Nos	78	G2
Kanin Nos, Mys	78	G2
Kanin, Poluostrov	78	G2
Kanjiza	72	F2
Kankaanpaa	63	K6
Kankakee	124	G6
Kankan	104	D3
Kanker	92	F4
Kanmaw Kyun	93	J6
Kannapolis	129	M3
Kannonkoski	62	L5
Kannoura	89	E9
Kannus	62	N4
Kano	105	G3
Kanoya	89	C10
Kanpur	92	F3
Kansas	123	P8
Kansas City *Kansas, U.S.A.*	124	C7
Kansas City *Missouri, U.S.A.*	124	C7
Kansk	84	F5
Kansong	88	B6
Kant	86	D3
Kantemirovka	79	F6
Kanthi	93	G4
Kanton Island	111	U2
Kanturk	59	E8
Kanuku Mountains	136	F3
Kanye	108	E5
Kao	111	T5
Kao-hsiung	87	N7

Kaokoveld	108	B3
Kaolack	104	B3
Kaoma	106	D5
Kapanga	106	D4
Kapchagayskoye Vodokhranilishche	86	D3
Kapellskar	63	H7
Kapidagi Yarimadasi	76	B2
Kapiri Mposhi	107	E5
Kapit	90	E5
Kapiti Island	115	E4
Kapiting	137	F3
Kaplan	128	F5
Kaplice	70	F4
Kapoeta	103	F7
Kaposvar	72	D2
Kapsan	88	B5
Kapsukas	71	K1
Kaptanpasa	77	J2
Kapuas	90	E6
Kapuas	90	D6
Kapuas Hulu, Pegunungan	90	E5
Kapudzhukh	94	H2
Kapuskasing *Canada*	124	J2
Kapuskasing *Canada*	124	J2
Kapustin Yar	79	H6
Kara *Togo*	104	F4
Kara *Turkey*	77	J3
Kara *Russia*	84	Ae3
Kara Balta	86	C3
Karabas *Kazakhstan*	86	C3
Karabas *Kazakhstan*	86	D2
Karabekaul	95	S2
Karabiga	76	B2
Kara-Bogaz-Gol	79	J7
Kara-Bogaz-Gol, Proliv	79	J2
Kara-Bogaz-Gol, Zaliv	79	J2
Karabuk	76	E2
Karabulak *China*	86	D3
Karabulak *Kazakhstan*	86	E2
Karaburun	76	B3
Karacabey	76	C2
Karacadag	77	H4
Karacakoy	76	C2
Karacali Dagi	77	H4
Karacasu	76	C4
Karacay	77	G4
Karachev	79	E5
Karacheyevsk	79	G7
Karachi	92	C4
Karad	92	D5
Karadeniz Bogazi	76	C2
Karadilli	76	D3
Karagach	84	A5
Karaganda	86	C2
Karagayly	86	D2
Karagel	95	L2
Karaginskiy, Ostrov	85	U5
Karagiye, Vpadina	79	J7
Karahalli	76	C3
Karaidel	78	K4
Karaikal	92	E6
Karaikkudi	92	E6
Karaisali	76	F4
Karaj	95	K4
Karak	94	B6
Kara Kala	95	N2
Karakax He	92	E1
Karakecili	76	E3
Karakelong	91	H5
Karakocan	77	J3
Karakoram	92	E1
Karakuduk	84	B6
Karakul	86	C4
Kara Kul	86	C3
Kara-Kul , Ozero	86	C4
Karakumskiy Kanal	95	R3
Karakurt	77	K2
Karaman	76	E4
Karamay	86	E2
Karamea	115	D4
Karamea Bight	115	C4
Karamursel	76	C2
Karand	94	H4
Karanja	92	E4
Karanlik	76	F3
Karanlik Burun	76	B3
Karapelit	73	J4
Karapinar	76	E4
Karasburg	108	C5
Kara Sea	84	A2
Karashoky	84	A6
Karasjok	62	L2
Karasu *Turkey*	76	D2
Karasu *Kazakhstan*	84	A6
Karasu *Kazakhstan*	86	E2
Karasuk	84	B6
Karatal	86	D2
Karatas	76	F4
Kara Tau	86	C3
Karatau, Khrebet *Kazakhstan*	123	P8
Karatau, Khrebet *Kazakhstan*	79	J7
Karatobe	79	J6
Karaton	79	J6
Karatsu	89	B9
Karaudanawa	136	F3
Karauli	92	E3
Karaulkeldy	79	K6
Karavas	75	G4
Karawang	90	D7
Karayazi	77	K3
Karbala	94	G5
Karbole	63	F6
Karcag	73	F2

Name	Page	Grid
Kardhamila	75	J3
Kardhitsa	75	F3
Kardla	63	K7
Karesuando	62	K2
Kargasok	84	C5
Kargat	84	C5
Kargi *Turkey*	76	D4
Kargi *Turkey*	76	F2
Kargopol	78	F3
Kariba	108	E3
Kariba, Lake	108	E3
Karibib	108	C4
Kariburo	88	H4
Karigasniemi	62	L2
Karikari, Cape	115	D1
Karima	103	F4
Karimata, Kepulauan	90	D6
Karimata, Selat	90	D6
Karimganj	93	H4
Karimnagar	92	E5
Karimunjawa, Kepulauan	90	E7
Karin	103	J5
Karistos	75	H3
Kariz	95	Q4
Karkaralinsk	86	D2
Karkaralong, Kepulauan	91	H5
Karkar Island	114	D2
Karkas, Kuh-e	95	L5
Karkkila	63	L6
Karlino	70	F1
Karliova	77	J3
Karl-Marx-Stadt	70	E3
Karlobag	72	C3
Karlovac	72	C3
Karlovo	73	H4
Karlovy Vary	70	E3
Karlsborg	63	F7
Karlskoga	63	F7
Karlskrona	63	F8
Karlsruhe	70	C4
Karlstad *Sweden*	63	E7
Karlstad *U.S.A.*	124	B2
Karlstadt	70	C4
Karmanovka	79	J6
Karmoy	63	A7
Karnafuli Reservoir	93	H4
Karnal	92	E3
Karnali	92	F3
Karnataka	92	E6
Karnobat	73	J4
Karonie	112	E5
Karora	103	G4
Karossa, Tanjung	91	F7
Karousadhes	74	E3
Karoy	86	D2
Karpathos *Greece*	75	J5
Karpathos *Greece*	75	J5
Karpathos Straits	75	J5
Karpathou, Stenon	75	J5
Karpenision	75	F3
Karpinsk	84	Ad5
Karpogory	78	G3
Karratha	112	D3
Karrats Fjord	120	R3
Karree Berge	108	D6
Kars *Turkey*	77	K2
Kars *Turkey*	77	K2
Karsakpay	86	B2
Karsamaki	62	L5
Karsanti	76	F4
Karshi *Kazakhstan*	79	J7
Karshi *Uzbekistan*	80	H6
Karsiyaka	76	B3
Karskoye More	84	A2
Karsun	78	H5
Kartal	76	C2
Kartayel	78	J3
Kartuni	133	T11
Kartuzy	71	H1
Karufa	91	J6
Karun	94	J6
Karvina	71	H4
Karwar	92	D6
Karym	84	Ae4
Karymskoye	85	J6
Kas	76	C4
Kasai	106	C3
Kasaji	106	D5
Kasama	107	F5
Kasane	108	E3
Kasanga	107	F4
Kasangulu	106	C3
Kasaragod	92	D6
Kasar, Ras	96	D7
Kasba Lake	119	Q3
Kasba Tadla	100	D2
Kasempa	106	E5
Kasese	107	F2
Kashaf	95	Q3
Kashan	95	K5
Kashary	79	G6
Kashgar	86	D4
Kashi	86	D4
Kashima	89	C9
Kashin	78	F4
Kashipur	92	E3
Kashira	78	F5
Kashiwazaki	89	G7
Kashkanteniz	86	C2
Kashkarantsy	78	F2
Kashmar	95	P4
Kasimov	78	G5
Kasin	92	D2
Kasiruta	91	H6
Kaskinen	62	J5
Kasko	62	J5
Kas Kong	93	K6
Kasli	84	Ad5
Kasmere Lake	119	Q4
Kasongo	106	E3
Kasongo-Lunda	106	C4
Kasos	75	J5
Kasos, Stenon	75	J5
Kaspiyskiy	79	H6
Kassala	103	G4
Kassandra	75	G2
Kassel	70	C3
Kasserine	101	G1
Kastamonu	76	E2
Kastaneai	75	J2
Kastelli	75	G5
Kastellorizon	76	C4
Kastoria	75	F2
Kastorias, Limni	75	F2
Kastornoye	79	F5
Kastron	75	H3
Kasulu	107	F3
Kasumi	89	E8
Kasumiga-ura	89	H7
Kasungu	107	F5
Kata	84	G5
Kataba	106	E6
Katagum	105	H3
Katahdin, Mount	125	R4
Katako Kombe	106	D3
Katanning	112	D5
Katastari	75	F4
Katav Ivanovsk	78	K5
Katchall	93	H7
Katen	88	F2
Katerini	75	G2
Katha	93	J4
Katherina, Gebel	103	F2
Katherine	112	G1
Kathmandu	92	G3
Kati	100	D6
Katihar	93	G3
Katikati	115	E2
Katiola	104	D4
Katla	62	V13
Katlabukh, Ozero	73	K3
Katmai Volcano	118	E4
Kato Nevrokopion	75	G2
Katoomba	113	L5
Kato Stavros	75	G2
Katowice	71	H3
Katrineholm	63	G7
Katrine, Loch	57	D4
Katsina	105	G3
Katsina Ala	105	G4
Katsuura	89	H8
Katsuyama	89	F7
Kattavia	75	J5
Kattegat	63	D8
Kauai	126	R9
Kauai Channel	126	R10
Kauhajoki	62	K5
Kauiki Head	126	S10
Kaujuitok	120	H3
Kaulakahi Channel	126	Q9
Kaunakakai	126	S10
Kaunas	71	K1
Kaura Namoda	105	G3
Kaushany	73	K2
Kautokeino	62	K2
Kavacha	85	V4
Kavaje	74	E2
Kavak	77	G2
Kavaklidere	76	C4
Kavalerovo	88	E3
Kavali	92	E6
Kavalla	75	H2
Kavar	95	L7
Kavarna	73	K4
Kavgamis	77	H4
Kavieng	114	E2
Kavir, Dasht-e	95	M4
Kavir-e Namak	95	N4
Kavungo	106	D5
Kavusshap Daglari	77	K3
Kaw	137	G3
Kawagoe	89	G8
Kawaguchi	89	G8
Kawaihae	126	T10
Kawakawa	115	E1
Kawambwa	107	E4
Kawardha	92	F4
Kawasaki	89	G8
Kawerau	115	F3
Kawhia	115	E3
Kawhia Harbour	115	E3
Kawimbe	107	F4
Kawkareik	93	J5
Kawthaung	93	J7
Kayak Island	118	G4
Kayan	91	F5
Kaydak, Sor	79	J7
Kaye, Cape	120	H3
Kayenta	127	G2
Kayes	100	C6
Kaymaz	76	D3
Kaynar	86	D2
Kaynarca	76	D2
Kayseri	76	F3
Kayuagung	90	C6
Kazachinskoye	84	H5
Kazachye	85	P2
Kazakh	77	L2
Kazakhskiy Melkosopochnik	86	C2
Kazakhskiy Zaliv	79	J2
Kazakhstan	79	J6
Kazan	78	H4
Kazan *Turkey*	76	E2
Kazan	119	R3
Kazandzhik	95	M2
Kazan Lake	119	R3
Kazanluk	73	H4
Kazan-retto	83	N4
Kazatin	79	D6
Kazbek	77	L1
Kazerun	95	K7
Kazgorodok	84	Ae6
Kazhim	78	J3
Kazi Magomed	94	J1
Kazim Karabekir	76	E4
Kaztalovka	79	H6
Kazumba	106	D4
Kazy	95	N2
Kazym	84	Ae4
Kazymskaya	84	Ae4
Kazymskiy Mys	84	Ae4
Kea *Greece*	75	H4
Kea *Greece*	75	H4
Keady	58	J4
Keal, Loch na	57	B4
Kearny	126	G4
Keaukaha	126	T11
Keban	77	H3
Keban Baraji	77	H3
Kebemer	104	B2
Kebezen	84	D6
Kebnekaise	62	H3
Kebock Head	56	B2
Kebri Dehar	103	H6
Kech a Terara	103	G6
Kechika	118	K4
Keciborlu	76	D4
Kecil, Kai	91	J7
Kecskemet	72	E2
Kedainiai	63	K9
Kedgwick	125	S3
Kedong	87	P2
Kedougou	104	C3
Kedva	78	J3
Keel	58	B5
Keelby	55	J3
Keele	118	K3
Keele Peak	118	J3
Keeler	126	D2
Keene	125	P5
Keeper Hill	59	F7
Keetmanshoop	108	C5
Keewatin *N.W. Territories, Canada*	119	R3
Keewatin *Ontario, Canada*	124	C2
Kefallinia	75	F3
Kefamenanu	91	G7
Kefken	76	D2
Keflavik	62	T12
Keglo Bay	121	N6
Kegulta	79	G6
Kehsi Mansam	93	J4
Keighley	55	H3
Keitele *Kaskisuomi, Finland*	62	L5
Keitele *Kuopio, Finland*	62	M5
Keith	56	F3
Keith Arm	119	L2
Keiyasi	114	Q8
Kekertaluk Island	120	N4
Keketa	114	C3
Kel	85	M3
Kelang	90	C5
Keld	55	G2
Keles	76	C3
Kelibia	101	H1
Kelkit *Turkey*	77	G2
Kelkit *Turkey*	77	H2
Keller Lake	119	L3
Kellett, Cape	118	K1
Kellog	84	D4
Kellogg	122	F4
Kelloselka	62	N3
Kells	58	J5
Kelme	63	K9
Kelmentsy	73	J1
Kelo	102	C6
Kelolokan	91	F5
Kelowna	122	E3
Kelsey Bay	122	B2
Kelso *New Zealand*	115	B6
Kelso *U.K.*	57	F5
Keluang	90	C5
Kelvedon	53	H3
Kem	78	E3
Kemah	77	H3
Kemaliye	77	H3
Kemalpasa	77	J2
Kemalpasar	76	B3
Kemano	118	K5
Kemer *Turkey*	76	C4
Kemer *Turkey*	76	C4
Kemer *Turkey*	76	D4
Kemerovo	84	D5
Kemi	62	L4
Kemijarvi *Finland*	62	L3
Kemijarvi *Finland*	62	M3
Kemijoki	62	L3
Kemmerer	123	J7
Kempen	64	F3
Kempendyayi	85	K4
Kemp, Lake	127	N4
Kemps Bay	132	H2
Kempsey	113	L5
Kempten	70	D5
Kempt, Lac	125	N3
Kempton	113	K7
Ken	92	F3
Kenadsa	100	E2
Kenai	118	E3
Kenai Mountains	118	E4
Kenai Peninsula	118	F3
Kendal	55	G2
Kendall, Cape	120	J5
Kendari	91	G6
Kendawangan	90	E6
Kendraparha	92	G4
Kendyrliki	86	F2
Kenema	104	C4
Kenete Karavastas	74	E1
Kenge	106	C3
Kengtung	93	J4
Kenhardt	108	D5
Kenilworth	53	F2
Kenitra	100	D2
Keniut	85	X4
Kenli	87	M4
Kenmare *Ireland*	59	C9
Kenmare *Ireland*	59	C9
Kenmore	57	D4
Kennacraig	57	C5
Kennebec	125	R4
Kenner	128	G5
Kennet	53	F3
Kennewick	122	E4
Kenninghall	53	J2
Kenn Reef	113	M3
Kenogami	121	K7
Keno Hill	118	H3
Kenora	124	C2
Kenosha	124	G5
Kent *U.K.*	53	H3
Kent *U.S.A.*	127	K5
Kentau	86	B3
Kentford	53	H2
Kentmere	55	G2
Kent Peninsula	119	P2
Kentucky *U.S.A.*	124	G8
Kentucky *U.S.A.*	124	H8
Kentucky Lake	124	F8
Kentwood	128	G5
Kenya	107	G2
Keokea	126	S10
Keokuk	124	E6
Keos	75	H4
Kepi	91	K7
Kepno	71	G3
Keppel Bay	113	L3
Kepsut	76	C3
Kerala	92	E6
Kerama-retto	89	H10
Keravat	114	E2
Kerch	79	F6
Kerchenskiy Proliv	79	F6
Kerema	114	D3
Keremeos	122	E3
Keren	103	G4
Kerguelen, Ile	142	D6
Keri	75	F4
Kericho	107	G3
Kerinci, Gunung	90	C6
Keriya He	92	F1
Kerki	95	S3
Kerkinitis, Limni	75	G2
Kerkira *Greece*	74	E3
Kerkira *Greece*	74	E3
Kerma	102	F4
Kermadec Islands	111	T8
Kermadec Trench	143	H6
Kerman	95	N6
Kerman Desert	95	P7
Kermen	73	J4
Kermit	127	L5
Kern	126	C2
Keros	78	J3
Kerpineny	73	K2
Kerrera	57	C4
Kerrville	127	N5
Kerry	59	C8
Kerry Head	59	C8
Kerrykeel	58	G2
Keruh	90	C4
Kerulen	87	L2
Kesalahti	63	N6
Kesan	76	B2
Kesap	77	H2
Kesennuma	88	H6
Keshvar	94	J3
Keskin	76	E3
Keski-Suomi	62	K5
Keskozero	78	E3
Keswick	55	F2
Keszthely	72	D2
Ket	84	D5
Keta	104	F4
Keta, Ozero	84	E3
Ketapang	90	D6
Ketchikan	118	J4
Kete	104	E4
Ketmen, Khrebet	86	E3
Ketoy, Ostrov	85	S7
Ketrzyn	71	J1
Kettering	53	G2
Kettle Ness	55	J2
Kettle River Range	122	E3
Kettlewell	55	G2

Name	Pg	Grid	Name	Pg	Grid	Name	Pg	Grid	Name	Pg	Grid
Kettusoja	62	N3	Kherson	79	E6	Kilakh	97	K5	Kingsbarns	57	F4
Keurus-selka	63	L5	Khe Sanh	93	L5	Kilauea	126	R9	Kingsbridge	52	D4
Keushki	84	Ae4	Kheta	84	G2	Kilauea Crater	126	T11	King's Bromley	53	F2
Kew	133	M4	Khiitola	63	N6	Kilbasan	76	E4	Kingsclere	53	F3
Kewanee	124	F6	Khilok	85	J6	Kilbeggan	59	H6	Kingscote	113	H6
Keweenaw	124	G3	Khios *Greece*	75	H3	Kilberry	58	J5	Kingscourt	58	J5
Keweenaw Bay	124	G3	Khios *Greece*	75	J3	Kilbirnie	57	D5	Kingsford	124	F4
Keweenaw Point	124	G3	Khirbat Isriyah	77	G5	Kilbrannan Sound	57	C5	Kingsley	55	H3
Keyano	121	M7	Khiva	80	H5	Kilbride *Ireland*	59	K7	King's Lynn	53	H2
Keyaygyr	86	D3	Khlebarovo	73	J4	Kilbride *U.K.*	57	A3	Kingsmill Group	111	R2
Keyi	86	E3	Khmelnik	79	D6	Kilbuck Mountains	118	D3	King Sound	112	E2
Key Largo	129	M8	Khmelnitskiy	79	D6	Kilchu	88	B5	Kings Peak	123	J7
Key, Lough	58	F4	Khodzhakala	95	N2	Kilcock	59	J6	Kingsport	129	L2
Keynsham	52	E3	Kholm *Afghanistan*	92	C1	Kilcolgan	59	E6	Kingston *Australia*	113	H6
Key West	129	M8	Kholm *Russia*	78	E4	Kilcormac	59	G6	Kingston *Canada*	125	M4
Keyworth	53	F2	Kholmogory	78	G3	Kilcoy	113	L4	Kingston *Jamaica*	132	J5
Kez	78	J4	Kholmsk	88	J2	Kilcullen	59	J6	Kingston *New Zealand*	115	B6
Kezhma	84	G5	Khomas Highland	108	C4	Kildare *Ireland*	59	J6	Kingston *U.S.A.*	125	P6
Khabarovo	84	Ad3	Khomeyn	95	K5	Kildare *Ireland*	59	J6	Kingston Bagpuize	53	F3
Khabarovsk	88	E1	Khomeynishahr	95	K5	Kildin, Ostrov	62	R2	Kingston-upon-Hull	55	J3
Khabarovsk Kray	85	P6	Khong	93	L6	Kildinstroy	62	Q2	Kingston-upon-Thames	53	G3
Khabur	94	E4	Khongkhoyuku	85	N4	Kilfinnane	59	F8	Kingstown	133	S8
Khadki	92	D5	Khonj	95	L8	Kilgore	128	E4	Kingsville	128	D7
Khairagarh	92	F4	Khoper	79	G5	Kilham	57	F5	Kingswood	52	E3
Khairpur *Pakistan*	92	C3	Khor *Russia*	88	E2	Kilickaya	77	J2	Kington	52	D2
Khairpur *Pakistan*	92	D3	Khor *Russia*	88	E2	Kilifi	107	G3	Kingussie	57	D3
Khakhar	85	P5	Khora Sfakion	75	H5	Kilimanjaro	107	G3	King William Island	120	G3
Khalafabad	94	J6	Khorat, Cao Nguyen	93	K5	Kilinailau Islands	114	F2	King William's Town	108	E6
Khalili	95	L8	Khordha	92	G4	Kilis	77	G4	Kiniama	107	E5
Khalkhal	94	J3	Khordogoy	85	K4	Kiliya	79	D6	Kinik	76	B3
Khalki	75	J4	Khoreyver	78	K2	Kilkee	59	C7	Kinloch	57	B3
Khalkis	75	G3	Khorgo	84	J2	Kilkeel	58	L4	Kinlochewe	56	C3
Khalmer-Yu	84	Ad3	Khorinsk	84	H6	Kilkelly	58	E5	Kinloch Hourn	57	C3
Khalturin	78	H4	Khorod	79	E6	Kilkenny *Ireland*	59	H7	Kinna	63	E8
Khamar Daban, Khrebet	84	G6	Khorol	88	C3	Kilkenny *Ireland*	59	H7	Kinnaird Head	56	F3
Khambhat	92	D4	Khorovaya	84	A3	Kilkhampton	52	C4	Kinnegad	59	H6
Khambhat, Gulf of	92	D4	Khorramabad *Iran*	94	J5	Kilkieran Bay	59	C6	Kinnerley	52	E2
Khamili	75	J5	Khorramabad *Iran*	95	N4	Killadysert	59	D7	Kinnert, Yam	94	B5
Khamir	96	F8	Khorramshahr	94	J6	Killala	58	D4	Kinoosao	119	Q4
Khamis Mushayt	96	F7	Khosf	95	P5	Killala Bay	58	D4	Kinross	57	E4
Kham Keut	93	K5	Khosheutovo	79	H6	Killaloe	59	F7	Kinsale	59	E9
Khammam	92	F5	Khosk	95	R4	Killarney	59	C8	Kinsalebeg	59	G9
Khamra	85	J4	Khosrowabad	94	J6	Killashandra	58	G4	Kinsarvik	63	B6
Khanabad	92	C1	Khotin	73	J1	Killeen	128	D5	Kinshasa	106	C3
Khan al Baghdadi	94	F5	Khouribga	100	D2	Killenaule	59	G7	Kinsley	127	N2
Khanaqin	94	G4	Khoyniki	79	D5	Killiecrankie	57	E4	Kinston	129	P3
Khanda	84	H6	Khristiana	75	H4	Killiecrankie, Pass of	57	E4	Kintampo	104	E4
Khandela	92	E3	Khroma	85	Q2	Killin	57	D4	Kintore	56	F3
Khandra	75	J5	Khuff	96	G4	Killinek Island	121	P5	Kintyre	57	C5
Khandwa	92	E4	Khulna	93	G4	Killini	75	G4	Kintyre, Mull of	57	C5
Khandyga	85	P4	Khulo	77	K2	Killorglin	59	C8	Kinuachdrachd	57	C4
Khangokurt	84	Ad4	Khunjerab Pass	92	E1	Killybegs	58	F3	Kiparissia	75	F4
Khanh Hoa	93	L6	Khunsar	95	K5	Killylea	58	J4	Kiparissiakos Kolpos	75	F4
Khanh Hung	93	L7	Khunti	92	G4	Kilmacthomas	59	H8	Kipawa, Lac	125	L3
Khani	85	L5	Khur	95	P4	Kilmallock	59	E8	Kipengere Range	107	F4
Khania	75	H5	Khurays	97	J4	Kilmaluag	56	B3	Kipili	107	F4
Khaniadhana	92	E4	Khurja	92	E3	Kilmarnock	57	D5	Kipini	107	H3
Khanion Kolpos	75	G5	Khuryan Munjan, Jazar	97	N8	Kilmaurs	57	D5	Kipnuk	118	C4
Khanka, Ozero	88	D3	Khust	79	C6	Kilmelford	57	C4	Kipseli	75	G3
Khanpur	92	D3	Khutu Datta	85	Q7	Kilmez	78	J4	Kirakira	114	K7
Khan Shaykhun	94	C4	Khuzdar	92	C3	Kilmurry	59	D7	Kiraz	76	C3
Khantau	86	C3	Khvaf	95	Q4	Kilnsea	55	K3	Kirazli	76	B2
Khantayka	84	D3	Khvalynsk	79	H5	Kiloran	57	B4	Kirbasi	76	D2
Khantayskoye, Ozero	84	E3	Khvor	95	M5	Kilosa	107	G4	Kirbey	84	H3
Khanty-Mansiysk	84	Ae4	Khvormuj	95	K7	Kilpisjarvi	62	J2	Kircubbin	58	L4
Khan Yunis	94	B6	Khvoy	94	G2	Kilrea	58	J3	Kirec	76	C3
Kharabali	79	H6	Khvoynaya	78	E4	Kilrush	59	D7	Kirenga	84	H5
Kharagpur	93	G4	Khwaja Muhammad, Koh-i-	92	D1	Kilsyth	57	D5	Kirenis	76	C4
Kharalakh	85	L3	Khyber Pass	92	D2	Kiltan	92	D6	Kirensk	84	H5
Kharan	95	N7	Khyrov	71	K4	Kilwa Masoko	107	G4	Kirgizskiy Khrebet	86	C3
Kharanaq	95	M5	Kiamba	91	G4	Kilwinning	57	F4	Kirgiz Step	79	J6
Kharaulakhskiy Khrebet	85	M2	Kiantajarvi	62	N4	Kilyos	76	C2	Kiri	106	C3
Kharbur	77	J5	Kiaton	75	G3	Kimbal, Mount	118	G3	Kiribati	111	S2
Kharga, El Wahat el	102	F3	Kiberg	62	P1	Kimbe Bay	114	E3	Kirik	77	J2
Kharg Island	97	K2	Kibombo	106	E3	Kimberley *Canada*	122	G3	Kirikhan	77	G4
Kharitah, Shiqqat al	96	H8	Kibondo	107	F3	Kimberley *South Africa*	108	D5	Kirikkale	76	E3
Khark	97	K2	Kibwezi	107	G3	Kimberley Plateau	112	F2	Kirillo	78	F4
Kharkov	79	F6	Kibworth Harcourt	53	G2	Kimi	75	H3	Kirin	87	P3
Kharku	97	K2	Kicevo	73	F5	Kimito	63	K6	Kirinyaga	107	G3
Khar Kuh	95	L6	Kicking Horse Pass	119	M5	Kimmeridge	53	E4	Kirka	76	D3
Kharlovka	78	F2	Kidal	100	F5	Kimolos	75	H4	Kirkagac	76	B3
Kharsawan	92	G4	Kidan, Al	97	M5	Kimry	78	F4	Kirk Bulag Dag	94	H3
Kharstan	85	Q2	Kidderminster	52	E2	Kimvula	106	C4	Kirkburton	55	H3
Khartoum	103	F4	Kidnappers, Cape	115	F3	Kimzha	78	G2	Kirkby	55	G3
Khartoum North	103	F4	Kidsgrove	55	G3	Kinabalu, Gunung	90	F4	Kirkby in Ashfield	55	H3
Kharutayuvam	78	K2	Kidwelly	52	C3	Kinbasket Lake	122	F2	Kirkby Lonsdale	55	G2
Khasalakh	85	M2	Kidyut, Wadi	97	K8	Kinbrace	56	E2	Kirkby Stephen	55	G2
Khasan	88	C4	Kiel	70	D1	Kincardine *Canada*	125	K4	Kirkcaldy	57	E4
Khasavyurt	79	H7	Kielce	71	J3	Kincardine *U.K.*	57	E4	Kirkcambeck	57	F5
Khash	95	Q7	Kielder	57	F5	Kindat	93	H4	Kirkcolm	54	D2
Khash	95	R6	Kielder Forest	57	F5	Kinder	128	F5	Kirkcudbright	54	E2
Khash, Dasht-i-	92	B2	Kielder Water	57	F5	Kinder Scout	55	H3	Kirkcudbright Bay	54	E2
Khashm el Girba	96	B9	Kieler Bucht	70	D1	Kindersley	123	K2	Kirkenes	62	P2
Khash Rud	95	R6	Kieta	114	F3	Kindia	104	C3	Kirkestinden	62	H2
Khashuri	77	K2	Kiev	79	E5	Kindu	106	E3	Kirkheaton	57	G5
Khasi Hills	93	H3	Kiffa	100	C5	Kinel	79	J5	Kirkintilloch	57	D5
Khaskovo	73	H5	Kifisos	75	G3	Kinel-Cherkasy	78	J5	Kirkland Lake	125	K2
Khatanga *Russia*	84	G2	Kifri	94	G4	Kineshma	78	G4	Kirk Langley	53	F2
Khatanga *Russia*	84	G2	Kigali	107	F3	Kingaroy	113	L4	Kirklareli	76	B2
Khatangskiy Zaliv	84	H2	Kigi	77	J3	Kingarth	57	C5	Kirklington	55	J3
Khatayakha	78	K2	Kiglapait, Cape	121	P6	King Christian Island	120	F2	Kirk Michael	54	E2
Khatyrka	85	X4	Kigoma	107	E3	King City	126	B2	Kirkoswald	55	G2
Khaybar, Harrat	96	E4	Kiholo	126	T11	King George Island	141	W6	Kirk Smeaton	55	H3
Khaypudyrskaya Guba	78	K2	Kii-sanchi	89	E9	King George Sound	112	D5	Kirksville	124	D6
Khayran, Ra's al	97	P5	Kii-suido	89	E9	Kinghorn	57	E4	Kirkton	57	F4
Khaysardakh	85	M4	Kikai-jima	89	B11	Kingisepp	63	M7	Kirkton of Culsalmond	56	F3
Khe Bo	93	K5	Kikiakki	84	C4	Kingiseppa	63	K7	Kirkton of Largo	57	F4
Kheisia	77	J5	Kikinda	72	F3	King Island	113	J6	Kirkuk	94	G4
Khemis Miliana	67	H4	Kikladhes	75	H4	King, Lake	112	D5	Kirkwall	56	F2
Khemisset	100	D2	Kikonai	88	H5	King Leopold Ranges	112	F2	Kirkwhelpington	57	F5
Khenchela	101	G1	Kikori	114	C3	Kingman	126	E3	Kirkwood	108	E6
Khenifra	100	D2	Kikwit	106	C3	Kingoonya	113	H5	Kirlangic Burun	76	D4
Kherrata	67	J4	Kil	63	E7	Kings	126	B2	Kirmir	76	E2
Khersan	95	K6	Kilafors	63	G6	King Salmon	118	D4	Kirov *Russia*	78	E5

Name		
Kirov *Russia*	78	H4
Kirova	86	D2
Kirovabad	79	H7
Kirovakan	77	L2
Kirovgrad	79	E6
Kirovo-Chepetsk	78	H4
Kirovsk *Russia*	62	Q3
Kirovsk *Turkmenistan*	95	Q3
Kirovskiy	88	D3
Kirriemuir	57	F4
Kirs	78	J4
Kirsanov	79	G5
Kirsehir	76	F3
Kirtgecit	77	K3
Kirthar Range	92	C3
Kirtlington	53	F3
Kirton	55	J3
Kiruna	62	J3
Kiryu	89	G7
Kisa	63	F8
Kisamou, Kolpos	75	G5
Kisangani	106	E2
Kisar	91	H7
Kisarazu	89	G8
Kiselevsk	84	D6
Kishanganj	93	G3
Kishangarh	92	D3
Kishb, Harrat	96	E5
Kishika-zaki	89	C10
Kishinev	79	D6
Kishiwada	89	E8
Kishorganj	93	H4
Kishorn, Loch	56	C3
Kisii	107	F3
Kiska Island	118	Ab9
Kiskunfelegyhaza	72	E2
Kiskunhalas	72	E2
Kislovodsk	79	G7
Kismaayo	107	H3
Kiso-Fukushima	89	F8
Kiso-sammyaku	89	F8
Kispest	72	E2
Kissidougou	104	C4
Kissimmee	129	M7
Kisumu	107	F3
Kita	100	D6
Kitajaur	62	J3
Kitakami *Japan*	88	H6
Kitakami *Japan*	88	H6
Kitakami-sanmyaku	88	J3
Kita-kyushu	89	C9
Kitale	107	G2
Kitami	88	J4
Kitami-sammyaku	88	H6
Kitangari	107	G5
Kitay, Ozero	73	K3
Kit Carson	127	L1
Kitchener	125	K5
Kitee	62	P5
Kitgum	107	F2
Kithira *Greece*	75	G4
Kithira *Greece*	75	G4
Kithnos *Greece*	75	H4
Kithnos *Greece*	75	H4
Kitikmeot	119	N1
Kitimat	118	K5
Kitinen	62	M3
Kitkiojoki	62	K3
Kitsuki	89	C9
Kittanning	125	L6
Kittila	62	L3
Kitui	107	G3
Kitunda	107	F4
Kitwe	107	E5
Kitzbuhel	68	D2
Kitzbuheler Alpen	68	D2
Kitzingen	70	D4
Kivalo	62	L3
Kivijarvi	62	L5
Kivu, Lake	107	E3
Kiyev	79	E5
Kiyevka	88	D4
Kiyevskoye Vodokhranilishche	79	E5
Kiyikoy	76	C2
Kizel	78	K4
Kizema	78	H3
Kizilagac	77	J3
Kizilcaboluk	76	C4
Kizilcadag	76	C4
Kizilhisar	76	C4
Kizilirmak	76	E2
Kizil Irmak	77	F2
Kizilkaya	76	D4
Kiziloren	76	E4
Kiziltepe	77	J4
Kizlyar	79	H7
Kizyl-Arvat	95	N2
Kizyl-Atrek	95	M3
Kizyl Ayak	95	S3
Kizyl-Su	95	L2
Kjollefjord	62	M1
Kjopsvick	62	L2
Kladanj	72	E3
Kladno	70	F3
Kladovo	73	G3
Klagenfurt	68	E2
Klaipeda	63	L9
Klamath *U.S.A.*	122	B7
Klamath *U.S.A.*	122	C7
Klamath Falls	122	D6
Klamath Mountains	122	C6
Klamono	91	J6
Klaralven	63	J6
Klatovy	70	E4

Name		
Klekovaca	72	D3
Klenak	72	E3
Klerksdorp	108	E5
Klichka	85	K7
Klimovichi	79	E5
Klin	78	F4
Klinovec	70	E3
Klintsovka	79	H5
Klintsy	79	E5
Klisura	73	H4
Kljuc	72	D3
Klobuck	71	H3
Klodzka *Poland*	71	G3
Klodzko *Poland*	71	G3
Klos	75	F2
Klosterneuberg	68	F1
Klosters	68	B2
Klrovskiy	79	H6
Kluane	118	H3
Kluane Lake	118	H3
Kluczbork	71	H3
Klyevka	84	A6
Klyuchevskaya Sopka	85	U5
Klyuchi	85	U5
Klyukvinka	84	D5
Kmagta	114	J6
Kmanjab	108	B3
K2, Mount	92	E1
Knapdale	57	C5
Knaresborough	55	H2
Knife	123	N4
Knight Island	118	F3
Knighton	52	D2
Knin	72	D3
Knjazevac	73	G4
Knockadoon Head	59	G9
Knockalla Mount	58	G2
Knockanaffrin	59	G8
Knockaunapeebra	59	G8
Knocklayd	58	K2
Knockmealdown Mountains	59	G8
Knocknaskagh	59	F8
Knottingley	55	H3
Knox, Cape	118	J5
Knoxville *Iowa, U.S.A.*	124	D6
Knoxville *Tennessee, U.S.A.*	129	L3
Knoydart	57	C3
Knud Rasmussen Land	120	P2
Knutholstind	63	C6
Knutsford	55	G3
Knyazhaya Guba	62	Q3
Knyazhevo	78	G4
Knysna	108	D6
Knyszyn	71	K2
Koba	90	D6
Kobarid	72	B2
Kobayashi	89	C10
Kobberminebugt	120	R5
Kobelyaki	79	E6
Kobenhavn	63	E9
Koblenz	70	B3
Kobowre, Pegunungan	91	K6
Kobrin	71	L2
Kobroor	91	J7
Kobuk	118	D2
Kobuleti	77	J2
Kobya	85	M4
Koca *Turkey*	76	B3
Koca *Turkey*	76	C3
Koca *Turkey*	76	E2
Kocapinar	77	K3
Kocarli	76	B4
Koceljevo	72	E3
Koch Bihar	93	G3
Kochechum	84	G3
Kochegarovo	85	K5
Kocher	70	C4
Kochi	89	D9
Koch Island	120	L4
Kochkorka	86	D3
Koch Peak	122	J5
Kochumdek	84	E4
Koden	71	K3
Kodiak	118	E4
Kodiak Island	118	E4
Kodima	78	G3
Kodinar	92	D4
Kodok	103	F6
Kodomari	88	H6
Kodyma	73	L2
Kofcaz	76	B2
Koffiefontein	108	D5
Koflach	68	E2
Koforidua	104	E4
Kofu	89	G8
Koge	63	E9
Kogilnik	73	K2
Ko, Gora	88	F2
Kohat	92	D2
Kohima	93	H3
Koh-i Qaisar	95	S5
Kohtla-Jarve	63	M7
Koide	89	G7
Koi Sanjaq	94	G3
Koitere	62	P5
Koivu	62	L3
Koje	89	B8
Kojonup	112	D5
Kokand	86	B3
Kokas	91	J6
Kokchetav	84	Ae6
Kokemaenjoki	63	K6
Kokenau	91	K6
Kokkola	62	K5

Name		
Koko	105	G4
Kokoda	114	D3
Kokomo	124	G6
Kokpekty	86	E2
Koksoak	121	N6
Kokstad	108	E6
Koktas	86	C2
Kokubu	89	C10
Kokuora	85	R2
Kokura	89	C9
Kokuy	85	K6
Kok-Yangak	86	C3
Kola	62	Q2
Kolaka	91	G6
Kolar	92	E6
Kolari	62	K3
Kolarovgrad	73	J4
Kolasin	72	E4
Kolay	77	F2
Kolberg	70	F1
Kolbuszowa	71	J3
Kolchugino	78	F4
Kolda	104	C3
Kolding	63	C9
Kole	106	D3
Kolguyev, Ostrov	78	H2
Kolhapur	92	D5
Kolin	70	F3
Kolki	71	L3
Kolkuskull	62	V12
Kollabudur	62	T12
Koln	70	B3
Kolno	71	J2
Koloa	126	R10
Kolobrzeg	70	F1
Kologriv	78	G4
Kolombangara	114	H5
Kolomna	78	F4
Kolono	91	G6
Koloubara	72	F3
Kolozsvar	73	G2
Kolpashevo	84	C5
Kolpino	78	E4
Kolskiy Poluostrov	78	F2
Koltubanovskiy	79	J5
Koluszki	71	H3
Kolva *Russia*	78	K3
Kolva *Russia*	78	K2
Kolwezi	106	E5
Kolyma	85	U3
Kolymskaya Nizmennost	85	T3
Kolymskiy, Khrebet	85	T4
Komadugu Gana	105	H3
Komandorskiye Ostrova	81	T4
Komarno	71	H5
Komarom	72	E2
Komatsu	89	F7
Komering	90	C6
Kommunarsk	79	F6
Komodo	91	F7
Komoe	104	E4
Kom Ombo	103	F3
Komoran	91	K7
Komsomolets, Ostrov	81	L1
Komotini	75	H2
Komovi	74	E1
Kompong Cham	93	L6
Kompong Chhnang	93	K6
Kompong Som	93	K6
Kompong Speu	93	K6
Kompong Sralao	93	L6
Kompong Thom	93	K6
Komrat	79	D6
Komsomolets, Zaliv	79	J6
Komsomolsk	79	E6
Komsomolskiy	79	J6
Komsomolsk-na-Amure	85	P6
Konakovo	78	F4
Koncanica	72	D3
Konch	92	E3
Konda *Indonesia*	91	J6
Konda *Russia*	84	Ae4
Kondagaon	92	F5
Kondinin	112	D5
Kondinskoye	84	Ae5
Kondoa	107	G3
Kondon	85	P6
Kondoponga	78	E3
Konduz	92	C1
Kone	114	W16
Konevo	78	F3
Kong	104	E4
Kongan	89	J10
Kong Christian den X Land	120	W3
Kong Karls Land	80	D2
Kongolo	106	E4
Kongsberg	63	C7
Kongsvinger	63	E6
Kong Wilhelms Land	120	X2
Koniecpol	71	H3
Konigsberg	71	H2
Konigs Wusterhausen	70	E2
Konin	71	H2
Konitsa	75	F2
Koniya	89	B11
Korkamaalv	62	J2
Konkoure	104	C3
Konnern	70	D3
Konnevesi	62	M5
Konosha	78	G3
Konotop	79	E5
Konqi He	86	F3
Konskie	71	J3
Konstantinovka	79	F6

Name		
Konstantinovsk	79	G6
Konstanz	68	B2
Kontagora	105	G3
Kontcha	105	H4
Kontiomaki	62	N4
Kontum	93	L6
Kontum, Plateau du	93	L6
Konya	76	E3
Konya Ovasi	76	E3
Konzhakovskiy Kamen , Gora	78	K4
Kootenai	122	G3
Kootenay	122	F3
Kootenay Lake	122	F3
Kopaonik	73	F4
Kopasker	62	W11
Kopavogur	62	U12
Koper	72	B3
Kopervik	63	A7
Kopet Dag, Khrebet	95	N2
Kopeysk	84	Ad5
Koping	63	F7
Kopka	124	F1
Kopmanholmen	62	H5
Koppang	63	D6
Kopparberg *Sweden*	63	F7
Kopparberg *Sweden*	63	F6
Koppi *Russia*	88	G1
Koppi *Russia*	88	H1
Kopru	76	D4
Koprubasi	76	C3
Koprulu	76	E4
Kopruoren	76	C3
Kopychintsy	73	H1
Kor	95	L6
Kora	77	K2
Korab	72	F5
Korahe	103	H6
Koraluk	121	P6
Korana	72	C3
Korba	69	C7
Korbach	70	C3
Korbu, Gunung	90	C5
Korce	75	F2
Korcula	72	D4
Korda	84	F4
Kord Kuv	95	M3
Korea Bay	87	N4
Korea, North	87	P4
Korea, South	87	P4
Korea Strait	89	B8
Korennoye	84	H2
Korenovsk	79	F6
Korf	85	V4
Korforskiy	88	E1
Korgan	77	G2
Korgen	62	E3
Korhogo	104	D4
Korido	91	K6
Korim	91	K6
Korinthiakos Kolpos	75	G3
Korinthos	75	G4
Koriyama	89	H7
Korkinitskiy Zaliv	79	E6
Korkodon	85	T4
Korkuteli	76	D4
Korla	86	F3
Kormakiti, Akra	76	E5
Kornat	72	C4
Koro	114	R8
Korocha	79	F5
Koroglu Daglari	76	E2
Koronia, Limni	75	G2
Koronowo	71	G2
Koros	72	F2
Korosten	79	D5
Korostyshev	79	D5
Korotaikha	78	L2
Korovin Volcano	118	Ad9
Korpilombolo	62	K3
Korsakov	88	J2
Korsnas	62	J5
Korsor	63	D9
Korti	103	F4
Kortrijk	64	E3
Korucu	76	B3
Koryakskaya Sopka	85	U6
Koryanskiy Khrebet	85	Z5
Koryazhma	78	H3
Korzybie	71	G1
Kos *Greece*	75	J4
Kos *Greece*	75	J4
Koschagyl	79	J6
Koscian	71	G2
Koscierzyna	71	G1
Kosciusko, Mount	113	K6
Kosciusko	128	H4
Kose	77	H2
Kos Golu	76	B2
Koshiki-retto	89	B10
Kosice	71	J4
Koski	63	K6
Koslan	78	H3
Koslin	71	G1
Kosma	78	H2
Kosong	88	B6
Kosong-ni	88	B5
Kossou, Lac de	104	D4
Kossovo	71	L2
Kostajnica	72	D3
Kosti	103	F5
Kostino	84	D3
Kostomuksha	62	P4
Kostopol	71	M3
Kostroma *Russia*	78	G4

Name	Page	Ref
Libourne	65	C6
Librazhd	75	F2
Libreville	106	A2
Librilla	67	F4
Libya	101	J3
Libyan Desert	102	E3
Libyan Plateau	102	E1
Licata	69	D7
Lice	77	J3
Lichfield	53	F2
Lichinga	109	G2
Lichtenburg	108	E5
Lichtenfels	70	D3
Lichuan	87	M6
Licking	124	J7
Licosa, Punta	69	E5
Lida	71	L2
Lidao	87	N4
Liddel Water	57	F5
Liddesdale	57	F5
Liden	62	G5
Lidingo	63	H7
Lidkoping	63	E7
Lidzbark Warminski	71	J1
Liebling	73	F3
Liechtenstein	70	C5
Liege	64	F3
Liegnitz	71	G5
Lielope	63	L8
Lienz	68	D2
Liepaja	63	L8
Lier	64	F3
Liestal	68	A2
Liezen	68	E2
Liffey	59	J6
Lifford	58	H3
Lifi Mahuida	139	C8
Lifou	114	X16
Ligger Bay	52	B4
Lighthouse Reef	132	D6
Ligonha	109	G3
Ligui	126	G3
Ligure, Appennino	68	B3
Ligurian Sea	68	B4
Lihir Group	114	E2
Lihou Reefs	113	L2
Lihue	126	R10
Lihula	63	K7
Lijiang	93	K3
Likasi	106	E5
Likhoslavl	78	F4
Liku	90	D5
Likupang	91	H5
L'Ile-Rousse	69	B4
Lille	64	E3
Lille Balt	63	C8
Lillebonne	64	D4
Lillehammer	63	D6
Lillesand	63	C7
Lillestrom	63	E7
Lillhamra	63	F5
Lillhardal	63	F5
Lillholmsjon	62	F5
Lillo	66	E3
Lillviken	62	G3
Lilongwe	107	F5
Liloy	91	G4
Lima *Paraguay*	138	E4
Lima *Peru*	136	B6
Lima *Portugal*	66	E2
Lima *Montana, U.S.A.*	122	H5
Lima *Ohio, U.S.A.*	124	H6
Limah	97	N4
Limankoy	76	C2
Limavady	58	J2
Limay	139	C7
Limbang	90	E5
Limbani	136	D6
Limbe *Cameroon*	105	G5
Limbe *Malawi*	107	G6
Limburg	70	C3
Limeira	138	G4
Limenaria	75	H2
Limen Vatheos	75	J4
Limerick *Ireland*	59	E8
Limerick *Ireland*	59	E7
Limfjorden	63	C8
Limin	75	H2
Limmen Bight	113	H1
Limni	75	G3
Limnos	75	H3
Limoeiro *Ceara, Brazil*	137	K5
Limoeiro *Pernambuco, Brazil*	137	K5
Limoges	65	D6
Limon	132	E9
Limon	123	N8
Limousin	65	D6
Limoux	65	E7
Limpopo	109	F4
Linaalv	62	J3
Linah	96	F2
Linapacan Strait	91	F3
Linares *Chile*	139	B7
Linares *Mexico*	128	C8
Linares *Spain*	66	E3
Lincang	93	K4
Lincoln *New Zealand*	115	D5
Lincoln *U.K.*	55	J3
Lincoln *Illinois, U.S.A.*	124	F6
Lincoln *Maine, U.S.A.*	125	R4
Lincoln *Nebraska, U.S.A.*	123	R7
Lincoln City	122	B5
Lincoln Sea	140	R2
Lincolnshire	55	J3
Lincolnton	129	M3
Lindau	70	C5
Linde	85	L3
Linden *Guyana*	136	F2
Linden *U.S.A.*	129	J3
Linderodsasen	63	E9
Lindesberg	63	F7
Lindi	107	G4
Lindley	108	E5
Lindos	75	K4
Lindsay *Canada*	125	L4
Lindsay *California, U.S.A.*	126	C2
Lindsay *Montana, U.S.A.*	123	M4
Lindu Point	114	S8
Linfen	93	M1
Lingao	93	L5
Lingayen	91	G2
Lingen	70	B2
Lingfield	53	G3
Lingga	90	C6
Lingga, Kepulauan	90	C6
Lingle	123	M6
Lingling	93	M3
Lingshi	87	L4
Lingshui	93	M5
Lingsugur	92	E5
Ling Xian	93	M3
Lingyuan	87	M3
Lingyun	93	L4
Linhai	87	N6
Linhares	138	H3
Linhe	87	K3
Linh, Ngoc	93	L5
Linkoping	63	F7
Linkou	88	C3
Linlithgow	57	E5
Linnhe, Loch	57	C4
Linosa	74	B5
Linru	93	M2
Lins	138	G4
Linsell	63	E5
Linslade	53	G3
Lintao	93	K1
Linton *U.K.*	53	H2
Linton *U.S.A.*	123	P4
Linwu	93	M3
Linxi	87	M3
Linxia	93	K1
Linyi *China*	87	M4
Linyi *China*	87	M4
Linz *Austria*	68	E1
Linz *Germany*	70	B3
Linze	86	J4
Lion, Golfe du	65	F7
Liouesso	106	C2
Lipa *Philippines*	91	G3
Lipa *Yugoslavia*	72	D3
Lipari, Isola	69	E6
Lipari, Isole	69	E6
Lipenska nadrz	70	F4
Lipetsk	79	F5
Lipiany	70	F2
Lipin Bor	78	F3
Liping	93	L3
Lipkany	79	D6
Lipljan	73	F4
Lipnishki	71	L2
Lipno	71	H2
Lippe	70	C3
Lipsoi	75	J4
Lipson	75	F3
Lipu	93	M4
Lipusz	71	G1
Lira	107	F2
Lircay	136	C6
Liri	69	D5
Lisabata	91	H6
Lisala	106	D2
Lisboa	66	B3
Lisbon *Portugal*	66	B3
Lisbon *U.S.A.*	123	R4
Lisburn	58	K3
Lisburne, Cape	118	B2
Liscannor Bay	59	D7
Lisdoonvarna	59	D6
Lishi	87	L4
Lishui	87	M6
Lisichansk	79	F6
Lisieux	64	D4
Liskeard	52	C4
L'Isle-Jourdain	65	D7
Lismore *Australia*	113	L4
Lismore *Ireland*	59	G8
Lismore *U.K.*	57	C4
Liss	53	G3
Listowel	59	D8
Lit	62	F5
Litang	93	K3
Litani	137	G3
Litchfield	124	F7
Litherland	55	G3
Lithgow	113	L5
Lithinon, Akra	75	H5
Litos	66	C2
Lithuania	63	K9
Litovko	85	P7
Little	128	E4
Little Abaco	132	J1
Little Aden	96	G10
Little Andaman	93	H6
Little Bahama Bank	132	H1
Little Barrier Island	115	E2
Little Belt Mountains	122	J4
Littleborough	55	G3
Little Bow	122	H2
Little Cayman	132	G5
Little Colorado	126	G3
Little Falls *Minnesota, U.S.A.*	124	C3
Little Falls *New York, U.S.A.*	125	N5
Littlefield	127	L4
Littlehampton	53	G4
Little Inagua Island	133	L4
Little Karoo	108	D6
Little Minch, The	56	B3
Little Missouri	123	M5
Little Nicobar	93	H7
Little Ouse	53	H2
Little Pamir	92	D1
Littleport	53	H2
Little Red	128	G3
Little Rock	128	F3
Little Rocky Mountains	123	K3
Little Scarcies	104	C4
Little Sitkin Island	118	Ab9
Little Smoky	119	M5
Little Snake	123	K7
Little South-west Miramichi	125	S3
Little Stricklanc	93	G2
Littleton *Colorado, U.S.A.*	123	M8
Littleton *New Hampshire, U.S.A.*	125	Q4
Little Wabash	124	F7
Little Waltham	53	H3
Liulin	87	L4
Liupan Shan	93	L1
Liuyang	93	M3
Liuzhou	93	L4
Livani	63	M8
Live Oak	129	L5
Livermore	126	B2
Livermore, Mount	127	K5
Liverpool *Australia*	113	L5
Liverpool *U.K.*	55	G3
Liverpool Bay *Canada*	118	K1
Liverpool Bay *U.K.*	55	F3
Livingston *Canada*	121	N7
Livingston *U.K.*	57	E5
Livingston *Montana, U.S.A.*	123	J5
Livingston *Texas, U.S.A.*	128	E5
Livingstone	106	E6
Livingstone, Chutes de	106	B4
Livingstone Falls	106	B4
Livingstone Mountains	107	F4
Livingstone Island	141	V6
Livingston, Lake	128	E5
Livno	72	D4
Livny	79	F5
Livojoki	62	M4
Livonia	124	J5
Livorno	68	C4
Liwiec	71	J2
Liwonde	107	G6
Li Xian	93	M3
Liyang	87	M5
Lizard	52	B4
Lizardo	137	H5
Lizard Point	52	B4
Ljosavatn	62	W12
Ljubinje	72	E4
Ljubisnja	72	E4
Ljubljana	72	C2
Ljungan	62	G5
Ljungby	63	E8
Ljusdal	63	G6
Ljusnan	63	F5
Llanarmon Dyffryn Ceiriog	52	D2
Llanbadarn Fynydd	52	D2
Llanbedr	52	C2
Llanberis	54	E3
Llanbrynmair	52	D2
Llandeilo	52	D3
Llandovery	52	D3
Llandrindod Wells	52	D2
Llandudno	54	F3
Llanelli	52	C3
Llanerchymedd	54	E3
Llanes	66	D1
Llanfaethlu	54	E3
Llanfair Caereinion	52	D2
Llanfairfechan	54	F3
Llanfair Talhaiarn	55	F3
Llanfyllin	52	D2
Llangefni	55	E3
Llanglydwen	52	C3
Llangollen	52	D2
Llangranog	52	C2
Llangurig	52	D2
Llanidloes	52	D2
Llanilar	52	C2
Llanos	136	D2
Llanquihue, Lago	139	B8
Llanrhystud	52	C2
Llanrwst	54	F3
Llantrisant	52	D3
Llantwit	52	C2
Llanwenog	52	C2
Llanwrtyd Wells	52	D2
Llawhaden	52	C3
Lleyn Peninsula	52	C2
Lliria	67	F3
Llivia	67	G1
Llobregat	67	G2
Lloydminster	119	P5
Lluchmayor	67	H3
Llyswen	52	D2
Loa	138	C4
Loanhead	57	E5
Lobatse	108	E5
Lobau	70	F3
Loberia	139	E7
Lobez	70	F2
Lobito	106	B5
Lobos	139	E7
Lobos, Island	126	G7
Locarno	68	B2
Lochaber	57	D4
Lochan Fada	56	C3
Loch Ard Forest	57	D4
Lochboisdale	57	A3
Lochearnhead	57	D4
Loches	65	D5
Lochgelly	57	E4
Lochgilphead	57	C4
Lochinver	56	C2
Lochmaben	57	E5
Lochmaddy	56	A3
Lochnagar	57	E4
Lochranza	57	C5
Loch Shin	56	D2
Lochy, Loch	57	D4
Lock	113	H5
Lockerbie	57	E5
Lockhart	128	D6
Lock Haven	125	M6
Lockport	125	L5
Locri	69	F6
Loddekopinge	63	E9
Loddon *Australia*	113	J6
Loddon *U.K.*	53	J2
Lodeve	65	E7
Lodeynoye Pole	78	E3
Lodge Grass	123	L5
Lodgepole	123	M7
Lodi *Italy*	68	B3
Lodi *U.S.A.*	126	B1
Lodingen	62	F2
Lodja	106	D3
Lodwar	107	G2
Lodz	71	H3
Loeriesfontein	108	C6
Lofoten	62	E2
Loftus	55	J2
Logan	122	J7
Logan, Mount	118	G3
Logansport *Indiana, U.S.A.*	124	G6
Logansport *Louisiana, U.S.A.*	128	F5
Loge	106	B4
Logishin	71	M2
Logone	102	C5
Logrono	66	E1
Logrosan	66	D3
Loh	114	T10
Lohardaga	92	F4
Loharu	92	E3
Lohit	93	J3
Lohja	63	L6
Loikaw	93	J5
Loimaa	63	K6
Loimijoki	63	K6
Loing	65	E5
Loi, Phu	93	K4
Loir	65	C5
Loire	65	B5
Loja *Ecuador*	136	B4
Loja *Spain*	66	D4
Lokantekojarvi	62	M3
Lokhpodgort	78	M2
Lokhvitsa	79	E5
Lokichokio	107	F2
Lokilalaki, Gunung	91	G6
Lokka	62	M3
Loknya	78	E4
Lokoja	105	G4
Lokshak	85	N6
Lokuru	114	H6
Lol	102	E6
Lola	104	D4
Lolland	63	D9
Lolo	122	G4
Loloda	91	H5
Lolo Pass	122	G4
Lolvavana, Passage	114	U11
Lom *Bulgaria*	73	G4
Lom *Norway*	63	C6
Lomami	106	D3
Lomas Coloradas	139	C8
Lomazy	71	K3
Lombarda, Serra	137	G3
Lombe	107	G4
Lombez	65	D7
Lomblen	91	G7
Lombok	90	F7
Lome	105	G4
Lomela	106	D3
Lomir	94	J2
Lomond Hills	57	E4
Lomond, Loch	57	D4
Lomonosov Ridge	140	A1
Lompobattang, Gunung	91	F7
Lompoc	126	B3
Lomza	71	K2
London *Canada*	125	K5
London *U.K.*	53	G3
Londonderry *U.K.*	58	H2
Londonderry *U.K.*	58	J3
Londonderry, Cape	112	F1
Londonderry, Isla	139	B11
Londoni	114	R8
Londrina	138	F4

M

Name	Page	Ref	Name	Page	Ref	Name	Page	Ref	Name	Page	Ref
Macae	138	H4	Madison *Indiana, U.S.A.*	124	H7	Mahia Peninsula	115	G3	Mala, Punta	136	B2
McAlester	128	E3	Madison *Montana, U.S.A.*	122	J5	Mahmudabad *India*	92	F3	Malaren	63	G7
McAllen	128	C7	Madison *Nebraska, U.S.A.*	123	R7	Mahmudabad *Iran*	95	L3	Malargue	139	C7
McAllister, Mount	113	K5	Madison *S. Dakota, U.S.A.*	123	R5	Mahmudia	73	K3	Malartic	125	L2
MacAlpine Lake	119	Q2	Madison *Winconsin, U.S.A.*	124	F5	Mahmudiye	76	D3	Malaspina	139	C8
Macapa	137	G3	Madisonville *Kentucky, U.S.A.*	124	G8	Mahnomen	124	B3	Malaspina Glacier	118	G4
Macara	136	B4	Madisonville *Texas, U.S.A.*	128	E5	Mahon	67	J3	Malatya	77	H3
McArthur	113	H2	Madiun	90	E7	Mahrah, Al	97	K8	Malatya Daglari	77	H3
Macau	137	K5	Mado Gashi	107	G2	Mahukona	126	T10	Malavate	137	G3
Macaubas	138	J6	Madoi	93	J2	Mahuva	92	D4	Malavi	94	H5
Macauley Islands	111	T8	Madona	63	M8	Maicao	136	C1	Malawi	107	F5
McBeth Fjord	120	N4	Madrakah, Ra's	97	N7	Maiche	65	G5	Malawi, Lake	107	F5
McBride	119	L5	Madras *India*	92	F6	Maicuru	137	G4	Malaybalay	91	H4
McCamey	127	L5	Madras *U.S.A.*	122	D5	Maidenhead	53	G3	Malayer	94	J4
McCammon	122	H6	Madre de Dios	136	D6	Maidi	91	H5	Malay Peninsula	90	C5
McCarthy	118	G3	Madre de Dios, Isla	139	A10	Maidstone	53	H3	Malaysia	90	D5
Macclesfield	55	G3	Madre, Laguna *Mexico*	128	D8	Maiduguri	105	H3	Malazgirt	77	K3
McClintock Channel	119	Q1	Madre, Laguna *U.S.A.*	128	D7	Maihar	92	F4	Malbork	71	H1
McClintock Range	112	F2	Madre Occidental, Sierra	127	H6	Maijdi	93	H4	Malcolm's Point	57	B4
McClure Strait	120	C3	Madre Oriental, Sierra	127	L7	Maikala Range	92	F4	Malden	124	F8
McComb	128	G5	Madre, Sierra	91	G2	Main *U.K.*	58	K3	Maldives	82	F6
McCook	123	P7	Madrid	66	E2	Main *Germany*	70	C4	Maldon	53	H3
McCreary	123	Q2	Madridejos	66	E3	Main Barrier Range	113	J5	Maldonado	139	F6
McDermitt	122	F7	Madrigalejo	66	D3	Main Channel	125	K4	Maldonado, Punta	131	K9
Macdonnell Ranges	113	G3	Madrona, Sierra	66	D3	Mai-Ndombe, Lac	106	C3	Male	82	F6
Macduff	56	F3	Madura *Australia*	112	F5	Maine *France*	64	C4	Malea, Akra	75	G4
Macedonia	73	F5	Madura *Indonesia*	90	E7	Maine *U.S.A.*	125	R4	Malegaon	92	D4
Maceio	137	K5	Madurai	92	E7	Maine Soroa	101	H6	Male Karpaty	71	G4
Maceio, Punta da	137	K4	Madura, Selat	90	E7	Maingkwan	93	J3	Malema	109	G2
Macenta	104	D4	Madzharovo	73	H5	Mainland *Orkney Is., U.K.*	56	E2	Maleme	75	G5
Macerata	68	D4	Maebashi	89	G7	Mainland *Shetland Is., U.K.*	56	A1	Maler Kotla	92	E2
McGehee	128	G4	Maerus	73	H3	Maintirano	109	H3	Malesherbes	64	E4
Macgillycuddy's Reeks	59	C9	Maesteg	52	D3	Mainua	62	M4	Maleta	84	H6
Macha	85	K5	Maestra, Sierra	132	J4	Mainz	70	C4	Malevangga	114	H5
Machachi	136	B4	Maevatanana	109	J3	Maio	104	L7	Malgobek	79	G7
Machakos	107	G3	Maewo	114	U11	Maipu	139	E7	Malgomaj	62	G4
Machala	136	B4	Mafa	91	H5	Maiquetia	133	P9	Malhat	77	K5
Machanga	109	G4	Mafeteng	108	E5	Maira	68	A3	Malheur	122	F6
Macharioch	57	C5	Mafia Island	107	G4	Maisi, Cabo	133	K4	Malheur, Lake	122	E6
Machias	125	S4	Mafikeng	108	E5	Maiskhal	93	H4	Mali	100	E5
Machichaco, Cap	66	E1	Mafra	66	B3	Maitland *New South Wales, Australia*	113	L5	Mali Hka	93	J3
Machilipatnam	92	F5	Mafraq	94	C5	Maitland *S. Australia, Australia*	113	H5	Mali Kanal	72	E3
Machiques	136	C2	Maga	114	S8	Maiz, Islas del	132	F8	Mali Kyun	93	J6
Machir Bay	57	B5	Magadan	85	S5	Maizuru	89	E8	Malimba, Mont	107	E4
Machynlleth	52	D2	Magadan Oblast	85	V3	Majagual	136	C2	Malin *Ireland*	58	H2
Macin	73	K3	Magadi	107	G3	Majene	91	F6	Malin *Ukraine*	79	D5
McIntosh	123	P5	Magallanes, Estrecho de	139	B10	Maji	103	G6	Malin Beg	58	E3
Macka	77	H2	Magangue	136	C2	Majiang	93	L3	Malindi	107	H3
Mackay	113	K3	Magara	76	E4	Majin	87	M6	Malin Head	58	H2
Mackay, Cape	120	D2	Magarida	114	D4	Majorca	67	H3	Malin More	58	E3
Mackay, Lake	112	F3	Magburaka	104	C4	Maka *Senegal*	104	C3	Malka	85	T6
MacKay Lake	119	N3	Magdagachi	85	M6	Maka *Solomon Is.*	114	K6	Malkachan	85	S5
McKean Island	111	U2	Magdalena *Bolivia*	136	E6	Makale	91	F6	Malkapur	92	E4
McKeesport	125	L6	Magdalena *Colombia*	136	C2	Makambako	107	F4	Malkara	76	B2
Mackenzie *Australia*	113	K3	Magdalena *Mexico*	126	F7	Makanza	106	C2	Malkinia	71	K2
Mackenzie *Canada*	118	J2	Magdalena *Mexico*	126	G5	Makarikha	78	K2	Malko Turnovo	73	J5
Mackenzie Bay *Antarctic*	141	E5	Magdalena *Mexico*	130	H7	Makarova	84	D2	Mallaig	57	C4
Mackenzie Bay *Canada*	118	H2	Magdalena, Isla	130	C5	Makarska	72	D4	Mallawi	102	F2
Mackenzie King Island	120	D2	Magdalena, Llano de la	130	D5	Makaryev	78	G4	Mallorca	67	H3
Mackenzie Mountains	118	H3	Magdalen Islands	121	P8	Makassar	91	F7	Mallow	59	E8
Mackinac, Straits of	124	H4	Magda Plateau	120	K3	Makassar, Selat	91	F6	Mallwyd	52	D2
McKinley, Mount	118	E3	Magdeburg	70	D2	Makat	79	J6	Malm	62	D4
McKinney	128	D4	Magdelena	127	J3	Makatini Flats	109	F5	Malmberget	62	J3
Macklin	123	K1	Magee, Island	58	L3	Makay, Massif du	109	J4	Malmedy	64	G3
McLaughlin	123	P5	Magelang	90	E7	Makeni	104	C4	Malmesbury *South Africa*	108	C6
Maclean Strait	120	F2	Magellan, Strait of	139	B10	Makenu	126	S10	Malmesbury *U.K.*	53	E3
Maclear	108	E6	Magenta, Lake	112	D5	Makeyevka	79	F6	Malmo	63	E9
McLeod, Lake	112	C3	Mageroya	62	L1	Makhachkala	79	H7	Malmohus	63	E9
Macmillan	118	J3	Maggiore, Lago	68	B3	Makharadze	77	K2	Malmyzh	78	J4
McMillan, Lake	127	K4	Maghagha	102	F2	Makhmur	94	F4	Malo	114	T11
McMinnville *Oregon, U.S.A.*	122	C5	Magharee Islands	59	B8	Makhyah, Wadi	97	J8	Malolo	114	Q8
McMinnville *Tennessee, U.S.A.*	129	K3	Maghera	58	J3	Maki	91	J6	Malone	125	N4
McMurdo	141	M3	Magherafelt	58	J3	Makinsk	84	A6	Malorita	71	L3
Macomb	124	E6	Magheramorne	58	L3	Makkah	96	D6	Malo Strait	114	T11
Macomer	69	B5	Magilligan Point	58	J2	Makkovik	121	Q6	Maloy	62	A6
Macon	65	F5	Magina	66	E4	Makkovik, Cape	121	Q6	Maloyaroslavets	78	F4
Macon *Georgia, U.S.A.*	129	L4	Maglic	72	E4	Makogai	114	R8	Malozemelskaya Tundra	84	Ab3
Macon *Missouri, U.S.A.*	124	D7	Maglie	69	G5	Makokou	106	B2	Malpartida de Caceres	66	C3
Macossa	109	F3	Magnolia	128	F4	Makondi Plateau	107	G5	Malpas	55	G3
McPherson	128	D1	Magoe	109	F3	Makov	71	H4	Malpelo, Isla	134	A2
Macquarie	113	K5	Magog	125	P4	Makra	75	H4	Malta	74	C5
Macquarie Harbour	113	K7	Magpie	121	P7	Makrai	92	E4	Malta *U.S.A.*	123	L3
Macquarie Island	141	L8	Magro	67	F3	Makran	92	B3	Malta Channel	74	C4
McRae	129	L4	Magude	109	F5	Makri	75	H2	Maltahohe	108	C4
Macroom	59	E9	Maguse Lake	119	R3	Makronisi	75	H4	Maltby	55	H3
McTavish Arm	119	M2	Maguse Point	119	S3	Maksatikha	78	F4	Maltepe	76	C2
Macuspana	131	N9	Magwe	93	H4	Maksim	78	K3	Malton	55	J2
Macuzari, Presa	127	H7	Magwe	93	H4	Maksimovka	88	F2	Malu	73	J3
McVicar Arm	119	L2	Mahabad	94	G3	Makteir	100	C4	Maluku	91	H6
Mad	122	C7	Mahabe	109	J3	Maku	94	G2	Maluku, Laut	91	H5
Madaba	94	B6	Mahabharat Range	92	G3	Makurazaki	89	C10	Malung	63	E6
Madade	109	F4	Mahabo	109	H4	Makurdi	105	G4	Maluu	114	K6
Madagascar	109	J3	Mahaddayweyne	107	J2	Makushin Volcano	118	Ae9	Malvan	92	D5
Madang	114	D3	Mahadeo Hills	92	E4	Mala	62	M4	Malvern	128	F3
Madaoua	101	G6	Mahagi	107	F2	Malabang	91	G4	Malvern Hills	52	E2
Madaripur	93	H4	Mahajanga	109	J3	Malabar Coast	92	D6	Malvinas, Islas	139	E10
Madawaska	125	M4	Mahakam	90	F5	Malabo	105	G5	Malykay	85	K4
Maddalena, Isola di	69	B5	Mahalapye	108	E4	Malacca, Strait of	90	C5	Malyy Anyuy	85	U3
Maddaloni	69	E5	Mahallat	95	K5	Malacky	71	G4	Malyy Lyakhovskiy, Ostrov	85	Q2
Maddy, Loch	56	A3	Mahanadi	92	F4	Mala Fatra	71	H4	Malyy Taymyr, Ostrov	81	M2
Madeira *Brazil*	136	E5	Mahanoy City	125	M6	Malaga *Colombia*	136	C2	Malyy Yenisey	84	F6
Madeira *Portugal*	100	B2	Mahao	88	A4	Malaga *Spain*	66	D4	Mama	85	J5
Madelia	124	C5	Maharashtra	92	E5	Malagarasi	107	F3	Mamankhalinka	79	J6
Maden *Turkey*	77	H3	Maharlu, Daryacheh-ye	95	L7	Malahide	59	K6	Mamanuca Group	114	Q8
Maden *Turkey*	77	J2	Maha Sarakham	93	K5	Malaita	114	K6	Mamaru	137	F4
Madera *Mexico*	127	H6	Mahavavy	109	J3	Malakal	103	F6	Mambasa	107	E2
Madera *U.S.A.*	126	B2	Mahbubnagar	92	E5	Malakanagiri	92	F5	Mamberamo	114	B2
Madetkoski	62	M3	Mahdah	97	M4	Malakand	92	D2	Mamburao	91	G3
Madhubani	92	G3	Mahdia *Guyana*	136	F2	Malakula	114	T12	Mamers	64	D4
Madhya Pradesh	92	E4	Mahdia *Tunisia*	101	H1	Malang	90	E7	Mamfe	105	G4
Madidi	136	D6	Mahe	92	E6	Malanje	106	C4	Mamlyutka	84	Ae6
Madinat ash Shab	96	G10	Mahebourg	109	L7	Malao	114	T11			
Madingo-Kayes	106	B3	Mahenge	107	G4						
Madingou	106	B3	Mahesana	92	D4						
Madin Jadid	77	H5	Mahi	92	D4						

Mamonovo 71 H1
Mamore 138 D3
Mamore Forest 57 D4
Mamoria 136 D5
Mamou 104 C3
Mampong 104 E4
Mamry, Jezioro 71 J1
Mamuju 91 F6
Man *India* 92 F3
Man *Ivory Coast* 104 D4
Mana 63 C7
Mana *Fr. Guiana* 137 G3
Mana *U.S.A.* 126 R9
Manacapuru 136 E4
Manacapuru, Lago de 136 E4
Manacor 67 H3
Manadir, Al 97 M5
Manado 91 G5
Managua 132 D8
Managua, Laguna de 132 D8
Manakara 109 J4
Manakhah 96 F9
Manambolo 109 H3
Manam Island 114 D2
Mananara *Madagascar* 109 J4
Mananara *Madagascar* 109 J3
Mananjary 109 J4
Manantavadi 92 E6
Manaoba 114 K6
Manapire 136 D2
Manapouri 115 A6
Manapouri, Lake 115 A6
Manas 93 H3
Manau 114 D3
Manaus 136 F4
Manavgat 76 D4
Manbij 94 C3
Mancha Real 66 E4
Manchester *U.K.* 55 G3
Manchester *Connecticut, U.S.A.* 125 P6
Manchester *Kentucky, U.S.A.* 124 J8
Manchester *New Hampshire, U.S.A.* 125 Q5
Manchester *Tennessee, U.S.A.* 129 J3
Mancora 136 A4
Mand 95 K7
Mandab, Bab el 103 H5
Mandal *Afghanistan* 95 Q5
Mandal *Norway* 63 B7
Mandala, Puncak 91 L6
Mandalay 93 J4
Mandalgovi 87 K2
Mandali 94 G5
Mandal-Ovoo 87 J3
Mandan 123 P4
Mandaon 91 G3
Mandar, Teluk 91 F6
Mandasawu, Poco 91 G7
Mandav Hills 92 D4
Mandeville 132 J5
Mandi 92 E2
Mandiore, Lago 138 E3
Mandla 92 F4
Mandoudhion 75 G3
Mandurah 112 D5
Manduria 69 F5
Mandvi 92 C4
Mandya 92 E6
Manea 53 H2
Manevichi 71 L3
Manfredonia 69 E5
Manfredonia, Golfo di 69 F5
Manga 138 J6
Mangakino 115 E3
Mangalia 73 K4
Mangalore 92 D6
Mangaon 92 D5
Mangapehi 115 E3
Manggautu 114 J7
Mangin Range 93 J4
Mangkalihat, Tanjung 91 F5
Manglares, Punta 136 B3
Mangochi 107 G5
Mangoky 109 H4
Mangole 91 H6
Mangonui 115 D1
Mangoro 109 J3
Mangotsfield 52 E3
Mangral 92 D4
Manguari 136 D4
Mangueira, Lagoa 138 F6
Mangui 87 N1
Manguinha, Pontal do 137 K6
Mangut 85 J7
Mangyshlak 79 J7
Mangyshlak, Poluostrov 79 J7
Mangyshlakskiy Zaliv 79 J7
Manhan 86 G2
Manhattan 123 R8
Manhica 109 F5
Manicore 136 E5
Manicouagan 121 N7
Manicouagan, Reservoir 121 N7
Manifah 97 J3
Manika, Plateau de la 106 E4
Manila 91 G3
Manipa, Selat 91 H6
Manipur 93 H4
Manisa 76 B3
Man, Isle of 54 E2
Manistee *U.S.A.* 124 G4
Manistee *U.S.A.* 124 H4
Manistique 124 G4

Manitoba 119 R4
Manitoba, Lake 123 Q2
Manitou Falls 123 T2
Manitou Island 124 G4
Manitoulin 124 J4
Manitowoc 124 G4
Maniwaki 125 N3
Manizales 136 B2
Manja 109 H4
Manjra 92 E5
Mankato 124 C4
Mankono 104 D4
Mankovka 73 L1
Manna 90 C6
Mannar 92 E7
Mannar, Gulf of 92 E7
Mannheim 70 C4
Manning, Cape 120 B2
Manning Strait 114 J5
Manningtree 53 J3
Mannu 69 B6
Manoa Abuna 136 D5
Manokwari 91 J6
Manolas 75 F3
Manonga 107 F3
Manono 107 E4
Manorbier 52 C3
Manorcunningham 58 G3
Manorhamilton 58 F4
Manoron 93 J6
Manosque 65 F7
Manouane, Reservoir 121 M7
Mano-wan 89 G7
Manpojin 87 P3
Manra 111 U2
Manresa 67 G2
Mansa 107 E5
Mansehra 92 D2
Mansel Island 120 L5
Mansfield *U.K.* 55 H3
Mansfield *Louisiana, U.S.A.* 128 F5
Mansfield *Ohio, U.S.A.* 124 J6
Mansfield *Pennsylvania, U.S.A.* 125 M6
Mansfield Woodhouse 55 H3
Mansle 65 D6
Manson Creek 118 L4
Mansoura 67 J4
Manston 53 J3
Mansurlu 77 F4
Manta 136 A4
Mantalingajan, Mount 91 F4
Mantaro 136 B6
Mantecal 136 D2
Mantes 64 D4
Mantiqueira, Serra da 138 G4
Mantova 68 C3
Mantsala 63 L6
Mantta 63 L5
Mantua 68 C3
Mantyharju 63 M6
Manua 111 V4
Manuel 131 K6
Manui 91 G6
Manu Island 114 C2
Manujan 95 N8
Manukau 115 E2
Manukau Harbour 115 E2
Manulla 58 D5
Manus Islands 114 D2
Manya 78 L3
Manyas 76 B2
Manych Gudilo, Ozero 79 G6
Manyoni 107 F4
Manzanares 66 E3
Manzanillo *Cuba* 132 J4
Manzanillo *Mexico* 130 G8
Manzanillo, Punta 136 B2
Manzariyeh 95 K4
Manzhouli 87 M2
Manzini 109 F5
Manzya 84 F5
Mao 102 C5
Maoershan 88 A3
Maoke, Pegunungan 91 K6
Maoming 93 M4
Mapai 109 F4
Mapam Yumco 92 F2
Mapire 133 Q11
Maple Creek 123 K3
Mappi *Indonesia* 91 K7
Mappi *Indonesia* 91 K7
Maprik 114 C2
Mapuera 136 F4
Maputo 109 F5
Maqdam, Ras 96 C7
Maqna 96 B2
Maqueda 66 D2
Maquinchao 139 C8
Maraba 137 H5
Maracaibo 136 C1
Maracaibo, Lago de 136 C2
Maraca, Ilha de 137 G3
Maracay 136 D1
Maradah 101 J3
Maradi 101 G6
Maragheh 94 H3
Marajo, Baia de 137 H4
Marajo, Ilha de 137 H4
Maralal 107 G2
Maramasike 114 K6
Maramba 106 E6
Maran 90 C5
Marand 94 G2

Maranguape 137 K4
Maranhao 137 H5
Maranhao Grande, Cachoeira 137 F4
Maran, Koh-i- 92 C3
Maranon 136 C4
Marans 65 C5
Marari 136 D5
Marasesti 73 J3
Marassume 137 H4
Marateca 66 B3
Marathokambos 75 J4
Marathon *Canada* 124 G2
Marathon *Florida, U.S.A.* 129 M8
Marathon *Texas, U.S.A.* 127 L5
Marau 90 E6
Marau Point 115 G3
Maravovo 114 J6
Marbella 66 D4
Marble Bar 112 D3
Marble Canyon 126 G2
Marburg 70 C3
Marcelino 136 D4
March 53 H2
Marche *Belgium* 64 F3
Marche *France* 65 D5
Marchena 66 D4
Marchena, Isla 136 A7
Mar Chiquita, Lago 138 D6
Marcigny 65 F5
Marcus Baker, Mount 118 F3
Marcus Island 83 P4
Mardan 92 D2
Mar del Plata 139 E7
Mardin 77 J4
Mare 114 Y16
Mareeba 113 K2
Maree, Loch 56 C3
Mareeq 103 J7
Mareuil 65 D6
Margai Caka 92 G1
Marganets 79 E6
Margaret, Cape 120 H3
Margaret River 112 F2
Margarita, Isla de 136 E1
Margaritovo 88 E4
Margate 53 J3
Margeride, Monts de la 65 E6
Margita 73 F3
Margo, Dasht-i 95 R6
Marguerite 121 N7
Marguerite Bay 141 V5
Mari 114 C3
Maria Elena 138 C4
Maria, Golfo de Ana 132 H4
Maria Madre, Isla 130 F7
Maria Magdalena, Isla 130 F7
Marianas Islands 83 N5
Marianas Trench 142 F4
Marian Lake 119 M3
Marianna *Arkansas, U.S.A.* 128 G3
Marianna *Florida, U.S.A.* 129 K5
Marianske Lazne 70 E4
Marias 122 J3
Marias, Islas 130 F7
Mariato, Punta 132 G11
Maria van Diemen, Cape 115 D1
Mariazell 68 E2
Marib 96 G9
Maribor 72 C2
Maridi 102 E7
Marie Byrd Land 141 S3
Marie Galante 133 S7
Mariehamn 63 H6
Marienbad 70 E4
Marienburg 71 H1
Mariental 108 C4
Marienwerder 71 H2
Mariestad 63 E7
Marietta *Georgia, U.S.A.* 129 K4
Marietta *Ohio, U.S.A.* 125 K7
Marigot 133 S7
Mariinsk 84 D5
Marina di Carrara 68 C3
Marina di Leuca 69 G6
Marina di Monasterace 69 F6
Marinette 124 G4
Maringa 106 D2
Maringa 138 F4
Marion *Illinois, U.S.A.* 124 F8
Marion *Indiana, U.S.A.* 124 H6
Marion *Ohio, U.S.A.* 124 J6
Marion *S. Carolina, U.S.A.* 129 N3
Marion *Virginia, U.S.A.* 125 K8
Marion, Lake 129 M4
Marion Reefs 113 L2
Maripa 136 D2
Marisa 91 G5
Mariscal Estigarribia 138 D4
Maritimes, Alpes 65 G6
Maritsa 73 H4
Marivan 94 H4
Marjamaa 63 L7
Marjayoun 94 B5
Marka 96 E7
Marka 107 H2
Markam 93 J3
Market Deeping 53 G2
Market Drayton 52 E2
Market Harborough 53 G2
Markethill 58 J4
Market Rasen 55 J3
Market Weighton 55 J3
Markha 85 K4
Markham 114 D3

Marlborough *Australia* 113 K3
Marlborough *Guyana* 136 F2
Marlborough *U.K.* 53 F3
Marlin 128 D5
Marlinton 125 K7
Marlow 53 G3
Marmagao 92 D5
Marmande 65 D6
Marmara *Turkey* 76 B2
Marmara *Turkey* 76 B2
Marmara Denizi 76 C2
Marmara, Sea of 76 C2
Marmara Golu 76 C3
Marmara, Sea of 76 C2
Marmaraereglisi 76 B2
Marmaris 76 C4
Marmblada 68 C2
Marmelos 136 E6
Marne 64 E4
Maro 102 C3
Maroantsetra 109 J3
Marolambo 109 J4
Marondera 109 F3
Maroni 137 G3
Maros 91 F6
Marotiri Islands 115 E1
Maroua 105 H3
Marovoay 109 J3
Marowyne 137 G3
Marple 55 G3
Marquette 124 G3
Marquise 64 D3
Marquises, Iles 143 J5
Marra, Jebel 102 D5
Marrakech 100 D2
Marrakesh 100 D2
Marrak Point 120 R5
Marrawah 113 J7
Marree 113 H4
Marresale 84 Ae3
Marrupa 109 G2
Marsa Alam 96 B4
Marsabit 107 G2
Marsala 69 D7
Marsden *Australia* 113 K5
Marsden *U.K.* 55 H3
Marseille 65 F7
Mar, Serra do 138 G5
Marsfjallet 62 G3
Marshall *Minnesota, U.S.A.* 124 C4
Marshall *Missouri, U.S.A.* 124 D7
Marshall *Texas, U.S.A.* 128 E4
Marshall Bennett Islands 114 E3
Marshall Islands 143 G4
Marshalltown 124 D5
Marshchapel 55 K3
Marshfield 124 E4
Marsh Island 128 G6
Marske-by-the-Sea 55 H2
Marsta 63 G7
Martaban 93 J5
Martaban, Gulf of 93 J5
Martapura 90 E6
Martes, Sierra 67 F3
Marthaguy 113 K5
Martha's Vineyard 125 Q6
Martigny 68 A2
Martigues 65 F7
Martin *Poland* 71 H4
Martin *Spain* 67 F2
Martin *S. Dakota, U.S.A.* 123 P6
Martin *Tennessee, U.S.A.* 128 H2
Martinavas 53 N6
Martinborough 115 E4
Martinique 133 S7
Martinique Passage 133 S7
Martin Lake 129 K4
Martin Point 118 G1
Martinsberg 68 E1
Martinsville 125 L8
Martock 52 E4
Marton *New Zealand* 115 E4
Marton *U.K.* 55 J3
Martorell 67 G2
Martos 66 E4
Martre, Lac La 119 M3
Martuk 79 K5
Martuni 79 H7
Martyn 78 K2
Martze 136 D4
Marudi 90 E5
Marugame 89 D8
Marum, Mount 114 U12
Marunga 114 E2
Marungu 107 E4
Marv Dasht 95 L7
Marvejols 65 E6
Marvine, Mount 122 J8
Marwar 92 D3
Mary 95 Q3
Maryborough 113 L4
Maryevka 84 Ae6
Maryland 125 M7
Maryport 55 F2
Mary, Puy 65 E6
Marystown 121 Q8
Marysville *California, U.S.A.* 126 B1
Marysville *Kansas, U.S.A.* 123 R8
Maryvale 113 L4
Maryville *Missouri, U.S.A.* 124 C6
Maryville *Tennessee, U.S.A.* 129 L3
Marzo, Cabo 132 J11
Masagua 132 B7
Masai Steppe 107 G3
Masaka 107 F3

Merauke 91 L7
Mercan Dagi 77 H3
Mercato Saraceno 68 D4
Merced 126 B2
Mercedario, Cerro 138 B6
Mercedes *Argentina* 139 C6
Mercedes *Argentina* 139 E6
Mercedes *Argentina* 138 E5
Mercedes *Uruguay* 138 E6
Mercimek 77 F4
Mercimekkale 77 J3
Mercurea 73 G3
Mercury Bay 115 E2
Mercy, Cape 120 P5
Mere 52 E3
Meredith, Cape 139 D10
Meredoua 100 F3
Mere Lava 114 U11
Mereworth 53 H3
Mergenovo 79 J6
Mergui 93 J6
Mergui Archipelago 93 J6
Meribah 113 J5
Meric 76 B2
Merida *Mexico* 131 Q7
Merida *Spain* 66 C3
Merida *Venezuela* 136 C2
Merida, Cordillera de 136 C2
Meriden 125 P6
Meridian 128 H4
Merig 114 T11
Merir 91 J5
Meriruma 137 G3
Merkys 63 L9
Mermaid Reef 112 D2
Merowe 103 F4
Merredin 112 D5
Merrick 57 D5
Merrill 124 F4
Merrillville 124 G6
Merrimack 125 Q5
Merritt 122 D2
Merritt Island 129 M6
Merriwa 113 L5
Mersa Fatma 96 E9
Mersea Island 53 H3
Merseburg 70 D3
Merse, The 57 F5
Mersey 55 G3
Merseyside 55 G3
Mersin 76 F4
Mersing 90 C5
Mersrags 63 K8
Merthyr Tydfil 52 D3
Mertola 66 C4
Mertvyy Kultuk, Sor 79 J6
Mertz Glacier 141 K5
Merzifon 76 F2
Merzig 70 B4
Mesa 126 G4
Mesaras, Kolpos 75 H5
Meschede 70 C3
Meselefors 62 G4
Meshik 118 D4
Meshraer Req 102 E6
Mesolongion 75 F3
Messina *Italy* 69 E6
Messina *South Africa* 108 F4
Messina, Stretto di 69 E6
Messingham 55 J3
Messini 75 F4
Messiniakos Kolpos 75 F4
Messo 84 B3
Messoyakha 84 B3
Mesta 75 H2
Mestiya 77 K1
Mestre 68 D3
Mesudiye 77 G2
Meta 136 D2
Metan 138 D5
Metapan 132 C7
Metaponto 69 F5
Metema 103 G5
Meteran 114 E2
Methven *New Zealand* 115 C5
Methven *U.K.* 57 E4
Methwin, Mount 112 E4
Metkovic 72 D4
Metlika 72 C3
Metropolis 124 F8
Metsovon 75 F3
Metu 103 G6
Metz 64 G4
Meulaboh 90 B5
Meureudu 90 B4
Meurthe 64 G4
Meuse 64 F3
Mexborough 55 H3
Mexia 128 D5
Mexicali 126 E4
Mexico 130 H6
Mexico *U.S.A.* 124 E7
Mexico City 131 K8
Mexico, Gulf of 117 K6
Meydancik 77 K2
Meydan e Gel 95 M7
Meydani, Ra's e 95 P9
Meymaneh 94 S4
Meymeh 95 K5
Meynypilgyno 85 X4
Meyrueis 65 E6
Mezdra 73 G4
Mezen *Russia* 78 G2
Mezen *Russia* 78 H2
Mezenc, Mont 65 F6
Mezenskaya Guba 78 G2
Mezenskiy 84 F2
Mezhdurechensk 84 D6
Mezhdusharskiy, Ostrov 80 G2
Mezhgorye 71 K4
Mezotur 72 F2
Mezquital 130 G6
Mezzana 68 C2
Mhangura 108 F3
Mhow 92 E4
Miahuatlan 131 L9
Miajadas 66 D3
Miami *Arizona, U.S.A.* 126 G4
Miami *Florida, U.S.A.* 129 M8
Miami *Ohio, U.S.A.* 124 H7
Miami Beach 129 M8
Mianabad 95 N3
Miandowab 94 H3
Mianeh 94 H3
Miang, Pou 93 K5
Mianwali 92 D2
Mianyang 93 K2
Miarinarivo *Madagascar* 109 J3
Miarinarivo *Madagascar* 109 J3
Miass 84 Ad5
Miastko 71 G1
Micang Shan 93 L2
Michalovce 71 J4
Michelson, Mount 118 G2
Michigan 124 H5
Michigan City 124 G6
Michigan, Lake 124 G5
Michipicoten 124 H3
Michipicoten Island 124 H3
Michurinsk 79 G5
Mickle Fell 55 G2
Mickleton 53 F2
Micronesia 142 F4
Micurin 73 J4
Middelburg *Netherlands* 64 E3
Middelburg *South Africa* 108 E5
Middelburg *South Africa* 108 E6
Middle Andaman 93 H6
Middle Barton 53 F3
Middlebury 125 P4
Middlefart 63 C9
Middlemarch 115 C6
Middlesboro 124 J8
Middlesbrough 55 H2
Middleton *Greater Manchester, U.K.* 55 G3
Middleton *Strathclyde, U.K.* 57 B4
Middleton Cheney 53 F2
Middle Tongue 55 G2
Middleton-on-the-Wolds 55 J3
Middleton Reef 113 M4
Middletown *U.K.* 52 D2
Middletown *New York, U.S.A.* 125 N6
Middletown *Ohio, U.S.A.* 124 H7
Middlewich 55 G3
Mid Glamorgan 52 D3
Midhurst 53 G4
Midi 96 F8
Midland *Canada* 125 L4
Midland *Michigan, U.S.A.* 124 H5
Midland *Texas, U.S.A.* 127 M5
Midleton 59 F9
Midongy Atsimo 109 J4
Midsomer Norton 52 E3
Midwest 123 L6
Midwest City 128 D3
Midyan 96 B3
Midyat 77 J4
Mid Yell 56 A1
Midzor 73 G4
Miechow 71 J3
Miedwie, Jezioro 70 F2
Miedzyrzecz 70 F2
Mielec 71 J3
Miena 113 K7
Mieres 66 D1
Mieso 103 H6
Mieszkowice 70 F2
Miford Sound 115 A6
Mighan 95 P6
Miguel Aleman, Presa 131 L8
Miguel Alves 137 J4
Miguel Hidalgo, Presa 127 H7
Mihaliccik 76 D3
Mihara 89 D8
Miharu 89 H7
Mihrad, Al 97 L6
Miida 96 E9
Mijares 67 F2
Mikha Tskhakaya 77 J1
Mikhaylova 84 D1
Mikhaylovgrad 73 G4
Mikhaylov Island 141 F6
Mikhaylovka *Russia* 88 C4
Mikhaylovka *Russia* 79 G5
Mikindani 107 G5
Mikkeli *Finland* 63 M6
Mikkeli *Finland* 63 M6
Mikolajki 71 J2
Mikonos 75 H4
Mikri Prespa, Limni 75 F2
Mikulov 71 G4
Mikun 78 J3
Mikuni 89 F7
Mikuni-sammyaku 89 G7
Mikura-jima 89 G9
Milaca 124 D4
Milagro 136 B4
Milan *Italy* 68 B3
Milan *U.S.A.* 128 H3
Milano 68 B3
Milas 76 B4
Milazzo 69 E6
Milbank 123 R5
Mildenhall 53 H2
Mildurra 113 J5
Mile 93 K4
Mileh Tharthar 94 F5
Miles 113 L4
Miles City 123 M4
Milford *U.K.* 58 G2
Milford *U.S.A.* 125 N7
Milford Haven 52 B3
Milford Sound 115 A6
Milgun 112 D4
Milh, Bahr al 94 F5
Miliana 101 F1
Miliane, Oued 69 C7
Milk 123 L3
Millas 65 E7
Millau 65 E6
Milledgeville 129 L4
Mille Lacs, Lac des 124 E2
Mille Lacs Lake 124 D3
Miller 123 Q5
Millerovo 79 G6
Millers Flat 115 B6
Millford 58 J4
Millington 128 H3
Mill Island *Antarctic* 141 G5
Mill Island *Canada* 120 L5
Millisle 58 L3
Millnocket 125 R4
Millom 55 F2
Millport 57 D5
Mills Lake 119 M3
Milltown 58 K2
Milltown Malbay 59 D7
Millville 125 N7
Millwood Lake 128 F4
Milngavie 57 D5
Milogradovo 88 E4
Milolii 126 T11
Milos *Greece* 75 H4
Milos *Greece* 75 H4
Milowka 71 H4
Milparinka 113 J4
Milpillas 131 K9
Milton *New Zealand* 115 B7
Milton *Florida, U.S.A.* 129 J5
Milton *Pennsylvania, U.S.A.* 125 M6
Milton Abbot 52 C4
Milton Ernest 53 G2
Milton Keynes 53 G2
Miluo 93 M3
Milwaukee 124 G5
Mimizan 65 C6
Mimon 70 F3
Mina Abd Allah 97 J2
Minab 95 N8
Mina de San Domingos 66 C4
Minahassa Peninsula 91 G5
Minamata 89 C9
Minas *Indonesia* 90 C5
Minas *Uruguay* 139 E6
Mina Saud 97 J2
Minas Gerais 138 G3
Minas, Sierra de las 132 C7
Minatitlan 131 M8
Minbu 93 H4
Minch, The 56 C2
Mincio 68 C3
Mindanao 91 G4
Mindelo 104 L7
Minden *U.S.A.* 128 F4
Minden *Germany* 70 C2
Mindoro 91 G3
Mindoro Strait 91 G3
Mindra 73 G3
Minehead 52 D3
Mine Head 59 G9
Mineola 128 E4
Mineral Wells 128 C4
Minerva Reefs 111 T6
Minervino Murge 69 F5
Minfeng 92 F1
Mingechaur 79 H7
Mingela 113 K2
Minglanilla 67 F3
Mingshui *Gansu, China* 86 H3
Mingshui *Heilongjiang, China* 87 P2
Mingulay 57 A4
Minicoy 92 D7
Minigwal 112 E4
Min Jiang 93 K3
Minle 86 J4
Minna 105 G4
Minneapolis 124 D4
Minnedosa 123 Q2
Minnesota *U.S.A.* 124 C3
Minnesota *U.S.A.* 124 C4
Minnitaki Lake 124 E1
Mino 66 B1
Minorca 67 J3
Minot 123 P3
Minsk 78 D5
Minsk Mazowiecki 71 J2
Minsterley 52 E2
Mintlaw 56 F3
Minto 125 S3
Minto Inlet 119 M1
Minto, Lac 121 L6
Minturn 123 L8
Minusinsk 84 E6
Minwakh 97 J8
Min Xian 93 K2
Minyar 78 K4
Miquelon 125 M2
Mira *Italy* 68 D3
Mira *Portugal* 66 B4
Mirabad 95 Q6
Miracema do Norte 137 H5
Miraflores 136 C2
Miraj 92 D5
Miramichi Bay 121 N8
Miramont 65 D6
Miram Shah 92 D2
Miranda *Brazil* 138 E4
Miranda *Brazil* 138 E4
Miranda de Ebro 66 E1
Miranda do Douro 66 C2
Mirande 65 D7
Mirandela 66 C2
Mirandola 68 C3
Mirapinima 136 E4
Miravci 73 G5
Mirbat, Ra's 97 M8
Mirbut 97 M8
Mirear Island 96 B5
Mirebeau 65 D5
Mirgorod 79 E6
Miri 90 E5
Miri Hills 93 H3
Mirimire 136 D1
Mirim, Lagoa 138 F6
Mirjaveh 95 Q7
Mirnyy *Antarctic* 141 G5
Mirnyy *Russia* 85 J4
Mironovo 84 H5
Mirpur Khas 92 C3
Mirriam Vale 113 L3
Mirtoan Sea 75 G4
Mirtoon Pelagos 75 G4
Miryang 89 B8
Mirzapur 92 F3
Misgar 92 D1
Mishan 88 C3
Mi-shima 89 C8
Mishkino 78 K4
Misima Island 114 T10
Miskolc 73 F1
Misool 91 J6
Misratah 101 J2
Missinaibi 121 K7
Mission *Canada* 122 C3
Mission *U.S.A.* 123 P6
Mission Viejo 126 D4
Mississauga 125 L5
Mississippi *U.S.A.* 128 G4
Mississippi *U.S.A.* 128 G5
Mississippi Delta 128 H6
Missoula 122 G4
Missouri *U.S.A.* 124 D7
Missouri *U.S.A.* 124 E7
Missouri, Coteau de 123 P4
Mistassibi 121 M8
Mistassini *Canada* 125 P2
Mistassini *Canada* 125 P2
Mistassini, Lac 121 M7
Mistelbach 68 F1
Mistretta 69 E7
Mitatib 96 C9
Mitchell *Australia* 113 J2
Mitchell *Australia* 113 K4
Mitchell *U.S.A.* 123 Q6
Mitchell, Mount 129 L3
Mitchelstown 59 F8
Mithankot 92 D3
Mithimna 75 J3
Mitilini 75 J3
Mito 89 H7
Mitre 111 R4
Mitrofanovskaya 78 K3
Mitsio, Nosy 109 J2
Mitsiwa 103 G4
Mitsiwa Channel 96 D9
Mittelland Kanal 70 B2
Mittelmark 70 E2
Mitumba, Chaine des 107 E4
Mitwaba 107 E4
Mitzic 106 B2
Mixteco 131 K8
Miyah, Wadi al 77 H5
Miyake-jima 89 G8
Miyake-shoto 89 G11
Miyako 88 H6
Miyako-jima 89 G11
Miyakonojo 89 C10
Miyaly 79 J6
Miyazaki 89 C10
Miyazu 89 E8
Miyoshi 89 D8
Mizdah 101 H2
Mizen Head *Cork, Ireland* 59 C10
Mizen Head *Wicklow, Ireland* 59 K7
Mizhi 87 L4
Mizil 73 J3
Mizoram 93 H4
Mizpe Ramon 94 B6
Mjolby 63 F7
Mjosa 63 D6
Mlada Boleslav 70 F3
Mladenovac 72 F3
Mlawa 71 J2
Mljet 72 D4
Moa *Cuba* 133 K4

Moa *Indonesia*	91	H7
Moab	127	H1
Moa Island	114	C4
Moala	114	R9
Moate	59	G6
Moatize	109	F3
Moba	107	E4
Mobaye	102	D7
Mobayi-Mbongo	106	D2
Moberly	124	D7
Mobile	129	H5
Mobile Bay	129	H5
Mobridge	123	P5
Mobutu Sese Seko, Lake	107	F2
Moca	114	S9
Mocajuba	137	G4
Mocambique	109	H3
Mocamedes	106	B6
Mocha, Isla	139	B7
Mochudi	108	E4
Mocimboa da Praia	109	H2
Moctexuma	127	H6
Moctezuma	131	K7
Mocuba	109	G3
Modder	108	E5
Modena *Italy*	68	C3
Modena *U.S.A.*	126	F2
Modesto	126	B2
Modica	69	E7
Modigliana	68	C3
Modling	68	F1
Modowi	91	J6
Moe	113	K6
Moelv	63	D6
Moengo	137	G2
Moffat	57	E5
Moffat Peak	115	B6
Mogadishu	107	J2
Mogadouro	66	C2
Mogdy	85	N6
Mogilev	78	E5
Mogilev-Podolskiy	79	D6
Mogi-Mirim	138	G4
Mogincual	109	H3
Moglice	75	F2
Mogocha	85	L6
Mogoi	91	J6
Mogok	93	J4
Mogollon Plateau	126	G3
Mogotoyevo, Ozero	85	R2
Mogoyn	86	H2
Mogoytuy	85	J6
Moguer	66	C4
Mohacs	72	E2
Mohaka	115	F3
Mohall	123	P3
Mohammadabad	95	Q6
Mohammadia	100	F1
Mohawk	125	N5
Moheli	109	H2
Mohill	58	G5
Mohoro	107	G4
Moi	63	B7
Moidart	57	C4
Moimenta da Beira	66	C2
Moindou	114	W16
Mointy	86	C2
Mo i Rana	62	F3
Moisie	121	N7
Moissac	65	D6
Moissala	102	C6
Mojave	126	C3
Mojave Desert	126	D3
Moji	89	C9
Mojones, Cerro	138	C5
Moju	137	H4
Mokai	115	E3
Mokelumne	122	D8
Moknine	101	H1
Mokohinau Island	115	E1
Mokokchung	93	H3
Mokolo	105	H3
Mokpo	87	P5
Mokra Gora	72	F4
Molaoi	75	G4
Molat	72	C3
Mold	55	F3
Moldavia	73	J2
Molde	62	B5
Moldova	73	J2
Moldova Noua	73	F3
Moldoveanu	73	H3
Moldovita	73	H2
Mole *Devon, U.K.*	52	D4
Mole *Surrey, U.K.*	53	G3
Molepolole	108	E4
Molfetta	69	F5
Molina de Aragon	67	F2
Molina de Segura	67	F3
Moline	124	E6
Molkom	63	E7
Mollakendi	77	H3
Mollaosman	77	K3
Mollendo	138	B3
Molln	70	D2
Molnlycke	63	E8
Molodechno	71	M1
Molodezhnaya	141	D5
Molodo *Russia*	85	L3
Molodo *Russia*	85	L3
Mologa	78	F4
Molokai	126	S10
Moloma	78	H4
Molotov	78	K4

Moloundou	105	J5
Molsheim	64	G4
Molson Lake	119	R5
Moluccas	91	H6
Moma *Mozambique*	109	H3
Moma *Russia*	85	Q3
Mombasa	107	R3
Mombetsu	88	J3
Momboyo	106	C3
Momi, Ra's	97	P9
Momol	71	L2
Mompos	136	C2
Mon	63	E9
Monach Islands	56	A3
Monach, Sound of	56	A3
Monaco	65	G7
Monadhliath Mountains	57	D3
Monaghan	58	J4
Monahans	127	L5
Mona, Isla	133	P5
Mona Passage	133	N5
Monarch Mount	118	K5
Monarch Pass	123	L8
Monar, Loch	56	C3
Monashe Mountains	122	E2
Monasterevin	59	H6
Monastir *Albania*	73	F5
Monastir *Italy*	69	B6
Monastir *Tunisia*	101	H1
Monastyriska	73	H1
Monatele	105	H5
Moncalieri	68	A3
Moncao	66	B1
Monchdorf	68	E1
Monchegorsk	62	Q3
Monchique	66	B4
Monclova	127	M7
Moncontour	64	B4
Moncton	121	P8
Mondego	66	C2
Mondonedo	66	C1
Mondovi	68	A3
Mondragone	69	D5
Mondsee	68	D2
Monemvasia	75	G4
Moneron, Ostrov	88	H2
Monesterio	66	C3
Moneymore	58	J3
Monfalcone	68	D3
Monforte	66	C3
Monforte de Lemos	66	C1
Monga	106	D2
Mongala	106	D2
Mongalla	103	F6
Mong Cai	93	L4
Mongga	114	H5
Mongge	91	J6
Mong Hang	93	J4
Monghyr	92	G3
Mong Lin	93	K4
Mongo	102	C5
Mongolia	86	G2
Mongororo	102	D5
Mongu	106	D6
Monhhaan	87	L2
Moniaive	57	E5
Monifieth	57	F4
Moniquira	136	C2
Monitor Range	122	F8
Monkira	113	J3
Monkland	52	E2
Monkoto	106	D3
Monmouth *U.K.*	52	E3
Monmouth *U.S.A.*	124	E6
Monnow	52	E3
Mono	105	F4
Mono Lake	126	C2
Monolithos	75	J4
Monopoli	69	F5
Monovar	67	F3
Monreal del Campo	67	F2
Monreale	69	D6
Monroe *Georgia, U.S.A.*	129	L4
Monroe *Louisiana, U.S.A.*	128	F4
Monroe *Michigan, U.S.A.*	124	J6
Monroe *N. Carolina, U.S.A.*	129	M3
Monroe *Wisconsin, U.S.A.*	124	F5
Monrovia	104	C4
Mons	64	E3
Monsaras, Ponta da	138	J3
Monselice	68	C3
Monserrat	67	F3
Montaigu	65	C5
Montalban	67	F2
Montalbo	66	E3
Montalcino	68	C4
Montalto	69	E6
Montalvo	136	B4
Montamarta	66	D2
Montana	122	K4
Montanchez	66	C3
Montanita	136	B3
Montargis	65	E5
Montauban	65	D6
Montauk Point	125	Q6
Montbard	65	F5
Montbeliard	65	G5
Montblanch	67	G2
Montbrison	65	F6
Montceau-les-Mines	65	F5
Montcornet	64	F4
Mont-de-Marsan	65	C7
Montdidier	64	E4
Monte Alegre	137	G4

Monte Azul	138	H3
Monte Bello	136	B5
Montebello	125	N4
Monte Carlo	68	A4
Monte Caseros	139	E6
Montecatini Terme	68	C4
Monte Cristi	133	M5
Montecristo, Isola di	69	C4
Montego Bay	132	J5
Montelimar	65	F6
Montemaggiore Belsito	69	D7
Montemorelos	128	C8
Montemor-o-Novo	66	B3
Montenegro	72	E4
Montepuez	109	G2
Montepulciano	68	C4
Monte Quemado	138	D5
Montereau-faut-Yonne	64	E4
Monterey	126	B2
Monterey Bay	126	B2
Monteria	136	B2
Montero	138	D3
Monterotondo	69	D4
Monterrey	128	B8
Monte Santu, Capo di	69	B5
Montes Claros	138	E3
Montevideo *Uruguay*	139	E6
Montevideo *U.S.A.*	124	C4
Monte Vista	127	J2
Montezuma Peak	127	J2
Montfort-sur-Meu	64	B4
Montgomery *U.K.*	52	D2
Montgomery *U.S.A.*	129	J4
Montguyon	65	C6
Monti	69	B5
Monticello *Arkansas, U.S.A.*	128	G4
Monticello *Florida, U.S.A.*	129	L5
Monticello *New York, U.S.A.*	125	N6
Monticello *Utah, U.S.A.*	127	H2
Montiel, Campo de	66	E3
Montignac	65	D6
Montilla	66	D4
Mont-Joli	125	R2
Mont Laurier	125	N3
Montlucon	65	E5
Montmagny	125	Q3
Montmedy	64	F4
Montmirail	64	E4
Montmorillon	65	D5
Monto	113	L3
Montoro	66	D4
Montpelier	122	J6
Montpellier *France*	65	E7
Montpellier *U.S.A.*	125	P4
Montraux	68	A2
Montreal	124	H3
Montreal	125	P4
Montreal Lake	119	P5
Montreal River Harbour	124	H3
Montrose *U.K.*	57	F4
Montrose *U.S.A.*	127	J1
Mont Saint-Michel	64	C4
Montseny	67	H2
Montserrat	133	R6
Mont Wright	121	N7
Monywa	93	J4
Monza	68	B3
Monzon	67	G2
Moonie	113	K4
Moopna	112	F5
Moora	112	D5
Mooraberree	113	J4
Moorcroft	123	M5
Moore, Lake	112	D4
Moorfoot Hills	57	E5
Moorhead	124	B3
Moorlands	113	H6
Moorlinch	52	E3
Moose	121	K7
Moosehead Lake	125	R4
Moose Jaw	123	M2
Moose Lake *Canada*	119	Q5
Moose Lake *U.S.A.*	124	D3
Moose Mountain Creek	123	N2
Moosonee	121	K7
Mopeia Velha	109	G3
Mopti	100	E6
Moqor	92	C2
Moquequa	138	B3
Mora *Cameroon*	105	H3
Mora *Portugal*	66	B3
Mora *Sweden*	63	F6
Moradabad	92	E3
Moradal, Sierra do	66	C3
Mora de Rubielos	67	F2
Morafenobe	109	H3
Morag	71	H2
Morales	132	C7
Moramanga	109	J3
Moran	123	J6
Morant Cays	132	K6
Morant Point	132	J6
Moratuwa	92	E7
Morava *Czechoslovakia*	71	G4
Morava *Yugoslavia*	73	F3
Moraveh Tappeh	95	M3
Morawa	112	D4
Moray Firth	56	E3
Morbi	92	D4
Mor Budejovice	70	F4
Morbylanga	63	G8
Morden	123	Q3
Mordogan	76	B3
Mordovo	79	G5
Moreau	122	N5

Morebattle	57	F5
Morecambe	55	G2
Morecambe Bay	55	E2
Moreda	66	E4
Moree	113	K4
Morehead *Papua New Guinea*	114	C3
Morehead *U.S.A.*	124	J7
Morehead City	129	P3
Morelia	131	J8
Morella	67	F2
More, Loch *U.K.*	56	D2
More, Loch *U.K.*	56	E2
Morena, Sierra	66	D3
Moreno	126	G6
Moreno, Bahia	138	B4
More og Romsdal	62	C5
Moresby Island	118	J5
Mores Island	132	J1
Moreton Bay	113	L4
Moreton-in-Marsh	53	F3
Moreton Island	113	L4
Morez	65	G5
Morgan City	128	G6
Morganton	129	M3
Morgantown	125	L7
Morgongava	63	G7
Mori *China*	86	F3
Mori *Japan*	88	H4
Moriarty	127	K3
Morioka	88	H6
Morlaix	64	B4
Morley	55	H3
Morlunda	63	F8
Mormanno	69	F6
Mornington, Isla	139	A9
Mornington Island	113	H2
Morobe	114	D3
Morocco	100	D2
Morogoro	107	G4
Moro Gulf	91	G4
Morokovo	85	W3
Moroleon	131	J7
Morombe	109	H4
Moron	132	H3
Moron *Mongolia*	86	J2
Moron *Mongolia*	87	L2
Moronade, Cerro des	130	G7
Morondava	109	H4
Moron de la Frontera	66	D4
Moroni	109	H2
Moron Us He	93	H2
Morotai	91	H5
Moroto	107	F2
Morozovsk	79	G6
Morpara	137	J6
Morpeth	55	H1
Morrilton	128	F3
Morrinhos	138	G3
Morrinsville	115	E2
Morris *Canada*	123	R3
Morris *U.S.A.*	124	C4
Morris Jesup, Kap	140	Q2
Morris, Mount	112	G4
Morristown	129	L2
Morro Bay	126	B3
Morro do Chapeu	137	J6
Morro, Punta	139	B5
Morros, Punta	131	P8
Morrosquillo, Golfo de	133	K10
Mors	63	C8
Morshansk	79	G5
Mortagne	64	D4
Mortain	64	C4
Mortara	68	B3
Morteau	65	G5
Morte Bay	52	C3
Mortes	137	G6
Morton *U.K.*	53	G2
Morton *U.S.A.*	122	C4
Morundah	113	K5
Morven *Australia*	113	K4
Morven *U.K.*	57	E3
Morvern	57	C4
Morwell	113	K6
Mosakula	63	L7
Mosby	63	B7
Moscow *U.S.A.*	122	F4
Moscow *Russia*	78	F4
Mosedale	55	F2
Mosel	70	B4
Moselle	64	G4
Moses Lake	122	E4
Moseyevo	78	H2
Mosgiel	115	C6
Mosha	78	G3
Moshchnyy, Ostrov	63	M6
Moshi	107	G3
Mosjoen	62	E4
Moskenesoya	62	E3
Moskosel	62	H4
Moskva	78	F4
Mosonmagyarovar	72	D2
Mosquera	136	B3
Mosquitia	132	E7
Mosquito Lake	119	Q3
Mosquitos, Costa de	132	F8
Mosquitos, Golfo de los	132	G10
Moss	63	D7
Mossaka	106	C3
Mossburn	115	B6
Mosselbaai	108	D6
Mossley	58	L3
Mossman	113	K2
Mossoro	137	K5

191

Nagahama	89	D9	Nana Barya	102	C6	Nasice	72	E3	Neapolis *Greece*	75	F2
Naga Hills	93	H3	Nanaimo	122	C3	Nasielsk	71	J2	Neapolis *Greece*	75	H5
Nagai	89	G6	Nanam	88	B5	Nasijarvi	63	K6	Nea Psara	75	G3
Nagaland	93	H3	Nanao	89	F7	Nasik	92	D5	Near Islands	118	Aa9
Nagano	89	G7	Nancha	88	B2	Nasir	103	F6	Neath	52	D3
Nagaoka	89	G7	Nanchang	87	M6	Nasir, Buhayrat	103	F3	Nebine	113	K4
Nagappattinam	92	E6	Nanchong	93	L2	Nasorolevu	114	R8	Nebit Dag	95	M2
Nagarjuna Sagar	92	E5	Nancowry	93	H7	Nasrabad	95	K4	Neblina, Pico da	136	D3
Nagasaki	89	B9	Nancy	64	G4	Nass	118	K4	Nebraska	123	N7
Nagashima	89	F8	Nanda Devi	92	E2	Nassau	129	P8	Nebraska City	124	C6
Nagato	89	C8	Nandan	93	L3	Nasser, Lake	103	F3	Nebrodi, Monti	69	E7
Nagaur	92	D3	Nanded	92	E5	Nassjo	63	F8	Nechako	118	L5
Nagercoil	92	E7	Nandurbar	92	D4	Nastapoka Islands	121	L6	Nechi	133	K11
Nagishot	103	F7	Nandyal	92	E5	Nastved	63	D9	Neckar	70	C4
Nagles Mountains	59	F8	Nanfeng	87	M6	Nata	108	E4	Necochea	139	E7
Nagornyy	85	L5	Nanga Eboko	105	H5	Natagaima	136	B3	Nedong	93	H3
Nagorsk	78	J4	Nangahpinoh	90	E6	Natal *Brazil*	137	K5	Nedstrand	63	A7
Nagoya	89	F8	Nanga Parbat	92	D1	Natal *Indonesia*	90	B5	Needles *Canada*	122	E3
Nagpur	92	E4	Nangatayap	90	E6	Natanz	95	K5	Needles *U.S.A.*	126	E3
Nagqu	93	H2	Nangong	87	M4	Natara	85	L3	Needles Point	115	E2
Nags Head	129	Q3	Nan Hai	83	K5	Natashquan	121	P7	Needles, The	53	F4
Nagykanizsa	72	D2	Nanjing	87	M5	Natchez	128	G5	Neepawa	123	Q2
Nagykata	72	E2	Nanking	87	M5	Natchitoches	128	F5	Neergaard Lake	120	L3
Nagykoros	72	E2	Nan, Mae Nam	93	K5	Natewa Bay	114	R8	Nefedovo	84	A5
Naha	89	H10	Nanning	93	L4	National City	126	D4	Nefta	101	G2
Nahariya	94	B5	Nanortalik	116	Q2	Natitingou	105	F3	Neftechala	94	J2
Nahavand	94	J4	Nanpan Jiang	93	K4	Natividade	137	H6	Neftegorsk	79	J5
Nahe	70	B4	Nanpara	92	F3	Natori	89	H6	Neftekamsk	78	J4
Nahoi, Cap	114	T11	Nanpi	87	M4	Natron, Lake	107	G3	Nefyn	52	C2
Nahuel Huapi, Lago	139	B8	Nanping	87	M6	Nattavaara	62	J3	Nefza	69	B7
Naikliu	91	G7	Nansei-shoto	89	H10	Natuna Besar	90	D5	Negele	103	G6
Nailsea	52	E3	Nansen Sound	120	H1	Natuna, Kepulauan	90	D5	Negev	94	B6
Nailsworth	52	E3	Nanshan Islands	90	E4	Naturaliste, Cape	112	D5	Negoiu	73	H3
Naiman Qi	87	N3	Nansha Qundao	90	E4	Naturaliste Channel	112	C4	Negombo	92	E7
Nain	95	L5	Nantais, Lac	121	M5	Nauen	70	E2	Negotin	73	G3
Nain	121	P6	Nantes	65	C5	Naueyi Akmyane	63	K8	Negrais, Cape	93	H5
Naini Tal	92	E3	Nantong	87	N5	Naujoji Vilnia	71	L1	Negra, Punta	136	A5
Nairai	114	R8	Nantua	65	F5	Naul	58	K5	Negritos	136	A4
Nairn	56	E3	Nantucket Island	125	Q6	Naumburg	70	D3	Negro *Argentina*	139	C7
Nairobi	107	G3	Nantucket Sound	125	Q6	Naungpale	93	J5	Negro *Amazonas, Brazil*	136	E4
Najafabad	95	K5	Nantwich	55	G3	Nauru	111	Q2	Negro *Santa Catarina, Brazil*	138	F5
Najd	96	E4	Nant-y-moch Reservoir	52	D2	Naurzum	84	Ad6	Negro *Uruguay*	138	F6
Najibabad	92	E3	Nanuku Passage	114	S8	Nausori	114	R9	Negros	91	G3
Najin	88	C4	Nanuku Reef	114	S8	Nautanwa	92	F3	Negru Voda	73	K4
N'Ajjer, Tassili	101	G3	Nanumanga	111	S3	Nautla	131	L7	Nehavand	94	J4
Najran	96	G8	Nanumea	111	S3	Nauzad	95	S5	Nehbandan	95	Q6
Najran, Wadi	96	G8	Nanusa, Kepulauan	91	H5	Navadwip	93	G4	Nehe	87	N2
Nakadori-shima	89	B9	Nanyang	93	M2	Navahermosa	66	D3	Nehoiasu	73	J3
Nakajo	89	G6	Nanyuki	107	G2	Naval	91	G3	Neijiang	93	K3
Nakamura	89	D9	Nao, Cabo de la	67	G3	Navalcarnero	66	D2	Nei Mongol Zizhiqu	87	L3
Nakano	89	G7	Naocacane, Lake	121	M7	Navalmoral de la Mata	66	D3	Neisse *Poland*	70	F3
Nakano-shima	89	B11	Naousa	75	G2	Navalpino	66	D3	Neisse *Poland*	71	G3
Nakatay	84	Ad5	Napa	126	A1	Navan	58	J5	Neiteyugansk	84	A4
Nakatsu	89	C9	Napabalana	91	G6	Navarin, Mys	85	X4	Neiva	136	B3
Nakatsugawa	89	F8	Napalkovo	84	A2	Navarino, Isla	139	C11	Neixiang	93	M2
Nakfa	103	G4	Napas	84	C5	Navarra	67	F1	Nekemte	103	G6
Nakhichevan	77	L3	Nape	93	L5	Navars	67	G2	Neksikan	85	R4
Nakhl *Egypt*	96	A2	Napier	115	F3	Navasota	128	D5	Nekso	63	H9
Nakhl *Oman*	97	N5	Naples *Italy*	69	E5	Navassa Island	133	K5	Nelidovo	78	E4
Nakhodka *Russia*	84	B3	Naples *U.S.A.*	129	M7	Navax Point	52	B4	Neligh	123	Q6
Nakhodka *Russia*	88	D4	Napo	136	C4	Navenby	55	J3	Nelkan	85	P5
Nakhon Pathom	93	J6	Napoleon	124	H6	Naver, Loch	56	D2	Nellore	92	E6
Nakhon Phanom	93	K5	Napoletano, Appennino	69	E5	Navia *Spain*	66	C1	Nelma	88	G2
Nakhon Ratchasima	93	K6	Napoli	69	E5	Navia *Spain*	66	C1	Nelson *Canada*	122	F3
Nakhon Sawan	93	K5	Napoli, Golfo di	69	E5	Naviti	114	Q8	Nelson *New Zealand*	115	D4
Nakhon Si Thammarat	93	J7	Naqadeh	94	G3	Navlya	79	E5	Nelson *U.K.*	55	G3
Nakina	121	J7	Nar	53	H2	Navojoa	127	H7	Nelson, Cape *Australia*	113	J6
Nakiri	89	F8	Nara *Japan*	89	E8	Navolato	130	F5	Nelson, Cape *Papua New Guinea*	114	D3
Naknek Lake	118	D4	Nara *Mali*	100	D5	Navpaktos	75	F3			
Nakskov	63	F9	Nara *Pakistan*	92	C4	Navplion	75	G4	Nelson Lagoon	118	Af8
Naktong	87	P4	Naracoorte	113	J6	Navrongo	104	E3	Nelspruit	108	F5
Nakuru	107	G3	Naran	87	L2	Navsari	92	D4	Nema	100	D5
Nakusp	122	F2	Narasapur	92	F5	Navua	114	R9	Neman	78	C4
Nalchik	79	G7	Narat	86	E3	Nawabshah	92	C3	Neman	71	K1
Nalgonda	92	E5	Narathiwat	93	K7	Nawada	92	G4	Nemira	73	J2
Nallamala Hills	92	E5	Narayanganj	93	H4	Nawah	92	C2	Nemirov	73	K1
Nallihan	76	D2	Narberth	52	C3	Nawasif, Harrat	96	F6	Nemiscau	121	L7
Nalut	101	H2	Narbonne	65	E7	Naws, Ra's	97	M8	Nemours	64	E4
Namaa, Tanjung	91	H6	Narborough Island	136	A7	Nawton	55	J2	Nemun	63	J9
Namacunde	106	C6	Narcea	66	C1	Naxos *Greece*	75	H4	Nemuro	88	K4
Namacurra	109	G3	Nardin	95	M3	Naxos *Greece*	75	H4	Nemuro-kaikyo	88	K4
Namak, Daryacheh-ye	95	K4	Narew *Poland*	71	J2	Nayagarh	92	G4	Nemuy	85	P5
Namaki	95	M6	Narew *Poland*	71	K2	Nayau	114	S8	Nenagh	59	F7
Namakzar	95	Q5	Narince	77	H4	Nay Band	95	L8	Nenana	118	F3
Namakzar, Daryacheh-ye	95	Q5	Narken	62	K3	Nay Band	95	N5	Nene	53	G2
Namangan	86	C3	Narkher	92	E4	Nayoro	88	J3	Nen Jiang	87	P1
Namapa	109	G2	Narli	77	G4	Nazare	137	K6	Nenjiang	87	P2
Namaponda	109	G3	Narmada	92	E4	Nazareth *Israel*	94	B5	Nenthead	55	G2
Namarroi	109	G3	Narman	77	J2	Nazareth *Peru*	136	B5	Neokhorion	75	F3
Namasagali	107	F2	Narnaul	92	E3	Nazarovo	84	E5	Neon Karlovasi	75	J4
Namatanai	114	E2	Narodnaya, Gora	84	Ad3	Nazas	130	G5	Neosho *Kansas, U.S.A.*	124	C7
Nambour	113	L4	Naro-Fominsk	78	F4	Nazca	136	C6	Neosho *Missouri, U.S.A.*	124	C8
Nam Can	93	K7	Narowal	92	D2	Naze	89	B11	Nepa *Russia*	84	H5
Nam Co	93	H2	Narpes	62	J5	Nazerat	94	B5	Nepa *Russia*	84	H5
Nam Dinh	93	L4	Narrabri	113	K5	Naze, The	53	J3	Nepal	92	F3
Nametil	109	G3	Narrandera	113	K5	Nazik	94	G2	Nephi	126	G1
Namib Desert	108	B4	Narrogin	112	D5	Nazik Golu	77	K3	Nephin Beg Range	58	C4
Namibe	106	B6	Narromine	113	K5	Nazilli	76	C4	Nera	69	D4
Namibia	108	C4	Narsimhapur	92	E4	Nazmiye	77	H3	Nerac	65	D6
Namlea	91	H6	Narsinghgarh	92	E4	Nazwa	97	N5	Nerchinsk	85	K6
Namoi	113	L5	Nart	87	M3	Nazyvayevsk	84	A5	Neretva	72	D4
Namosi Peak	114	R8	Nartabu	91	J6	Ncheu	107	F5	Neriquinha	106	D6
Nampa	122	F6	Naruko	88	H6	Ndalatando	106	B4	Neris	63	L9
Nampula	109	G3	Narva	63	N7	Ndele	102	D6	Nermete, Punta	136	A5
Namse La	92	F3	Narvik	62	G2	Ndeni	114	N7	Neryuktey-l-y	85	K4
Namsen	62	E4	Naryan Mar	78	J2	Ndjamena	102	C5	Neryuvom	84	Ad3
Namsos	62	D4	Narymskiy Khrebet	86	E2	Ndjote	106	B3	Nes	63	C6
Namti	93	J3	Naryn *Russia*	84	F6	Ndola	107	E5	Nesbyen	63	C6
Namtok	93	J5	Naryn *Kirghizia*	86	C3	Nea	62	D5	Neskaupstadur	62	Y12
Namuka-i-Lau	114	S9	Naryn *Kirghizia*	86	D3	Nea Filippias	75	F3	Nesna	62	E3
Namuli	109	G3	Nasarawa	105	G4	Neagh, Lough	58	K3	Nesscliffe	52	E2
Namur	64	F3	Naseby	115	C6	Neah Bay	122	B3	Ness, Loch	56	D3
Namutoni	108	C3	Nashua	125	Q5	Neale, Lake	112	G3	Nesterov *Russia*	71	K3
Namwala	106	E6	Nashville	129	J2	Nea Moudhania	75	G2	Nesterov *Ukraine*	71	K1

Nesterovo 84 H6
Neston 55 F3
Nestos 75 H2
Nesvizh 71 M2
Netanya 94 B5
Netherlands 64 F2
Neto 69 F6
Nettilling Lake 120 M4
Nettleham 55 J3
Netzahualcoyotl, Presa 131 N9
Neubrandenburg 70 E2
Neuchatel 68 A2
Neuchatel, Lac de 68 A2
Neufchateau *Belgium* 64 F4
Neufchateau *France* 64 F4
Neufchatel 64 D4
Neufelden 68 D1
Neumunster 70 C1
Neunkirchen *Austria* 68 F2
Neunkirchen *Germany* 70 B4
Neuquen *Argentina* 139 C7
Neuquen *Argentina* 139 C7
Neuruppin 70 E2
Neuse 129 P3
Neusiedler See 68 F2
Neuss 70 B3
Neustadt 70 C5
Neustettin 71 G2
Neustrelitz 70 E2
Neu-Ulm 70 D4
Nevada *Missouri, U.S.A.* 124 C8
Nevada *U.S.A.* 122 F8
Nevada, Sierra *Argentina* 138 C5
Nevada, Sierra *Spain* 66 E4
Nevada, Sierra *U.S.A.* 126 C2
Nevado, Cerro 139 C7
Nevado, Sierra del 139 C7
Nevel 78 E4
Nevelsk 88 H2
Nevers 65 E5
Neve, Sierra da 106 B5
Nevesinje 72 E4
Nevezis 63 L9
Nevinnomyssk 79 G7
Nevis, Loch 57 C4
Nevsehir 76 F3
Nevyansk 84 Ad5
New 125 K8
New Abbey 55 F2
New Albany 124 H7
New Alresford 53 F3
Newark *New Jersey, U.S.A.* 125 N6
Newark *Ohio, U.S.A.* 124 J6
Newark-on-Trent 55 J3
New Bedford 125 Q6
New Bedford River 53 H2
New Bern 129 P3
Newberry 129 M3
Newbiggin 55 G2
Newbiggin-by-the-Sea 55 H1
Newbigging 57 E5
New Braunfels 128 C6
Newbridge 59 J6
New Britain 114 E3
New Brunswick *Canada* 121 N8
New Brunswick *U.S.A.* 125 N6
Newbuildings 58 H3
Newburgh *U.K.* 57 E4
Newburgh *U.S.A.* 125 N6
Newbury 53 F3
New Bussa 105 F4
Newby Bridge 55 G2
New Castle 125 K6
Newcastle *Australia* 113 L5
Newcastle *South Africa* 108 E5
Newcastle *U.K.* 58 L4
Newcastle *Indiana, U.S.A.* 124 H7
Newcastle *Wyoming, U.S.A.* 123 M6
Newcastle Emlyn 52 C2
Newcastleton 57 F5
Newcastle-under-Lyme 55 G3
Newcastle-upon-Tyne 55 H2
Newcastle Waters 113 G2
Newcastle West 59 D8
Newchurch 52 D2
New Cumnock 57 D5
Newdegate 112 D5
New Delhi 92 E3
Newell, Lake 122 J2
New England Range 113 L5
Newenham, Cape 118 C4
Newfoundland *Canada* 121 P6
Newfoundland *Canada* 121 Q8
New Galloway 57 D5
New Georgia 114 H6
New Georgia Island 114 H6
New Glasgow 121 P8
New Guinea 114 C2
New Halfa 96 B9
New Hampshire 125 Q5
New Hampton 124 D5
New Hanover 114 E2
Newhaven 53 H4
New Haven 125 P6
New Iberia 128 G5
Newick 53 H4
New Ireland 114 E2
New Jersey 125 N6
New Kandla 92 D4
New Liskeard 125 L3
New London 125 P6
Newman, Mount 112 D3
New Market 125 L7
Newmarket *Ireland* 59 D8
Newmarket *U.K.* 53 H2
Newmarket-on-Fergus 59 E7
New Martinsville 125 K7
New Meadows 122 F5
New Mexico 127 J3
Newmill 57 F5
Newmilns 57 D5
New Milton 53 F4
Newnan 129 K4
New Orleans 128 G5
New Philadelphia 125 K6
New Pitsligo 56 F3
New Plymouth 115 E3
Newport *Ireland* 58 C5
Newport *Dyfed, U.K.* 52 C2
Newport *Essex, U.K.* 53 H3
Newport *Gwent, U.K.* 52 E3
Newport *Isle of Wight, U.K.* 53 F4
Newport *Shropshire, U.K.* 52 E2
Newport *Arkansas, U.S.A.* 128 G3
Newport *Kentucky, U.S.A.* 124 H7
Newport *Rhode Island, U.S.A.* 125 Q6
Newport *Tennessee, U.S.A.* 129 L3
Newport *Vermont, U.S.A.* 125 P4
Newport News 125 M8
Newport Pagnell 53 G2
New Providence 132 J2
Newquay 52 B4
New Quay 52 C2
New Richmond 125 T2
New Romney 53 H4
New Ross 59 J8
Newry 58 K4
Newry Canal 58 K4
New Smyrna Beach 129 M6
New South Wales 113 K5
Newton *Dumfries and Galloway, U.K.* 57 E5
Newton *Lancashire, U.K.* 55 G3
Newton *Iowa, U.S.A.* 124 D6
Newton *Kansas, U.S.A.* 128 D1
Newton *Mississippi, U.S.A.* 128 H4
Newton Abbot 52 D4
Newton Aycliffe 55 H2
Newtonferry 56 A3
Newton Flotman 53 J2
Newtongrange 57 E5
Newtonmore 57 D3
Newton on Trent 55 J3
Newton Poppleford 52 D4
Newton Stewart 54 E2
Newtown 52 D2
New Town 123 N4
Newtownabbey 58 L3
Newtownards 58 L3
Newtownbreda 58 L3
Newtownbutler 58 H4
Newtown-Crommelin 58 K3
Newtowncunningham 58 G3
Newtownmountkennedy 59 K6
Newtownstewart 58 H3
New Ulm 124 C4
New York *U.S.A.* 125 M5
New York *U.S.A.* 125 P6
New York Erie Canal 125 M5
New Zealand 115 B3
Nexpa 130 H8
Neya 78 G4
Neybasteh 95 Q5
Neyland 52 C3
Neyriz 95 M7
Neyshabur 95 P3
Nezhin 79 E5
Ngabe 106 C3
Ngabordamlu, Tanjung 91 J7
Ngadda 105 H3
Ngangla Ringco 92 F2
Nganglong Kangri 92 F2
Ngangze Co 93 G2
Ngaoundere 105 H4
Ngaruawahia 115 E2
Ngaruroro 115 F3
Ngau 114 R9
Ngauruhoe 115 E3
Nggatokae 114 J6
Nggela Pile 114 K6
Nggela Sule 114 K6
Nggele Levu 114 S8
Ngoila 105 H5
Ngong 107 G3
Ngoring Hu 93 J2
Ngorongoro Crater 107 G3
NGouri 102 C5
Ngozi 107 E3
Nguigmi 101 H6
Ngulu Atoll 91 K4
Nguna 114 U12
Ngunju, Tanjung 91 G8
Nguru 105 H3
Nhamunda 136 F4
Nha Trang 93 L6
Nhill 113 J6
Niafounke 100 E5
Niagara 124 G4
Niagara Falls 125 L5
Niah 90 E5
Niamey 101 F6
Niangara 107 E2
Nias 90 B5
Nibe 63 C8
Nicaj Shale 74 E1
Nicaragua 132 D8
Nicaragua, Lago de 132 E9
Nicastro 69 F6
Nice 65 G7
Nichicun, Lake 121 M7
Nichinan 89 C10
Nicholas, Cape 120 G3
Nicholas Channel 132 G3
Nicholls Town 132 H2
Nicholl's Town 129 P8
Nicholson 113 H2
Nickol Bay 112 D3
Nicobar Islands 93 H7
Nicosia *Cyprus* 76 E5
Nicosia *Italy* 69 E7
Nicotera 69 E6
Nicoya, Golfo de 132 E10
Nicoya, Peninsula de 132 E10
Nida 71 J3
Nidd 55 H3
Nidzica 71 J2
Niebull 70 C1
Niederbronn 64 G4
Niedere Tauern 68 D2
Niefang 105 H5
Niemisel 62 J3
Nienburg 70 C2
Nieuw Amsterdam 137 F2
Nieuw Nickerie 137 F2
Nieuwpoort 64 E3
Nigde 76 F4
Niger 105 G4
Niger 101 G5
Nigeria 105 G4
Nigg 56 D3
Niigata 89 G7
Niihama 89 D9
Niihau 126 Q10
Nii-jima 89 G8
Niimi 89 D8
Nijar 66 E4
Nijmegan 64 F3
Nikaria 75 J4
Nikel 62 P2
Nikitas 75 G2
Nikki 105 F4
Nikolaev 71 K4
Nikolayev 79 E6
Nikolayevka 84 Ae6
Nikolayevsk-na-Amure 85 Q6
Nikolsk *Russia* 79 H5
Nikolsk *Russia* 78 H4
Nikolskiy 86 B2
Nikopol 79 E6
Niksar 77 G2
Nikshahr 95 Q8
Niksic 72 E4
Nikulino 84 D4
Nikumarora 111 U2
Nil 103 F2
Nila 91 H7
Nilgiri Hills 92 E6
Nil, Nahren 103 F2
Nilsia 62 N5
Nimach 92 D4
Nimba Mountains 104 D4
Nimes 65 F7
Nimmitabel 113 K6
Nimule 103 F6
Nina Bang Lake 120 L3
Nine Degree Channel 92 D7
Ninety Mile Beach 115 D1
Ninfas, Punta 139 D8
Ninfield 53 H4
Ningan 88 B3
Ningbo 87 N6
Ningde 87 M6
Ningdu 87 M6
Ningguo 87 M5
Ninghe 87 M4
Ninghua 87 M6
Ningjing Shan 93 J2
Ningqiang 93 L2
Ningshan 93 L2
Ningwu 87 L4
Ningxia 93 L1
Ningyang 87 M4
Ninh Hoa 93 L6
Ninigo Group 114 C2
Ninnis Glacier 141 K5
Ninyako Vogumma 84 B2
Nioaque 138 E4
Niobrara 123 P6
Niono 100 D6
Nioro du Sahel 100 D5
Niort 65 C5
Nios 75 H4
Nipigon 124 F2
Nipigon, Lake 124 F2
Nipisiguit 125 S3
Nipissing, Lac 125 L3
Niquelandia 137 H6
Nir 94 H2
Nirmal 92 E5
Nirmal Range 92 E5
Nis 73 F4
Nisa 66 C3
Nisab 96 H9
Nisava 73 G4
Nishinoyama 89 E8
Nishi-suido 89 B8
Nisiros 75 J4
Nisling 118 H3
Nisporeny 73 K2
Nissan 63 E8
Nisum Bredning 63 C8
Nitchequon 121 M7
Niteroi 138 H4
Nith 57 E5
Nithsdale 57 E5
Nitra 71 H4
Niuafoou 111 T5
Niuatoputapu 111 U5
Niue 111 V5
Niulakita 111 S4
Niulan Jiang 93 K3
Niutao 111 S3
Nivelles 64 F3
Nivernais 65 E5
Nivshera 78 J3
Niwbwrch 54 E3
Nizamabad 92 E5
Nizhneangarsk 84 H5
Nizhneimbatskoye 84 D4
Nizhnekamsk 78 J4
Nizhnekamsko Vodokhranilishche 78 J4
Nizhneudinsk 84 F6
Nizhnevartovsk 84 B4
Nizhneye Bugayevo 84 Ab3
Nizhniy Lomov 79 G5
Nizhniy Yenangsk 78 H4
Nizhnyaya Bugayevo 78 J2
Nizhnyaya Chulym 84 B6
Nizhnyaya Omka 84 A5
Nizhnyaya Salda 84 Ad5
Nizhnyaya Shakhtama 85 K6
Nizhnyaya Tunguska 84 H5
Nizhnyaya Tura 78 K4
Nizhnyaya Voch 78 J3
Nizip 77 G4
Nizke Tatry 71 H4
Nizmennyy, Mys 88 E4
Njombe 107 F4
Njoroveto 114 H5
Njurundabommen 63 L5
Nkambe 105 H4
Nkayi 108 E3
Nkhotakota 107 F5
Nkongsamba 105 G5
Nmai Hka 93 J3
Noasca 68 A3
Noatak 118 C2
Nobeoka 89 C9
Nobres 137 F6
Nocera 69 E5
Nogales *Mexico* 126 G5
Nogales *U.S.A.* 126 G5
Nogata 89 C9
Nogent-le-Rotrou 64 D4
Nogent-sur-Seine 64 E4
Noginsk 78 F4
Noginskiy 84 E4
Nogoa 113 K3
Nogoya 138 E6
Noheji 88 H5
Noire 93 K4
Noire, Montagnes 64 B4
Noirmoutier 65 B5
Noirmoutier, Ile de 65 B5
Nok Kundi 92 B3
Nola *Central African Republic* 102 C7
Nola *Italy* 69 E5
Nolinsk 78 H4
Nomad 114 C3
Noma-misaki 89 C10
Nome 118 B3
Nomuka 111 U6
Nonburg 78 J2
Nonda 113 J3
Nondugl 114 C3
Nongan 87 P3
Nong Khai 93 K5
Nongoma 109 F5
Nonouti 111 R2
Nonthaburi 93 K6
Nontron 65 D6
Nookta Island 122 A3
Nootka Sound 122 A3
Nora 103 H4
Noranda 125 L2
Nordaustlandet 140 L2
Nordborg 63 E9
Nord Cap 62 T11
Norddepil 62 Z14
Norden 70 B2
Nordenham 70 C2
Nordenshelda, Arkhipelag 84 F1
Norderney 70 B2
Nordfjord 62 A6
Nordfjordeid 62 A6
Nordfold 62 F3
Nord-Friesische Inseln 63 C9
Nordhausen 70 D3
Nordhorn 70 B2
Nordkapp 62 L1
Nordkinn-halvoya 62 M1
Nord Kvaloy 62 H1
Nordland 63 E4
Nordmaling 62 H5
Nordostsee Kanal 70 C2
Nordoyar 62 Z14
Nordre Isortoq 120 R4
Nordre Strmfjord 120 R4
Nordstrand 70 C1
Nordurfjordur 62 U11
Nordvik 84 J2
Nordvik, Mys 84 J2
Nore 59 H8
Norfolk *U.K.* 53 H2
Norfolk *Nebraska, U.S.A.* 123 R6

Plauen 70 E3
Plav 72 E4
Playa Azul 130 H8
Pleasanton 128 C6
Pleihari 90 E6
Pleiku 93 L6
Plenty, Bay of 115 F2
Plentywood 123 M3
Plesetsk 78 G3
Plessisville 125 Q3
Pleszew 71 G3
Pletipi Lake 121 M7
Pleven 73 H4
Plitra 75 G4
Pljevlja 72 E4
Plock 71 H2
Plockenstein 70 E4
Ploermel 65 B5
Ploiesti 73 J3
Plomb du Cantal 65 E6
Plombieres 65 G5
Ploner See 70 D1
Plonsk 71 J2
Ploty 70 F2
Plovdiv 73 H4
Plumpton 55 G2
Plym 52 C4
Plymouth *Devon, U.K.* 52 C4
Plymouth *Monserrat, U.K.* 133 R6
Plymouth *Indiana, U.S.A.* 124 G6
Plymouth *New Hampshire, U.S.A.* 125 Q5
Plymouth Sound 52 C4
Plynlimon 52 D2
Plyussa *Russia* 63 N7
Plyussa *Russia* 63 N7
Plzen 70 E4
Pniewy 71 G2
Po *Burkina Faso* 104 E3
Po *Italy* 68 C3
Pobeda, Gora 85 R3
Pobedy, Pik 86 D3
Pobiedziska 71 G2
Pobla de Segur 67 G1
Pocatello 122 H6
Pocatky 70 F4
Pochep 79 E5
Pochinok 78 E5
Pochutla 131 L10
Pocomoke City 125 N7
Pocone 138 E3
Pocos de Caldas 138 G4
Podcherye 78 K3
Po della Pila, Bocche del 68 D3
Podgorica 72 E4
Podgornoye 84 C5
Podkamennaya Tunguska 84 E4
Podlaska, Nizina 71 K2
Podolsk 78 F4
Podor 104 C2
Podporozhye 78 E3
Pofadder 108 C5
Poggibonsi 68 C4
Pohang 89 B7
Pohjois-Karjala 62 N5
Pohorela 71 J4
Pohorje 72 C2
Poiana Teiului 73 J2
Poinsett, Cape 141 H5
Pointe-a-Pitre 133 S6
Pointe-Noire 106 B3
Point Etienne 100 B4
Point Fortin 133 S9
Point Hope 118 B2
Point Lake 119 N2
Point Pleasant 124 J7
Poipet 93 K6
Poitiers 65 D5
Poitou 65 C5
Poix 64 D4
Pokataroo 113 K4
Pokhara 92 F3
Pokka 62 L2
Pokrovka *Kirghizia* 86 D3
Pokrovka *Russia* 88 C4
Pokrovsk 85 M4
Pokrovskoye 84 Ae5
Polacca Wash 126 G3
Pola de Laviana 66 D1
Polan 95 Q9
Polana 71 H4
Poland 71 G2
Polar Plateau 141 A1
Polati 76 E3
Pole Khatun 95 Q3
Pol-e Safid 95 L3
Polesie Lubelskie 71 K3
Polessk 71 J1
Polesye 79 D5
Polgar 73 F2
Poliaigos 75 H4
Policastro, Golfo di 69 E6
Poligny 65 F5
Poligus 84 E4
Polikastron 75 G2
Polikhnitos 75 J3
Polillo Islands 91 G3
Polis 76 E5
Polisan, Tanjung 91 H5
Politovo 78 H3
Poliyiros 75 G2
Polkyko 84 F2
Pollachi 92 E6
Pollino, Monte 69 F6

Polmak 62 N2
Polmont 57 E5
Polna 63 N7
Polnovat 84 Ae4
Polonnoye 79 D5
Polotsk 63 N9
Polperro 52 C4
Polski Trumbesh 73 H4
Poltava 79 E6
Poltavka 84 A6
Poltsamaa 63 L7
Polunochnoye 84 Ad4
Poluostrov Shirokostan 85 P2
Poluy 84 Ae3
Polyanovo 84 Ae4
Polyarnik 85 Y3
Polyarnyy 62 Q2
Polynesia 143 H4
Polyuc 131 Q8
Pombal *Para, Brazil* 137 G4
Pombal *Paraiba, Brazil* 137 K5
Pombal *Portugal* 66 B3
Pomerania 70 E2
Pomona 126 D3
Pomorskie, Pojezierze 70 F2
Pomorskiy Proliv 78 H2
Pompano Beach 129 M7
Pompeyevka 88 C1
Pomyt 84 Ae4
Ponca City 128 D2
Ponce 133 P5
Ponce de Leon Bay 129 M8
Poncheville, Lac 125 M1
Pondicherry 92 E6
Pond Inlet 120 L3
Pondo 114 E2
Ponerihouen 114 W16
Ponferrada 66 C1
Pongoma 78 E2
Ponnaiyar 92 E6
Ponnani 92 E6
Pono 114 A3
Ponomarevka 78 J5
Ponoy *Russia* 78 F2
Ponoy *Russia* 78 G2
Pons 65 C6
Pont 57 G5
Ponta de Pedras 137 G4
Ponta Grossa 138 F5
Pont-a-Mousson 64 G4
Ponta Pora 138 E4
Pontardulais 52 C3
Pontarlier 65 G5
Pontchartrain, Lake 128 G5
Ponte de Barca 66 B2
Ponte de Pedra 137 F6
Pontedera 68 C4
Ponte de Sor 66 B3
Pontefract 55 H3
Ponteland 55 H1
Ponte Nova 138 H4
Ponterwyd 52 D2
Pontevedra 66 B1
Ponthierville 106 E3
Pontiac 124 J5
Pontianak 90 D6
Pontivy 64 B4
Pont-l'Abbe 65 A5
Pontoetoe 137 F3
Pontois 64 E4
Pontremoli 68 B3
Pontrilas 52 E3
Ponts 67 G2
Pontypool 52 D3
Pontypridd 52 D3
Ponziane, Isole 69 D5
Poole 53 F4
Poole Bay 53 F4
Poolewe 56 C3
Pooley Bridge 55 G2
Poona 92 D5
Poopo, Lago 138 C3
Poor Knights Islands 115 E1
Popayan 136 B3
Popigay *Russia* 84 H2
Popigay *Russia* 84 J2
Poplar Bluff 124 E8
Poplarville 128 H5
Popocatepetl, Volcan 131 K8
Popokabaka 106 C4
Popoli 69 D4
Popomanaseu, Mount 114 K6
Popondetta 114 D3
Porbandar 92 C4
Porcher Island 118 J5
Porcuna 66 D4
Porcupine 118 G2
Pordenone 68 D3
Pordim 73 H4
Pore 136 C2
Porec 72 B3
Pori 63 J6
Porirua 115 E4
Porjus 62 H3
Porkhov 63 N8
Porlakshofn 62 U13
Porlamar 136 E1
Porlock 52 D3
Porlock Bay 52 D3
Pornic 65 B5
Porog *Russia* 78 F3
Porog *Russia* 78 K3
Poronaysk 85 Q7
Poros *Greece* 75 G4

Poros *Greece* 75 G4
Porosozero 78 E3
Porozhsk 78 J3
Porozovo 71 L2
Porpoise Bay 141 J5
Porrentury 68 A2
Porsangen 62 L1
Porsanger-halvoya 62 L1
Porsgrunn 63 C7
porshofn 62 X11
Porsuk 76 D3
Porsuk Baraji 76 D3
Porsyakha 84 A3
Portachuelo 138 D3
Portadown 58 K4
Portaferry 58 L4
Portage 124 F5
Portage la Prairie 119 R5
Portal 123 N3
Port Alberni 122 B3
Port Albert 113 K6
Portalegre 66 C3
Portales 127 L3
Port Alice 122 A2
Port Angeles 122 C3
Port Antonio 132 J5
Portarlington 59 H6
Port Arthur *Australia* 113 K7
Port Arthur *U.S.A.* 128 F6
Port Askaig 57 B5
Port Augusta 113 H5
Port-au-Prince 133 L5
Port Austin 124 J4
Portavogie 58 M4
Port-Berge 109 J3
Port Blair 93 H6
Portboil 53 N7
Port Burwell 121 P5
Port Cartier 121 N7
Port Chalmers 115 C6
Port Charlotte 129 L7
Port Clarence 118 B2
Port Clinton 124 J6
Port Coquitlam 122 C3
Port Darwin 139 E10
Port-de-Paix 133 L5
Port Dickson 90 C5
Portel 66 C3
Port Elgin 125 K4
Port Elizabeth 108 E6
Port Ellen 57 C5
Port Erin 54 E2
Porterville 126 C2
Port-Eynon 52 C3
Port Francqui 106 D3
Port Gentil 106 A3
Port Glasgow 57 F4
Port Harcourt 105 G5
Port Hardy 118 K5
Porthcawl 52 D3
Port Heiden 118 D4
Port Herald 107 G6
Porthleven 52 B4
Port Huron 124 J5
Port Il'ich 94 J2
Portimao 66 B4
Port Isaac 52 C4
Port Isaac Bay 52 C4
Portishead 52 E3
Port Jackson 113 L5
Port Jervis 125 N6
Port Kaituma 136 F2
Port Kembla 113 L5
Port Kenney 113 G5
Portknockie 56 F3
Port Lairge 59 H8
Portland *Australia* 113 J6
Portland *New Zealand* 115 E1
Portland *Indiana, U.S.A.* 124 H6
Portland *Maine, U.S.A.* 125 Q5
Portland *Oregon, U.S.A.* 122 C5
Portland Bay 113 J6
Portland, Bill of 52 E4
Portland, Cape 113 K7
Portland, Isle of 52 E4
Portland Point 132 J6
Portland Promontory 121 L6
Port Laoise 59 H6
Port Lavaca 128 D6
Port-Leucate 65 E7
Port Lincoln 113 H5
Portlock Reefs 114 C3
Port Loko 104 C4
Port Louis 109 L7
Port McArthur 113 H2
Port Macquarie 113 L5
Port Menier 121 P8
Port Moresby 114 D3
Portnacroish 57 C4
Portnahaven 57 B5
Port Nelson 119 S4
Port Nolloth 108 C5
Portnyagino, Ozero 84 H2
Porto 66 B2
Porto Alegre 138 F4
Porto Alexandre 106 B6
Porto Amboim 106 B5
Porto Camargo 138 F4
Porto d'Ascoli 69 D4
Porto dos Gauchos 137 F6
Porto Esperanca 138 E3

Porto Esperidiao 138 E3
Portoferraio 69 C4
Port-of-Spain 136 E1
Porto Grande 137 G3
Portogruaro 68 D3
Porto Lucena 138 F5
Portom 62 J5
Portomaggiore 68 C3
Porto Nacional 138 H6
Porto Novo *Benin* 105 F4
Porto Novo *Cape Verde* 104 L7
Port Orford 122 B6
Porto San Stefano 69 C4
Porto Sao Jose 138 F4
Porto Seguro 137 K7
Porto Socompa 138 C4
Porto Tolle 68 D3
Porto Torres 69 B5
Porto-Vecchio 69 B5
Porto Velho 136 E5
Portoviejo 136 A4
Portpatrick 54 D2
Port Pegasus 115 A7
Port Phillip Bay 113 J6
Port Pirie 113 H5
Portraine 59 K6
Portreath 52 B4
Portree 56 B3
Portrush 58 J2
Port Said 103 F1
Port Saint Joe 129 K6
Port Saint Johns 108 E6
Port-Saint-Louis 65 F7
Port Sandwich 114 T12
Port Saunders 121 Q7
Port Shepstone 108 F6
Portskerra 56 E2
Portsmouth *U.K.* 53 F4
Portsmouth *New Hampshire, U.S.A.* 125 Q5
Portsmouth *Ohio, U.S.A.* 124 J7
Portsmouth *Virginia, U.S.A.* 125 M8
Portsoy 56 F3
Port Stephens 113 L5
Portstewart 58 J2
Port Sudan 103 G4
Port Talbot 52 D3
Porttipahdan tekojarvi 62 M2
Port Townsend 122 C3
Portugal 66 B3
Portuguesa 136 D2
Portumna 59 F6
Port Washington 124 G5
Port William 54 E2
Porvenir *Bolivia* 136 D6
Porvenir *Chile* 139 B10
Porvoo 63 L6
Posadas 138 E5
Posen 71 G2
Poshekhonye Volodarsk 78 F4
Posht-e Badam 95 M5
Poso 91 G6
Posof 77 K2
Post 127 M4
Postavy 63 M9
Poste Weygand 100 F4
Postmasburg 108 D5
Postojna 72 C3
Posusje 72 D4
Posyet 88 C4
Potamia 75 F4
Potamos 75 G4
Potapovo 84 D3
Potchefstroom 108 E5
Poteau 128 E3
Potenza 69 E5
Potes 66 D1
Potgietersrus 108 E4
Poti 77 J1
Potiskum 105 H3
Potlogi 73 H3
Potnarvin 114 U13
Potomac 125 M7
Potosi 138 C3
Potsdam *U.S.A.* 125 N4
Potsdam *Germany* 70 E2
Pott 114 V15
Potters Bar 53 H3
Pottstown 125 N6
Pottsville 125 M6
Pouebo 114 W16
Poughkeepsie 125 P6
Poulaphouca Reservoir 59 J6
Poulter 55 H3
Poulton-le-Fylde 55 G3
Poundstock 52 C4
Pouso Alegre 138 G4
Pouzauges 65 C5
Povenets 78 E3
Poverty Bay 115 G3
Povorino 79 G5
Povungnituk 121 L6
Povungnituk Bay 121 L6
Powder 123 M5
Powell 123 K5
Powell, Lake 126 F2
Powell River 122 B3
Power Head 59 F9
Powys 52 D2
Poya 114 W16
Poyang Hu 87 M6
Poyraz 77 H3
Poysdorf 68 F1
Poytya 63 K6

Raychikhinsk **85** M7
Rayen **95** N7
Rayeskiy **78** J5
Rayleigh **53** H3
Raymondville **128** D7
Ray Mountains **118** E2
Raysut **97** L8
Razan **94** J5
Razan **94** J4
Razdelnaya **79** E6
Razdolnoye **88** C4
Razgrad **73** J4
Razmak **92** C2
Raznas Ezers **63** M8
Raz, Pointe du **64** A4
Reading *U.K.* **53** G3
Reading *U.S.A.* **125** N6
Realico **139** D7
Rea, Lough **59** E6
Rearsby **53** F2
Reawick **56** A2
Reay **56** E2
Rebecca, Lake **112** E5
Rebi **91** J7
Reboly **62** P5
Rebrikha **84** C6
Rebrovo **73** G4
Rebun-to **88** H3
Recanati **68** D4
Recea **73** G3
Recherche, Archipelago of the **112** E5
Rechitsa **79** E5
Rechna Doab **92** D2
Recife **137** L5
Recklinghausen **70** B3
Recknitz **70** E2
Reconquista **138** E5
Recreio **136** F5
Red *Canada* **123** R2
Red *U.S.A.* **128** F5
Redalen **63** D6
Red Bay **121** Q7
Redbird **123** M6
Red Bluff **122** C7
Red Bluff Lake **127** L5
Redcar **55** H2
Redcliffe **113** L4
Red Cloud **123** Q7
Red Deer *Canada* **122** G2
Red Deer *Canada* **122** H1
Red Deer *Canada* **123** J2
Red Deer *Saskatchewan, Canada* **119** Q5
Redding **122** C7
Redditch **53** F2
Redencao **137** J5
Redfield **123** Q5
Redhakhol **92** F4
Redhill **53** G3
Red Hills **127** N2
Red Lake *Canada* **123** S2
Red Lake *Canada* **123** T2
Red Lake *U.S.A.* **124** C3
Red Lake *U.S.A.* **123** R4
Red Lodge **123** K5
Redmond **122** D5
Redon **65** B5
Redondela **66** B1
Redondo **66** C3
Red Rock **124** F2
Redruth **52** B4
Red Sea **103** G3
Red Tank **113** K5
Red Wharf Bay **54** E3
Red Wing **124** D4
Redwood City **126** A2
Reed City **124** H5
Reedsport **122** B6
Ree, Lough **58** G5
Reetton **115** C5
Refahiye **77** H3
Refresco **138** C5
Rega **70** F2
Regen **70** E4
Regensburg **70** E4
Reggane **100** F3
Reggio di Calabria **69** E6
Reggio nell Amelia **68** C3
Regina *Brazil* **137** G3
Regina *Canada* **123** M2
Reguengos de Monsaraz **66** C3
Rehna **70** D2
Rehoboth **108** C4
Rehoboth Beach **125** N7
Rehovot **94** B6
Reidh, Rubha **56** C3
Reidsville **129** N2
Reiff **56** C2
Reigate **53** G3
Reighton **55** J2
Re, Ile de **65** C5
Reims **64** F4
Reina Adelaida, Archipielago de la **139** B10
Reindeer Lake **119** Q4
Reine **62** E3
Reinga, Cape **115** D1
Reinheimen **62** B5
Reinosa **66** D1
Reitz **108** E5
Relizane **100** F1
Remada **101** H2
Rembang **90** E7
Remeshk **95** P8
Remiremont **65** G4
Remontnoye **79** G6
Remoulins **65** F7
Remscheid **70** B3
Rena *Norway* **63** D6
Rena *Norway* **63** D6
Renaix **64** E3
Renard Islands **114** E4
Rendova Island **114** H6
Rendsburg **70** C1
Renfrew *Canada* **125** M4
Renfrew *U.K.* **57** D5
Rengat **90** D6
Rengo **139** B6
Renish Point **56** B3
Renk **103** F5
Renmark **113** J5
Renmin **87** P2
Rennell Island **114** K7
Rennes **64** C4
Reno *Italy* **68** C3
Reno *U.S.A.* **122** E8
Reo **91** G7
Repetek **95** R2
Repolovo **84** Ae4
Republican **123** R7
Repulse Bay *Australia* **113** K3
Repulse Bay *Canada* **120** J4
Requena *Peru* **136** C5
Requena *Spain* **67** F3
Rere **114** K6
Resadiye *Turkey* **76** B4
Resadiye *Turkey* **77** G2
Resen **73** F5
Resia, Passo de **68** C2
Resistencia **138** E5
Resita **73** F3
Resolution Island *Canada* **121** P5
Resolution Island *New Zealand* **115** A6
Resolution Lake **121** P6
Restigouche **125** S3
Retalhuleu **132** B7
Rethel **64** F4
Rethimnon **75** H5
Retiche, Alpi **68** C2
Retsag **72** E2
Retuerta de Bullaque **66** D3
Reunion **109** L7
Reus **67** G2
Reuss **68** B2
Reut **73** J2
Reutlingen **70** C4
Revel **65** D7
Revelstoke **122** E2
Reventador, Volcan **136** B4
Revillagigedo Island **118** J5
Revillagigedo, Islas **130** D8
Rewa **92** F4
Rewari **92** E3
Rexburg **122** J6
Reyes, Point **122** C9
Reyhanli **77** G4
Rey, Isla del **132** H10
Reykjaheidi **62** W12
Reykjahhd **62** W12
Reykjanesta **62** T13
Reykjavik **62** U12
Reynivellir *Iceland* **62** U12
Reynivellir *Iceland* **62** W12
Reynosa **128** C7
Rezekne **63** M8
Rhatikon Pratigau **68** B2
Rhayader **52** D2
Rheda-Wiedenbruck **70** C3
Rhee **53** G2
Rhein **70** B3
Rheine **70** B2
Rhewl **55** F3
Rhiconich **56** D2
Rhine **64** G4
Rhinelander **124** F4
Rhino Camp **107** F2
Rhir, Cap **100** D2
Rho **68** B3
Rhode Island **125** Q6
Rhodes **75** J4
Rhodopi Planina **73** G4
Rhondda **52** D3
Rhone **65** F7
Rhoose **52** D3
Rhosneigr **55** E3
Rhuddlan **55** F3
Rhum **57** B3
Rhum, Sound of **57** B4
Rhydaman **52** C3
Rhyl **55** F3
Rhynie **56** F3
Riachao do Jacuipe **138** K6
Riacho de Santana **138** J6
Riano **66** D1
Riansares **66** E3
Riau, Kepulauan **90** C5
Riaza **66** E2
Ribadeo **66** C1
Ribadesella **66** D1
Ribas do Rio Pardo **138** F4
Ribat **95** R5
Ribatejo **66** B3
Ribble **55** G2
Ribe **63** C9
Ribeirao Preto **138** G4
Ribeiro do Pombal **137** K6
Riberac **65** D6
Riberalta **136** D6
Ribnica **72** C3
Ribnitz-Damgarten **70** E1
Riccall **55** H3
Rice Lake *Canada* **125** L4
Rice Lake *U.S.A.* **124** E4
Richard Collinson Inlet **119** N1
Richards Island **118** H2
Richardson **128** D4
Richardson Mountains **118** H2
Richelieu **125** P4
Richfield **126** F1
Richland **122** E4
Richlands **125** K8
Richmond *Australia* **113** J3
Richmond *New Zealand* **115** D4
Richmond *South Africa* **108** D6
Richmond *Greater London, U.K.* **53** G3
Richmond *North Yorkshire, U.K.* **55** H2
Richmond *Indiana, U.S.A.* **124** H7
Richmond *Kentucky, U.S.A.* **124** H8
Richmond *Virginia, U.S.A.* **125** M8
Richmond Range **115** D4
Rickmansworth **53** G3
Ricla **67** F2
Ricobayo, Embalse de **66** D2
Ridgecrest **126** D3
Ridgeland **129** M4
Ridgway **125** L6
Riding Mountain **123** P2
Ridsdale **57** F5
Ried **68** D1
Rienza **68** C2
Riesa **70** E3
Riesco, Isla **139** B10
Rietfontein **108** D4
Rieti **69** D4
Rifle **123** L8
Rifstangi **62** W11
Riga **63** L8
Riga, Gulf of **63** K8
Rigan **95** P7
Rigistan **92** B2
Rigolet **121** Q7
Rihab, Ar **94** G6
Rihand **92** F4
Riiser-Larsen Sea **141** B5
Rijeka **72** C3
Rika **71** K4
Rika, Wadi al **96** G5
Rimah, Wadi al **96** E3
Rimal, Ar **97** L6
Rimavska Sobota **71** J4
Rimbo **63** H7
Rimini **68** D3
Rimna **73** J3
Rimnicu Sarat **73** J3
Rimnicu Vilcea **73** H3
Rimouski **125** R2
Rinca **91** F7
Rinchinlhumbe **86** H1
Ringe **63** D9
Ringebu **63** D6
Ringgold Isles **114** S8
Ringkobing **63** C8
Ringkobing Fjord **63** C9
Ringmer **53** H4
Ringselet **62** L3
Ringvassoy **62** H2
Ringwood **53** F4
Rinia **75** H4
Rinjani, Gunung **90** F7
Rinns Point **57** B5
Riobamba **136** B4
Rio Branco *Brazil* **136** D5
Rio Branco *Uruguay* **138** F6
Rio Bravo **128** D8
Rio Bueno **139** B8
Rio Caribe **136** E1
Rio Claro **136** E1
Rio Colorado **139** D7
Rio Cuarto **138** D6
Rio de Janeiro *Brazil* **138** H4
Rio de Janeiro *Brazil* **138** H4
Rio de Oro, Baie de **100** B4
Rio Gallegos **139** C10
Rio Grande *Argentina* **139** C10
Rio Grande *Brazil* **138** F6
Rio Grande *U.S.A.* **130** H6
Rio Grande City **128** C7
Rio Grande de Santiago **130** G7
Rio Grande do Norte **137** K5
Rio Grande do Sul **138** F5
Riohacha **136** C1
Rio Hato **132** G10
Rio Lagartos **131** Q7
Riom **65** E6
Riom-es-Montagnes **65** E6
Rio Mulatos **138** C3
Rionegro **136** C2
Rio Negro *Brazil* **138** G5
Rio Negro *Spain* **66** C1
Rio Negro, Embalse del **138** E6
Rio Negro, Pantanal do **138** E3
Rioni **77** J1
Rio Pardo de Minas **138** H3
Rio Primero **138** D6
Rio Sao Goncalo **138** H4
Riosucio *Colombia* **136** B2
Riosucio *Colombia* **136** B2
Rio Verde **138** F3
Ripley *Ohio, U.S.A.* **124** J7
Ripley *Tennessee, U.S.A.* **128** H3
Ripley *W. Virginia, U.S.A.* **125** K7
Ripoll **67** H1
Ripon **55** H2
Ripponden **55** H3
Risca **52** D3
Rishiri-to **88** H3
Rishon le Zion **94** B6
Risle **64** D4
Risor **63** C7
Risoyhamn **62** F2
Ritchie's Archipelago **93** H6
Ritter, Mount **122** E9
Ritzville **122** E4
Riva **68** C3
Rivas **132** E9
Rivera **138** E6
River Falls **124** D4
Riverina **113** K5
Riversdale **108** D6
Riverside **126** D4
Riverton *Australia* **113** H5
Riverton *Canada* **123** R2
Riverton *New Zealand* **115** B7
Riverton *U.S.A.* **123** K6
Riviere-du-Loup **125** R3
Rivoli **68** A3
Riwaka **115** D4
Riwoqe **93** J2
Riyan **97** J9
Rize **77** J2
Rizhskiy Zaliv **63** K8
Rizokarpaso **76** F5
Rjukan **63** C7
Rjuven **63** B7
Roa **66** E2
Road Town **133** Q5
Roan Fell **57** F5
Roanne **65** F5
Roanoke *N. Carolina, U.S.A.* **129** P2
Roanoke *U.S.A.* **125** L8
Roanoke *U.S.A.* **125** L8
Roanoke Rapids **129** P2
Roan Plateau **123** K8
Robat **95** R6
Robat Karim **95** K4
Robat Thand **95** Q7
Robel **70** E2
Robert Brown, Cape **120** K4
Roberton **57** E5
Robertsbridge **53** H4
Robertsfors **62** J4
Robert S. Kerr Reservoir **128** E3
Robertson Range **112** E3
Robertsport **104** C4
Roberval **125** P2
Robinson **124** G7
Robinson Ranges **112** D4
Robleda **66** C2
Robledollano **66** D3
Robles La Paz **136** C1
Roblin **123** P2
Robore **138** E3
Rob Roy Island **114** H5
Robson, Mount **119** M5
Roca, Cabo da **66** B3
Roca Partida, Isla **130** C8
Roca Partida, Punta **131** M8
Roccella Ionica **69** F6
Rocha **139** F6
Rocha da Gale, Barragem **66** C4
Rochdale **55** G3
Rochechouart **65** D6
Rochefort **65** C6
Rochelle **124** F6
Rochester *Kent, U.K.* **53** H3
Rochester *Northumberland, U.K.* **57** F5
Rochester *New Hamshire, U.S.A.* **125** Q5
Rochester *New York, U.S.A.* **125** M5
Rochester *Winconsin, U.S.A.* **124** D4
Rochford **53** H3
Rochfortbridge **59** H6
Rock **124** F5
Rockefeller Plateau **141** R3
Rock Falls **124** F6
Rockford **124** F5
Rockglen **123** L3
Rockhampton **113** L3
Rockingham *Australia* **112** D5
Rockingham *U.S.A.* **129** N3
Rockingham Bay **113** K2
Rock Island **124** E6
Rockland *Maine, U.S.A.* **125** R4
Rockland *Michigan, U.S.A.* **124** F3
Rock Springs *Montana, U.S.A.* **123** L4
Rock Springs *Wyoming, U.S.A.* **123** K7
Rockwood **125** R4
Rocky Ford **127** L1
Rocky Mount **129** P3
Rocky Mountain House **119** N5
Rocky Mountains **116** G3
Rocroi **64** F4
Rodberg **63** C6
Rodby **63** D9
Rodeby **63** F8
Rodel **56** B3
Roden **52** E2
Rodez **65** E6
Rodhos *Greece* **75** J4
Rodhos *Greece* **75** K4
Rodi Garganico **69** E5
Roding **53** H3
Rodinga **113** G3

Name	Page	Ref
Santaren Channel	132	H3
Santa Rita	136	C1
Santa Rosa *Argentina*	139	C6
Santa Rosa *Argentina*	139	D7
Santa Rosa *Bolivia*	136	D6
Santa Rosa *Brazil*	138	F5
Santa Rosa *California, U.S.A.*	126	A1
Santa Rosa *New Mexico, U.S.A.*	127	K3
Santa Rosa de Cabal	136	B3
Santa Rosa de Copan	132	C7
Santa Rosa Island	126	B4
Santa Rosalia	126	F7
Santa Rosa Range	122	F7
Santa Teresa Gallura	69	B5
Santa Vitoria do Palmar	139	F6
Santa Ynez	126	B3
Santee	129	M4
Santerno	68	C3
Sant Eufemia, Golfo di	69	F6
Santhia	68	B3
Santiago *Brazil*	138	F5
Santiago *Chile*	139	B6
Santiago *Dominican Republic*	133	M5
Santiago *Panama*	132	G10
Santiago *Peru*	136	B4
Santiago, Cerro	132	G10
Santiago de Chuco	136	B5
Santiago de Compostela	66	B1
Santiago de Cuba	133	K4
Santiago del Estero	138	D5
Santiago do Cacem	66	B3
Santiago Ixcuintla	130	G7
Santiago Papasquiaro	130	G5
San Tiburcio	130	J5
Santo Amaro	137	K6
Santo Andre	138	G4
Santo Angelo	138	F5
Santo Antao	104	L7
Santo Antonio do Ica	136	D4
Santo Domingo *Dominican Republic*	133	N5
Santo Domingo *Mexico*	126	E5
Santo Domingo de la Calzada	66	E1
Santo Domingo de los Colorados	136	B4
Santorini	75	H4
Santos	138	G4
Santos Dumont *Amazonas, Brazil*	136	D5
Santos Dumont *Minas Gerais, Brazil*	138	H4
Santo Tomas	126	D5
Santo Tome	138	E5
San Valentin, Cerro	139	B9
San Vicente de la Barquera	66	D1
San Vicente del Caguan	136	C3
San Vincent	132	C8
San Vincente	91	G2
San Vito, Capo	69	D6
Sanyati	108	E3
Sanyshand	87	L3
Sao Borja	138	E5
Sao Bras de Alportel	66	C4
Sao Carlos *Rondonia, Brazil*	136	E5
Sao Carlos *Sao Paulo, Brazil*	138	G4
Sao Domingos	137	H6
Sao Felix	137	G5
Sao Francisco *Acre, Brazil*	136	D6
Sao Francisco *Bahia, Brazil*	137	K5
Sao Francisco do Sul	138	G5
Sao Francisco, Ilha de	138	G5
Sao Joao del Rei	138	H4
Sao Joao do Araguaia	137	H5
Sao Joao do Piaui	137	J5
Sao Joao, Ilhas de	137	H4
Sao Jose	136	D4
Sao Jose do Gurupi	137	H4
Sao Jose do Rio Preto	138	G4
Sao Jose dos Campos	138	G4
Sao Leopoldo	138	F5
Sao Lourenco	138	E3
Sao Luis	137	J4
Sao Manuel	136	F5
Sao Marcos	138	G3
Sao Marcos, Baia de	137	J4
Sao Maria da Boa Vista	137	K5
Sao Mateus	138	K7
Sao Miguel dos Campos	137	K5
Sao Miguel do Tapuio	137	J5
Saona, Isla	133	N5
Saone	65	F5
Sao Nicolau	104	L7
Sao Paulo *Brazil*	138	G4
Sao Paulo *Brazil*	138	G4
Sao Paulo de Olivenca	136	D4
Sao Pedro do Sul	66	B2
Sao Raimundo Nonato	137	J5
Sao Romao	138	G3
Sao Roque, Cabo de	137	K5
Sao Sebastiao do Paraiso	138	G4
Sao Tiago	104	L7
Sao Tome	105	G5
Sao Tome	105	G5
Sao Tome and Principe	105	G5
Sao Tome, Cabo de	138	H4
Saouda, Qornet es	77	G5
Saoura, Oued	100	E2
Sao Vicente	138	G4
Sao Vincente, Cabo de	66	B4
Sao Vincente	104	L7
Sapai	75	H2
Sapanca	76	D2
Sapanca Golu	76	D2
Sape	91	F7
Sapele	105	G4
Sapientza	75	F4
Saposoa	136	B5
Sapporo	88	H4
Sapri	69	E5
Sapulut	90	F5
Saqqez	94	H3
Sarab	94	H3
Sara Buri	93	K6
Saragossa	67	F2
Saraguro	136	B4
Sarajevo	72	E4
Sarakhs	95	Q3
Sarakli	75	G2
Saraktash	79	K5
Saralzhin	79	J6
Saranac Lake	125	P4
Sarande	74	E3
Saran, Gunung	90	E6
Saranpaul	84	Ad4
Saransk	78	H5
Sarapul	78	J4
Sarapul'skoye	88	F1
Sarasota	129	L7
Sarata	73	K2
Saratoga	126	A2
Saratoga Springs	125	P5
Saratov	79	H5
Saravan	95	R8
Saravane	93	L5
Sarawak	90	E5
Saraykent	76	F3
Saray *Turkey*	76	B2
Saray *Turkey*	77	L3
Saraychik	79	J6
Saraykoy *Turkey*	76	C4
Saraykoy *Turkey*	76	F3
Sarayonu	76	E3
Sarbaz	95	Q8
Sarbisheh	95	P5
Sarcham	94	J3
Sarda	92	F3
Sardarshahr	92	D3
Sardegna	69	B5
Sardinia	69	B5
Sardis Lake	128	H3
Sareks	62	G3
Sar-e Pol	92	C1
Sar-e Yazd	95	M6
Sargans	68	B2
Sargodha	92	D2
Sarh	102	C6
Sari	95	L3
Saria	75	J5
Sarickaya	76	D2
Sarigol	76	C3
Sarikamis	77	K2
Sarikaya	76	F3
Sarinay	86	C4
Sarine	68	A2
Sarioglan	77	F3
Sarisu	77	K3
Sariwon	87	P4
Sariyar Baraji	76	D2
Sariz	77	G3
Sark	53	M7
Sarkikaraagac	76	D3
Sarkisla	77	G3
Sarkoy	76	B2
Sarlat-la-Caneda	65	D6
Sarmi	91	K6
Sarmiento	139	C9
Sarna	63	E6
Sarneh	94	H5
Sarnen	68	B2
Sarnia	124	J5
Sarny	79	D5
Saronikos Kolpos	75	G4
Saronno	68	B3
Saros Korfezi	76	B2
Sarowbi	92	C2
Sar Planina	72	F5
Sarpsborg	63	H7
Sarralbe	64	G4
Sarre	64	G4
Sarrebourg	64	G4
Sarria	66	C1
Sarshive	94	H4
Sartang	85	N3
Sartatovskoye Vodokhranilishche	79	H5
Sartene	69	B5
Sarthe	65	C5
Sartu	87	N2
Saruhanli	76	B3
Sarvabad	94	H4
Sarvar	72	D2
Sarvestan	95	L7
Sarviz	72	E2
Sarych, Mys	79	E7
Sary-Ishikotrau, Peski	86	D2
Sary Ozek	86	D3
Sary-Shagan	86	C2
Sary-Tash	86	C4
Sarzana	68	B3
Sasamungga	114	H5
Sasaram	92	F4
Sasd	72	E2
Sasebo	89	B9
Saskatchewan *Canada*	119	P5
Saskatchewan *Canada*	119	Q5
Saskatoon	123	L1
Saskylakh	84	J2
Sasovo	78	G5
Sassandra *Ivory Coast*	104	D4
Sassandra *Ivory Coast*	104	D5
Sassari	69	B5
Sassnitz	70	E1
Sasstown	104	D5
Sassuolo	68	C3
Sas-Tobe	86	C3
Sasyk, Ozero	73	K3
Satadougou	100	C6
Satara	92	D5
Sater	63	F6
Satley	55	H2
Satmala Range	92	E5
Satna	92	F4
Satoraljaujhely	71	J4
Satpura Range	92	E4
Sattahip	93	K6
Satu Mare	73	G2
Satun	93	K7
Satyga	84	Ad5
Sauceda	127	M8
Saucillo	127	K6
Sauda	63	B7
Saudarkrokur	62	V12
Saudi Arabia	96	F3
Sauerland	70	B3
Saugeen	124	K4
Sauk City	124	F5
Saulieu	65	F5
Sault Sainte Marie *Canada*	124	H3
Sault Sainte Marie *U.S.A.*	124	H3
Saumarez Reef	113	L3
Saumlakki	91	J7
Saumur	65	C5
Saunders, Cape	115	C6
Saundersfoot	52	C3
Saurimo	106	D4
Sava	72	E3
Savaii	111	U4
Savalou	105	F4
Savannah *Tennessee, U.S.A.*	129	H3
Savannah *U.S.A.*	129	M4
Savannah *U.S.A.*	129	M4
Savannakhet	93	K5
Savant Lake	124	E1
Savantvadi	92	D5
Savanur	92	E6
Savar	62	J5
Savastepe	76	B3
Save	105	F4
Save *France*	65	D7
Save *Mozambique*	109	F4
Saveh	95	K4
Saveni	73	J2
Saverne	64	G4
Savinja	72	C2
Savirsin	73	G2
Savitaipale	63	M6
Savnik	72	E4
Savoie	65	G6
Savona	68	B3
Savo Nggatokae	114	J6
Savonlinna	63	N6
Savsat	77	K2
Savsjo	63	F8
Savukoski	62	N3
Savur	77	J4
Savusavu	114	R8
Savusavu Bay	114	R8
Sawab, Wasi as	77	J5
Sawadah, As	96	G5
Sawara	88	H4
Sawatch Mountains	123	L8
Sawbridgeworth	53	H3
Sawel	58	H3
Sawqirah, Ghubbat	97	N7
Sawqirah, Ra's	97	N7
Sawston	53	H2
Sawtooth Mountains *Idaho, U.S.A.*	122	G5
Sawtooth Mountains *Minnesota, U.S.A.*	124	E3
Sawtry	53	G2
Sawu	91	G8
Sawu, Laut	91	G7
Saxby Downs	113	J3
Saxmundham	53	J2
Saxthorpe	53	J2
Sayak	86	D2
Saydy	85	N3
Sayhan-Ovoo	87	J2
Sayhut	97	K9
Saylac	103	H5
Sayula	130	H8
Sayulita	130	G7
Sayun	97	J9
Say-Utes	79	J7
Sazan	74	E2
Sazava	70	F4
Sazin	92	D1
Scafell Pikes	55	G2
Scalasaig	57	B4
Scalby	55	J2
Scalea	69	E6
Scalloway	56	A2
Scalpay	56	C3
Scamblesby	55	J3
Scammon Bay	118	B3
Scapa Flow	56	E2
Scaraben	56	E2
Scaramia, Capo	69	E7
Scarba	57	C3
Scarborough *Canada*	125	L5
Scarborough *Trinidad and Tobago*	133	S9
Scarborough *U.K.*	55	J2
Scarinish	57	B4
Scarp	56	A2
Scarpanto	75	J5
Scarpe	64	E3
Scarriff	59	C7
Schaal See	70	D2
Schaffhausen	68	B2
Scharhorn	70	C2
Schefferville	121	N7
Scheibbs	68	E1
Scheitling	68	E2
Schelde	64	E3
Schenectady	125	P5
Schiedam	64	F3
Schiehallion	57	D4
Schiermonnikoog	64	G2
Schio	68	C3
Schitu Duca	73	J2
Schlei	70	C1
Schleiz	70	D3
Schleswig	70	C1
Schneidemuhl	71	G2
Schoningen	70	D2
Schonsee	70	E4
Schouten Islands	114	C2
Schouwen	64	E3
Schreiber	124	G2
Schwabische Alb	70	C4
Schwandorf	70	E4
Schwaner, Pegunungan	90	E6
Schwarmstedt	70	C2
Schwarze Elser	70	E3
Schwarzwald	70	C5
Schwaz	68	C2
Schwedt	70	F2
Schweinfurt	70	D3
Schwerin	70	D2
Schweriner See	70	D2
Schwieloch See	70	F2
Schwyz	68	B2
Sciacca	69	D7
Scilly, Isles of	52	L5
Scioto	124	J7
Sckuls	68	C2
Scobey	123	M3
Sconser	56	B3
Score Head	56	A1
Scoresby, Cape	120	H3
Scotia Ridge	139	F10
Scotia Sea	139	F1
Scott Base	141	M3
Scottburgh	108	F6
Scott, Cape	118	K5
Scott City	127	M1
Scott Glacier	141	P1
Scott Lake	119	P4
Scott Reef	112	E1
Scottsbluff	123	N7
Scottsboro	129	J3
Scottsdale	126	G4
Scourie	56	C2
Scrabster	56	E2
Scranton	125	N6
Screeb	59	C6
Scridain, Loch	57	B4
Scunthorpe	55	J3
Scuol	68	C2
Scurrival Point	57	A3
Scutari	74	E1
Seaford *U.K.*	53	H4
Seaford *U.S.A.*	125	N7
Seaforth, Loch	56	B3
Seaham	55	H2
Seahorse Point	120	K5
Seahouses	55	H1
Seal	119	R4
Sea Lake	113	J6
Seal, Cape	108	D6
Seal Cape	118	D4
Seamer	55	J2
Searcy	128	G3
Searles Lake	126	D3
Seascale	55	F2
Seaside	122	C5
Seathwaite	55	F2
Seaton	52	D4
Seaton Sluice	55	H1
Seattle	122	C4
Sebago Lake	125	Q5
Sebangka	90	C5
Sebastian Vizcaino, Bahia de	126	E6
Sebderat	103	G4
Seben	76	D2
Sebenico	72	C4
Sebes	73	G3
Sebesului, Muntii	73	G3
Sebezh	63	N8
Sebinkarahisar	77	H2
Sebring	129	M7
Sebta	66	D5
Sebuku	90	F6
Secchia	68	C3
Sechura, Bahia de	136	A5
Sechura, Desierto de	136	A5
Secretary Island	115	A6
Secunderabad	92	E5
Seda	66	C3
Sedalia	124	D7
Sedan	64	F4
Sedano	66	E1
Sedbergh	55	G2

Name	Page	Grid	Name	Page	Grid
Shepherd Bay	120	H4	Shulan	87	P3
Shepherd Islands	114	U12	Shumagin Islands	118	Af9
Shepparton	113	K6	Shumen	73	J4
Sheppey, Isle of	53	H3	Shumerlya	78	H4
Shepshed	53	F2	Shungnak	118	D2
Shepton Mallet	52	E3	Shuqrah	96	G10
Sheragul	84	G6	Shura	77	K4
Sherard, Cape	120	K3	Shurab	95	K5
Sherborne	52	E4	Shurab	95	N5
Sherbro	104	C4	Shusf	95	Q6
Sherbro Island	104	C4	Shush	94	J5
Sherbrooke	125	Q4	Shushenskoye	84	E6
Sherburne Reef	114	D2	Shushtar	94	J5
Sherburn in Elmet	55	H3	Shuswap Lake	122	E2
Shereik	96	A7	Shuya	78	G4
Sheridan *Arkansas, U.S.A.*	128	F3	Shuya	89	G7
Sheridan *Wyoming, U.S.A.*	123	L5	Shwebo	93	J4
Sheringham	53	J2	Shwegyin	93	J5
Sherlovaya Gora	85	K6	Shweli	93	J4
Sherman	128	D4	Shyok	92	E2
's-Hertogenbosch	64	F3	Siahan Range	92	B3
Shetland	56	A1	Siah Koh	95	S5
Shetland Islands	56	A1	Sialkot	92	D2
Shetpe	79	J7	Siargao	91	H4
Shevchenko	79	J7	Siau	91	H5
Shewa Gimira	103	G6	Siauliai	63	K9
Sheya	85	K4	Sibenik	72	C4
Sheyang	87	N5	Siberut	90	B6
Sheyenne	123	Q4	Siberut, Selat	90	B6
Shiant Islands	56	B3	Sibi	92	C3
Shiant, Sound of	56	B3	Sibirskaya Nizmennost	84	G2
Shiashkotan, Ostrov	85	S7	Sibirtsevo	88	D3
Shibam	97	J9	Sibiryakovo, Ostrov	84	B2
Shibata	89	G7	Sibiti	106	B3
Shibecha	88	K4	Sibiu	73	H3
Shibetsu *Japan*	88	J3	Sibolga	90	B5
Shibetsu *Japan*	88	K4	Sibsagar	93	H3
Shibin el Kom	102	F1	Sibsey	55	K3
Shibotsu-jima	88	L4	Sibu	90	E5
Shibushi	89	C10	Sibut	102	C6
Shickshock Mountains	125	S2	Sibutu	91	F5
Shiel Bridge	56	C3	Sibutu Passage	91	F5
Shieldaig	56	C3	Sibuyan	91	G3
Shiel, Loch	57	C4	Sibuyan Sea	91	G3
Shihan, Wadi	97	L8	Sicasica	138	C3
Shihezi	86	F3	Sichuan	93	K2
Shiikh	103	J6	Sichuan Pendi	93	L3
Shijiazhuang	87	L4	Sicie, Cap	65	F7
Shikarpur	92	C3	Sicilia	69	D7
Shikoku	89	D9	Sicilian Channel	69	C7
Shikoku-sanchi	89	D9	Sicily	69	D7
Shikong	87	K4	Sicuani	136	C6
Shikotan-to	88	L4	Sidatun	88	E3
Shikotsu-ko	88	H4	Sideby	63	J5
Shildon	55	H2	Sidheros, Akra	75	J5
Shilega	78	G3	Sidhirokastron	75	G2
Shiliguri	93	G3	Sidi Akacha	67	G4
Shilka *Russia*	85	K6	Sidi Barram	102	E1
Shilka *Russia*	85	L6	Sidi Bel Abbes	100	E1
Shillingstone	52	E4	Sidi Ifni	100	C3
Shillong	93	H3	Sidi Kacem	100	D2
Shilovo	78	G5	Sidima	88	E1
Shimabara	89	C9	Sidlaw Hills	57	E4
Shimada	89	G8	Sidmouth	52	D4
Shimanovsk	85	M6	Sidmouth, Cape	113	J1
Shimian	93	K3	Sidney *Canada*	122	C3
Shimizu	89	G8	Sidney *Montana, U.S.A.*	123	M4
Shimoda	89	G8	Sidney *Ohio, U.S.A.*	124	H6
Shimoga	92	E6	Sidon	94	B5
Shimonoseki	89	C9	Sidorovsk	84	C3
Shinano	89	G7	Siedlce	71	K2
Shinas	97	N4	Siegen	70	C3
Shindand	95	R5	Siemiatycze	71	K2
Shin Falls	56	D3	Siem Reap	93	K6
Shingu	89	E9	Siena	68	C4
Shinjo	88	H6	Sieniawa	71	K3
Shinness	56	D2	Sierpc	71	H2
Shinshar	77	G5	Sierra Colorada	139	C3
Shinyanga	107	F3	Sierra Leone	104	C4
Shiogama	89	H6	Sierra Vista	127	G5
Shiono-misaki	89	C9	Sierre	68	A2
Shiosawa	89	G7	Sifnos	75	H4
Shiping	93	K4	Sifton Pass	118	K4
Shipley	55	H3	Sigatoka *Fiji*	114	Q8
Shippensburg	125	M6	Sigatoka *Fiji*	114	Q9
Shippigan Island	121	P8	Sigean	65	E7
Shipston-on-Stour	53	F2	Sighetu Marmatiei	73	G2
Shipton	55	H2	Sighisoara	73	H2
Shipton-under-Wychwood	53	F3	Sigli	90	B4
Shipunovo	84	C6	Siglufjordur	62	V11
Shirakawa	89	H7	Sigmaringen	70	C4
Shirane-san *Japan*	89	G8	Signy	141	W6
Shirane-san *Japan*	89	G7	Sigovo	84	D4
Shiraz	95	L7	Sigtuna	63	G7
Shire	107	F6	Siguenza	66	E2
Shirebrook	55	H3	Siguiri	104	D3
Shiretoko-misaki	88	K3	Sigulda	63	L8
Shiriya-saki	88	H5	Siin	66	C1
Shir Kuh	95	M6	Siikajoki	62	L4
Shirten Holoy Gobi	86	H3	Siikavuopio	62	J2
Shirvan	95	N3	Siilinjarvi	62	M5
Shishaldin Volcano	118	Af9	Siin	88	E2
Shivpuri	92	E3	Siipyy	63	J5
Shivwits Plateau	126	F2	Siirt	77	J4
Shiwan Dashan	93	L4	Sikar	92	E3
Shiyan	93	M2	Sikasso	100	D6
Shizhu	93	L3	Sikeston	124	F8
Shizugawa	88	H6	Sikhote Alin	88	E3
Shizuishan	87	K4	Sikinos	75	H4
Shizuoka	89	G8	Sikkim	93	G3
Shkoder	74	E1	Sil	66	C1
Shkumbin	74	E2	Sila	97	K4
Shmidta, Ostrov	81	L1	Silchar	93	H4
Shobara	89	D8	Sile	76	C2
Shokalskogo, Ostrov	84	A2	Silesia	71	G3
Shorapur	92	E5	Silgarhi	92	F3
Shorawak	95	S6	Silifke	76	E4
Shoreham-by-Sea	53	G4	Siligir	84	J3
Shorkot	92	D2	Siling Co	93	G2
Shoshone	122	G6	Silistra	73	J3
Shoshone Mountains	122	F8	Silivri	76	C2
Shoshoni	123	K6	Siljan	63	F6
Shostka	79	E5	Silkeborg	63	C8
Shouguang	87	M4	Sillajhuay	138	C3
Shouning	87	M6	Sillan, Lough	58	J4
Showa	141	C5	Sillon de Talbert	64	B4
Showak	96	B9	Siloam Springs	128	E2
Shozhma	78	G3	Silom	114	E2
Shpikov	73	K1	Silopi	77	K4
Shpola	79	E6	Silovayakha	78	L2
Shrankogl	68	C2	Silsbee	128	E5
Shreveport	128	F4	Silute	63	J9
Shrewsbury	52	E2	Silvan	77	J3
Shrewton	53	F3	Silver Bay	124	E3
Shrigonda	92	D5	Silver City	127	H4
Shropshire	52	E2	Silvermines Mountains	59	F7
Shrule	59	D5	Silver Spring	125	M7
Shuab, Ra's	97	P9	Silverstone	53	F2
Shuanghezhen	87	P3	Silverton *U.K.*	52	D4
Shuangliao	87	N3	Silverton *U.S.A.*	127	J2
Shuangyashan	87	Q2	Simanggang	90	E5
Shubar-Kuduk	79	K6	Simard, Lac	125	L3
Shubra el-Khema	102	F1	Simareh Karkheh	94	H5
Shucheng	87	M5	Simav *Turkey*	76	C3
Shuga	84	B6	Simav *Turkey*	76	C2
Shuicheng	93	K3	Simayr	96	E8
Shuikou	87	M6	Simcoe	125	K5
Shujaabad	92	D3	Simcoe, Lake	125	L4

Name	Page	Grid	Name	Page	Grid
Simeonovgrad	73	H4	Sines, Cabo de	66	B4
Simeulue	90	B5	Sinetta	62	L3
Simferopol	79	E7	Sinfra	104	D4
Simi	75	J4	Singa	103	F5
Simiti	136	C2	Singapore	90	C5
Simitli	73	G5	Singaraja	90	F7
Simla	92	E2	Sing Buri	93	K6
Simleu Silvaniei	73	G2	Singida	107	F3
Simmern	70	B3	Singitikos, Kolpos	75	G2
Simojarvi	62	M3	Singkang	91	G6
Simojoki	62	L4	Singkawang	90	D5
Simonka	71	J4	Singkep	90	C6
Simplicio Mendes	137	J5	Singleton	53	G4
Simplon Pass	68	B2	Singleton, Mount	112	G3
Simpson Bay	119	N2	Singosan	87	P4
Simpson Desert	113	H3	Siniatsikon	75	F2
Simpson Peninsula	120	J4	Siniscola	69	B5
Simrishamn	63	F9	Sinj	72	D4
Simsor	77	J3	Sinjai	91	G7
Simushir, Ostrov	85	S7	Sinjajevina	72	E4
Sinabang	90	B5	Sinjar	77	J4
Sinabung	90	B5	Sinkat	103	G4
Sinac	72	C3	Sinnamary	137	G2
Sinafir	96	B3	Sinnes	63	B7
Sinaia	73	H3	Sinni	69	F5
Sinai Peninsula	103	F2	Sinnicolau Mare	72	F2
Sinaloa	130	F4	Sinoe	104	D4
Sinanaj	74	E2	Sinoe, Lacul	73	K3
Sinaxtla	131	L9	Sinop	76	F2
Sincan *Turkey*	76	C3	Sinpo	88	B5
Sincan *Turkey*	77	G3	Sinpung-dong	88	B5
Since	133	K10	Sintang	90	E5
Sincelejo	136	B2	Sint Maarten	133	R5
Sinclair's Bay	56	E2	Sinton	128	D6
Sind	92	E3	Sintra	66	B3
Sinda	88	F1	Sinu	136	B2
Sindal	63	D8	Sinuiju	87	N4
Sindangbarang	90	D7	Sinyavka	71	M2
Sindel	73	J4	Sinyaya	63	N8
Sindhuli Garhi	92	G3	Siocon	91	G4
Sindirgi	76	C3	Siofok	72	E2
Sindominic	73	H2	Sion	68	A2
Sincor	78	J3	Sionascaig, Loch	56	C2
Sind Sagar Doab	92	D2	Sion Mills	58	H3
Sinegorye	78	J4	Sioule	65	E5
Sinelnikovo	79	F6	Sioux City	124	B5
Sines	66	B4	Sioux Falls	123	R6
			Sioux Lookout	119	S5
			Sipalay	91	G4
			Siping	87	N3
			Sip Song Chau Thai	93	K4
			Sipul	114	D3
			Sipura	90	B6
			Siquia	132	E8
			Siquijor	91	G4

Name	Page	Grid
Sira *India*	92	E6
Sira *Norway*	63	B7
Sir Abu Nuayr	97	M4
Siracusa	69	E7
Sirajganj	93	G4
Sir Alexander, Mount	119	M5
Siran	77	H2
Sir Bani Yas	97	L4
Sir Edward Pellew Group	113	H2
Siret *Romania*	73	J2
Siret *Romania*	73	J2
Sirhan, Wadi	94	D6
Siri Kit Dam	93	K5
Sirik, Tanjung	90	E5
Sir James McBrien, Mount	118	R3
Sirjan, Kavir-e	95	L6
Sirk	95	N8
Sirna	75	J4
Sirnal	77	K4
Sirohi	92	D4
Siros *Greece*	75	H4
Siros *Greece*	75	H4
Sirri	95	M9
Sirr, Nafud as	96	K5
Sirsa	92	D3
Sir Sanford, Mount	122	F2
Sirsi	92	D6
Sirte	101	J2
Sirte, Gulf of	101	J2
Sirvan	77	K3
Sisak	72	D3
Sisaket	93	K5
Sisophon	93	K6
Sisseton	123	R5
Sissonne	64	E4
Sistan	95	P8
Sistan, Daryacheh-ye-	95	Q6
Sisteron	65	F4
Sistig-Khem	84	F6
Sistranda	62	C5
Sitamau	92	F3
Sitapur	92	F3
Sitges	67	G2
Sithonia	75	G2
Sitia	75	J5
Sitian	86	F3
Sitidgi Lake	118	J2
Sitio da Abadia	138	H6
Sitka	118	H4
Sittang	93	J5
Sittingbourne	53	H3
Sittwe	93	H4
Situbondo	90	E7
Siuri	93	G4
Siuruanjoki	62	M4
Sivas	77	G3
Sivasli	76	C3
Siverek	77	H4
Siverskiy	63	P7

South Andaman 93 H6
South Baldy 127 J4
South Baymouth 124 J4
South Bend Indiana, U.S.A. 124 G6
South Bend Washington, U.S.A. 122 C4
South Benfleet 53 H3
Southborough 53 H3
South Boston 125 L8
South Canadian 128 D3
South Cape Fiji 114 R8
South Cape U.S.A. 126 T11
South Carolina 129 M3
South China Sea 87 L7
South Creake 53 H2
South Dakota 123 N5
South Dorset Downs 52 E4
South Downs 53 G4
Southeast Cape 118 B3
South East Cape 113 K6
Southend 119 Q4
Southend-on-Sea 53 H3
Southern Alps 115 C5
Southern Cross 112 D5
Southern Indian Lake 119 R4
Southern Pine Hills 128 H5
Southern Pines 129 N3
Southern Uplands 57 E5
Southery 53 H2
South Esk 57 E4
South Foreland 53 J3
South Forty Foot Drain 53 G2
South Geomagnetic Pole 141 K5
South Georgia 139 J10
South Glamorgan 52 D3
South Harbour 56 A2
South Haven 124 G5
South Hayling 53 G4
South Henik Lake 119 R3
South Hill 125 L8
South Korea 87 P4
South Lake Tahoe 126 C1
South Magnetic Pole 141 K5
Southminster 53 H3
South Molton 52 D3
South Morar 57 C4
South Nahanni 118 K3
South Negril Point 132 H5
South Orkney Islands 141 W4
South Platte 123 N7
South Point 133 K3
South Pole 141 A1
Southport 55 F3
South River 125 L4
South Ronaldsay 56 F2
South Sandwich Islands 141 Y7
South Saskatchewan 123 L2
South Seal 119 R4
South Shields 55 H2
South Sister 122 D5
South Skirlaugh 55 J3
South Sound 59 C6
South Taranaki Bight 115 E3
South Twin Island 121 K7
South Tyne 55 G2
South Uist 56 A3
Southwell 55 J3
Southwest Bay 139 J10
Southwest Cape 115 A7
South West Cape 113 K7
South-west Miramichi 121 N8
Southwold 53 J2
South Woodham Ferrers 53 H3
South Yemen 97 J8
South Yorkshire 55 H3
South Zeal 52 D4
Sovata 73 H2
Sovets 78 H4
Sovetsk 71 J1
Sovetskaya Gavan 88 H1
Soya-Kaikyo 88 J3
Soya-misaki 88 H3
Soyana 78 G2
Soylemez 77 J3
Soyo 106 B4
Sozopol 73 J4
Spa 64 F3
Spain 66 D2
Spalato 72 D4
Spalding 53 G2
Spaldwick 53 G2
Spanish Town 132 J5
Sparkford 52 E3
Sparks 122 E8
Sparta 75 G4
Spartanburg 129 M3
Spartel, Cap 100 D1
Sparti 75 G4
Spartivento, Capo Italy 69 B6
Spartivento, Capo Italy 69 F7
Sparwood 122 G3
Spas Demensk 78 E5
Spasskaya Guba 78 E3
Spassk Dalniy 88 D3
Spatha, Akra 75 G5
Spean Bridge 57 D4
Spearfish 123 N5
Spence Bay 120 H4
Spencer Indiana, U.S.A. 124 G7
Spencer Iowa, U.S.A. 124 C5
Spencer W. Virginia, U.S.A. 125 K7
Spencer, Cape 113 H6
Spencer Gulf 113 H5
Spences Bridge 122 D2

Spennymoor 55 H2
Spenser Mountains 115 D5
Sperrin Mountains 58 H3
Spessart 70 C3
Spetsai 75 G4
Spey 56 E3
Spey Bay 56 E3
Speyer 70 C4
Spicer Islands 120 L4
Spiddle 59 D6
Spiekeroog 70 B2
Spiez 68 A2
Spili 75 H5
Spilsby 55 K3
Spinazzola 69 F5
Spithead 53 F4
Spitsbergen 80 C2
Spittal 68 D2
Spittal of Glenshee 57 E4
Spjelkavik 62 B5
Split 72 D4
Spokane U.S.A. 122 E4
Spokane U.S.A. 122 F4
Spoleto 69 D4
Spooner 124 E4
Spornoye 85 S4
Spremberg 70 F3
Spring 124 C8
Springbok 108 C5
Springdale Canada 121 Q8
Springdale U.S.A. 128 E2
Springer 127 K2
Springerville 127 H3
Springfield New Zealand 115 C5
Springfield Colorado, U.S.A. 127 L2
Springfield Illinois, U.S.A. 124 F7
Springfield Massachusetts, U.S.A. 125 P5
Springfield Missouri, U.S.A. 124 D8
Springfield Ohio, U.S.A. 124 J7
Springfield Oregon, U.S.A. 122 C5
Springfield Tennessee, U.S.A. 129 J2
Springfield Vermont, U.S.A. 125 P5
Springfontein 108 E6
Spring Garden 136 F2
Spring Mountains 126 E2
Springs 108 E5
Springs Junction 115 D5
Spruce Knob 125 L7
Spurn Head 55 K3
Squamish 122 C3
Squillace, Golfo di 69 F6
Srbica 72 F4
Srebrnica 72 E3
Srediny 85 S5
Sredinnyy Khrebet 85 U5
Sredna Gora 73 H4
Srednekolymsk 85 S3
Sredne Olekma 85 L5
Sredne Russkaya Vozvyshennost 79 F5
Sredne-Sibirskoye Ploskogorye 84 H3
Sredneye Kuyto, Ozero 62 P4
Sredni Rodopi 73 H5
Sredniy Kalar 85 K5
Sremska Mitrovica 72 E3
Sretensk 85 K6
Sre Umbell 93 K6
Srikakulam 92 F5
Sri Lanka 92 F7
Srinagar 92 D2
Sroda 71 G2
Sroda Slaska 71 G3
Stack, Loch 56 D2
Stade 70 C2
Stadhampton 53 F3
Stadthagen 70 C2
Staffin 56 B3
Stafford 53 E2
Staffordshire 53 F2
Staines 53 G3
Staintondale 55 J2
Stakhanov 79 F6
Stalac 73 F4
Stalham 53 J2
Stalingrad 79 G6
Stalybridge 55 G3
Stamford Australia 113 J3
Stamford Connecticut, U.S.A. 125 P6
Stamford New York, U.S.A. 125 N5
Stamford Texas, U.S.A. 127 N4
Stamford U.K. 53 G2
Stamford Bridge 55 J3
Stamfordham 57 G5
Stampiky 109 J3
Stamsund 62 E2
Standerton 108 E5
Standish U.K. 55 G3
Standish U.S.A. 124 J4
Stanford 123 J4
Stanford-le-Hope 53 H3
Stanger 108 F5
Stanhope 55 G2
Stanislav 71 L4
Stanke Dimitrov 73 G4
Stanley Durham, U.K. 55 H2
Stanley Falkland Islands, U.K. 139 E10
Stanley U.S.A. 123 N3
Stanley Zaire 107 E2
Stanley Mission 119 Q4
Stanleyville 106 E2
Stann Creek 132 C6
Stanos 75 F3

Stanovoye Nagorye 85 J5
Stanovoy Khrebet 85 L5
Stansted 53 H3
Stanthorpe 113 L4
Stanton 53 H2
Stapleford 53 F3
Stara Planina 73 G4
Staraya Russa 78 E4
Staraya Vorpavla 84 Ae4
Stara Zagora 73 H4
Starcross 52 D4
Stargard 70 F2
Starikovo 85 R2
Starke 129 L6
Starkville 128 H4
Starmyri 62 X12
Starnberg 70 D5
Starnberger See 70 D5
Staroaleyskoye 84 C6
Starobelsk 79 F6
Starodub 79 E5
Starodubskoye 88 J2
Starogard 71 H2
Starokazachye 73 K2
Starokonstantinov 79 D6
Starominskaya 79 F6
Starosielce 71 K2
Start Bay 52 D4
Start Point Devon, U.K. 52 D4
Start Point Orkney Is., U.K. 56 F1
Stary Sacz 71 J4
Staryy Oskol 79 F5
Staryy Sambor 71 K4
State College 125 M6
Staten Island 139 D10
Statesboro 129 M4
Statesville 129 M3
Staunton U.K. 52 E3
Staunton U.K. 52 E3
Staunton U.S.A. 125 L7
Staunton on Wye 52 E2
Stavanger 63 A7
Staveley Cumbria, U.K. 55 G2
Staveley Derbyshire, U.K. 55 H3
Staveley N. Yorkshire, U.K. 55 H2
Stavelot 64 F3
Stavropol 79 G6
Stavropolskaya Vozvyshennost 79 G6
Stawiski 71 K2
Staxton 55 J2
Steensby Inlet 120 L3
Steensby Peninsula 120 J3
Steens Mountain 122 E6
Steenstrups Glacier 120 Q2
Steeping 55 K3
Steere, Mount 112 D3
Stefanesti 73 J2
Stefansson Island 120 E3
Stege 63 E9
Steigerwald 70 D4
Steinbach 123 R3
Steinhuder Meer 70 C2
Steinkjer 62 D4
Stellenbosch 108 C6
Steller, Mount 118 G3
Stenay 64 F4
Stendal 70 D2
Stenhousemuir 57 E4
Stenness 56 A1
Stenness, Loch of 56 E2
Stentrask 62 H3
Stepan 71 M3
Stepanakert 94 H2
Stephens, Cape 115 D4
Stephenville Canada 121 Q8
Stephenville U.S.A. 128 C4
Stepnogorsk 84 A6
Stepnyak 84 A6
Sterkstroom 108 E6
Sterlibashevo 78 K5
Sterling Colorado, U.S.A. 123 N7
Sterling Illinois, U.S.A. 124 F6
Sterling Heights 124 J5
Sterlitamak 78 K5
Steshevskaya 78 F3
Stettin 70 F2
Steubenville 125 K6
Stevenage 53 G3
Stevens Point 124 F4
Stevenson 57 D5
Stewart 118 H3
Stewart Island 115 A7
Stewart Islands 111 P3
Stewarton 57 D5
Stewartstown 58 J3
Steynsburg 108 E6
Steyr 68 E1
St-Gildas, Pointe de 65 B5
Stibb Cross 52 C4
Stickford 55 K3
Stikine 118 J4
Stikine Mountains 118 K4
Stilis 75 G3
Stillwater Minnesota, U.S.A. 124 D4
Stillwater Oklahoma, U.S.A. 128 D2
Stilo, Punta 69 F6
Stinchar 57 D5
Stip 73 G5
Stirling Australia 113 G3
Stirling U.K. 57 E4
Stirling Range 112 D5
Stjernoya 62 K1
Stjordal 62 D5

Stockach 70 C5
Stockbridge 53 F3
Stockerau 68 F1
Stockholm Sweden 63 H7
Stockholm Sweden 63 H7
Stockport 55 G3
Stocksbridge 55 H3
Stockton California, U.S.A. 126 B2
Stockton Kansas, U.S.A. 123 Q8
Stockton Heath 55 G3
Stockton-on-Tees 55 H2
Stockton Plateau 127 L5
Stode 62 G5
Stoer, Point of 56 C2
Stoke Ferry 53 H2
Stoke-on-Trent 55 G3
Stokesley 55 H2
Stokes Point 113 J7
Stokhod 71 L3
Stokkseyri 62 U13
Stokmarknes 62 F2
Stolbovoy, Ostrov 85 P2
Stolbtsy 71 M2
Stolica 71 J4
Stolin 79 D5
Stolp 71 G1
Stolsheimen 63 B6
Stone 53 E2
Stonehaven 57 F4
Stonehouse Gloucestershire, U.K. 52 E3
Stonehouse Strathclyde, U.K. 57 E5
Stony 118 D3
Stora 63 C8
Stora Lulevatten 62 H3
Storavan 62 H4
Storby 63 H6
Stord 63 A7
Store Balt 63 D9
Store Heddinge 63 E9
Storen 62 D5
Storjord 62 F3
Storlien 62 E5
Storm Bay 113 K7
Storm Lake 124 C5
Stornoway 56 B2
Storozhevsk 78 J3
Storozhinets 73 H1
Storr, The 56 B3
Storsjon 62 F5
Storslett 62 J2
Storsteinfjellet 62 G2
Stort 53 H3
Storuman Sweden 62 G4
Storuman Sweden 62 G4
Stosch, Isla 139 A9
Stour Dorset, U.K. 53 E4
Stour Suffolk, U.K. 53 H3
Stourbridge 53 E2
Stourport-on-Severn 52 E2
Stowmarket 53 J2
Stow-on-the-Wold 53 F3
Stoyba 85 N6
Stozac 72 E4
Strabane 58 H3
Strachur 57 C4
Stradbroke 53 J2
Strait of Belle Isle 121 Q7
Strakonice 70 E4
Stralsund 70 E1
Strand 108 C6
Stranda 62 B5
Strandhill 58 E4
Strangford 58 L4
Strangford Lough 58 L4
Strangnas 63 G7
Stranorlar 58 G3
Stranraer 54 D2
Strasbourg 64 G4
Strasheny 73 K2
Strasswalchen 68 D2
Stratfield Mortimer 53 F3
Stratford Canada 125 K5
Stratford New Zealand 115 E3
Stratford U.S.A. 127 L2
Stratford-upon-Avon 53 F2
Strathaven 57 D5
Strathblane 57 D5
Strathbogie 56 F3
Strath Carron 56 D4
Strathclyde 57 D5
Strath Dearn 56 E3
Strath Earn 57 E4
Strath Halladale 56 E2
Strathmore Canada 122 H2
Strathmore Highland, U.K. 56 D2
Strathmore Tayside, U.K. 57 F4
Strath Naver 56 D2
Strath of Kildonan 56 E2
Strath Oykel 56 D2
Strath Spey 56 E3
Strathy Point 56 D2
Stratos 75 F3
Stratton U.K. 52 C4
Stratton U.S.A. 125 Q4
Straubing 70 E4
Straumnes 62 T11
Straumsjoen 62 F2
Strausberg 70 E2
Strawberry Mountains 122 E5
Strawberry Reservoir 122 J7
Streaky Bay Australia 113 G5
Streaky Bay Australia 113 G5
Streator 124 F6

Name	Page	Grid
Tabora	107	F4
Tabou	104	D5
Tabriz	94	H2
Tabuk	96	C2
Tabuka	89	C9
Tabut	97	L9
Tabwemasana	114	T11
Taby	63	H7
Tacheng	86	F2
Tacloban	91	G3
Tacna *Peru*	138	B3
Tacna *U.S.A.*	126	F4
Tacoma	122	C4
Tacora, Cerro de	138	C3
Tacuarembo	138	E6
Tadcaster	55	H3
Tademait, Plateau du	101	F3
Tadjoura	103	H5
Tadmur	77	H5
Tadoule Lake	119	R4
Tadoussac	125	R2
Tadpatri	92	E6
Tadworth	53	G3
Taegu	89	B8
Taehuksan	87	P5
Taejon	87	P4
Taf	52	C3
Tafahi	111	U5
Tafalla	67	F1
Tafassasset	101	G4
Tafassasset, Tenere du	101	H4
Taff	52	D3
Taff, At	97	M4
Tafila	94	B6
Tafi Viejo	138	C5
Tafresh	95	K4
Taft	95	M6
Taftan, Kuh-e	95	Q7
Taganrog	79	F6
Taganrogskiy Zaliv	79	F6
Tagbilaran	91	G4
Taghmon	59	J8
Tagliamento	68	D3
Tagolo Point	91	G4
Tagounite	100	D3
Tagu	73	H2
Taguatinga	138	H6
Tagudin	91	G2
Tagula	114	E4
Tagula Island	114	E4
Tagum	91	H4
Tagus	66	C3
Tahan, Gunung	90	C5
Tahat, Mont	101	G4
Ta He	87	N1
Tahe	87	N1
Taheri	95	L8
Tahiryuak Lake	119	N1
Tahiti	143	J5
Tahlab, Dasht-i	92	B3
Tahlequah	128	E3
Tahoe Lake *Canada*	119	P1
Tahoe, Lake *U.S.A.*	122	E8
Tahoka	127	M4
Tahoua	101	G6
Tahrud	95	N7
Tahta	102	F2
Tahtali Daglari	77	G3
Tahuamanu	136	D6
Tahulandang	91	H5
Taian	87	M4
Taibai Shan	93	L2
Taibus Qi	87	M3
Tai-chung	87	N7
Taier	115	C6
Taieri	115	C6
Taigu	87	L4
Taihape	115	E3
Taihe *Anhui, China*	93	N2
Taihe *Jiangxi, China*	93	M3
Tai Hu	87	N5
Taimba	84	F4
Tain	56	D3
Tai-nan	87	N7
Tainaron, Akra	75	G4
Taining	87	M6
Taipale	62	N5
Tai-pei	87	N6
Taiping	90	C5
Taipingbao	86	J4
Taipinggou	88	C1
Taira	89	H7
Taisei	88	G4
Taisha	89	D8
Taitao, Peninsula de	139	B9
Tai-tung	87	N7
Taivalkoski	62	N4
Taiwan	87	N7
Taiwan Haixia	87	M7
Taiyetos Oros	75	G4
Taiyuan	87	L4
Taiza	89	E8
Taizhou	87	M5
Taizz	96	G10
Tajabad	95	M6
Tajikistan	86	B4
Tajima	89	G7
Tajin-dong	88	B5
Tajito	126	F5
Tajo	66	D3
Tajrish	95	K4
Tajumuclo, Volcan de	132	B7
Tajuna	66	E2
Tak	93	J5
Takab	94	H3
Takada	89	G7
Takaka	115	D4
Takamatsu	89	E8
Takanabe	89	C9
Takaoka	89	F7
Takapuna	115	E2
Takasaki	89	G7
Takatshwane	108	D4
Takaungu	107	G3
Takayama	89	F7
Takefu	89	F8
Takengon	90	B5
Takeo	93	K6
Takestan	95	J3
Takhadid	94	G7
Takhi-i-Suleiman	95	K3
Takhta Bazar	95	R4
Takhtabrod	84	Ae6
Takikawa	88	H4
Takinoue	88	J3
Taku	118	J4
Takum	105	G4
Takwa	114	K6
Talagang	92	D2
Talamanca, Cordillera de	132	F10
Talangbetutu	90	C6
Talara	136	A4
Talar-i-Band	92	B3
Talas	86	C3
Talasea	114	E3
Talaton	52	D4
Talaud, Kepulauan	91	H5
Talavera de la Reina	66	D3
Talayuelas	67	F3
Talbot Inlet	120	L2
Talca	139	B7
Talcahuano	139	B7
Talcher	92	G4
Taldy-Kurgan	86	D2
Talgarth	52	D3
Taliabu	91	G6
Talihina	128	E3
Tali Post	102	F6
Talisay	91	G3
Talitsa	84	Ad5
Taliwang	91	F7
Talkeetna	118	E3
Talkeetna Mountains	118	F3
Talladega	129	J4
Tallahassee	129	K5
Tallinn	63	L7
Tall Kalakh	77	G5
Tall Kayf	77	K4
Tall Kujik	77	K4
Tallow	59	F8
Tall Tamir	77	J4
Talmenka	84	C6
Talnoye	79	E6
Taloda	92	D4
Talodi	102	F5
Talok	91	F5
Talovka	84	E5
Taloye	85	M4
Talsi	63	K8
Taltal	138	B5
Taltson	119	N3
Talu	114	F3
Taluma	85	L5
Talvik	62	K1
Tama	124	D6
Tamabo Range	90	F5
Tamale	104	E4
Tamames	66	C2
Tamana	111	S2
Tamano	89	D8
Tamanrasset *Algeria*	100	F4
Tamanrasset *Algeria*	101	G4
Tamar *Australia*	113	K7
Tamar *U.K.*	52	C4
Tamar, Alto de	133	K11
Tamarite de Litera	67	G2
Tamatave	109	J3
Tamaulipas, Llanos de	128	C8
Tamazunchale	131	K7
Tambacounda	104	C3
Tambangsawah	90	C6
Tambelan, Kepulauan	90	D5
Tambey	84	A2
Tambo	113	K3
Tambora, Gunung	91	F7
Tamboril	137	J4
Tambov	79	G5
Tambre	66	B1
Tambura	102	E6
Tamchaket	100	C5
Tame	136	C2
Tamega	66	C2
Tamiahua, Laguna de	131	L7
Tamil Nadu	92	E6
Tamis	72	F3
Tamit, Wadi	101	J2
Tammerfors	63	M6
Tammisaari	63	K6
Tampa	129	L7
Tampa Bay	129	L7
Tampere	63	M6
Tampico	131	L6
Tamsagbulag	87	M2
Tamuin	131	K7
Tamworth *Australia*	113	L5
Tamworth *U.K.*	53	F2
Tana *Chile*	138	C3
Tana *Kenya*	107	H3
Tana *Norway*	62	M1
Tanabe	89	E9
Tana bru	62	N2
Tanafjorden	62	N1
Tana Hayk	103	G5
Tanahbala	90	B6
Tanahgrogot	90	F6
Tanahjampea	91	G7
Tanahmasa	90	B6
Tanahmerah	114	C3
Tanah Merah	90	C4
Tanami	112	F3
Tanana	118	E2
Tananarive	109	J3
Tanchon	88	B5
Tandag	91	H4
Tandek	91	F4
Tandil	139	E7
Tando Adam	92	C3
Tandragee	58	K4
Taneatua	115	F3
Tanega-shima	89	C10
Tan Emellel	101	G3
Tanen Tong Dan	93	J5
Tanew	71	K3
Tanezrouft	100	E4
Tanf, Jbel al	77	H6
Tanga *Tanzania*	107	G4
Tanga *Russia*	85	J6
Tanga Islands	114	E2
Tanganyika, Lake	107	F4
Tangarare	114	J6
Tanger	100	D1
Tanggula Shan	93	G2
Tanggula Shankou	93	H2
Tangra Yumco	92	G2
Tangshan	87	M4
Tangwang He	88	B2
Tangwanghe	88	B1
Tangyuan	88	B2
Tan Hill	53	F3
Tanhua	62	M3
Taniantaweng Shan	93	J2
Tanimbar, Kepulauan	114	A3
Tanjung	90	F6
Tanjungbalai	90	B5
Tanjungkarang Telukbetung	90	D7
Tanjungpandan	90	D6
Tanjungpura	90	B5
Tanjungredeb	91	F5
Tanjungselor	91	F5
Tankapirtti	62	M2
Tankovo	84	D4
Tankse	92	E2
Tanlovo	84	A3
Tanna	114	U13
Tannu Ola	84	E6
Tannurah, Ra's	97	K3
Tanout	101	G6
Tan-shui	87	N6
Tanta	102	F1
Tan-Tan	100	C3
Tantoyuca	131	K7
Tanumshede	63	D7
Tanzania	107	G4
Taoan	87	N2
Tao He	93	K2
Tao, Ko	93	J6
Taolanaro	109	J5
Taormina	69	E7
Taos	127	K2
Taoudenni	100	E4
Taourirt	100	E2
Tapa	63	L7
Tapachula	131	N10
Tapah	90	C5
Tapajos	137	F4
Tapaktuan	90	B5
Tapan	90	D6
Tapanahoni	137	F3
Tapauá	136	D5
Taperoa	137	K6
Tappahannock	125	M8
Tappi-saki	88	H5
Tapsuy	78	L3
Tapti	92	D4
Tapuaenuku	115	D4
Tapul Group	91	G4
Taqah	97	M8
Taqtaq	94	G4
Taquari	138	E3
Taquari, Pantanal do	138	E3
Tara	84	A5
Tarabulus	101	H2
Taradale	115	F3
Tara, Hill of	58	J5
Tarakan	91	F5
Tarakli	76	D2
Tarakliya	73	K3
Taramana	91	G7
Taramo-jima	89	G11
Taran	84	A2
Tarancon	66	E2
Taransay	56	A3
Taransay, Sound of	56	A3
Taranto	69	F5
Taranto, Golfo di	69	F5
Tarapoto	136	B5
Tararua Range	115	E4
Tarascon	65	F7
Tarasovo	78	H2
Tarauaca *Brazil*	136	C5
Tarauaca *Brazil*	136	C5
Taravo	69	B5
Tarazona	67	F2
Tarazona de la Mancha	67	F3
Tarbagatay, Khrebet	86	E2
Tarbert *Ireland*	59	D7
Tarbert *Strathclyde, U.K.*	57	C5
Tarbert *Western Isles, U.K.*	56	B3
Tarbes	65	D7
Tarbet	57	D4
Tarbolton	57	D5
Tarboro	129	P3
Tarcaului, Muntii	73	J2
Tarcoola	113	G5
Tardienta	67	F2
Tardoki-yani, Gora	88	F1
Taree	113	L5
Tarendo	62	K3
Tareya	84	E2
Tarfa, Ra's at	96	F8
Tarfa, Wadi el	103	F2
Tarfaya	100	C3
Tarfside	57	F4
Targhee Pass	122	J5
Tarhunah	101	H2
Tarif	97	L4
Tarifa	66	D4
Tarija	138	D4
Tariku	114	B2
Tarim	97	J8
Tarim Basin	86	E3
Tarim He	86	E3
Tarim Pendi	86	E3
Taritatu	114	B2
Tarkasale	84	A3
Tarkastad	108	E6
Tarkhankut, Mys	79	E6
Tarkio	124	C6
Tarkwa	104	E4
Tarlac	91	G2
Tarleton	55	G3
Tarma	136	B6
Tarn	65	D7
Tarna	72	F2
Tarnaby	62	F4
Tarnobrzeg	71	J3
Tarnow	71	J4
Tarnsjo	63	G6
Taro	68	B3
Taron	114	E2
Taroom	113	K4
Taroudannt	100	D2
Tarporley	55	G3
Tarragona	67	G2
Tarrasa	67	H2
Tarrega	67	G2
Tarsus	76	F4
Tartagal	138	D4
Tartas	65	C7
Tartu	63	P7
Tartung	90	B5
Tartus	94	B4
Tartus	77	F5
Tarutino	73	K2
Tarzout	67	G4
Tasci	77	F3
Tashakta	86	F2
Tashauz	80	G5
Tashigang	93	H3
Tashk, Daryacheh-ye	95	L7
Tashkent	86	B3
Tashkepri	95	R3
Tashla	79	J5
Tashtagol	84	D6
Tasikmalaya	90	D7
Tasiujaq	121	N6
Taskesken	86	E2
Taskopru	76	F2
Tas-Kumsa	85	N3
Taslicay	77	K3
Tasman Bay	115	D4
Tasmania	113	K7
Tasman Mountains	115	D4
Tasnad	73	G2
Tasova	77	G2
Tas-Tumus	85	N2
Tasty	86	B3
Tasucu	76	E4
Tasuj	77	L3
Tataba	91	G6
Tatabanya	72	E2
Tatarbunary	73	K3
Tatarka	84	B6
Tatarsk	84	B5
Tataurovo	85	J6
Tateyama	89	G8
Tathlina Lake	119	M3
Tathlith	96	F7
Tathlith, Wadi	96	F6
Tatnam, Cape	119	S4
Tatry	71	H4
Tatsinskiy	79	G6
Tatsuno	89	E8
Tatta	92	C4
Tatum	127	L4
Tatvan	77	K3
Tau	111	V4
Tauari	137	F4
Taubate	138	G4
Tauchik	79	J7
Taumarunui	115	E3
Taung-gyi	93	J4
Taungnyo Range	93	J5

Name	Map	Grid
Tierp	63	G6
Tierra Amarilla	127	J2
Tierra Blanca	131	L8
Tierra del Fuego, Isla Grande de	139	C10
Tietar	66	D2
Tiete	138	F4
Tifton	129	L5
Tifu	91	H6
Tiger	122	F3
Tigharry	56	A3
Tigil *Russia*	85	T5
Tigil *Russia*	85	T5
Tignish	121	P8
Tigre *Peru*	136	B4
Tigre *Venezuela*	136	E2
Tigres, Baia dos	106	B6
Tigris	94	H6
Tigzerte, Oued	100	D3
Tigzirt	67	J4
Tihamat ash Sham	96	E7
Tihamat Asir	96	F8
Tihsimir	77	J3
Tijoca	137	H4
Tijuana	126	D4
Tikal	132	C6
Tikamgarh	92	E4
Tikanlik	86	F3
Tikhoretsk	79	G6
Tikhvin	78	E4
Tikitiki	115	G2
Tikopica	111	Q4
Tikrit	77	K5
Tiksi	85	M2
Tilburg	64	F3
Tilbury	53	H3
Tilemsi, Vallee du	100	F5
Till	57	F5
Tillaberi	100	F6
Tillanchang	93	H7
Tillicoultry	57	E4
Tilomar	91	H7
Tilos	75	J4
Tilsit	71	J1
Tilt	57	E4
Timanskiy Kryazh	78	H3
Timar	77	K3
Timaru	115	C6
Timashevsk	79	F6
Timbakion	75	H5
Timbedra	100	D5
Timbo *Guinea*	104	C3
Timbo *Liberia*	104	D4
Timbuktu	100	E5
Timfristos	75	F3
Timimoun	100	F3
Timiris, Cap	100	B5
Timis	73	G3
Timisoara	73	F3
Timkapaul	84	Ad4
Timmernabben	63	G8
Timmins	125	K2
Timok	73	G3
Timolin	59	J7
Timor	91	H7
Timor, Laut	91	H7
Timoshino	78	F3
Timsher	78	J3
Tinaca Point	91	H4
Tinaco	133	N10
Tinahely	59	K7
Tinakula	114	M7
Tindivanam	92	E6
Tindouf	100	D3
Tineo	66	C1
Tinglev	63	C9
Tingo Maria	136	B5
Tingsryd	63	F8
Tingvoll	62	C5
Tinhare, Ilha de	137	K6
Tinogasta	138	C5
Tinompo	91	G5
Tinos *Greece*	75	H4
Tinos *Greece*	75	H4
Tintinara	113	J6
Tinto *Spain*	66	C4
Tinto *U.K.*	57	E5
Tinto Hills	57	E5
Tinwald	115	C5
Tiomilaskogen	63	E6
Tipaza	67	H4
Tipitapa	132	D8
Tippecanoe	124	G6
Tipperary *Ireland*	59	F8
Tipperary *Ireland*	59	G7
Tipton	124	H6
Tiptree	53	H3
Tiquicheo	131	J8
Tiracambu, Serra do	137	H4
Tiran	96	B3
Tirana	74	E2
Tirane	74	E2
Tirano	68	C2
Tiraspol	79	D6
Tire	76	B3
Tirebolu	77	H2
Tiree	57	C4
Tirga Mor	56	B3
Tirgoviste	73	H3
Tirgu Bujor	73	J3
Tirgu Carbunesti	73	G3
Tirgu Frumos	73	J2
Tirgu Jiu	73	G3
Tirgu Mures	73	H2
Tirgu Neamt	73	J2
Tirgu Ocna	73	J2
Tirich Mir	92	D1
Tirnava Mare	73	H2
Tirnava Mica	73	H2
Tirnavos	75	G3
Tirol	68	C2
Tirpul	95	Q4
Tirso	69	B6
Tirua Point	115	E3
Tiruchchirappalli	92	E6
Tirumangalam	92	E7
Tirunelveli	92	E7
Tirupati	92	E6
Tiruppur	92	E6
Tiruvannamalai	92	E6
Tisa	72	F3
Tisisat Falls	103	G5
Tissa	71	K4
Tissington	55	H3
Tista	93	G3
Tisza	72	F2
Tit-Ary	85	M2
Titchfield	53	F4
Titicaca, Lago	138	C3
Titograd	72	E4
Titova Mitrovica	73	F4
Titovo Uzice	72	E4
Titovo Velenje	72	C2
Titov Veles	73	F5
Titran	62	C5
Tittmoning	70	E4
Titu	73	H3
Titusville	129	M6
Tiumpan Head	56	B2
Tivaouane	104	B2
Tiveden	63	F7
Tiverton	52	D4
Tivoli	69	D5
Tiwi	97	P5
Tiyas	77	G5
Tizimin	131	Q7
Tizi Ouzou	101	F1
Tiznit	100	D3
Tjamotis	62	H3
Tjornuvik	62	Z14
Tjotta	62	E4
Tlaltenango	130	H7
Tlapa	131	K9
Tlapehuala	131	J8
Tlaxiaco	131	L9
Tlemcen	100	E2
Toad River	118	K4
Toamasina	109	J3
Tobago	133	S9
Toba Kakar Ranges	95	Q4
Tobercurry	58	E4
Tobermory *Canada*	125	K4
Tobermory *U.K.*	57	B4
Toberonochy	57	C4
Tobi	91	J5
Tobin Lake	112	F3
Tobi-shima	88	G6
Toboali	90	D6
Tobol	84	Ae5
Tobolsk	84	Ae5
Tobseda	78	J2
Tobysh	78	J3
Tocache Nuevo	136	B5
Tocantins	137	H4
Toccoa	129	L3
Toco	133	S9
Toconao	138	C4
Tocopilla	138	B4
Tocuyo	133	N9
Todeli	91	G6
Todi	68	B2
Todi	69	D4
Todmorden	55	G3
Todog	86	E3
Todos os Santos, Baia de	137	K6
Todos Santos *Bolivia*	138	C3
Todos Santos *Mexico*	130	D6
Todos Santos, Bahia de	126	D5
Toe Head *Ireland*	59	D10
Toe Head *U.K.*	56	A3
Toetoes Bay	115	B7
Tofino	122	B3
Toft	56	A1
Tofte	63	D7
Tofua	111	T5
Toga	114	T10
Togi	89	F7
Togiak	118	C4
Togian, Kepulauan	91	G6
Togni	96	B7
Togo	104	F4
Togtoh	87	L3
Toguchi	89	H10
Togur	84	C5
Tohamiyam	103	G4
Tohatchi	127	H3
Tohma	77	G3
Toi-misaki	89	C10
Tojo	89	D8
Tok	118	G3
Tokachi	88	J4
Tokachi-Dake	88	J4
Tokaj	73	F1
Tokanui	115	B7
Tokar	103	G4
Tokara-kaikyo	89	C10
Tokara-retto	89	B11
Tokat	77	G2
Tokelau	111	U3
Tokiwa	88	J3
Tokke	63	C7
Toklar	77	G3
Tokmak	86	D3
Tokolon	84	H5
Tokoro	88	K3
Tokoroa	115	E3
Toksun	86	F3
Tok-to	89	C7
Toktogul	86	C3
Tokuno-shima	89	J10
Tokushima	89	E8
Tokuyama	89	C8
Tokyo	89	G8
Tolar, Cerro	138	C5
Tolbonuur	86	G2
Tolbukhin	73	J4
Toledo *Spain*	66	D3
Toledo *U.S.A.*	124	J6
Toledo Bend Reservoir	128	F5
Toledo, Montes de	66	D3
Tolentino	68	D4
Toliara	109	H4
Tolitoli	91	G5
Tolka	84	C4
Tolmezzo	68	D2
Tolmin	72	B2
Tolochin	78	D5
Tolosa	67	E1
Tolo, Teluk	91	G6
Tolsta Head	56	B2
Tolstoye	73	H1
Tolstoy, Mys	85	T5
Toluca	131	K8
Toluca, Nevado de	131	K8
Tolyatti	79	H5
Tomah	124	E4
Tomahawk	124	F4
Tomakomai	88	H4
Tomani	90	F5
Tomaniivi	114	R8
Tomar *Portugal*	66	B3
Tomar *Kazakhstan*	86	D2
Tomari	88	J2
Tomarza	77	F3
Tomasevo	72	E4
Tomashevka	71	K3
Tomaszow Lubelski	71	K3
Tomaszow Mazowiecka	71	J3
Tombador, Serra do	136	F6
Tombe	103	F6
Tombigbee	129	H5
Tombo	106	B4
Tombouctou	100	E5
Tombua	106	B6
Tomelilla	63	E9
Tomelloso	66	E3
Tomini, Teluk	91	G6
Tomioka	89	H7
Tomkinson Ranges	112	F4
Tomma	62	E3
Tommot	85	M5
Tomo	136	D2
Tomochic	127	J6
Tompa	84	H5
Tompo	85	P4
Tomsk	84	D5
Tonbridge	53	H3
Tondano	91	G5
Tonder	70	C1
Tone	52	E3
Tonelagee	59	K6
Tonga	111	U6
Tonga *Sudan*	102	F6
Tongareiro	115	E3
Tongatapu	111	U6
Tongatapu Group	111	T6
Tonga Trench	143	H5
Tongcheng	93	M3
Tongchuan	93	L1
Tongdao	93	L3
Tonggu	93	M3
Tongguan	93	M2
Tonghai	93	K4
Tonghe	88	B2
Tonghua	87	P3
Tongjiang	88	D2
Tongking, Gulf of	93	L5
Tongliao	87	N3
Tongling	87	M5
Tonglu	87	M6
Tongnae	89	B8
Tongoa	114	U12
Tongren	93	L3
Tongtianheyan	93	H2
Tongue *U.K.*	56	D2
Tongue *U.S.A.*	123	L5
Tongue, Kyle of	56	D2
Tongue of the Ocean	132	J2
Tong Xian	87	M4
Tongxin	93	L1
Tongyu	87	N3
Tongzi	93	L3
Tonichi	127	H6
Tonk	92	E3
Tonkabon	95	K3
Tonle Sap	93	K6
Tonneins	65	D6
Tonnerre	65	E5
Tono	88	H6
Tonopah	126	D2
Tonosi	132	G11
Tonsberg	63	D7
Tonstad	63	B7
Tonya	77	H2
Tooele	122	H7
Toowoomba	113	L4
Topeka	124	C7
Toplane	74	E1
Toplica	73	F4
Toplita	73	H2
Topocalma, Punta	138	B6
Topola	72	F3
Topolcani	73	F5
Topoli	79	J6
Topolkki	63	N6
Topolovgrad	73	J4
Topozero, Ozero	62	P4
Toppenish	122	D4
Toprakli	76	F3
Toraka Vestale	109	H3
Tora-Khem	84	F6
Torbali	76	B3
Torbat-e-Heydariyeh	95	P4
Torbat-e Jam	95	Q4
Tor Bay *Australia*	112	D5
Tor Bay *U.K.*	52	D4
Tordesillas	66	D2
Tore	56	D3
Tore	62	K4
Torfastadir	62	U12
Torgau	70	E3
Torgo	85	K5
Torhout	64	E3
Torino	68	A3
Torkaman	94	H3
Tormes	66	D2
Tornealven	62	K3
Tor Ness	56	E2
Torne-trask	62	H2
Torngat Mountains	121	P6
Tornio	62	L4
Toro, Cerro de	138	C5
Toroiaga	73	H2
Torokina	114	F3
Torokszentmiklos	72	F2
Toronaios, Kolpos	75	G2
Toronto	125	L5
Toropets	78	E4
Tororo	107	F2
Toros Dagi	76	F4
Toros Daglari	76	E4
Torpoint	52	C4
Torquay	52	D4
Torrance	126	C4
Torrao	66	B3
Torre Annunziata	69	E5
Torre Baja	67	F2
Torreblanca	67	G2
Torrecilla en Cameros	66	E1
Torre del Greco	69	E5
Torrelaguna	66	E2
Torrelavega	66	D1
Torremolinos	66	D4
Torrens Creek	113	K3
Torrens, Lake	113	H5
Torrente	67	F3
Torreon	127	L8
Torres Island	114	T10
Torres Novas	66	B3
Torres Strait	114	C4
Torres Vedras	66	B3
Torrevieja	67	F4
Torr Head	58	K2
Torridge	52	C4
Torridon, Loch	56	C3
Torrijos	66	D3
Torrington *Connecticut, U.S.A.*	125	P6
Torrington *Wyoming, U.S.A.*	123	M6
Torrox	66	E4
Torsas	63	F8
Torsby	63	E6
Torshavn	62	Z14
Torsken	62	L2
Tortkuduk	84	A6
Tortola	133	Q5
Tortona	68	B3
Tortosa	67	G2
Tortosa, Cabo de	67	G2
Tortue, Ile de la	133	L4
Tortuga, Isla	126	G7
Tortuga, Isla la	136	D1
Tortum	77	J2
Torul	77	H2
Torun	71	H2
Tory Island	58	F2
Torysa	71	J4
Tory Sound	58	F2
Torzhok	78	F4
Torzym	70	F2
Tosa-shimizu	89	D9
Tosa-wan	89	D9
Toscaig	56	C3
Tosco-Emiliano, Appennino	68	C4
Tostado	138	D5
Tosya	76	F2
Totana	67	F4
Totes	64	D4
Totma	78	G4
Totnes	52	D4
Totness	137	F2
Totora	138	C3
Totota	104	C3
Totoya	114	S9
Totton	53	F4
Tottori	89	E8
Touba	104	D4

Produced by Engineering Surveys
Reproduction Ltd.

Cartographic Design and Production Manager
Keith Brook

Senior Cartographic Editor
Zoë Goodwin

Cartographic Editor
Lindsay Evans

Cartographers
Nicky Chapman
Mike Larby
Gill Dalton
David Handley-Clarke
Chris Major

Cartographic Illustrator
Janos Marffy

Text by
Simon Palfrey

Pictorial Section Design
Sue Cook

Commissioning Editor
Andrew Preston

The publishers wish to thanks all those involved in the production of
this atlas, and in particular the photo technicians at ESR Ltd, Richard
Ross, John Gill, Michael Hodson Designs, Apollo Colour Repro Ltd,
E.S. Computing Ltd, Typogram Ltd, Link-Line Ltd.

Photographic Acknowledgements
Gamma, Paris; James Davis Travel Photography; Compix;
Daily Telegraph Colour Library; J. Allan Cash;
Colour Library Books Ltd; Philippine Embassy, London;
Pakistan Embassy, London; Qatar Embassy, London;
Contact Press Images; Cyprus Tourism Organisation,
Planet Earth Pictures Ltd.